T0243560

Advance Praise

"Dr. Brews's coverage of humankind's economic progress is as comprehensive as it is original, and he explains how our past and present often impair our futures in a profound way. His analysis of the United States and its imbalances is pertinent to Americans and those in leading countries. *Lead, Follow, or Fail* provides actionable suggestions that will be useful to organizations, governments, and individuals as they seek to understand the pathways to leadership and the challenges that must be managed. It is a beautiful walk through time culminating with valuable insights that are critical in assessing current positions and future actions."

—**LLOYD JOHNSON**, Retired Senior Executive at Accenture and Board Chair at AARP

"I've seen firsthand how Dr. Brews's insistence that all students graduate data proficient and analytical capable has changed the lives of the many thousands studying at the Darla Moore School of Business, and his well-founded understanding of nation-building and what is needed to remain globally competitive reaches even more in these pages. Powerful and weighty, his ideas are worthy of close study."

—**DARLA MOORE**, American Financier and Philanthropist

"Meticulously researched and data rich, *Lead, Follow, or Fail*'s coverage of industrial versus post-industrial business provides invaluable insights for business professionals wherever they compete. Most impressive is how Peter Brews explains the creative work Leaders must do to remain ahead as others Follow. He connects the big ideas of today's innovators with emerging trends in technology as well as with new structures of government and policy. The result is a new road map for developing strategy and understanding competitive markets."

—**DR. ALBERT SEGARS**, Author of *The Idea Chase* and PNC Distinguished Professor of Strategy and Entrepreneurship, Kenan-Flagler Business School at the University of North Carolina at Chapel Hill

"*Lead, Follow or Fail*'s coverage of business worldwide is comprehensive, and its articulation of the challenges Leaders, Followers, and Failures face and how to remedy them is important for all to consider in business and beyond. Dr. Brews's statement that an isolationist conflicted America is bad for the country and the world is timely, and his notion that a more equitable, cleaner, better-balanced nation is within reach should be heeded by all Americans especially. The message of hope embedded in these pages is required reading for all concerned about the future."

—**DR. KENDALL ROTH**, Distinguished Professor Emeritus and Executive Director, Center for International Business Education and Research, University of South Carolina

"Among the most outstanding executive educators I have worked with, I watched Peter Brews be challenged by senior executives in many countries. With astonishing levels of insight and humanity, his unequalled ability to engage in debate was both memorable and thought-provoking. *Lead, Follow, or Fail* follows in this tradition and is not just a meticulous analysis of business leadership for our age, but also an engaging and compelling read that makes a clarion call for change."

—**ALPH KEOGH**, Managing Director, OnBoard UG

"*Lead, Follow or Fail* provokes, challenges, and educates even more than the author's award-winning classes did. Its background research and depth enrich the conversation considerably. For those wanting insight into who we are, how we got here, and the choices we face going forward, this is a must-read!"

—**ALAN GOLDING**, Senior Strategy and Operations Officer, The World Bank, and former UNC Executive MBA student

LEAD, FOLLOW, OR FAIL

LEAD, FOLLOW, OR FAIL

The Human Struggle for Productivity, and How Nations, Organizations, and People Will Prosper in Our Changing World

DR. PETER J. BREWS

IDEAPRESS PUBLISHING
WASHINGTON, DC

IDEAPRESS
PUBLISHING

Copyright © 2024 by Dr. Peter J. Brews

All rights reserved. No part of this book may be reproduced, stored, or transmitted by any means—whether auditory, graphic, mechanical, or electronic—without written permission of both publisher and author, except in the case of brief excerpts used in critical articles and reviews. Unauthorized reproduction of any part of this work is illegal and is punishable by law.

Ideapress Publishing | www.ideapresspublishing.com

All trademarks are the property of their respective companies.

Cover Design by Matt Chase
Interior Design: Jessica Angerstein

Cataloging-in-Publication Data is on file with the Library of Congress.

Hardcover ISBN: 978-1-64687-165-0

Special Sales
Ideapress books are available at a special discount for bulk purchases for sales promotions and premiums, or for use in corporate training programs. Special editions, including personalized covers, a custom foreword, corporate imprints, and bonus content, are also available.

1 2 3 4 5 6 7 8 9 10

This book is dedicated to my wife, Dorinda, whose love and support sustain me and whose expert editing and eagle eyes underscore the smart and talented person that she is.

It is written for my children, Kristen and Michael, and for the generations that follow, as it is they who will pay for mistakes my generation has made should they remain unaddressed.

My thanks also go to the tens of thousands of business students and business executives I have had the honor to educate in my over 30 years in higher education. We learned together how business differs around the world, and how national heritage influences business and political choices as global competitiveness is built.

Contents

Figures i
Tables iii
Abbreviations v
Author's Message to Readers 1
Introduction 3

CHAPTER 1 UNDERSTANDING THE BIG PICTURE:
Our Human Struggle for Productivity from Pre- to Post-Industrial Production, or Failing, Following, and Leading 7

The Advance of Global Economic Output: Millennia of Scarcity Followed by Two Centuries of Astounding Success 9
Cataloging the Human Struggle for Productivity: Eras, Times, Populations, Sectors 17
The Human Struggle for Productivity: With Progress, Failure Endures and Followers and Leaders Stumble 23
Forecasting the Human Struggle for Productivity: Avoiding the Apocalypse 28
Forecasting the Future of Human Productivity: Prosperity as Following and Leading Dominate 38
Conclusion and Synthesis 42

CHAPTER 2 THE PRE-INDUSTRIAL ERA:
Failures Enduring Scarcity and Want 45

Pre-Industrial Era Political Economy: Failure amid Meritocratic Bureaucracy, Feudalism, and Mercantile Capitalism 47
Feudalism: Kings and Princes Dominating People 48

China's Imperial Bureaucracy: Early Progress, Isolation, and Failure 51
Mercantile Capitalism and Hard Power Accumulate Wealth 53
Pre-Industrial Era Land Cultivation: Subsistence Farming and Failure's Perpetuation 55
Pre-Industrial Era Economic Capital: Sailing Ships Extending Hard Power, and Hand Tools and Beasts of Burden Prolonging Scarcity and Want 58
Pre-Industrial Era Human Resources Management: Serfdom, Slavery, Guilds, and Man's Inhumanity to Man 62
Pre-Industrial Era Entrepreneurship: Christopher Columbus and Plunder through Hard Power 67
Columbus's Life and Times: Plenty from Brutality and Oppression 68
Twenty-First-Century Pre-Industrial Subsistence: Rural to Urban Failure 71
Conclusion and Synthesis 74

CHAPTER 3 THE INDUSTRIAL ERA:
Follower Abundance from Input Mobilization and Economic Diversification 77

Industrialization as Transformer of Nations and Peoples 78
Industrialization's Voracious Demand for Capital, Labor, Energy, and Materials 80
Industrialization's Capital Intensity: Deferring Gratification as Productive Bases Are Built 81
Industrialization's Labor Intensity: Leaders Building Infrastructure and Businesses to Employ Workers on the Assembly Line 86
America's Early Industrial Leadership: Robber Barons or Visionary Icons Enabling a World of Plenty 86
Industrialization's Workforce: Labor for Routine Assembly Line Work 90
Industrialization's Human Resources Management: Specialization and Scientific Management, Thinkers, and Doers 94
Organized Labor and the Sharing of Abundance 97
Industrialization's Materials Intensity: Endless Search for Energy and Raw Materials 101

Industrialization's Energy: Fossil Fuels and Our Carbon-Based World 102
Industrialization's Insatiable Demand for Raw Materials 105
Industrial Era Entrepreneurship: Henry Ford and a Car for the Everyman 110
Ford's Early Years: Farmer to Mechanic/Engineer 111
Ford Motor Company at Full Stride: The Model T, Highland Park and Rouge, and Enlightened Capitalist Henry Ford 113
Industrial Organization at Its Best: The Multidivisional, Professionally Managed, Hierarchically Controlled Firm 120
Comparing Columbus and Ford: Plundering Pre-Industrial Pioneer versus Enlightened Industrial Capitalist 123
Industrialization Era Political Economy: Generations of Sacrifice and Deferred Gratification 125
Modern Democracy and Early Industrialization: Complementary or in Conflict? 127
Empirical Evidence: Contradictions in Poorly Designed Studies 129
First Mover Industrialization: Generations of Toil Starting in Great Britain, Perfected in the United States 133
First Mover Industrialization: Triumph of the Visible Invisible Hand 138
Regime Type in First Mover Early Industrializations: Democracy Light 142
Fast Follower Industrialization: Triumph of Interventionist Governments, Markets, and Deferred Gratification 147
Fast Follower Political Economy: Authoritarian Developmentalists Getting the Growth Job Done 165
Fast Follower Economic Success: Growth Begets Growth as Inputs Accumulate 169
The Economic Nation-Building Virtual Cycle: Maintaining Stability and Achieving Growth, Then Fostering Development 178
Economic Nation-Building in Practice: Six Nations and the Stability, Growth, Development Framework 183
Conclusion and Synthesis 207

CHAPTER 4 THE POST-INDUSTRIAL ERA: Leader Creative Core Innovation, Business in Tightly Controlled Networks, and Humans Doing What Smart Machines Cannot Do 211

Post-Industrialization: Mobilizing Knowledge and Information to Enhance the Human Condition 212

Post-Industrial Lessons from the Front Lines: Automated Information, Stores, Vehicles, Factories, and Earthworks, and from Product to Service to Solution in a Networked World 214

Post-Industrial Robotics and the Pervasive Automation of Production 215

Post-Industrial Air Travel: Automated Travel and Aircraft Products to Services and Solutions 218

Post-Industrial Retailing: Automated Retail and the Retail Apocalypse 221

Post-Industrial Automobile Automation: From Factories to Highways 225

Post-Industrial Earthmoving: Dozer Solutions at Work 230

Post-Industrial Economic Capital: Computer Operated, Automated, and Networked 234

Post-Industrial Production: CNC to CAD/CAM and CIM, and the Rise of Automated Factory and Production Systems 237

Post-Industrial Organization: Networked, Less Hierarchical, More Focused/Specialized, Global and Local, Big and Small, Centralized and Decentralized 242

Post-Industrial Organization in Practice: Cisco and the Internet Generation Company 244

Cisco's Internet-Based Structure: Tightly Integrated Collectives of Specialized Businesses, Partners, and Suppliers 248

Post-Industrial Infrastructure: Bandwidth for Far-Flung Networks 254

Post-Industrial Human Resources: Doing Only What Machines Cannot Do 263

Post-Industrial Creative Work: New Products, Services, or Solutions from Creative Cores 269

Post-Industrial Transformative Work: Post-Industrial Operational Efficiency through Network-Based Business Process Restructuring 274

Post-Industrial Manual Work: Smarter Humans Working with Smart Machines ... 284
Post-Industrial Entrepreneurship: Bill Gates and Microsoft Software Running Every Computer ... 285
Gates's Formative Years and Amassing the World's Biggest Personal Fortune in Two Decades ... 287
Microsoft's Rise to Prominence: IBM's PC and MS-DOS, and Windows, Excel, Word, and Office ... 290
Microsoft's Organizational Model: Managing the Best and Brightest, with Millionaires Galore ... 296
Columbus, Ford, and Gates: No Business to Industrial Business to Post-Industrial Business ... 304
Post-Industrial Era Political Economy: Divergence and Convergence with the Possible Triumph of Democracy ... 313
Conclusion and Synthesis ... 318

CHAPTER 5 SUSTAINING THE HUMAN STRUGGLE FOR PRODUCTIVITY:
Global Diversity, Remedying Imbalances, Our Search for Clean Energy, and Scenarios for the Twenty-First Century ... 321

Early Twenty-First-Century Global Diversity: Not as Flat a World as Some Think ... 323
Twenty-First-Century Global Diversity: BOP to MOP to TOP, or Competing in Low-End, Good-Enough, and Premium Markets ... 326
Premium-Market MNCs: World-Class Products and Supply Chains with Global, Regional, National, and Local Operations ... 332
MNCs Competing in Low-End or Good-Enough Markets: Avoiding Square Pegs in Round Holes ... 337
Global Warming/Climate Change: A Massive Disruptor to Mitigate at All Costs ... 341
Leaders in Retreat: Democracy and Hospital Passes in an Upside-Down World ... 345

Twenty-First-Century Economic Scenarios: Peace with Scarcity Vanquished (BGG), Imbalance with Instability Enduring (UGG), or an Inhospitable, Apocalyptic World (GM) 358
Balanced Global Growth: Emergence of a Stable, Prosperous World 359
Unbalanced Global Growth and Leader Problems of Wealth: Inequity amid Wealth and Excess without Discipline 364
Unbalanced Global Growth and Follower/Failure Problems of Poverty: Economic Takeoff Stalled or Growth Never Started 374
Global Meltdown: Everything Everywhere All at Once, a World to Avoid at All Costs 380
Most Likely Scenario: Unbalanced Global Growth in a World Muddling Through 383
Unbalanced to Balanced Global Growth: Global Insights and Our Need to Work Together 385
Unbalanced to Balanced Global Growth: Followers and Failures Led by Those Understanding the Long Road Ahead 391
Unbalanced to Balanced Global Growth: Leaders in Balance Showing the Way to a Cleaner World 395
Unbalanced to Balanced Global Growth: Individual Insights as We All Build a Better World 399

Author's Biography: Dr. Peter J. Brews 411
Index 413

Figures

Figure 1: The Human Struggle for Productivity 10
Figure 2: US Real GDP Growth: 1930–2022 15
Figure 3: The Human Struggle for Productivity: Eras, Times, Populations, and Sectors 21
Figure 4: The Human Struggle for Productivity: Relative Positions 24
Figure 5: The Life Cycle Model 29
Figure 6: World Population: 10,000 BCE–2100 34
Figure 7: The Future of the Human Struggle for Productivity: S Curve Model 39
Figure 8: The Economic Nation-Building Triangle 178
Figure 9: GDP per Capita (US$ OER), China versus India: 1970–2020 200
Figure 10: Indian Annual GDP Growth: 1961–2021 205
Figure 11: OECD Broadband Subscriptions per 100 Inhabitants and GDP/Capita (US$ PPP), 2009 versus 2022 258
Figure 12: eHR Activity Mapping 280
Figure 13: Pre-eHR Employee Profile Change Map 281
Figure 14: Post-eHR Employee Profile Change Map 281
Figure 15: The Human Struggle for Productivity: From BOP to MOP to TOP 329
Figure 16: American Home Prices, Building Costs, Interest Rates, and Population: 1891–2014 347
Figure 17: Private Consumption Spending and Mortgage Equity Withdrawals as US GDP Percentages: 1953–2007 348
Figure 18: Federal Total Debt (% of US GDP): 1966–2023 349
Figure 19: GAO US Public Debt Projection (% GDP): 2022–2050 350
Figure 20: Select Government Revenues: 1950–2021 (% GDP) 355
Figure 21: Select Government Primary Balances: 1950–2021 (% GDP) 356
Figure 22: The Human Struggle for Productivity: Balanced Global Growth 362
Figure 23: The Human Struggle for Productivity: Unbalanced Global Growth 380
Figure 24: The Human Struggle for Productivity: Global Meltdown 383

Tables

Table 1: Top 10 City Populations: 1900 and 2018 73
Table 2: Industrial versus Pre-Industrial Societies 79
Table 3: Private Sector Trade Union Membership in the United States: 1900–2014 99
Table 4: Distribution of the 200 Largest Manufacturing Firms in the United States, United Kingdom, Germany, and Japan by Industry, Circa 1930 137
Table 5: Fast Follower Industrialization: Japan, South Korea, and Taiwan 150
Table 6: Fast Follower Industrialization: Hong Kong and Singapore 152
Table 7: Major Industries, Products, and Competitive Advantages of Hong Kong, Singapore, South Korea, and Taiwan 162
Table 8: Sources of Economic Growth: Hong Kong, Singapore, South Korea, Taiwan, China, Japan, and Non-Asian G5 Industrialized Countries 174
Table 9: India versus China: Comparative Data 201
Table 10: Educational Attainment, Earnings, and Unemployment in the United States: 2022 266
Table 11: Improving Existing Operations versus Forming Strategy 275
Table 12: Industrial versus Post-Industrial Organizations 308
Table 13: Comparative Industrial versus Post-Industrial Organization Data 310
Table 14: 2023 GDP, GDP per Capita, Population, and Gini Indices 324
Table 15: Categorization of Nike Activities: Global, Regional, National, and Local 334
Table 16: Government Debt, Revenues, Primary Balance, Interest (% GDP): 2022 353

Abbreviations

ADR: Authoritarian developmentalist regime

ADS: Automated driving system

AI: Artificial intelligence

ANC: African National Congress

ATM: Automated teller machine

AWS: Amazon Web Services

BEA: Bureau of Economic Analysis

BGG: Balanced global growth

BOP: Bottom of the Pyramid

BPR: Business process reengineering

CAD: Computer-aided design

CAM: Computer-aided manufacturing

CATIA: Computer-aided three-dimensional interactive application

CIM: Computer-integrated manufacturing

CME: Coordinated market economy

CNC: Computer numerical control

CO_2: Carbon dioxide

CP/M: Control Program for Microcomputers

DMSB: Darla Moore School of Business

DR: Democratic regime

EMEA: European, Middle East, and Africa

FAQ: Frequently asked question

FSJC: Federal Society of Journeymen Cordwainers

FY: Fiscal year

GAO: Government Accountability Office

Gbps: Gigabits per second

GM: Global meltdown

GPS: Global Positioning System

GUI: Graphical user interface

GWP: Gross world product

HPAEs: Japan, South Korea, Taiwan, Singapore, Indonesia, Thailand, and Malaysia

HR: Human resources

IaaS: Infrastructure as a service

IoT: Internet of Things

IP: Internet protocol

IPCC: Intergovernmental Panel on Climate Change

IPO: Initial public offering

IPP: Independent power project

IT: Information technology

JV: Joint venture

LAN: Local area network

LME: Liberal market economy

Mbps: Megabits per second

MEs: Mediterranean economies

MNC: Multinational corporation

MOP: Middle of the Pyramid

MVP: Market value per person (MVP)

NASA: National Aeronautics and Space Administration

NC: Numerical control

NDB: New Development Bank

NEO: Near-Earth object

NHTSA: National Highway Traffic Safety Administration

OER: Official exchange rate

OS: Operating system

PaaS: Platform as a service

PISA: Program for International Student Assessment

PLM: Product lifecycle management

PPP: Purchasing power parity

PQLI: Physical Quality of Life Index

ROA: Return on assets

ROCE: Return on capital employed

ROI: Return on investment

SaaS: Software as a service

TCE: Transaction cost economics

TFP: Total factor productivity

TOP: Top of the Pyramid

TSMC: Taiwan Semiconductor Manufacturing Company

UGG: Unbalanced global growth

UN: United Nations

WTO: World Trade Organization

AUTHOR'S MESSAGE TO READERS

This book's material has been tested and sharpened by countless interactions in MBA and executive education classes over my decades as an educator. My classes often changed the lives of attendees, and readers access in these pages the same material students did under my thought-provoking and award-winning tutelage. Reading it will likely change your life too.

Armed with facts about the human struggle for productivity in all its dimensions, with considerable data (macroeconomic and otherwise) at your fingertips, and being fully informed of how the past's long shadow often inhibits the present and skewers our future, you will gain a deep understanding of what it takes to build and sustain competitiveness and be much better prepared for your workplace wherever you are in the world. You will also be a better-informed global citizen, ready to ensure we all work together to make the twenty-first century a triumph for all inhabiting our wonderful but fragile planet.

I do hope Americans in particular share this book's message with others. As is detailed in these pages, there is much to fix in our country, and many ideas molded by data and the tyranny of logic are suggested in Chapters 4 and 5 to achieve the required repairs. If implemented, though at times painful but never unbearably so, they will move our country onto a more sustainable path. With an economy powered by clean energy and still the envy of the world—and driven by an educated, diverse, growing workforce armed to sustain high-value, innovation-led growth—a cleaner, less consumptive, more equitable America is within our reach. But change is needed!

American exceptionalism benefited the world for over a century, and this will not stop should a rebalanced America and its people continue working alongside others to make the twenty-first century our first truly global century—not the American century, as the twentieth century is often called, or the Chinese century, as some speculate will eventually describe the present century.

To understand and appreciate what this means and your role in making it happen, read on . . .

INTRODUCTION

This book is about the human struggle for productivity and how after hundreds of thousands of years of hunter-gathering and subsistence farming, our productive abilities suddenly blossomed over the past two centuries into a world now divisible into three eras: the Pre-Industrial Era (pre-1800), the Industrial Era (1800–1950), and the Post-Industrial Era (1950 onward). How nations, organizations, and individuals shaped the productive miracle that has transpired and, more importantly, how all will advance and prosper in the ongoing struggle moving forward are explained.

Chapter 1 reveals how global economic output evolved over recorded history and clarifies why Leaders, Followers, and Failures best characterize the eras that emerged. Two models, the Life Cycle and S Curve, indicate the paths our struggle for productivity may follow over the foreseeable future, and six factors that could cause our future to conform to the Life Cycle's four stages of early birth, high growth, maturity, and decline/death are identified. Considering a meteor strike, nuclear conflict, biological disaster, human population explosion, raw material scarcity, and global warming/climate change, only the last factor has the potential to cause global meltdown, the third and worst of the three future scenarios presented. But with global warming/climate change mitigated, the other factors are unlikely to stop progress, and the more optimistic S Curve better captures the futures we may face. Chapter 1 explains why this is so.

Chapters 2 to 4 catalog the conditions encountered in each era and provide an unmatched description of the conditions across our economic landscape today, revealing a world more unequal than at any time in history. Though most in the post-industrial world enjoy living standards immeasurably better than their ancestors of only 100 years ago, almost half of Earth's eight billion people still live in pre-industrial subsistence. The key uncertainty over the coming century is how many of those now failing and excluded become Followers and join the human struggle for productivity as they modernize.

Chapter 2 describes the world of our past and explains why scarcity endured until around 200 years ago. To understand the present and prepare for the future, the past and its legacy must be accounted for. Chapter 3 captures the rigors of industrialization and the discipline and deferred gratification required to start and complete the multigenerational process. The Industrial Era is considered the world of the present for those still mired in pre-industrial conditions.

Chapter 4 then reveals the conditions now emerging across the post-industrial world, denoted as the world of the future for those currently building it and especially for those still living in industrial or pre-industrial conditions. Post-industrial robotics, air travel, retailing, automobile manufacturing, and earthmoving provide up-to-date descriptions of the Post-Industrial Era in all of its intricacy.

Analyzing our human struggle for productivity in three eras clarifies how economic, organizational, and political economy characteristics change as productivity advances. How productive organization evolved from vertically integrated corporations controlled by human hierarchies in the Industrial Era to the automated and disaggregated supplier, partner, and customer networks of the Post-Industrial Era is also explained, as is how post-industrial creative and transformative work differ from manual assembly line work done by workers in industrial times.

Caterpillar's partnership with Trimble Navigation to automate earth-moving and Boeing's GoldCare show how industrial products and services evolved into complex, technology-based solutions now operating across the Internet of Things in post-industrial markets. Nike, Microsoft, Amazon, and others are also analyzed to reveal how the value of post-industrial human capital differs so markedly from that of the Industrial Era.

Chapters 3 to 5 further outline what political and business leaders must do to sustain Leader positions, what leaders of Followers must do to catch up, and what Failures must do to become Followers to escape conditions they face. To inform Failures of the paths to follow, the First Movers into the Industrial Era—the Americans and Europeans—are contrasted with the Fast Followers who mostly industrialized in the twentieth century—Japan, Hong Kong, Singapore, Taiwan, and South Korea. Fast Followers and not First Movers should be studied to understand industrialization.

After summarizing the economic diversity in our world today and considering what it takes to compete in these varied contexts, Chapter 5 underscores the urgent threat our warming planet presents. Balanced global growth, unbalanced global growth, and global meltdown then capture the scenarios our collective future may face. After arguing that unbalanced global growth will likely eventuate, this book closes with the steps all should take to ensure that balanced global growth ultimately prevails.

The closing pages focus on what Americans should do to ensure their country remains a Leader so that the world regains a confident advocate able to work alongside others and the best future prevails for us all. The biggest enemy facing America is not the Chinese or those crossing its borders illegally in search of better lives. It is those wishing to isolate the country from a changing world as their fears and insecurities are pandered to. Only leaders who acknowledge the challenges facing the country—

many identified in these pages—and who offer bipartisan solutions to conquer them will mobilize Americans to save their country from itself.

The material in this book stands on the shoulders of many, ranging from Thomas Hobbes to Thomas Malthus to Adam Smith to Karl Marx to Alfred Chandler to Frederick Taylor to Peter Drucker to Michael Hammer to James Champy to Angus Maddison to Jean-Baptiste Say to John Maynard Keynes to Nobel laureates Simon Kuznets, Robert Solow, and Oliver Williamson. Their contributions are woven into the fabric of the productive advances described.

Finally, to summarize key points and ideas and to aid understanding, learning, and retention, a conclusion and synthesis is provided at the end of the first four chapters. Care is also taken to define key concepts and constructs for those less familiar with the terms used. To list some, input-led and innovation-led growth, the Internet of Things, purchasing power parity, political economy, subsistence existence, and industrial policy are all defined or clarified for readers. Likewise, readers will encounter many new concepts, such as First Mover and Fast Follower industrialization; authoritarian developmentalists versus authoritarian plunderers; the complementary, conflicting, and sequential hypotheses to explain the modern distributive democracy/early industrialization relationship; democracy light; post-industrial creative and transformative work; organizational creative cores; societal hospital passes; and Leader problems of wealth and Follower problems of poverty, to name a few.

CHAPTER 1

UNDERSTANDING THE BIG PICTURE

Our Human Struggle for Productivity from Pre- to Post-Industrial Production, or Failing, Following, and Leading

Imagine you have lived for as long as reliable human records have been kept, say for the past 7,000 years or so, and you were asked to evaluate economic progress over these many thousands of years.[1] Did the living conditions and material freedoms enjoyed by humans improve? Are we better off today than we were 2,000 years ago? If so, was progress linear, or was a nonlinear pattern followed? Based on empirical data, you might give mankind a failing grade, and why so low is easy to explain. Over most of your journey, you would have lived in agrarian subsistence, eking out a tenuous living off the land, engaged in either hunting-gathering or

1 Homo sapiens, or "wise man," has been on Earth longer than the 7,000 years evaluated here. Mitochondrial DNA reveals we are traceable back to a most recent common African female ancestor of around 200,000 years ago (Mitochondrial Eve), while male DNA goes back to a common paternal ancestor of around 150,000 years ago (Y-chromosomal Adam), who was also African. (Brandon Specktor, "Scientists Think They've Found 'Mitochondrial Eve's' First Homeland," Live Science, October 28, 2019, accessed May 1, 2023, https://www.livescience.com/mitochondrial-eve-first-human-homeland.html). Genetic, paleontological, and linguistic evidence also show anatomically modern humans existed only in Africa until around 100,000 years ago, then leaving Africa to populate the world (John Reader, *Africa: A Biography of the Continent* [New York: Vintage Books, 1997], 97). Man's first globalization was his move out of Africa into Europe and Asia, and then across the Bering Strait into the Americas.

small-scale, peasant-based farming. Weather would have been your most worrisome variable. If rain came you would give thanks and eat. If rain was sparse, starvation was possible, even likely.

Second to weather, other humans—likely the tribe next door—would have been your gravest concern. Because of man's inhumanity to man, you might have been enslaved by Egyptians in 1600 BC, captured by Romans at the birth of Christ, or seized by Attila the Hun after he invaded your homeland in AD 440. Maybe you would have died from bubonic plague in Europe in the fourteenth century or watched many thousands die from the smallpox, measles, influenza, and typhus the European conquistadores introduced to the New World in the sixteenth century. These epidemics killed around 75 percent of the region's indigenous population[2] and led English philosopher Thomas Hobbes to conclude that life in the mid-seventeenth century was potentially "solitary, poor, nasty, brutish, and short."[3]

After surveying the lot of the everyman for most of your time on Earth, you might conclude that Hobbes's description was not that far off the mark. Scarcity, struggle, and plundering summarized life for most. But Hobbes did not think that life was unavoidably or inevitably "solitary, poor, nasty, brutish, and short." To him, the lack of good government left life unpleasant and jarring for most. He was correct. Good government and strong institutions are as vital to lifting societies out of poverty today as they were when Hobbes penned *Leviathan* in 1651.

Fortunately, the difficulty you would have observed began diminishing a century or so later with the Industrial Revolution's advent. If you surveyed the lives of some in Great Britain at the beginning of the twentieth century or in the United States or Europe a few decades later (better to do after the Great Depression), the progress made in the last few moments of your 7,000 years would have amazed you. After over 150,000 years of stumbling around (see footnote 1), the material living

---

2 Niall Ferguson, *Empire: How Britain Made the Modern World* (London: Penguin Books, 2003), 58.
3 Thomas Hobbes, chap. 13, para. 9 in *Leviathan or The Matter, Forme and Power of a Common Wealth Ecclesiasticall and Civil* (London: Printed by William Wilson for Andrew Crooke, 1651).

conditions in the last 250 years in some societies changed considerably for the better. Middle-class living standards in the 1950s and 1960s were substantially higher than those of the French nobility before the French Revolution. Apart from his house—the Palace of Versailles—and his thousands of servants, Louis XVI would have been deeply impressed, maybe even envious.

Though the last French sovereign's reaction to twentieth-century life is speculative, capturing the conditions encountered over your journey is not. Chapters 2 to 4 offer such descriptions primarily so that what the coming century holds for mankind is determinable. Our history and present time very much affect what the future may hold. Chapter 5 then presents the three futures we may face and clarifies what should be done to ensure the best future eventuates for us all.

The Advance of Global Economic Output: Millennia of Scarcity Followed by Two Centuries of Astounding Success

Economically, millennia of human struggle have been followed by two centuries of astounding success, producing material standards of living unimaginable to those alive in 1800. Figure 1 captures how global economic output grew over investigation. As indicated, output remained relatively flat over recorded time until around 1800, when the Industrial Revolution began. Growth then picked up dramatically, such that by the mid-twentieth century it was exponential.

Figure 1: The Human Struggle for Productivity

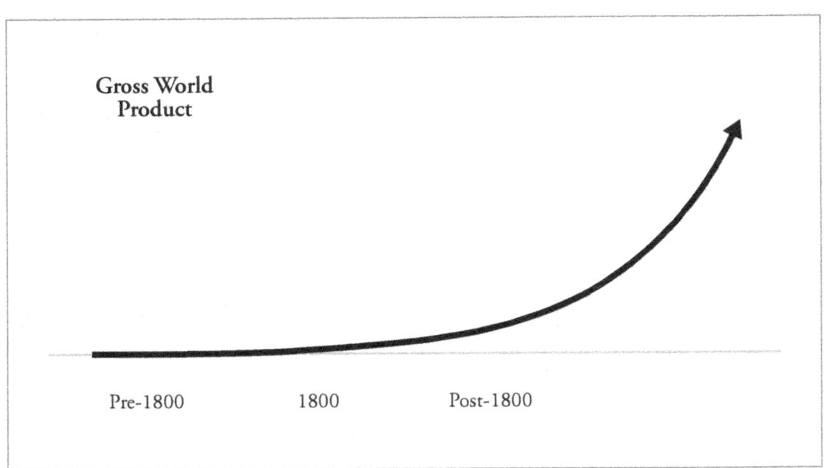

Economic historians performing the complicated task of estimating gross world product (GWP) over time indicate that global output, calibrated in international dollars ($), grew from $1.21 trillion in 1820 to $3.41 trillion by 1900 as the Industrial Revolution gathered pace, reached $8.41 trillion by 1950, increased sevenfold to $59.87 trillion by 2000, and added an impressive $53.76 trillion in 18 years to reach $113.63 trillion in 2018.[4] This data mirrors the exponential growth from the mid-twentieth century depicted in Figure 1 and reports that the $113.63 trillion GWP produced by 7.47 billion people in 2018 was divided regionally and nationally as follows:

4 Jutta Bolt and Jan Luiten van Zanden, "Maddison Style Estimates of the Evolution of the World Economy. A New 2020 Update," Maddison Project Database (2020), accessed November 10, 2023, https://www.rug.nl/ggdc/historicaldevelopment/maddison/releases/maddison-project-database-2020. International dollars ($) buy the same quantity and quality of goods and services no matter when spent. Inflation and cost of living adjustments are made, and purchasing power is fixed over time and across countries. GDP measures total goods and services produced over a specific time by a defined unit (e.g., a country or region), usually for a year, calculated typically at market prices based on nominal exchange rates or at prices based on purchasing power parity, or PPP. Footnote 443 explains how these two measures are calculated. GWP growing from $1.21 trillion to $113.63 trillion and the regional data reported is from Our World in Data, "Gross Domestic Product (GDP) by World Region," Oxford Martin School, Oxford University, accessed November 10, 2023, https://ourworldindata.org/grapher/gdp-world-regions-stacked-area. Oxford University's Martin School aggregates data from the Maddison Project Database, version 2020, and cites this data as its source.

- East Asia, including China's $18.15 trillion produced by 1.39 billion people, at $26.43 trillion (23 percent of GWP)
- Western Offshoots, including America's $18.14 trillion produced by 327.84 million people, at $21.22 trillion (19 percent of GWP)
- South and Southeast Asia, including India's $8.84 trillion produced by 1.30 billion people, at $18.56 trillion (16 percent of GWP)
- Western Europe, 421 million people, at $16.74 trillion (15 percent of GWP)
- Middle East, 534.10 million people, at $9.84 trillion (9 percent of GWP)
- Latin/South America, 620.43 million people, at $8.73 trillion (8 percent of GWP)
- Eastern Europe, 406.41 million people, at $8.40 trillion (7 percent of GWP)
- Sub-Saharan Africa, 1.05 billion people, at $3.70 trillion (3 percent of GWP)

With inflation and purchasing power differences accounted for, the data shows how productivity was spread around the world in 2018. East Asia, which includes China, was responsible for 23 percent of GWP, while America and the other Western Offshoots (Canada, Australia, and New Zealand), with 395 million people, accounted for 19 percent. South and Southeast Asia, which includes India, produced 16 percent of GWP, while western Europe, with 421 million people, produced 15 percent. The Middle East, Latin America, and Eastern Europe produced 9, 8, and 7 percent, respectively, with Latin/South America's larger population producing less than those of the Middle East or Eastern Europe. Least productive, sub-Saharan Africa's over 1 billion people account for only 3 percent of GWP.

Global production inequality is better revealed when population is divided into output to yield averages per person. In 1820, average annual GWP per capita was $1,102 and reached $2,212 by 1900, $3,351 by

1950, and $9,915 by 2000. By 2018, average global output per capita had climbed to $15,212.

Decomposing this average into smaller units, America's 2018 annual per capita production of $55,335 exceeded western Europe's $39,790, which, though only 72 percent of the American average, was still three times that of China's $13,102. India's average annual output of $6,806 was close to half of China's, and sub-Saharan Africa at $3,532 was only about half of India's. Eastern Europe's 406.41 million residents each produced $20,681, while the 534.1 million people in the Middle East produced $18,430 each, mostly from oil production. Of these three regions, Latin/South America was lowest at $14,076, though still above China and India.

The above averages do not take into account how income is distributed. As income is distributed unequally everywhere, citizens in each country/region produced even less than the average number suggests. The poor in India and sub-Saharan Africa lived on even less than the $19 and $10 per day that their average outputs suggest (obtained by dividing the annual output per capita by 365), as did the average American who relied on less than the $152 per day the data reports. The wide inequality in global production noted in the data and what it means is also addressed in Chapter 5, where the economic diversity both between and within countries and the implications of the unequal status quo are evaluated.

Flat, however, is too stark to describe pre-nineteenth-century output growth and material life. Before 1800 there were ups and downs and better versus worse times. Roman living standards at the peak of the Roman Empire were higher than in Europe during the Dark Ages. After the Roman Empire's fall, Europe endured a long period of economic and agricultural decline. Notwithstanding these ups and downs, however, given the impressive progress since 1750, any productive accomplishments prior to the Industrial Revolution, relatively speaking, are worthy of the label *flat*. There was little advance until the Industrial Revolution, which once underway delivered unprecedented gains.

The recent impressive growth in global output depicted in Figure 1 compared with the low growth that endured previously is confirmed by others. John Maynard Keynes, the renowned English economist who wrote the economic theory that guided the world out of the Great Depression, noted that human living standards did not change for 4,000 years preceding the Industrial Revolution, that European and American living standards had increased fourfold since 1700, and that factory output per capita in the United States was 40 percent higher in 1925 than in 1919.[5]

Maddison presents similar data comparing the annual Gross Domestic Product (GDP) per capita of China and western Europe from 400 to 1998.[6] GDP is the market value of all final goods or services produced in a country over a specific period. Chinese GDP per capita shows a trajectory similar to that in Figure 1, though in 1950 the Chinese GDP per capita was still where it was almost 10 centuries earlier at around US$450 per annum. It then grew substantially over the next 50 years to reach almost US$3,000 by 1998. The global pre-1800 flatness is mimicked in China but shows the country's advance only began in the 1970s rather than in the eighteenth century, when industrialization started in Europe.

China's economic path replicates those preceding it in their respective struggles for productivity, and again the pattern is repeated—many thousands of years of dismal performance followed by exponential growth once industrialization is underway. Confirming the almost exponential increases enjoyed after economic takeoff, Chinese GDP per capita in 2022 was estimated at US$17,600, six times higher in one generation (25 years).[7]

Maddison also notes that western European GDP per capita only doubled from 1000 to 1750—from less than US$500 to around

---

5 John Maynard Keynes, "Economic Possibilities for our Grandchildren (1930)," in *Essays in Persuasion* (New York: Harcourt Brace, 1932), 358–73.

6 Angus Maddison, *The World Economy: A Millennial Perspective* (Paris: Development Centre of the Organisation for Economic Co-operation and Development, 2001), 42.

7 *The World Factbook*, "Explore All Countries," Central Intelligence Agency, Washington, DC, updated 2021, accessed May 1, 2023, https://www.cia.gov/the-world-factbook/countries/.

US$1,000—underscoring that the Western Europe line from 1000 was close to flat too. Doubling output per capita over 750 years is an annual average growth of only 0.0924623 percent, far less than 0.1 percent annually. With GDP per capita in western Europe reaching around US$18,000 per annum by 1998, the overall tenor depicted in Figure 1 is confirmed in Europe. As economies mature, however, the rate does slow down: the European Union's 2021 GDP per capita was estimated at US$44,100, more than twice its figure in 1998.[8] Developing economies with annual growths of 8 percent double output in just over nine years.

To support the dramatic increase in economic growth seen over the last century or so, note that the growth rates enjoyed by some industrializing nations in the last quarter of the twentieth century greatly exceeded those the United States and European economies achieved in their early industrializations. In addition, over the eighteenth century an average annual global growth rate of only around 0.33 percent was achieved, followed by an unimpressive 1 percent per annum over the nineteenth century. In the first 60 years of the twentieth century, however, global output increased by 2.4 percent per annum and reached 4 percent per annum in the last 40 years of the twentieth century.[9] As knowledge about industrialization increased, so did overall economic growth rates.

Apart from the obvious rise in material living standards observed for some over the past 250 years, an additional argument supports the idea that for those living in the industrialized world, conditions are indeed better. A period of reduced volatility, denoted by economists as the Great Moderation, is now empirically clear: not only have living standards improved for those in the developed industrial economies, but the overall macroeconomic risks faced by these economies have decreased significantly too. A technical definition of risk relates to measuring the variation of a set of numbers around the average of those numbers: the more

8 *The World Factbook*, "Explore All Countries."

9 Robert E. Lucas, "The Industrial Revolution: Past and Future," *2003 Annual Report Essay* (The Federal Reserve Bank of Minneapolis, 2004), 3.

the observed variation around the average, the greater the risk accompanying the numbers in the data concerned.

According to this definition of risk—variation around an average—the American economy is far less risky today than it was 75 years ago. Figure 2 presents US Department of Commerce Bureau of Economic Analysis (BEA) data reporting annual real US GDP growth from 1930 until 2022, and in this data is a clear decrease in variation (i.e., a reduction in risk over time).[10] The dispersion of annual GDP growth rates (indicated in the larger dots) around the average (captured in the small dot trend line) decreases notably over the period reflected in the data. The downward trend of US GDP growth in Figure 2 confirms again that growth declines as an economy matures.

Figure 2: US Real GDP Growth: 1930–2022

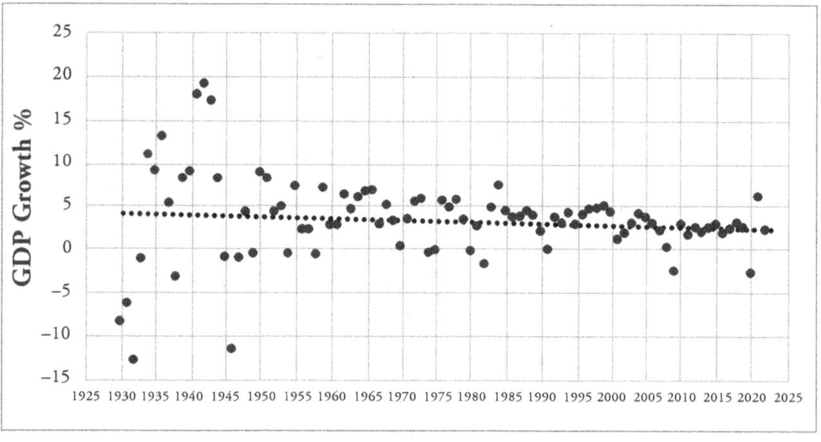

The data in Figure 2 is one of the most profound sets of economic data on record. Ben Bernanke, former chair of the American Federal Reserve Board, described the Great Moderation as "striking."[11] According to the

10 US Department of Commerce Bureau of Economic Analysis (BEA), "Gross Domestic Product," accessed May 1, 2023, https://www.bea.gov/data/gdp/gross-domestic-product. The real annual economic growth in Figure 2 is in chained 2012 dollars.

11 Ben S. Bernanke, "The Great Moderation," Remarks by Governor Ben S. Bernanke (at the meetings of the Eastern Economic Association, Washington, DC, on February 20, 2004), accessed May 1, 2023, https://www.federalreserve.gov/boarddocs/speeches/2004/20040220/.

BEA data, in the 1930s, annual growth rates in US real GDP ranged from –12.9 percent in 1932 to 12.9 percent in 1936. Moreover, in the years from 1930 to 1933, America lost a cumulative 29 percent of its productive capacity, while from 1934 to 1937, an equivalent cumulative 37.7 percent growth in real output was achieved, more than recouping the capacity lost over the previous four years.

The Great Depression destroyed the economic security of a generation, contributed to the start of World War II, and left an indelible memory on all misfortunate enough to live through it. During World War II, however, growth in the American economy was inordinately high, ranging from 8 percent in 1939 and 1944 and between 17 and 18.9 percent from 1941 to 1943.

But the wide dispersion of US GDP growth in the 1930s and 1940s did not last. By the 1950s it had narrowed noticeably and became even less volatile from the 1960s onward. Most impressively, from 1990 to 2022, average annual economic growth rates in the United States ranged between –2.8 percent in 2020 to 5.9 percent in 2021—the recent volatility from the COVID-19 pandemic. In addition, since 1990, only three years have shown negative real GDP growth, these being in 1991, 2009, and 2020, at rates of –0.1, –2.6, and –2.8 percent, respectively. Even in the economic adjustment after the housing bubble burst in 2007, before the 2020–21 pandemic (arguably the most significant economic event since the Great Depression), America lost almost 3 percent of its capacity over a single year. Measured in variation around an average, the US economy since 1950 has been far less risky than it was in the 1930s and 1940s.

This moderation is not only noticed in the United States. A 2006 multicounty study reported the same effect in 16 of 25 countries studied; real GDP growth was far less volatile than it was previously in these 16. In addition, the declines in volatility were all noted to be large, averaging more than 50 percent.[12] Most notable is that this widespread Great Moderation was not accomplished by a grand global economic plan. It mostly just happened; though as Chapter 3 describes, good fiscal and monetary policy explains some of the moderation. Good government is part of the story, but this still does not make the moderation *planned.* That at a macroeconomic level the leading economies in the world are becoming more stable supports the idea that humans in these countries are better off now than they were just 75 years ago. Those asserting that the world is becoming more unstable economically are wrong. Progress is being made.

The successes enjoyed over the past 250 years lend support to at least a partially positive answer to the question posed in your investigation: many across the world today are far better off than they would have been living only 100 years ago. Given the choices middle- and upper-class Americans, Europeans, and Asians now have, it is hard to argue they are not better off than their ancestors were only one or two generations ago. This does not apply, however, to all or possibly to the majority of the over 8 billion humans now on Earth.[13] As Figure 3 points out, most are still excluded from these gains; whether the majority of humans are better off is debatable. For those enjoying middle- or upper-class lives across the industrialized world, it is not.

Cataloging the Human Struggle for Productivity: Eras, Times, Populations, Sectors

Dividing humanity's overall economic journey into three eras offers more detail on our human struggle for productivity. Alvin Toffler also categorized human economic experiences into three waves: the first when agriculture replaced hunter-gathering, the second after the Industrial

12 Stephen G. Cecchetti, Alfonso Flores-Lagunes, and Stefan Krause, "Assessing the Sources of Changes in the Volatility of Real Growth," (working paper 11946, National Bureau of Economic Research, January 2006), https://doi.org/10.3386/w11946.

13 Worldometer, "Current World Population," accessed May 1, 2023, https://www.worldometers.info/world-population/. This is a continually increasing estimate.

Revolution, and the third describing post-industrial society.[14] These are named here the Pre-Industrial Era, which accounts for recorded time before 1800; the Industrial Era, which lasted from around 1800 until 1950; and the Post-Industrial Era, which commenced in the 1950s and continues today.

Populations can also be categorized according to which era their living standards most closely correspond. One estimate is that 42.5 percent[15] of the world's 8.033 billion people[16] were not urbanized in 2023, meaning that around this percent still live rurally in pre-industrial conditions. However, as Chapter 2 explains, many of the 57.5 percent in urban settings around the world are now living in urban as opposed to rural subsistence and are not really industrialized. Rather, they live in urban subsistence. Figure 3 provides estimates of the percentage of humans living in each era based on better data.

Chapter 5 divides the global population into three segments of a pyramid from the base to the top according to purchasing power and provides additional data on the size and nature of each segment. A categorization of markets from low-end to good-enough to premium matches the segments identified. In addition, Table 14 reports worldwide GDP per capita and population size of regions and countries, and the seven most advanced economies in the world are listed as 776 million of our 7.836 billion global population with average GDP's per capita of US$67,166 compared to the 155 emerging/developing country US$15,183 average. This data provides additional support for the population size estimates in Figure 3.

Eras can also be categorized according to the dominant economic sectors accompanying them: in the Pre-Industrial Era subsistence agriculture occupies most, in the Industrial Era manufacturing dominates, and in the Post-Industrial Era services become the main economic activity. A

14 Alvin Toffler, *Future Shock* (London: The Bodley Head Ltd., 1970); and Alvin Toffler, *The Third Wave* (New York: William Morrow, 1981).

15 *The World Factbook*, "Explore All Countries."

16 Worldometer, "Current World Population."

2005 estimate placed services in advanced industrial economies at more than two-thirds of GDP.[17] Figure 3 reflects this shift from agriculture to manufacturing to services.

One clarification, however, regarding the transition from agriculture to manufacturing to services, is imperative. As industrialization unfolds, agriculture mechanizes, and through use of physical economic capital (i.e., machines), food output increases exponentially while employment in agriculture plummets. In 1900, over 40 percent of Americans worked in agriculture; today agriculture accounts for less than 2 percent of American GDP, and American agribusiness produces enough food for Americans and many others across the world. More importantly, in the pre-industrial to industrial transition, agricultural production does not diminish, only the number of humans working in the fields do.

The same is now underway as the shift from industrial to post-industrial manufacturing takes place. Goods are still being made; however, as the number of goods produced increases, the number of humans employed in direct manufacturing declines. As they did to agricultural workers, smart and adept machines are replacing human labor and the human hands once needed on the factory floor. Chapter 4 explains how the industrial world is being altered by post-industrial technical advances just as industrialization changed agriculture. Yet agriculture and manufacturing remain key components of economic activity; food and manufactured goods are still consumed in the Post-Industrial Era. How they are produced is what changes the most.

Finally, nations can also be assigned to an era depending on the economic conditions enjoyed by the majority of their citizens and depending upon how diversified their economies are. For example, around 80 percent of the American economy is in services, and this, together with an estimated 2022 real GDP per capita of around US$63,700,

---

17 George Liagouras, "The Political Economy of Post-Industrial Capitalism," *Thesis Eleven* 81, no. 1 (May 2005): 20–35, https://doi.org/10.1177/0725513605051612.

places America in the Post-Industrial Era.[18] Conversely, with a GDP per capita of around US$6,600 and with 63.6 percent of its citizens still living in rural areas and 15.4 percent of its economy in agriculture, India remains mostly pre-industrial.[19]

Regardless, categorizing nations into such large buckets should be done carefully. Elements of all three eras are present in most countries. For example, the Chinese economy is mostly industrial, but almost 7.9 percent of Chinese still rely on agriculture to survive, and only 64.6 percent of the Chinese population is urbanized.[20] Where China is exactly categorized depends on the weight given to each dimension; such categorization is not an exact science. Its real GDP per capita of US$17,600 shows the country is on its way to full industrialization or is at least further ahead than South Africa.[21] In contrast, South Africa has a modern industrial economy, but only 20 to 30 percent of the population actively participates in it. As the majority of South Africans still live in pre-industrial conditions, South Africa remains more developing than developed and more pre-industrial than industrial. Figure 3 summarizes all these dimensions in each of the three eras.

Placement of world population into the three eras at the ratios of 50, 40, and 10 percent, respectively, highlights a fact of which many are unaware. About half of humanity is still living in pre-industrial conditions and is yet to enjoy industrialization's benefits. This underscores the major economic challenge facing the world over the coming century: bringing the benefits of industrialization and modernization to those excluded from these gains. Further, this questions even the hyperbole of a *global* economy or a *global* market; neither exists today. Only half the world's population actively participates in this global economy.

---

18 *The World Factbook*, "Explore All Countries." The GDP estimate is based on purchasing power parity. For more on GDP estimated at purchasing power parity, or PPP, see footnote 493.
19 *The World Factbook*, "Explore All Countries."
20 *The World Factbook*, "Explore All Countries."
21 *The World Factbook*, "Explore All Countries."

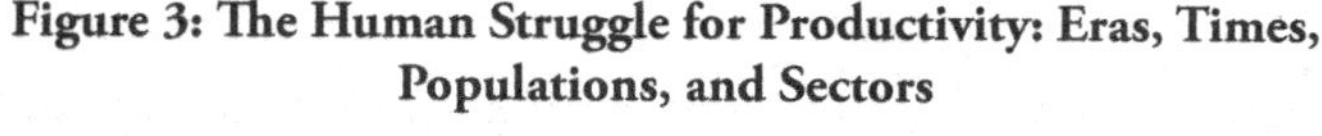

Figure 3: The Human Struggle for Productivity: Eras, Times, Populations, and Sectors

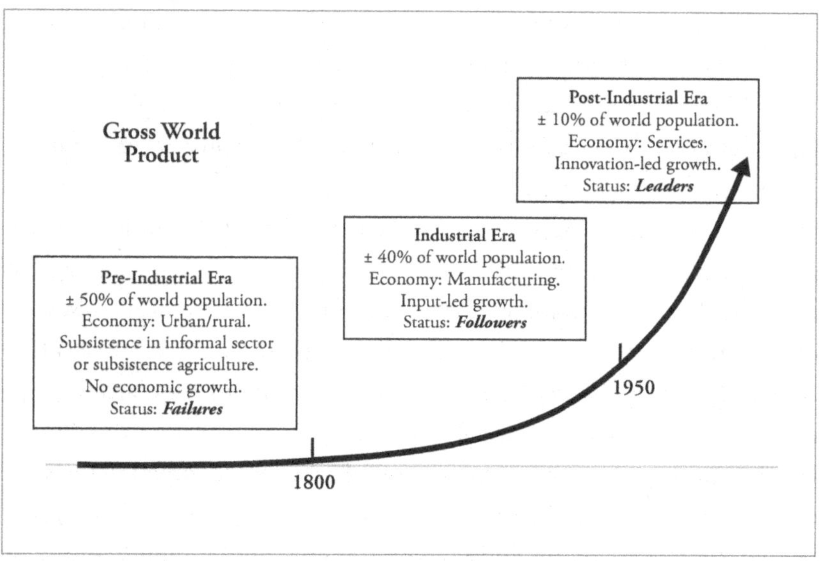

The three eras also explain the title of this book and emphasize the positions nations, firms, and individuals occupy in the human struggle for productivity: collectively we participate either as Leaders (Post-Industrial), Followers (Industrial), or Failures (Pre-Industrial). These roles are also indicated in Figure 3. Note that Failure in these pages is narrowly defined as economic failure alone, with Chapter 2 describing the world of the past that denoted all as Failures until industrialization began, and Chapter 3 revealing how industrialization's First Movers and Fast Followers escaped the economic scarcity plaguing humanity for time immemorial. Chapters 3 and 4 cover how nations, organizations, and individuals move from Failures to Followers and then to Leaders.

A final dimension worth highlighting from Figure 3 is how the nature and quality—and not only the quantum—of economic growth changes as societies advance from Failures to Followers to Leaders. Little or no economic growth occurred in the Pre-Industrial Era. Then in the Industrial Era, Figure 3 indicates input-led economic growth becomes the driver, while innovation-led growth characterizes the Post-Industrial Era. Chapters 3 and 4 explain input- and innovation-led growth, where they differ, and why Leaders invariably enjoy lower economic growth than do Followers as they catch up and industrialize.

Differentiating input-led from innovation-led growth also explains how Followers become Leaders. Once a nation is industrialized and has productive agents that compete globally at the efficient frontier of an industry, they are Leaders. These Leaders demonstrate by innovation-led growth that they possess the ability to stay ahead. In the language of this book, such innovation places these productive agents at the pinnacle of post-industrial productivity, given that production at the leading edge of human productivity is required to stay ahead. Leadership positions are also harder to dislodge if competitive advantage is distributed widely across an industry (for example, Germany's competitive advantage in automobile production). This capability may also be defended in national champions such as Samsung and Hyundai in South Korea or Taiwan's Taiwan Semiconductor Manufacturing Company.

Fully industrialized nations may boast few or even no leadership positions and still remain stable. Their average standard of living will not be as high as those who hold leadership positions, and most—if not all—of their economic activity will be national as opposed to global in nature. This is to be expected since the vast majority of economic activity is local, done by nationals for nationals in a country. Lastly, following really only applies for as long as a nation is catching up, and once caught up, a nation's economic position may not remain static. Competitive positions may be lost even by Leaders, causing them to become Followers for a time, and nations may also face challenges that cause economic decline regardless even of the competitiveness of some in their geographies. We now turn to the relative positions held by nations and regions to illustrate this last possibility.

CHAPTER 1

The Human Struggle for Productivity: With Progress, Failure Endures and Followers and Leaders Stumble

Figures 1 and 3 reflect the cumulative economic output of all engaged in the human struggle for productivity, but important perspectives are missing from both. Neither parcels out the relative contribution of individual nations nor reflects the travails of nations and regions still unable to join the struggle. Nations that reach the efficient frontier of global production but remain there for a time and then regress as others surge ahead are not reflected either.

For example, the Industrial Revolution started in Great Britain but was perfected in the United States. Great Britain dominated the world from the 1750s until the end of the nineteenth century, when America eclipsed Great Britain. America dominated until the end of the twentieth century, and China—and possibly others—will challenge this position over the coming decades. Though hard to capture in a two-dimensional space such as Figures 1 and 3, the relative individual positions of some nations and regions are depicted in Figure 4.

Figure 4 contains the familiar cumulative leading-edge graph seen in Figures 1 and 3 but also reflects conceptually—not numerically—the trajectories of some nations and regions from the 1950s to 2023. Nations remaining at the efficient frontier of global production remain on the familiar quantitative curve. Once they begin losing competitiveness, trajectories veer off, as is shown in the dashed slopes depicted in the four other curves. This veering off the leading-edge curve reflects a loss of competitiveness and a slowing of economic growth in the cases of the United States, Japan, and the USSR/Russia.

The most depressing line in Figure 4 (in the short-dash black) reflects the trajectory of sub-Saharan Africa. When taking into account population growth compared with regional output growth, average African living standards are lower today than they were in 1970. While America, Europe, and many in the Asia Pacific, Middle East, and Latin/South America progressed over the twentieth century, most in sub-Saharan

Africa did not. The notion of flat or even declining productivity is most applicable to sub-Saharan Africa; excluding South Africa, little industrialization or effective Following is seen across the subcontinent. The lack of economic growth in sub-Saharan Africa is conceptually captured by the short-dash black line.

Figure 4: The Human Struggle for Productivity: Relative Positions

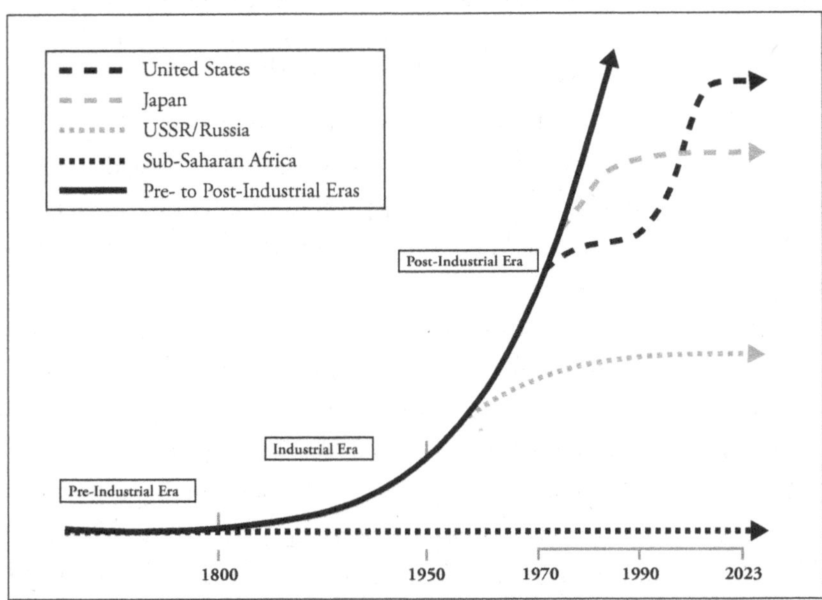

Explaining why sub-Saharan Africa remains at the back of the economic development table while others have progressed is important. One theory alleges the north-to-south shape of the African continent combined with a lack of domesticable animals caused the failure.[22] Because agriculture in northern Africa differed from agriculture at the equator or southern Africa, African settlements were unable to scale agriculture and remained small, isolated, and unproductive, expending much energy just struggling to survive. This absence of a capability that could be scaled has its modern equivalent. Chapter 5 underscores that essential to the success

22 Jared Diamond, *Guns, Germs, and Steel: The Fates of Human Societies* (New York: W. W. Norton and Company, 1997).

of any global company is possession of an economic capability that can be globalized. Without transferable capabilities, expansion fails.

By contrast, the east–west geography of continental Europe may have allowed Europeans to produce an agricultural surplus—agriculture in eastern Europe was not that different from farming on the western side—thus freeing labor to specialize and form larger, better organized settlements that supported faster population growth and higher levels of technical development. The scalability of agriculture on an east–west basis was most clearly seen in the European expansion into North America. After surviving their first winter with local help—accounting for America's most prominent secular holiday, Thanksgiving—had the early American settlers been unable to use their Europe-based agricultural knowledge in American soil, their settlements more than likely would have failed. Fortunately, America was on the same east–west axis geographically as Europe.

More proximate reasons also explain Africa's poor economic performance. The nineteenth-century scramble for Africa and how European colonization damaged the subcontinent is first among these, and an examination of the years of African independence from 1955 onward concluded that much of the most recent failure is due to poor leadership.[23] Geography, colonialization, and poor leadership all might explain the African discount, and as Figure 4 indicates, compared with conditions in other parts of the world, living conditions in sub-Saharan Africa remain depressingly low and, in some locations, declined over the twentieth century.

The long-dash black line captures the US trajectory from the 1970s until now. As indicated, America declined around the 1970s as Japanese and German manufacturing recovered from World War II and rose to prominence. However, emergence of the information technology (IT) and communications revolution in the late 1980s and 1990s, followed by development of the internet, revived American competitiveness such

23 Martin Meredith, *The State of Africa: A History of Fifty Years of Independence* (London: Free Press, 2005).

that by the end of the century, America was again close to the efficient frontier of production. This is reflected by the long-dash black line again mimicking the slope of the black line by the early 1990s, indicating a return to competitive growth in America. The country remained on this trajectory until the end of the twentieth century. Now, after the internet bubble, the 2007 subprime mortgage economic crisis, and the COVID-19 pandemic, American competitiveness again faces some challenges, indicated by the flattening in the long-dash black line after 2000.

Chapter 5 provides insights into America's post-2000 loss of competitiveness. As readers will see, the decline is attributable to a variety of factors, including an increase in debt—both public and private—as the country borrowed rather than created its prosperity, a rising inequality that indicates average Americans are falling behind, an increase in healthcare costs that if unabated will likely become unaffordable, and taxes too low to sustain the expenditures the US federal government chooses to incur. Even the best businesses will not thrive in a society where the social contract is fraying and social cohesion is deteriorating.

The long-dash gray line captures Japan's trajectory, which from the 1960s until the 1980s enjoyed growth at the efficient frontier of global manufacturing in some sectors—mostly consumer electronics and automobiles—but since the 1990s has encountered trouble. Japan's strong economic growth in the 1970s and 1980s stopped in the early 1990s, and the time from then until the present are considered lost decades. The flattening of the long-dash gray line indicates this loss of competitiveness. Japan is currently the world's most indebted country, with its gross public debt to GDP ratio estimated at 261 percent.[24]

---

24 International Monetary Fund (IMF), "Gross Public Debt, Percent of GDP," Public Finances in Modern History Database, accessed December 20, 2023, https://www.imf.org/external/datamapper/d@FPP/USA/FRA/JPN/GBR/SWE/ESP/ITA/ZAF/IND?year=2022. Notes the IMF: "The Public Finances in Modern History Database documents 200 years of the history of budget deficits and government debts. The current version covers 151 countries over the period 1800–2022, subject to data availability." Accessed December 20, 2023, https://www.imf.org/external/datamapper/datasets/FPP.

Finally, the short-dash gray line reflects the trajectory of the former Soviet Union—the USSR, now the Russian Federation—which followed a model that achieved partial industrialization by the 1950s but that in the 1970s was becoming unsustainable and by the mid-1980s needed radical restructuring. After World War II and especially in the 1950s and 1960s, the former USSR outperformed the United States in the production of many basic industrial goods. In addition, the Sputnik launch in 1957 and placing the first man in Earth orbit in 1961 (Yuri Gagarin) underscored the USSR's advancing technical capability, giving impetus to Soviet Premier Nikita Khrushchev's 1956 threat that communism would "bury" capitalism. From the 1960s onward, however, flaws in the centrally planned state-owned economic model became more and more obvious such that by the 1980s, then Soviet Premier Mikhail Gorbachev was unable to keep the USSR intact. The flattening of the short-dash gray line from the 1970s onward depicts this decline.

Including individual lines, in addition to the overall cumulative measure of output reflected in Figures 1 and 3, contributes two important ideas. First, it is not certain that all nations or regions will join the human struggle for productivity. Some may remain enduring Failures. Chapter 5 considers this outcome as economic scenarios for the twenty-first century are explored. Second, even those that reach the efficient frontier of production and dominate for a while may not remain dominant forever.

Figure 4's various dashed lines also underscore how Failure, Follower, or Leader may be applied more dynamically to individual nations and regions. As the trajectories reflect, over time Leaders may lose their edge and lag and fall behind others; Failure is only occupied by nations who have not yet joined the struggle for productivity as Followers. Chapter 2 considers the conditions encountered by Failures and describes why failure has been present for so long. Chapter 3 then explains the actions that move nations from failing to following and shows that those who diversified economically over the twentieth century did so by replicating steps taken by others before them, hence the descriptor Followers.

Chapter 4 finally explains how leadership is sustained at the leading edge of the human struggle for productivity.

In Chapters 3 and 4, Leading, Following, or Failing is considered at organizational and individual levels too, leading to a central question asked in this book: As you reflect upon the human struggle for productivity, which of the three categories are you and your community closest to? Are you Leading, Following, or Failing? Further, while no nation has regressed from Leader back to Failure, this is not the case for organizations. Organizations fail continually, outcompeted by others better than they are. Survival of the fittest is a central tenet of modern capitalism regardless of where it is practiced. Understanding how Leading, Following, and Failing differ—and how those before you moved from Failure to Follower, or from Follower to Leader—offers insights into how failing or regression back to following from leading are avoided.

Forecasting the Human Struggle for Productivity: Avoiding the Apocalypse

Before considering more deeply the conditions faced by Failures, Followers, or Leaders, how the overall data depicted in Figure 1 might progress in the future is an important question to ponder. What will the graph look like at 2100 or beyond? Two models, the Life Cycle and S Curve, provide paths the human struggle for productivity might follow over the foreseeable future. Figure 5 presents the Life Cycle model, which divides growth into four segments: early birth, high growth, maturity, and finally, decline and death.

The Life Cycle model explains much to do with economic man. Industries, companies, products, services, and technologies typically follow the phases in the model. Humans do too: after birth we experience periods of early and high growth, reach maturity—human bodies peak in their 20s and 30s—and by our late 40s or 50s, we face decline and finally death in our 60s or hopefully beyond. If humanity's progress aligns with Figure 5's pattern, Failure will eventually describe the overall human experiment.

Figure 5: The Life Cycle Model

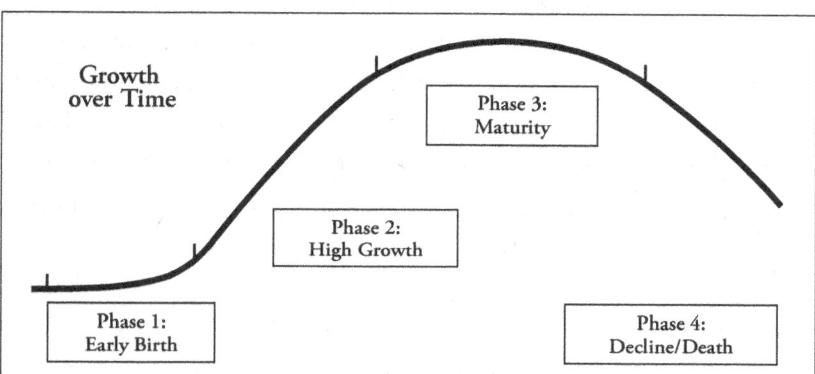

To determine if mankind's overall struggle for productivity will follow the phases depicted in the Life Cycle model, rephrasing the question helps. Rather than speculating on whether the Life Cycle model best explains human productivity over time, a better question is what factors could make the pattern follow the path depicted in this model? Six make the short list: a meteor strike, widespread nuclear conflict, a biological disaster, human population explosion, raw material scarcity, and global warming/climate change. The last factor is named global warming/climate change to underscore it is global warming that is causing climate change. Of these six, this last factor is of most concern.

The rest of this chapter explains why the first five are unlikely to cause Figure 1 to conform to the Life Cycle model and then suggests what shape Figure 1 might follow presuming the Life Cycle model is avoided. Chapter 5 explains why global warming/climate change in particular might force convergence toward the Life Cycle model over the next century. Whether this occurs depends on how quickly we reduce the carbon being added to our atmosphere.

Forecasting the Human Struggle for Productivity: Avoiding the Apocalypse

A meteor strike is the first event that might shorten humanity's time on Earth. One explanation for the dinosaurs' quick disappearance is that such an event occurred 65 million years ago. Geological evidence suggests a large meteor hit the Yucatan Peninsula around this time, and it is hypothesized that the resultant explosion created a significant change in the Earth's atmosphere such that 75 percent of the planet's living species perished.[25] Not all scientists, however, agree with this theory. Some assert the Yucatan impact was not big enough to cause such widespread damage. Nevertheless, a massive meteor strike is listed as the first potential danger to the longevity of humans on Earth.

Though small, the threat is taken seriously by the National Aeronautics and Space Administration (NASA), an independent US government agency responsible for aviation and spaceflight. The agency's Center for Near-Earth Object Studies at the Jet Propulsion Lab of the California Institute of Technology scans for incoming objects that might endanger Earth, and its Near-Earth Object Program is investigating if any near-Earth objects (NEOs) could collide with Earth with calamitous effects. The center's website provides some comfort about the threat:

> No one should be overly concerned about an Earth impact of an asteroid or comet. The threat to any one person from auto accidents, disease, other natural disasters and a variety of other problems is much higher than the threat from NEOs. Over long periods of time, however, the chances of the Earth being impacted are not negligible so that some form of NEO insurance is warranted. At the moment, our best insurance rests with the NEO scientists and their efforts to first

25 Center for Near-Earth Object Studies, "NEO Basics: Life on Earth," NASA-Jet Propulsion Laboratory/California Institute of Technology, accessed May 1, 2023, https://cneos.jpl.nasa.gov/about/life_on_earth.html.

> find these objects and then track their motions into the future. We need to first find them, then keep an eye on them.[26]

According to NASA, there is little need to worry too much about this threat. If an incoming projectile is identified, methods to divert or destroy it will be identified.

Widespread nuclear conflict is a second factor that could stop human progress in its tracks. Ironically, the effect of such conflict is not unlike that of a large meteor strike, and with the demise of the Soviet Union and the end of the Cold War, the likelihood of this occurring diminished considerably. To be significant enough to jeopardize the sustainability of human life, a large-scale nuclear exchange that causes nuclear winter is required. A few nuclear devices detonated, while disastrous for those at the blasts' epicenters, would not imperil man's overall survival.

In the twentieth century, massive nonnuclear conflict between the world's richest nations—World Wars I and II—slowed progress but did not derail our ongoing march forward. The same can be said of the two nuclear bombs detonated over Japan in 1945. The world survived the destruction of two world wars and two nuclear explosions, and the global economy emerged stronger after reconstruction in Europe and Japan in the 1950s and 1960s.

World wars led by great powers of the twentieth-century type now seem behind us. The formation of the European Union and convergence of the interests of the world's leading economic powers have made such events even less likely. Some worry, however, that nations like Russia or China either individually or in partnership might become global hegemonic forces, but in the long run, this outcome also may be unlikely. Given its recent economic progress, China will not have to invade the world to exercise its power; where needed, it may be able to buy it. Soft

---

26 Center for Near-Earth Object Studies, "NEO Basics: Target Earth," NASA-Jet Propulsion Laboratory/California Institute of Technology, accessed May 1, 2023, https://cneos.jpl.nasa.gov/about/target_earth.html.

power is always a better tool upon which to extend national influence than military power.

Noted historian Paul Kennedy's caution that economic power is first needed so military power can then be built must also be kept in mind.[27] Russia has already tried to dominate using hard power, but its failed economic model meant its supremacy could not be sustained. China's military expenditure, however, is second only to that of the United States,[28] and some worry that a Chinese invasion of Taiwan might trigger a conflict between these two nations. Hopefully, the likelihood of such a conflict is small. It would likely be tragic for humanity.

A question often asked is, Could terrorism along the lines of other 9/11-type attacks derail human progress? Though unspeakable in both concept and execution, events of this magnitude, like the detonation of a few nuclear bombs, are not widespread enough to have enduring long-term effects. Ten thousand dissidents—or however many terrorist groups mobilize—will likely not bring down the world and stop the human experiment. They can, however, make life more dangerous and uncomfortable in the short term and tragic for innocent victims in the wrong place at the wrong time.

Related to terrorism is the fact that human conflict also changed over the twentieth century: localized conflicts in failed or failing states have replaced wars between the richer developed nations. Unfortunately, failed states are perfect contexts for terrorism and other abuses to flourish. Disruptions by failed states, however, are unlikely to halt mankind's overall advance. As long as dominant great powers do not resort to war

---

27 Paul Kennedy, *The Rise and Fall of the Great Powers: Economic Change and Military Conflict from 1500 to 2000* (New York: Random House, 1987).

28 US military expenditure in 2022 was US$867 billion: Statista Research, "Military Spending in the United States from the Fiscal Year of 2000 to 2022," June 15, 2023, accessed September 3, 2023, https://www.statista.com/statistics/272473/us-military-spending-from-2000-to-2012/. (Note: Statista Research is not the source of surveys or statistics but an aggregator of information from others. The website provides access to its sources.) China's was estimated at US$229 billion: Amrita Jash, "China's 2022 Defense Budget: Behind the Numbers," *China Brief* 22, no. 8 (2022), The Jamestown Foundation, accessed June 15, 2023, https://jamestown.org/program/chinas-2022-defense-budget-behind-the-numbers/.

to resolve their disagreements, human conflict is unlikely to lead to the end of humanity.

Third on the list of potential disrupters is a biological disaster. This concern is not new. Plagues have been documented since 400 BC, with the European bubonic plagues of the fourteenth and fifteenth centuries the most damaging on record. The populations of Europe and the Middle East reduced by approximately one-third in the Black Death of the 1300s, and its economic effects were momentous. Economic depression resulted, and a stagnant Europe almost at its Malthusian limits (page 35) was eventually replaced by an economy sustained by two-thirds of the population, using the same amount of land, capital, stock of coins, and bullion. Real wages rose and then fell as populations recovered, and prices spiked initially, followed by a long period of deflation.[29]

Though disastrous for those involved, large segments of the population always survived plagues, and the long-term effects seem relatively small. The global HIV and AIDS epidemic in the late twentieth century shows this too. Millions of lives were lost because of the HIV virus, but its spread is now checked, and with the retroviral treatments available, the disease's worst effects are kept at bay. The COVID-19 pandemic in 2020–21 also stopped progress for a short time, and the rapid development of vaccines and other treatments quickly moved the threat from pandemic to endemic. The possibility of a biological calamity stopping humanity is accordingly small.

Explosive population growth is a fourth potential concern. Remarkably, the growth of human population is similar to the exponential economic growth seen in Figure 1. For most of history, population growth remained low, but over the past 300 years, this rate increased dramatically. Figure 6 shows how population levels have changed over the past 12,000 years and includes a forecast of the world population

---

29 Ronald Findlay and Kevin H. O'Rourke, "Commodity Market Integration, 1500–2000," in *Globalization in Historical Perspective*, ed. Michael D. Bordo, Alan M. Taylor, and Jeffrey G. Williamson (University of Chicago Press, Chicago: 2003), 13–64.

until 2100, clearly showing the growth since 1700 and the exponential increase especially over the past 100 years.

Based on the data in Figure 6, at AD 1 the world population was 188 million; by 1000 it reached 295 million and in 1800, 990 million. The first billion was noted soon thereafter, rising to 1.654 billion by 1900. By 1950, 2.536 billion was recorded, reaching 6.143 billion in 2000 and underscoring the recent exponential growth. In 2050 the data forecasts that around 9.735 billion will be alive, reaching 10.874 billion by 2100. Importantly, the exponential curve is expected to begin flattening later in the century.

Figure 6: World Population: 10,000 BCE–2100[30]

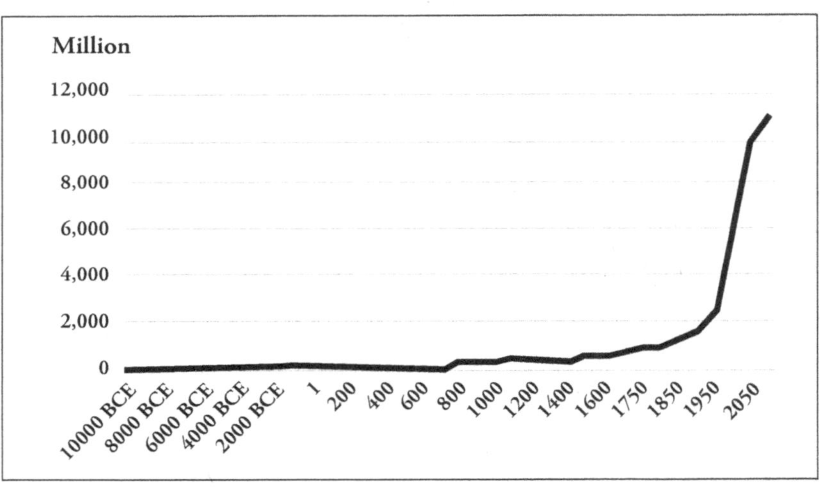

Uncontrolled population growth ahead of a society's ability to sustain itself has long been of concern to political economists and philosophers alike. Thomas Malthus, the father of population studies, argued in 1798 that unchecked population growth would eventually lead to disaster.[31] As an ordained minister and a trained mathematician, Malthus worried

30 Statista Research, "Estimated Global Population from 10,000 BCE to 2100," June 21, 2022, accessed May 1, 2023, https://www.statista.com/statistics/1006502/global-population-ten-thousand-bc-to-2050.

31 Thomas Robert Malthus, *An Essay on the Principle of Population* (London: Eeves and Turner, 1798).

population growth would eventually become geometric (exponential) while food supply growth remains arithmetic. He concluded that his now infamous notion of "Malthusian culling" (famine, disease, warfare, etc.) would control unchecked population growth.

One hundred and seventy years later, Paul Ehrlich predicted Malthusian culling would occur in the 1970s and 1980s owing to the population explosion occurring at the time and called for stringent population control to avoid the catastrophe.[32] Fortunately, the culling did not materialize, mostly because the Green Revolution in the 1960s and 1970s significantly increased food production.

Demographers have known since the 1930s that industrialization is the best—and possibly the only—practical, effective contraceptive for most nations. This does discount China's One Child Policy, remarkably successful at curbing population growth to the point that a significant decrease in the country's population is now forecast. Such a policy, however, is unlikely to be politically feasible in other large, high-growth populations in countries such as India, Pakistan, Nigeria, or Indonesia. China's authoritarian governance and its ability to impose discipline and control is unlikely to be replicated in these countries. In these contexts, economic growth is likely the only method to curb population growth.

The fertility rates of women in every society that has industrialized dropped dramatically soon after that society began modernizing. Technically known as fertility transition, why this happens is explained in Chapter 3. Given this fact, uncontrolled human population growth will cease on its own if the 50 percent of the global population currently excluded from economic activity join the struggle for productivity. The spread of productivity to those excluded from economic participation around the world is, for this reason, imperative.

Congruent with the notion of world population peaking, the United Nations (UN), noting 8 billion was reached in November 2022, expects the world population will peak at 10.4 billion in 2080, a number lower

---

32 Paul R. Ehrlich, *The Population Bomb* (New York: Ballantine Books, 1968).

than predicted in Figure 6.[33] Industrialization has in fact caused a new, unexpected trend. Many industrialized countries now have the opposite problem: population decline. For example, Germans, Italians, and Japanese are not replacing themselves,[34] and aging baby boomers in the United States are also at risk of not having enough younger Americans to support them in their old age.

Thus, while in many developing countries population growth is still too high, in some developed countries, it is too low. Given these facts, two macrotrends in global population over the twenty-first century are likely: as industrialization spreads, population growth will decline, and the average age across the world will increase, but regardless of how fast productivity reaches underdeveloped societies, the developing-country proportion of the global population will increase. Finally, and building on trends noted in countries not replacing themselves, a new demographic concern has become that world population will decline after peaking and be as harmful to our collective well-being as overpopulation may have been.[35] How rapid depopulation might affect China and others is considered in Chapters 4 and 5.

Raw material scarcity, or running out of resources, is a fifth factor that could scuttle the human experiment. Prior to industrialization, such a concern was inconceivable. But industrialization is both materials and energy intensive (as Chapter 3 indicates), and for this reason material scarcity warrants attention. The first notable analysis surfacing the possibility of raw materials running out was the Club of Rome's *The Limits to Growth* report, published in 1972. In the report the interaction of five trends was evaluated: accelerating industrialization, explosive population

33 United Nations, "World Population to Reach 8 Billion This Year, as Growth Rate Slows," July 11, 2022, accessed May 1, 2023, https://news.un.org/en/story/2022/07/1122272.

34 Women in Japan had 2.16 children in 1970; by 2005 the ratio was down to 1.26. In 2023 the rate was 1.37, still far below the replacement rate of 2.1 children: Macrotrends, "Japan Fertility Rate 1950–2023," accessed May 1, 2023, https://www.macrotrends.net/countries/JPN/japan/fertility-rate.

35 Dean Spears, "The World's Population May Peak in Your Lifetime. What Happens Next?" *New York Times*, September 18, 2023, last corrected September 26, 2023, accessed November 16, 2023, https://www.nytimes.com/interactive/2023/09/18/opinion/human-population-global-growth.html.

growth, potential widespread malnutrition, resource depletion, and the effects of a deteriorating environment. The report concluded:

> If the present growth trends in world population, industrialization, pollution, food production, and resource depletion continue unchanged, the limits to growth on this planet will be reached sometime within the next one hundred years. The most probable result will be a rather sudden and uncontrollable decline in both population and industrial capacity.[36]

According to the Club of Rome report, like exponential population growth, raw material scarcity was thought to be a factor that might contribute to Malthusian culling. Over 30 million copies were sold, and the report attracted considerable interest and sparked controversy. Surrounded by the glut of cheap goods in the last quarter of the twentieth century, some rejected the work as overly negative or alarmist, while others alleged the modeling used in the report was too conservative or Malthusian in its import. The response seems much like the reaction to global warming/climate change in the United States until recently.

Before 2007, anyone stating concerns about global warming/climate change in the United States ran the risk of being labeled an *Al Gore wacko* by more conservative Americans. When such concepts were mentioned to business executives, they were often dismissed as tree-hugger invective unworthy of attention. Attitudes began shifting in 2007, and by the presidential election of 2008, Americans began realizing global warming/climate change was real. Both candidates had serious proposals on dealing with global warming/climate change in their election platforms, and over the eight years of President Obama, the threat was taken seriously. Regrettably, the Trump administration put climate change/global warming on the back burner, but the Biden administration again treated the threat seriously. This topic is more comprehensively covered in Chapter 5.

---

36 Donella H. Meadows et al., *The Limits to Growth: A Report for the Club of Rome's Project on the Predicament of Mankind* (New York: Universe Books, 1972), accessed May 1, 2023, https://www.clubofrome.org/publication/the-limits-to-growth/.

Regardless, the sustainable consumption levels, should the entire global population reach middle-class industrialized living standards, will probably be lower than those enjoyed in America today, and a new consumption model will likely evolve over the coming decades to reflect this reality. Chapter 5 also considers this likelihood in more detail. Explicit in this consideration is the need to change consumption patterns to conserve resources as well change energy use to ameliorate the effects of global warming/climate change.

Moreover, though water scarcity induced by global warming/climate change might endanger the survival of poor communities in developing nations, this threat will not stop the overall human experiment. In extreme emergency, desalination can be done; an increase in the price of water will be the main effect. In the short run, resource supply and demand imbalances disrupt markets, but in general, as prices of scarce resources increase, substitutes are found (i.e., technology intervenes), or humans adapt and learn to do without that particular resource.

Chapter 5 also considers the impact and challenges presented by global warming/climate change, and we will not know if we have dodged the global warming/climate change bullet for decades. But to escape the worst effects of our changing climate, the preponderance of scientific analysis suggests immediate concerted action is needed and that failure to act quickly could assign humanity to an inexorable decline. Under these conditions, the Life Cycle model of early birth, high growth, maturity, and decline/death might better explain the future of the human experiment.

Forecasting the Future of Human Productivity: Prosperity as Following and Leading Dominate

With technology mitigating the effect of meteor strikes and biological disasters, productivity's spread containing exponential growth in the human population, and new technologies, clean energy, and new consumption models being developed in the face of global warming/climate change and growing resource scarcity, the human struggle for productivity will not conform to Figure 5's Life Cycle model. It will instead follow Figure 7's S Curve model, which predicts growth is initially exponential, but as maturity is reached, it slows and flattens into an elongated S.

Based on the model, Figure 7 indicates GWP since the start of the Industrial Revolution and suggests that output will increase exponentially over most of the twenty-first century but begin to slow as the end of the century approaches. Whether output flattens to a point that remains horizontal to the x-axis as indicated in Figure 7—indicating little or no growth in output over the twenty-second century—or whether growth continues upward but only at a slower pace or whether growth continues in fits and spurts as new technological frontiers are reached in the twenty-second century is hard to say. More than likely the slope will continue to rise in the twenty-second century but at a rate lower than that over most of the twenty-first century.

Figure 7: The Future of the Human Struggle for Productivity: S Curve Model

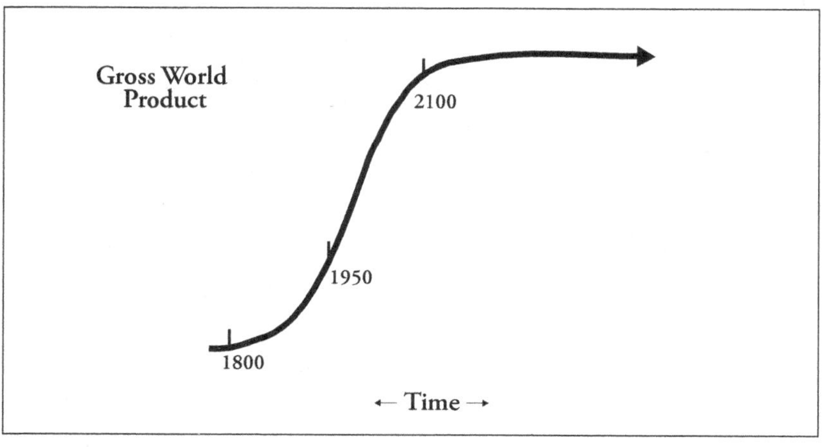

A key question is when does the fast growth in the curve peak and start slowing? To answer this question, refer back to the population percentages in the three eras in Figure 3. Every time a nation joins the human struggle for productivity as a Follower, productive experiments in the world increase, as does world output. With this logic, the rate of increase in growth will only begin slowing appreciably when most societies that may join the struggle for productivity have done so and are reaching full industrialization. Chapter 3 covers the challenges of industrialization and the time it typically takes to accomplish the task. As this period is at least two to three generations (50 to 75 years) for most nations, it is unlikely that the majority of the world will be fully industrialized before 2100. The rate of growth will only begin to slow early in the twenty-second century, as is depicted in Figure 7.

This means the stresses from the spread of productivity are likely to increase for the next 75 years and that competition will likely increase over the next two generations. Such growth also means more consumers and new markets, and the core challenge facing all will be whether they can produce the goods and services that modernizing nations will buy. If they can, they will participate in the expanding global economy too.

Another reason can be cited to support the idea that Figure 7 better describes the future of economic man than does Figure 5. The Life Cycle model best captures the paths of microsystems, modeling the global economy represents capturing the path of the world's largest economic macrosystem. Succinctly put, macrosystems behave differently from microsystems—for every human that dies, another is born; for every product obsolesced, another appears.[37] Macrosystems follow a different path from microsystems that appear and disappear along the way.

Support for the eventual slowing of growth and the relative flattening of the line in Figure 7 post-2100 is also drawn from the experiences of industrialized economies to date. Growth economists now understand that earlier economic growth rates are far higher than when nations

---

37 John Maynard Keynes, *The General Theory of Employment, Interest, and Money* (Hampshire, England: Palgrave Macmillan, 1936). Keynes termed this a "fallacy of composition": inferring that what is true for a small part of a system is also true for the whole system.

mature economically.[38] As Chapter 3 explains, fast growth in early industrialization derives from adding educated people into the labor force and by surrounding better-educated humans with newly formed economic capital. This is core to the activities of Followers as they industrialize and drives the faster input-led growth typically experienced in early industrialization.

But once most of the labor force is educated and employed, and once the physical economic capital needed to support these workers is fully formed, diminishing returns to adding capital and labor appear—and growth slows. At this point, rather than achieving growth through simply increasing the labor supply or by adding capital (i.e., by input-led growth), innovation (or as growth economists label it, *total factor productivity improvement*) is required. This innovation-led growth is considered in Chapter 4. Fast and ongoing improvement at this level turns out to be far more challenging, and the growth rate accordingly slows.

If average economic growth in mature societies slows, once all societies are industrialized the slope of the line in Figure 7 will moderate to a slower rate of growth. It is difficult to specify exactly what this longer-term sustainable rate of growth will be, but it will not be the annual 8 to 12 percent often enjoyed by newly industrializing countries. More than likely, it will be closer to those recorded by developed countries once they are fully industrialized (i.e., somewhere between 1 to 3 percent per annum). Thus, the exponential level of growth experienced over the next two to three generations as the billions excluded join the human struggle for productivity will not last forever. The same logic applies to companies: startups grow faster than mature companies do.

Figure 7 also presents a long-term outcome for the human struggle for productivity that predicts the predominance of Leaders and Followers

38 Growth economists study and explain how and why long-term economic growth happens. Possibly the first of this genre was Scottish economist Adam Smith who, in *An Inquiry into the Nature and Causes of the Wealth of Nations* (London: Methuen, 1776), argued that division of labor, pursuit of self-interest, and the freedom to trade are the essential ingredients to stimulate economic growth. As pointed out in Chapters 3 and 4, growth theory and growth economist perspectives are now far more sophisticated.

over Failures. In its most optimistic form, the hope is that all nations industrialize over the next 100 years or so (i.e., balanced global growth) and that concurrent with this spread of productivity to the rest of humanity, all find niches they may populate and hold to sustain their overall economic growth. A less optimistic prediction holds that by 2100, while more nations will be industrialized, some may still be Following or remain in the Failure camp (i.e., unbalanced global growth).

The less favorable prediction is based on the imbalances noted in both developed and developing nations today and on the possibility that people in some countries might get old before they get rich. The reasoning supporting such a conclusion is considered in Chapter 5 when the prospects for global economic growth over the twenty-first century are examined. Three scenarios are presented: balanced global growth (essentially the optimistic scenario that conforms almost identically to Figure 7), unbalanced global growth, and global meltdown. Unbalanced global growth may present an overall pattern similar to the path in Figure 7, except that where maturity is reached and growth starts slowing is earlier, and the level of output reached is lower. Figure 23 in Chapter 5 denotes how unbalanced global growth might look after taking these developments into account, while Figure 24 indicates how the scenario that conforms to Figure 5, global meltdown, might look should our struggle for productivity stumble and possibly fail.

Conclusion and Synthesis

Humans have been on Earth for over 150,000 years, but their efforts to reduce the scourge of material scarcity did not yield much until industrialization commenced in the eighteenth century. From this time on, progress has been impressive and permits division of the overall human struggle for productivity into three eras: Pre-Industrial (pre-1800, world of the past); Industrial (1800–1950, world of the present for those not industrialized); and Post-Industrial (1950 and beyond, world of the future).

The threefold era categorization presents a framework to determine how economic, social, organizational, and political economy characteristics evolve as human productivity advances, and it also provides the basis for this book's core thesis: nations, firms, and individuals play three roles in the human struggle for productivity, either as Failures, Followers, or Leaders. Those with economic capabilities remaining in the pre-industrial world are failing; those who have commenced economic diversification through industrialization and are doing what others have done before them are following; and those already industrialized that wish to sustain their economic growth even further must pioneer their place to post-industrial status, and if they do so, they are leading.

Moreover, though some around the world today enjoy material standards of living immeasurably better that their ancestors of only 100 years ago, around half of the 8 billion alive today still live in pre-industrial conditions. They are failing, and a key uncertainty over the twenty-first century is how many of those excluded from productive economic activity will join the human struggle for productivity. Chapters 2 to 4 reveal the characteristics of our journey from pre- to post-industrial production.

The Life Cycle and S Curve models are the two paths the human struggle for productivity might follow over the foreseeable future, and of the six factors that might force convergence to the Life Cycle model's early birth, high growth, maturity, and decline/death—meteor strike, widespread nuclear conflict, biological disaster, human population explosion, raw material scarcity, and global warming/climate change—only global warming/climate change is identified as of concern.

Absent the limits that unconstrained global warming/climate change might impose, the most likely path the future of human productivity will follow is the S Curve, which predicts initial exponential growth that slows as maturity is reached. Most likely is that human output will continue to grow at a rate of between 1 to 3 percent per annum from maturity onward.

The precise path that the human struggle for productivity will follow over the twenty-first century remains unclear, and three scenarios—balanced global growth, unbalanced global growth, and global meltdown—capture the range of futures that may unfold over the coming century. The first two scenarios represent paths corresponding to the S Curve model, with balanced global growth being the best. Global meltdown conforms to the path depicted in the Life Cycle model. The details of these contending scenarios are better deferred, however, until a deeper understanding of the human struggle for productivity is attained. Before how the future may unfold is revealed, the tribulations of Failures and the paths of Followers and Leaders must be fully appreciated. We turn first to the world of Failures, the Pre-Industrial Era.

CHAPTER 2

THE PRE-INDUSTRIAL ERA

Failures Enduring Scarcity and Want

Economists argue that the fundamental economic problem is scarcity, and to appreciate the conditions encountered in the Pre-Industrial Era, recourse to this basic precept is a good starting point. Scarcity explains many—but not all—of the stresses plaguing humanity in the pre-industrial world. Moreover, why the situation persisted for so long is easy to account for with hindsight. Knowing which ingredients had to be added so that industrialization started and the *industrial cake* could be baked makes recipe omissions easy to identify after the fact. Chapter 3 covers these ingredients; only their absence is noted here.

Economists also state that three primary factors are exploited in production: land (anything on or under the land), labor (humans), and economic capital (not money or finance, but machines, implements, or any productive instrument or capability other than the land and labor used in production). Finally, entrepreneurship is the fourth factor that combines land, labor, and economic capital into new goods and services offered to the market. This fourth factor was recognized last: until the 1980s, most economic texts reflected land, labor, and capital as the three main factors of production.

Based on these four factors, why scarcity plagued humanity for so long is easy to explain. First, though humans had use of the land, they could not farm or access these land-based resources effectively. Second, though humans were available to work, their training did not equip them to do much beyond what their fathers and mothers had done for generations before them. Poorly trained workers followed by poorly trained descendants did not produce much. Third, the economic capital available at the time was limited and did not improve the productivity of the other factors noticeably. Fourth, because land was difficult to access, and as labor was relatively unproductive and the economic capital not that effective in leveraging productivity, returns to entrepreneurship were also low. Combine these constraints and persistent scarcity is inevitable.

Gunnar Myrdal argued economic processes are circular and reinforce each other, including both economic and noneconomic factors in circular and cumulative causation. For example, he argued that insufficient nutrition leads to low labor productivity, resulting in negative feedback on food production that then impacts nutrition.[39] Myrdal pioneered a new theoretical identity for economics in a field now known as institutional economics. According to this approach, solving great economic problems requires holistic analysis that includes economics, psychology, sociology, and even politics. Mimicking Myrdal's "cumulative circle of poverty," a *cumulative circle of scarcity* existed in pre-industrial times.

The scarcity and scramble for resources characterizing the pre-industrial world also had an unwelcome and unintended consequence: endemic war. Written records provide accounts of pervasive human conflict; the stresses to amass resources to either conduct war or provide security in the face of external threats drained most societies. Moreover, to sustain their political and physical survival, elites typically lived off and extracted resources from relatively unproductive peasants. These crude, human-led hierarchies typically demanded allegiance, service, and in the extreme,

39 Gunnar Myrdal, *Asian Drama: An Inquiry into the Poverty of Nations*. 3 vols. (New York: Pantheon, 1968).

lives. Independence and individual freedom remained the domain of the rich and powerful, and even this privileged status could be lost in an instant when a conqueror or new ruler seized power, underscoring the Hobbesian dictum that life was "solitary, poor, nasty, brutish, and short."

To understand the conditions plaguing pre-industrial times, we now turn to a more comprehensive evaluation of the Pre-Industrial Era. First, the political economy of the Pre-Industrial Era is examined, followed by land cultivation and consideration of the economic capital available over the era. Then pre-industrial human resources management and entrepreneurship are examined, and the chapter concludes with pre-industrial city survival in the twenty-first century, characterized by the transition from rural to urban subsistence that is now the lot of hundreds of millions, possibly billions, across the developing world. Even as aspirant Followers begin their economic marches forward, pre-industrial life remains in an unexpected location.

Pre-Industrial Era Political Economy: Failure amid Meritocratic Bureaucracy, Feudalism, and Mercantile Capitalism

Three political systems capture the variety of political economies in use over pre-industrial times.[40] First, and most widely used, was feudalism. Second, governance through a meritocratic imperial bureaucracy was an important model pioneered in China long before the time of Christ. Finally, mercantile capitalism, implemented in Europe between the sixteenth and eighteenth centuries, facilitated the European rise to power over these three centuries. These three systems are considered in the rest

40 Todaro and Smith provide a useful definition of this important construct: "Political economy goes beyond traditional economics to study, among other things, the social and institutional processes through which certain groups of economic and political elites influence the allocation of scarce productive resources now and in the future, either exclusively for their own benefit or for that of the larger population as well" (Michael P. Todaro and Stephen C. Smith, *Economic Development*, 9th ed., [Boston: Addison-Wesley, 2005], 9). How governing elites use or abuse power to reduce scarcity for themselves and/or societies they govern is political economy's central concern.

of this chapter, and Chapter 3 shows that elements of two are still present today.

Feudalism: Kings and Princes Dominating People

Though use of the term in a general fashion is controversial, feudalism best captures the political economy of the Pre-Industrial Era.[41] Most prevalent in western Europe, but also imposed in non-European countries, feudalism has been used to describe England from 1066 until the mid-fifteenth century and even conditions in post-revolutionary France in the mid-nineteenth century. Moreover, until 1868 the emperor and his chief general (the shogun) headed Japanese feudalism. After civil wars in the fifteenth century, land in Japan was partitioned for peasant farmers to farm in exchange for security provided by the military and land-owning classes. Farmers paid a portion of their agricultural output for security and in turn received the right to farm. Samurai and daimyos were accountable to the shogun. Finally, warring feudal princes contributed to China's fragmentation such that unification of the country became imperative. Feudalism also preceded meritocratic bureaucracy in China.

European feudalism mostly involved kings granting land to favored subjects in return for military service. These tenants-in-chief (or barons in England) then allocated land to knights, who on-leased plots to villeins or serfs. Tenants-in-chief retained the right to own land from the Crown as long as they rendered service to the king and did not commit treason or felony, and when they died, heirs inherited their titles and rights. Each level swore allegiance to those above them, and each was required to perform service in return for favors: barons served on the king's governing councils and supplied knights and resources when required; knights' primary obligations were to provide military service

41 Using one term to summarize the political economies of almost a millennium is ambitious (Elizabeth A. R. Brown, "The Tyranny of a Construct: Feudalism and Historians of Medieval Europe," *The American Historical Review* 79, no. 4 [October 1974]: 1063–88). However, feudalism in one form or another pervaded most societies from around 1100 until recently, permitting such a generalization in the survey here.

to their lord or king; serfs provided free labor, food, and service when demanded by their knights and had few, if any, rights. In the ideal European feudal world, kings ruled, barons and knights fought, serfs worked, and the clergy prayed.[42]

By the 1500s nobility and the rich in Europe lived in castles or stone houses and enjoyed diverse diets that included meat, fish, and fowl. Household servants were employed in the manorial house, and the lady of the house managed the household while lords spent their time hunting or at war. Most life took place in the great hall, where households slept and ate. Lords typically slept in their own private room above the great hall. Land was also leased to serfs, who could neither marry nor leave their lord's manor without permission. Lords could not sell their serfs, but if a parcel of land was sold, the serfs attached to that land fell under the acquiring party's authority; serfs could not abandon their leased land without permission. Freemen did exist, and these tenant farmers owed little or no service to any lord. At the height of feudalism, however, freemen were less than 10 percent of those who were serfs.

The most extreme forms of feudalism ended in Europe by the sixteenth century, the collapse brought about by the convergence of many factors, including plagues that created a people shortage and increased the bargaining power of labor. The printing press's arrival in 1439 and creation of European universities also eroded the Christian Church's knowledge monopoly and over time democratized knowledge expansion. Universities evolved from studium generale, schools that possessed three characteristics: they invited students from all parts; they were places of higher education in that at least one of the higher faculties (theology,

---

42 By the Middle Ages the Christian Church was a powerful institution across Europe. Sustained by tithes and land holdings, Hatcher estimates monks reaching the age of 25 in England in the fifteenth century would have lived to between 46 and 49 years of age, close to longevity estimates for 25-year-old tenants-in-chief (see footnote 60). The clergy enjoyed privileged positions in feudal society, and monks were better fed, clothed, and sheltered and had better medical care than most; accordingly, their adult life expectancy was probably comparable with the wealthiest in their societies (John Hatcher, "Mortality in the Fifteenth Century: Some New Evidence," *Economic History Review* 39, no. 1 [February 1986]:19–38). The Church also had a monopoly on literacy until printing presses emerged in the fifteenth century.

law, or medicine) was taught; and they were places where many masters taught subjects. In the thirteenth century, only three met these criteria: Paris for theology and arts, Bologna for law, and Salerno for medicine.[43] Universities at Oxford and Cambridge were established in 1167–68 and 1209, respectively, but lacked the notoriety of the Paris, Bologna, and Salerno schools. Underscoring the significant and enduring impact of universities, Hastings Rashdall noted:

> The institutions which the Middle Age has bequeathed to us are of greater and more imperishable value than even its Cathedrals. And the University is a distinctly medieval institution, as much so as constitutional Kingships, or Parliament, or Trial by Jury. . . . A complete history the Universities of the Middle Ages would be in fact a history of medieval thought—of the fortunes, during four centuries, of literary culture, of the whole of the Scholastic Philosophy and Scholastic Theology, of the revived study of the Civil Law, of the formation and development of the Canon Law, of the faint, murky, cloud-wrapped dawn of modern Mathematics, modern Medicine, and modern Science.[44]

Over this entire period, the only meaningful technology transfer from western Europe was to the English colonies in America. In 1776, when declaring independence, the American colonies had nine universities for 2.5 million people and boasted an emerging intellectual elite conversant with state-of-the-art European knowledge and scientific advances. There were only two universities for 17 million people in the Spanish and Portuguese colonies, both in Mexico, focusing only on theology and law.[45] This data provides early indicators as to why America emerged as the twentieth century's great power, while other New World European colonies did not reach anywhere close to this status.

---

43 Hastings Rashdall, *The Universities of Europe in the Middle Ages, Volume 1: Salerno, Bologna, Paris* (Oxford: Oxford Clarendon Press, 1895).
44 Rashdall, *The Universities of Europe in the Middle Ages*, 5.
45 Maddison, *The World Economy: A Millennial Perspective*, 24.

From the sixteenth to the nineteenth centuries, the Renaissance and the Age of Enlightenment, combined with citizen-led revolutions and other constitutional law developments, eventually moderated some of the imbalances inherent in the feudalism that had ordered Europe for over 1,000 years. Parliamentary monarchy in England created a compromise between rulers and ruled, so power was more widely shared.[46] In addition, advances in maritime technology, banking and finance, and the natural sciences enabled western Europeans to rise to dominance by the eighteenth century.

Though China and Japan largely remained isolated, Africa and the Americas did not escape the European expansion and its colonial scramble for resources as the region industrialized. The consolidation of European nation-states and their imposition of mercantile capitalism also facilitated the rise of great powers based in Europe. Initially, this rise was due to sea power and the Europeans' ability to obtain resources from societies unable to resist their advance. By the late nineteenth century, however, industrial power had become the most significant factor explaining the ascendancy of the Eurocentric world. Chapter 3 more comprehensively explains the appearance of this so-called "European exceptionalism."

China's Imperial Bureaucracy: Early Progress, Isolation, and Failure

While feudalism represents the most widespread form of governance in the Pre-Industrial Era, China pioneered a system over 2,000 years ago that was centuries ahead of its time. Weber, the noted German sociologist, argued this Chinese imperial bureaucracy arose because warring feudal princes threatened to fragment the country in the centuries before Christ.[47] The unification of China under the Chi'in Prince in 221 BC and the subsequent overthrow of Chi'in rule by the Han dynasty finally

46 For example, and a testimony to their power, in 1688 James II was deposed by powerful English aristocrats supported by City of London merchants. Helped by Dutch Prince William of Orange, who was placed on the English throne after the deposition, English business gained access to the banking and finance capabilities pioneered by the Dutch in Amsterdam.
47 Max Weber, *The Religion of China*, ed. Hans H. Gerth (New York: Free Press, 1968).

permitted the consolidation of an imperial bureaucracy into a stable governance system.[48] Principles such as short periods of office, prohibitions against bureaucrats governing in their home provinces, and exams to qualify candidates produced an administrative system based on merit and competence and not hereditary succession. Challenging civil service exams to qualify bureaucrats were installed by the seventh century, causing some to conclude Chinese bureaucracy attained some modern traits long before these institutions emerged in the West.[49]

By the year 1000, China was the world's biggest economy, governed by a meritocratic bureaucracy in a unitary state that taxed agricultural surplus. Moreover, from the eighth to the thirteenth centuries, half the Chinese population moved from northern China to south of the Yangtze River, populating an area that when planted with more suitable quick-ripening rice seed represented possibly the world's first green revolution. Marketable agricultural surplus resulted, freeing up Chinese workers for activities other than a continuous scramble for food. Chapter 3 describes how development and application of surplus is key to industrialization and modernization. This Chinese ability to generate surplus was centuries ahead of its time.

China failed, however, to sustain its surplus generation and apply it to improve the living standards of its people, and though living standards improved, the gains were modest.[50] The imperial gentry and professional bureaucrats became rent seekers, restricting commercial or individual trading through regulation and "bureaucratic squeeze."[51] "Rent seeking" is attributable to Adam Smith: "As soon as the land of any country has all become private property, the landlords, like all other men, love to

48 The Han dynasty lasted for over 400 years and is considered among the greatest periods of Chinese history. During this dynasty China became an official Confucian state, its population grew to over 50 million, and the country prospered agriculturally and commercially. Most Chinese still refer to themselves as "Han" Chinese.

49 Alexander Woodside, *Lost Modernities: China, Vietnam, Korea, and the Hazards of World History* (Cambridge, MA: Harvard University Press, 2006).

50 Angus Maddison, *Chinese Economic Performance in the Long Run*, 2nd ed. (Paris, France: OECD Development Center, 2007), 16.

51 Maddison, *Chinese Economic Performance in the Long Run*, 17.

reap where they never sowed, and demand a rent even for its natural produce."[52]

Growing rich at the expense of others is considered the heart of rent seeking, and these behaviors were eventually encountered in the Chinese state bureaucracy. Private enterprise was discouraged, and the state retained the right to operate larger undertakings. Instead of promoting populace well-being, the machinery imposed overhead with little return and contributed to China's underperformance for centuries. Even meritocratic bureaucracies are open to corruption. How events in imperial China in the early fifteenth century led to its withdrawal and isolation from world affairs is explained on pages 59–61. This exit left the global arena open for less technically advanced Europeans to step into and dominate over the coming centuries.

Mercantile Capitalism and Hard Power Accumulate Wealth

The third political economy that appeared in the Pre-Industrial Era is mercantile capitalism, or mercantilism. This system emerged in Europe in the sixteenth century and dominated European political thinking for 250 years from 1500 to 1750. Predicated upon the idea that national wealth was measured by state accumulation of bullion, mercantilism held that the only way to accumulate gold or silver outside of possessing mineable mineral reserves was through running positive trade balances by exporting more than was imported. This principle explains the logic underlying the Spanish conquest of the Americas. The conquistadores took control of regions of Central and South America, mostly in hope of finding gold and silver.

Mercantilists also considered economics a zero-sum game, and based on this idea that one person's gain was another's loss, inward-oriented protectionism was a dominant part of the policy regime. The favored

52 Adam Smith, "Of the Component Parts of the Price of Commodities," book 1, chap. 6, para. 8 in *The Wealth of Nations.*

economic policy was accordingly the promotion of exports and discouraging of imports through tariffs:

> Most of the mercantilist policies were the outgrowth of the relationship between the governments of the nation-states and their mercantile classes. In exchange for paying levies and taxes to support the armies of the nation-states, the mercantile classes induced governments to enact policies that would protect their business interests against foreign competition. These policies took many forms. Domestically, governments would provide capital to new industries, exempt new industries from guild rules and taxes, establish monopolies over local and colonial markets, and grant titles and pensions to successful producers. In trade policy the government assisted local industry by imposing tariffs, quotas, and prohibitions on imports of goods that competed with local manufacturers.[53]

Mercantilism granted European states a prominent role in the management of economic welfare.

> Europe consisted of states big and small, each steered by the pride and interest of the ruler, but increasingly by self-aware nationalism. All vied. All knew the significance of money for standing and power.
>
> The primacy of money in the service of power found expression in economic thought. Mercantilism was not a doctrine nor a set of rules. It was a general recipe for political-economic management: whatever enhances the state was right. Even Adam Smith had his mercantilist moments: the Navigation Acts,[54] he noted, may have cost the British consumer, but they worked wonderfully to put down Dutch sea power.[55]

---

53 Laura LaHaye, "Mercantilism," in *The Concise Encyclopedia of Economics*, ed. David R. Henderson (Indianapolis, IN: Liberty Fund), accessed May 1, 2023, https://www.econlib.org/library/Enc1/Mercantilism.html.

54 The Navigation Acts were passed by the British parliament between 1651 and 1673 to outlaw foreign carrying trade and to ensure all goods imported or exported from Britain were done so in ships owned by Englishmen. The 1651 Act restricted import of plantation commodities from Asia, Africa, and America except in English ships.

55 David S. Landes, *The Wealth and Poverty of Nations: Why Some Are So Rich and Some So Poor* (New York: W. W. Norton & Company, 1998), 443.

Given the competitive context in Europe between 1500 and 1750, mercantilism's emergence is unsurprising. Growth through exports or resource acquisition—either through trade or conquest—perfectly complemented increasing maritime power and European nation-state expansion. Though it provided tools to increase hegemony and extend global reach, mercantilism eventually proved unsuitable for sustaining long-term national economic growth. Nevertheless, the mercantilist mindset underscored that nation-states were important actors on the international economic stage, providing an early example of the interventionist states that appeared in the twentieth century to modernize countries such as Japan, South Korea, Singapore, and China. The twentieth-century Asian developmentalist state (explained in Chapter 3) follows in the mercantilist tradition.

Further, in the impressive advances seen in the Fast Followers of the twentieth century, the principle of a meritocratic bureaucracy is also revisited. Most of the so-called Asian Tigers possessed such bureaucracies. Thus, of the three political economy models reviewed here, only feudalism proved of no value to the modernizing post-1800 world. But in the Pre-Industrial Era, neither imperial China's bureaucracy nor the tools of mercantilism sufficiently improved productivity such that a widespread improvement in the average standard of living resulted. Developments outside of political economy in the microeconomic and technological arenas were needed to accomplish this objective.

Pre-Industrial Era Land Cultivation: Subsistence Farming and Failure's Perpetuation

In the European Middle Ages, most peasants lived in small towns composed of around 30 to 60 families, tending small plots with a few oxen available to help with plowing and tilling.[56] Most peasant families

56 Maddison, *The World Economy: A Millennial Perspective*, 40. Maddison reports that in 1500 only 6.1 percent of the western European population lived in towns of more than 10,000; in China, 3.8 percent did. By 1820, 12.3 percent of the population in western Europe was urbanized, indicating the early impact of industrialization. But still the great majority of the population was rural. In China the number was still around 3.8 percent in 1820.

owned a cow, perhaps a goat or a pig, and a few chickens, all sources of food and also of warmth in the winter. Meat was a luxury, and peasant diets were simple and monotonous. In Europe, coarse breads and grains were the staple diet, and stew called pottage was typically served as the one hot meal enjoyed each day.

Subsistence farming is "farming in which nearly all of the crops or livestock raised are used to maintain the farmer and the farmer's family, leaving little, if any, surplus for sale or trade."[57] It was the primary method to produce food for survival, the goal being to permit family food self-sufficiency. But because of its low productivity, little or no surplus to sell on the open market was produced. Subsistence farmers were also generalists: Smith's fabled division of labor was yet to reach them.[58] They not only grew food but were responsible also for meeting other basic needs through their own individual efforts:

> The culture of the subsistence peasant is rooted in the ecology of the social life which emerged when farming was first invented about ten thousand years ago, in what has been called the Neolithic Revolution . . . where families grew, raised or hunted what they ate, built their own homes, raised their own children, and made their own clothing. The world . . . was one in which labor was closely tied to consumption; people and their neighbors made what they used or ate. They lived on homesteads without much cash, or regular access to extensive markets, and reproduced their own society for hundreds of generations.[59]

As infant mortality was high, the fertility rate of women was also. Labor worked the land, and large families diversified risk. This underscores that large families in the pre-industrial world are not because of the

57 *Encyclopaedia Britannica Online*, s. v. "*subsistence farming*," accessed May 1, 2023, https://www.britannica.com/topic/subsistence-farming.

58 Smith, "That the Division of Labour is Limited by the Extent of the Market," book 1, chaps. 1 and 3 in *The Wealth of Nations*. In his analysis of a pin factory in Chapter 1, Smith asserted division of labor and specialization was at the center of increasing human productivity. The benefits of specialization and division of labor are considered in Chapter 3.

59 Tony Waters, *The Persistence of Subsistence Agriculture: Life Beneath the Level of the Marketplace* (Lanham, MD: Lexington Books, 2006), 3.

absence of TV or the lack of birth control. Large families were a rational economic decision: children were sources of labor to work in the fields, and they were also pension plans for aging parents. This was economic diversification, pre-industrial style.

Life expectancy was also low though differing significantly between rich and poor (i.e., between peasants and nobles). Adult male tenants-in-chief—landowners holding land from the Crown—who had reached 25 years of age between 1305 and 1325 were estimated to live to 50.7 years but dropped to 48.3 years for those reaching 25 between 1335 and 1348 because of the bubonic plague.[60] This data is not representative of average life expectancy as reaching 25 was a prior condition. Average life expectancy at birth in England around 1550 was estimated at 33.7 years, increasing only to 40.8 years by the early nineteenth century.[61]

Subsistence existence continued in post-revolutionary France until the mid-nineteenth century and even drew Karl Marx's ire:

> The small-holding peasants form an enormous mass whose members live in similar conditions but without entering into manifold relations with each other. . . . Their field of production, the small holding, permits no division of labor in its cultivation, no application of science, and therefore no multifariousness of development, no diversity of talent, no wealth of social relationships. Each individual peasant family is almost self-sufficient, directly produces most of its consumer needs, and thus acquires its means of life more through an exchange with nature than in intercourse with society.[62]

Marxian analysis confirms feudalism and subsistence existence persisted in Europe until industrial capitalism intervened in the nine-

---

60 M. A. Jonker, "Estimation of Life Expectancy in the Middle Ages," *Journal of the Royal Statistical Society Series A: Statistics in Society* 166, no. 1 (January 2003): 105–17, https://doi.org/10.1111/1467-985X.00261.

61 E. A. Wrigley et al., *English Population History from Family Reconstitution 1580–1837* (Cambridge, England: Cambridge University Press, 1997), https://doi.org/10.1017/CBO9780511660344.

62 Karl Marx, *The Eighteenth Brumaire of Louis Bonaparte*, chap. 7, translated by Saul K. Padover from the German edition of 1869.

teenth century. Moreover, at the time Marx worried that "small-holding peasants" were not being liberated by industrialization's advance. Instead, the ruling aristocracy's yoke was replaced by the exploitation of industrial capitalists, leading to Marx's often quoted statement: "The hand-mill gives you society with the feudal lord; the steam-mill, society with the industrial capitalist."[63] Embedded in this proposition, however, is the premise that technology determines productivity and that people's well-being depends on how productive they and their societies are.[64] This idea is explored further in Chapters 3 and 4, along with Marx's forecast that to resolve labor's alleged exploitation, a working class revolution was needed so that labor could acquire the means of production. Fortunately, this prediction proved incorrect.

How such a revolution was avoided is explained in Chapter 3, when events at the Ford Motor Company and the actions taken by Henry Ford in the first decades of the twentieth century provided the antidote to the exploitation Marx was so concerned about.

Pre-Industrial Era Economic Capital: Sailing Ships Extending Hard Power, and Hand Tools and Beasts of Burden Prolonging Scarcity and Want

One important contributor to the lack of productivity in the Pre-Industrial Era was the inadequacy of the economic capital. Possibly the most sophisticated form of economic capital available in the fifteenth and sixteenth centuries was the sailing ship. This asset is not chosen randomly as the archetypal economic capital of pre-industrial times; maritime capability propelled many European countries to great power status from the fifteenth to the nineteenth centuries.

First were the Portuguese who built interests in Africa, Brazil, and Asia off their navigators' prowess, followed by the Spanish in the Amer-

63 Karl Marx and Frederick Engels, *Collected Works*, vol. 6 (Moscow, Russia: Progress Publishers, 1975), 166.
64 William H. Shaw, "'The Handmill Gives You the Feudal Lord': Marx's Technological Determinism," *History & Theory* 18, no. 2 (May 1979): 155–76, https://doi.org/10.2307/2504754.

icas, and then the Dutch, who by the latter part of the sixteenth century had a maritime fleet with carrying capacity the size of the combined English, French, and German fleets and who boasted colonies in the Caribbean, South America, southern Africa, and parts of Asia.

European colonial hubris is best underscored by the 1494 Treaty of Tordesillas, the result of Alexander VI's papal bulls dividing the world between the Spanish and Portuguese from north to south along a meridian relative to the Cape Verde Islands. Spain obtained the right to govern newly discovered lands west of the demarcation line, and Portugal was granted dominion over all lands east of the meridian. That every South American nation speaks Spanish except Brazil is a result of this treaty; Brazil was the only portion of South America east of the line. That Spain had no African colonies while Portugal played an important role establishing the seafaring routes around southern Africa and claimed Angola and Mozambique as colonies is another consequence of the treaty.

Maritime capacity also contributed to the Dutch Golden Age enjoyed over the seventeenth century, a time during which a country "small in size and limited in population was capable of acquiring a measure of power equal to that of the large, traditionally established monarchies."[65] The world's first multinational corporation (MNC), the Dutch East India Company (or VOC, Vereenigde Oostindische Compagnie), was built off Dutch seafaring capability; and the British Empire, which eventually reached from India and Australia to southern Africa to North America, was constructed and sustained by Britain's legendary seafaring capabilities.

Moreover, if seafaring was a key enabling factor to attain and sustain great power status in the Pre-Industrial Era, the opposite proved true too. Failure to use seafaring power excluded nations from influence, no more obvious than in the case of China. At the beginning of the fifteenth century, the world's greatest power was not European. It was China, which

---

65 P. L. Muller, *Onze Gouden Eeuw. de Republiek der Vereenigde Nederlanden in haar bloeitijd*, vol. 1 (Leiden, South Holland, The Netherlands: Sijthoff, 1896), 44.

in 1421 sent out a massive armada of ships to map the world.[66] Operating ships hundreds of feet in length, crewed by hundreds of sailors, Chinese seafarers reached Africa, North America, and South America in this pioneering voyage of discovery. Under then Emperor Zhu Di, China displayed its might all over the world through dispatch of armadas with treasure ships bearing gifts and trade goods. Even Columbus may have used Chinese maps to find his way to America.

Soon after the 1421 expedition embarked, however, conditions inside China deteriorated. Emperor Zhu's imperial ambitions proved too costly, and on September 7, 1424, his son ascended the throne and on the same day stopped the treasure ship voyages and began dismantling the Chinese navy. This closing led to 550 years of isolation and stagnation, reversed only when Deng Xiaoping reopened China in the 1970s.

The European ascendancy from the fifteenth century might have been either prevented or contained had China stayed engaged and continued using its seafaring power to exploit Africa and the Americas. But whether a China-centric—as opposed to a Eurocentric—world would have sparked the Industrial Revolution is a more complex question. Maddison explains Europe's rise was less due to Chinese slippage and more to do with European exceptionalism:

> There were several reasons why Europe was better placed to promote the emergence of modern capitalism.
>
> The most fundamental was the recognition of human capacity to transform the forces of nature by rational investigation and experiment. Thanks to the Renaissance and the Enlightenment, Western elites gradually abandoned superstition, magic, and submission to religious authority. The Western scientific tradition that underlies the modern approach to technical change and innovation had clearly emerged by the seventeenth century and had begun to impregnate the educational system. China's education system was steeped in the ancient classics

---

66 For information on the 1421 expedition and its effects on China, see Gavin Menzies, *1421: The Year China Discovered the World* (London: Bantam Books, 2002).

> and bureaucratic orthodoxy. It was not able to develop the fundamental bases of modern science.
>
> Europe had a system of nation-states in close propinquity. They were outward looking, had significant trading relations and relatively easy intellectual interchange. This stimulated competition and innovation.[67]

This brief coverage of Chinese history and the country's failure to remain open underscores the importance of seafaring in pre-industrial great power rivalry. Once China had exited the stage, Europeans and their less impressive ships eagerly filled the vacuum. Though the exact dimensions of the actual ships are lost to time, replicas of the *Pinta, Niña,* and *Santa Maria*—used by Columbus to chart a course to the New World in 1492—have been constructed based on similar ships in service at around the same time. Seeing replicas today typically evokes surprise: they are tiny. Columbus's flagship, the *Santa Maria,* was estimated to be around 75 feet long and 25 feet wide, displacing between 200 to 600 tons with a crew of 52. The other two vessels were much smaller, lighter, and faster than the flagship, and with crews of 18 to 20, they displaced only around 150 to 300 tons each. In such vessels sailors braved the elements to chart a course to the New World in a journey of around six weeks. Traversing a medium-sized lake in these vessels seems risky, let alone navigating the Atlantic Ocean.

That small transport vessels were the most impressive economic capital of the Pre-Industrial Era is indicative of the conditions experienced in the era. Production-oriented economic capital was mostly hand tools and implements used to supplement manual labor. In fact, the most important economic capital was not manmade implements at all. Beasts of burden—sources of food, fibers, transport, warmth, and farming assistance—such as cows, horses, goats, sheep, chickens, and the like, were far more valuable. In most societies in the Pre-Industrial Era, wealth was measured more by how much livestock was owned and not by machines or tools possessed.

---

67 Maddison, *Chinese Economic Performance in the Long Run*, 17.

In addition, human capital in the form of slavery was probably the second major form of productive capacity and is addressed next. Supported by such unimpressive economic capital, human productivity remained low and scarcity reigned; alleviation had to wait for the gains industrialization would offer. Hobbes's "nasty, brutish, and short" lives continued for most; only a small elite enjoyed relief.

Pre-Industrial Era Human Resources Management: Serfdom, Slavery, Guilds, and Man's Inhumanity to Man

Compounding the weaknesses of the political and administrative systems operating in the Pre-Industrial Era (and in addition to the poor economic capital and inability to organize for production that characterized the times) were the inadequate employment and training institutions used. Serfdom and slavery were the most widespread employment institutions utilized, and guilds represented the third notable institution of employment and work organization in pre-industrial times. Unfortunately, guilds did not permit productivity to be scaled widely enough to benefit the masses, and as is indicated later in this section, even the overall economic impact of guilds is controversial. But they were certainly superior to serfdom and slavery.

Serfs were bonded servants, forced to work on their lord's land in return for his protection and right to work on land leased by him. The term *serf* derives from the Latin word *servus*, meaning "slave." This derivation underscores the thin line between slavery and serfdom. Moreover, heirs of serfs inherited their parents' societal position, ensuring that their labor was also available to the lords to whom their parents swore allegiance. Serfs' work time was divided between working their own and their lord's land. Serfs could raise crops they chose on leased lands and pay taxes and fees through such cultivation.

Records of slavery go back at least to early biblical times: slaves existed around 1800 BC in Babylon. The Code of Hammurabi circa 1750 BC indicated Babylonian society was divided into three classes, with around a third being slaves. Slavery in ancient Greece and ancient Rome, and more recently the slave trade practiced by the European powers from the sixteenth to nineteenth centuries, underscores the ubiquity and longevity of the practice. In 1800, 16.9 percent of the American population was slaves, and by 1860 this number had declined to 12.6 percent.[68] The 1860 US census also indicated that slaves accounted for 32.27 percent of the 15 slaveholding states' population.[69] Slaves made up over 45 percent of the lower South and a little under 30 percent of the upper South.

The coup de grâce to underscore the Pre-Industrial Era's scarcity and scramble for resources was the fact that humans—typically from another population group or tribe—were often treated as instruments of production, owned and exploited against their will as capital investments to serve or produce for others.

By the eighteenth century, the infamous "Triangular Trade" reached its zenith among those practicing slavery in the Eurocentric world. Ships left England laden with cargo for West Africa, collected slaves in West African ports in exchange for their cargo, and conveyed these slaves to the West Indies to trade for molasses or other agricultural commodities, which were then transported back to England to complete the cycle. Around 12 million Africans were taken to the Americas between the sixteenth and nineteenth centuries, though less than 6 percent ended up in the United States.[70] The vast majority were transported to Brazil and put to work by Portuguese masters. Also important to note is that black-

68 "1800 Census: Return of the Whole Number of Persons within the Several Districts of the United States" (US Department of State, 1800), accessed May 1, 2023, http://www2.census.gov/prod2/decennial/documents/1800-return-whole-number-of-persons.pdf, and "1860 Census: Population of the United States" (US Department of State, 1860), accessed May 1, 2023, https://www2.census.gov/library/publications/decennial/1860/population/1860a-02.pdf. In the 1800 census, the enumeration of "Persons in the several Districts of the United States" recorded 5,309,758 free and enslaved in the country, 894,452 of whom were slaves. In the 1860 census, thirty-four states, seven territories, and the District of Columbia reported the United States had a population of 31,443,321, with 3,953,760 being slaves, and 487,970 "free colored" persons.
69 "1860 Census: Population of the United States," vii.
70 Ronald Segal, *The Black Diaspora: Five Centuries of the Black Experience Outside Africa*, (New York: Farrar, Straus and Giroux, 1995), 4; and the Trans-Atlantic Slave Trade Database, accessed May 1, 2023, http://www.slavevoyages.org/tast/index.faces.

on-black slavery and Arab-on-black slavery was practiced in Africa long before white-on-black slavery emerged in the sixteenth century.

The economics of slavery were compelling for merchants, traders, and entrepreneurs alike. The annual return from slaving voyages over the last 50 years of British slaving was between 8 and 10 percent,[71] while at the other end of the slavery value chain, the practice was profitable for the plantation-based Southern antebellum economy, even permitting profits for owners in the more barren seaboard and border states involved (e.g., Virginia and North Carolina).[72] Moreover, slavery's viability did not only involve putting humans to work with harsh controls and discipline. The sale of slave children was an important part of the business return.

The third economic institution of service and training impacting economic man in pre-industrial times was guilds, which by the Middle Ages in Europe comprised two types: craft and merchant. Craft guilds certified conditions under which workers could become members of their profession and perform certain handicrafts. Merchant guilds, in contrast, controlled the conduct of trade within a specified geographic monopoly, with powers including the ability to prevent nonmembers from trading in their towns and the means to discipline members for dishonest or illegal behaviors. The vast majority of merchant guilds were trader associations with exclusive rights to practice local commercial activities within their city limits.[73]

Like most human institutions, guilds could be forces of good or bad. In craft guilds, opportunities for mischief were many: members could abuse apprentices and journeymen over their training, and by controlling guild entry, access to labor markets and competition was restricted. Similar opportunities for rent seeking and self-interest protection were

71 Niall Ferguson, *Empire*, 74.
72 Alfred H. Conrad and John R. Meyer, "The Economics of Slavery in the Ante Bellum South," *The Journal of Political Economy* 66, no. 2 (April 1958): 95–130.
73 Roberta Dessí and Sheilagh Ogilvie, "Social Capital and Collusion: The Case of Merchant Guilds," CESifo Working Paper 1037, CESifo, Munich, Germany, September 2003, accessed May 1, 2023, https://www.cesifo.org/en/publications/2003/working-paper/social-capital-and-collusion-case-merchant-guilds.

also available to merchant guilds. But whether guilds economically benefited societies or were institutions that protected narrow self-interest is difficult to answer.

Adam Smith concluded guilds were collusive and anti–free trade,[74] and Marx and Engels dismissed them as oppressive. *The Communist Manifesto* categorized guild masters and journeymen as oppressor and oppressed, and it assigned guild members to the privileged capitalist classes while apprentices and journeymen fell into the oppressed proletariat. Later in the manifesto, Marx and Engels stated the following:

> In the earlier epochs of history, we find almost everywhere a complicated arrangement of society into various orders, a manifold gradation of social rank. In ancient Rome we have patricians, knights, plebeians, slaves; in the Middle Ages, feudal lords, vassals, guild-masters, journeymen, apprentices, serfs; in almost all of these classes, again, subordinate gradations.[75]

Marx and Engels further argued that feudal industry was a system of industrial production monopolized by closed guilds, and Dessí and Ogilvie concluded similarly that merchant guilds colluded with local rulers such that harmful economic and social outcomes resulted.[76]

More recent research suggests guilds' roles were more positive. Epstein observed craft guilds created transferable skills through apprenticeships and that these institutions prospered for more than 500 years because they sustained specialized interregional labor markets, stimulated technical diffusion through migrant labor, and provided inventors temporary monopoly rents.[77] Putnam alleged medieval guild traditions built modern social capital in northern Italy and that this social capital was

---

74 Adam Smith, "Of Wages and Profit in the Different Employments of Labour and Stock," *The Wealth of Nations*, book 1, chap. 10, part 2, para. 17.

75 Karl Marx and Friedrich Engels, "Bourgeois and Proletarians," chap. 1 in *Manifesto of the Communist Party* (London: Communist League, 1848).

76 Dessí and Ogilvie, "Social Capital and Collusion."

77 S. R. Epstein, "Craft Guilds, Apprenticeship, and Technological Change in Preindustrial Europe," *The Journal of Economic History* 58, no. 3 (September 1998): 684–713, accessed May 1, 2023, https://doi.org/10.1017/S0022050700021124.

vital to the region's current economic success,[78] while Dasgupta described merchant guilds as social networks that built social capital that promoted economic growth.[79]

Whether guilds economically contributed positively or negatively will not be settled here. Over their centuries of operation, more than likely economic welfare was sometimes promoted, and at other times, the interests of elites were protected and served. Though imperfect, when compared with serfdom and slavery, guilds were a clear improvement. Craft guilds represent among the first formal institutions of worker training, but though master craftsmen and merchant guild members enjoyed living standards way above the average, these gains were neither widespread nor substantial. A genuine industrial revolution was needed to attain this, only possible once more productive forms of economic capital appeared to complement and support labor in its enduring struggle for productivity. Endemic scarcity remained until this economic capital, housed in newfangled buildings called factories, appeared.

How inexpertly land, labor, and economic capital were employed in the struggle for productivity over the Pre-Industrial Era has now been surveyed. These all explain the lack of productivity that characterized the time. To conclude coverage of the economics of the era, the role of the entrepreneur must finally be considered. As the fourth vital factor of production, how entrepreneurs fared in pre-industrial times is an important topic, and an ideal candidate for an investigation of pre-industrial entrepreneurship is Christopher Columbus, Admiral of the Ocean Sea. It is to the life and times of this famous—and infamous—explorer that we now turn.

78 Robert D. Putnam, *Bowling Alone: The Collapse and Revival of American Community*, (New York: Simon & Schuster, 2000). Putnam defined "social capital" as "features of social life—networks, norms, and trust—that facilitate cooperation and coordination for mutual benefit" (Robert Putnam, "Democracy in America at Century's End," in *Democracy's Victory and Crisis*, ed. Axel Hadenius [New York: Cambridge University Press, 1997], 31). However, for a critique of social capital as a construct to rely upon in such research, see J. Sobel, "Can We Trust Social Capital?" *Journal of Economic Literature* 40, no. 1 (March 2002): 139–54.

79 Partha Dasgupta, "Economic Progress and the Idea of Social Capital," in *Social Capital: A Multifaceted Perspective*, eds. Partha Dasgupta and Ismail Serageldin (Washington, DC: World Bank, 2000), 325–424.

Pre-Industrial Era Entrepreneurship: Christopher Columbus and Plunder through Hard Power

Columbus is chosen to represent pre-industrial entrepreneurship for many reasons. First, as noted earlier, he was in possession of the most sophisticated form of economic capital available at the time, the sailing ship. Second, as a *transport* entrepreneur, he represents the entrepreneurial activity most valued at the time: not ventures to increase the productive capacity of humans directly, but endeavors to facilitate the movements of materials, goods, and people around the world and through these expand political power and amass economic wealth. Third, records of how he organized, financed, and executed his venture as well as the rewards he enjoyed are all available.

Columbus is also an ideal candidate because of the controversy surrounding his life and times and what this controversy says about entrepreneurship in the Pre-Industrial Era. As far back as 1939, Columbus was "alternately praised and belittled, groomed for canonization and charged with piracy, lauded as a scientist and branded as an ignoramus."[80] A call for revision of how he was portrayed in American textbooks was made in the 1980s,[81] and a plethora of books and articles in the late twentieth century revisited the Columbian Legacy. Disaffection with Columbus's place in history reached a crescendo around the five hundredth anniversary of his voyage of discovery,[82] when many cast him as looter and plunderer, though some alleged he was "mugged along the way."[83]

That a prominent entrepreneur of pre-industrial times prospered from unethical or immoral behavior is unsurprising. With man's inhumanity to man so prevalent in the era, entrepreneurship that reflects the

80 Charles E. Nowell, "The Columbus Question: A Survey of Recent Literature and Present Opinion," *The American Historical Review* 44, no. 4 (July 1939): 802–22.

81 James Axtell, "Europeans, Indians, and the Age of Discovery in American History Textbooks," *The American Historical Review* 92, no. 3 (June 1987): 621–32.

82 Kirkpatrick Sale, *The Conquest of Paradise: Christopher Columbus and the Columbian Legacy* (New York: Alfred A. Knopf, 1990); Hans Koning, *Columbus: His Enterprise* (New York: Monthly Review Press, 1976, revised 1992).

83 Garry Wills, "Goodbye Columbus," *The New York Review of Books*, November 22, 1990, 6–9.

use of hard power to obtain scarce resources often at the immense cost to others is imminently predictable.

Columbus's Life and Times: Plenty from Brutality and Oppression

Columbus was born to humble circumstances in 1451 and made his first serious voyage in 1475 at the age of 24. His entrepreneurial vision was to find a route to Asia sailing west from Europe. He turned to serious exploration of this dream in 1484 and first sought the support of John II of Portugal to fund what later became his *La Empresa de las Indias*, or "Enterprise of the Indies." A commission appointed by the Portuguese king rejected the idea, as members were skeptical Columbus had any likelihood of success in the journey. Portuguese rejection prompted Columbus to move to Spain to lobby the rich and prominent there, though he left Portugal "furtively and in haste, probably because he feared arrest for debt."[84] While promoting the venture he remained poor, seeking support from any backer he could convince.

In Spain, Don Luis de la Cerda, wealthy owner of a merchant fleet, eventually agreed to provide three or four caravels for the venture, but fearing royal permission was needed, he informed Queen Isabella. The Spanish sovereign's interest was piqued, and she ordered Columbus to present his ideas to her in May 1486, after which the venture entered limbo while the sovereign considered her support.

While the Spanish rulers dithered, Henry VII of England and Charles VIII of France were also asked for support but to no avail. Seven years passed from Columbus's arrival in Spain until the venture was funded, the lag due to a variety of factors. The Spanish monarchy's attention was diverted to more pressing issues, including a war to evict Muslims from Catholic Spain, and the uncertainty surrounding the enterprise itself meant many committees and councils reviewed the proposal on behalf of

84 Samuel Eliot Morison, *Admiral of the Ocean Sea: A Life of Christopher Columbus* (Boston: Little, Brown and Company, 1942), 79.

potential backers. Pioneering of the nature that Columbus was proposing was risky; money rarely comes easily or quickly for such enterprises.

In early 1492 the Spanish monarchs eventually agreed to support the venture, though not only for economic return: a devout Catholic, Queen Isabella commissioned Columbus to take her faith to the pagans he encountered. Columbus's rewards for the journey were mostly captured in two documents, an Articles of Agreement of April 17, and the *Titulo* or Title of April 30, 1492. In these, Columbus was appointed *Don Cristobal Colon*, Admiral of the Ocean Sea, over all islands and mainland he discovered (these rights enjoyed by his heirs and successors into perpetuity) and was named viceroy and governor general of all islands and mainland discovered or acquired. He was also given the right to 10 percent of the gold, silver, pearls, gems, spices, and other merchandise obtained by barter; to mining within the limits of the domains he discovered; and to pay an eighth of the total expenses and enjoy an eighth of the profits earned from voyages.

To finance the expedition 1,400,000 maravedis were borrowed from the Santa Hermandad endowment and later repaid by the Spanish Crown, and Columbus himself invested 250,000 maravedis, more than likely from friends. The balance either came from Luis de Santángel—keeper of King Ferdinand's Privy Purse—or from the Aragon treasury. The total cost represented about US$14,000 in mid-twentieth-century dollars.[85]

Finally, on August 3, 1492, Columbus left Spain and sailed west to the Canary Islands and then across the Atlantic Ocean. Sixty-five days later, on October 12, 1492, Bahamian land was sighted. After sailing around the other Bahamian islands, Columbus reached Cuba, then went east to Quisqueya, renamed Hispaniola, where on December 24, 1492, his flagship, the *Santa Maria*, floundered. Satisfied of a positive local reception, Columbus left the *Santa Maria* crew at newly named Navidad to return and report his success.

---

85 Morison, *Admiral of the Ocean Sea*, 103.

Following his first voyage, Columbus returned with a significantly larger fleet of 17 ships and 1,200 men in September 1493, reaching islands in the West Indies and Puerto Rico. A third voyage followed in 1498, following rumors that a great continent was to be found south of Columbus's first discoveries, and he reached Venezuela in August 1498. A fourth voyage followed in 1503, based on speculation that a strait permitted access back to the Indian Ocean. Columbus never found this strait nor reached the Pacific Ocean. He returned to Spain in November 1504 and died in May 1506 at 53 years of age.

Columbus's life and times provide valuable insight into entrepreneurship in the Pre-Industrial Era. First, the venture underscores the risk pre-industrial entrepreneurs faced and took. His Enterprise of the Indies was certainly risky, far more so even than the risks astronauts faced going to the moon 450 years later. Second, it took over seven years to raise the financial capital to fund his first voyage, this after being rejected by at least three European monarchs. These were not the deep, liquid capital markets open to entrepreneurs today. Third, the journey confirms that entrepreneurship during this time was typically plundering in nature. Columbus's venture was consistent with the notion that wealth in these times was best acquired by going next door and simply taking from those unable to defend themselves. Columbus mostly just extended the boundaries of next door. Continents were open for conquest for those brave enough to commit to such adventures. And the returns were substantial: domain over lands, even continents, was won.

Columbus's venture also underscored that in the Pre-Industrial Era, private agents alone did not have the capacity to launch ventures without the backing of a national authority. In the case of territorial conquest, cooperation between governments and private citizens was necessary. This persisted even until the nineteenth century with the activities of entrepreneurs such as Cecil John Rhodes, who set out to paint all of Africa "British red." Columbus's conquests pioneered the business/government alliance that western Europeans relied upon for the next four centuries in their engagement with the New World.

Armed with superior technology and organizational capabilities, and with Bible in one hand and gun in the other, the Europeans arrived as conquerors and imposed their governance, faith, and will on the lands and peoples conquered. Historians support this conceptualization of Europe's engagement with conquered societies:

> The process of Western ascension involved violence against other parts of the world. European colonisation of the Americas involved the extermination, marginalisation, or conquest of its indigenous population. European contact with Africa was for three centuries concentrated on the slave trade. There were European wars with Asian countries from the mid-eighteenth to the mid-twentieth century designed to establish or maintain colonies and trading privileges.[86]

Columbus died a very wealthy man; for inhabitants in the lands he and those following him conquered, the outcome was far less impressive, but such was the nature of pre-industrial entrepreneurship: nasty and brutal, though not poor or short for the entrepreneurs involved. Further assessment of Columbus's actions is provided in Chapter 3, when he is compared with Industrial Era entrepreneur Henry Ford, and when both Ford and Columbus are compared with Post-Industrial Era entrepreneur Bill Gates.

Twenty-First-Century Pre-Industrial Subsistence: Rural to Urban Failure

Why scarcity and failure remained endemic over the Pre-Industrial Era has now been explained. To conclude the era's coverage, the situation facing billions now living in *modern* pre-industrial conditions must be considered. A significant change has occurred over the past century: rural subsistence is gradually being replaced by a phenomenon better described

86 Maddison, *The World Economy: A Millennial Perspective*, 49.

as *urban subsistence*. Many twenty-first-century pre-industrial urban residents now reside in the location where failure persists for millions, if not billions.

Table 1 shows the top 10 city populations at the beginning of the past two centuries. Astounding is that in 1900, 8 of the 10 most populous cities were in western Europe and the United States, but by 2018 only one (Tokyo) remained and only one European city was included (Istanbul). America, with three in 1900, had none by 2018. Finally, the top 10 by 2018 were far more populated than in 1900. In 1900 the world's top 10 cities had just fewer than 26 million inhabitants in total. By 2018 they reported almost 155 million, with this number increasing to over 241 million if broader city metropolitan areas were included. Because no international agreement exists regarding the definition of metropolitan areas, Table 1 only reports city populations.

That most newcomers to the 2018 list are located in developing countries emphasizes the fact that over the past 50 years significant urbanization has taken place across the developing regions of Africa, Asia, and Latin America especially, giving rise to so-called exploding cities in these regions.[87] It is in the favelas and slums of these massive metropolises that urban (as opposed to rural) subsistence is now being encountered. Many wishing to embark upon the struggle for productivity now reside in locations and conditions unlike those of the generations before them.

87 Eugene Linden, "The Exploding Cities of the Developing World," *Foreign Affairs* 75, no. 1 (January–February 1996), 52–65.

Table 1: Top 10 City Populations: 1900 and 2018

1900*		2018**	
City	**Population**	**City**	**Population**
London, UK	6,480,000	Shanghai, China	24,153,000
New York, US	4,242,000	Beijing, China	18,590,000
Paris, France	3,330,000	Karachi, Pakistan	18,000,000
Berlin, Germany	2,707,000	Istanbul, Turkey	14,657,000
Chicago, US	1,717,000	Dhaka, Bangladesh	14,543,000
Vienna, Austria	1,698,000	Tokyo, Japan	13,617,000
Tokyo, Japan	1,497,000	Moscow, Russia	13,197,596
St. Petersburg, RUS	1,439,000	Manila, Philippines	12,877,000
Manchester, UK	1,435,000	Tianjin, China	12,784,000
Philadelphia, US	1,418,000	Mumbai, India	12,400,000
Total population	**25,963,000**		**154,818,596**

* Tertius Chandler, *Four Thousand Years of Urban Growth: An Historical Census* (Lewiston, NY: St. David's University Press, 1987).
** City Mayors Foundation, "Largest cities in the world," accessed May 1, 2023, http://www.citymayors.com/statistics/largest-cities-population-125.html.

Visit a city of the developing world today, from Rio de Janeiro in Brazil to Johannesburg in South Africa to Mumbai in India or Bangkok in Thailand, and the conditions of urban subsistence are obvious. In these cities two groups exist, side by side, day by day. They are the very rich and the very poor, with limited middle classes in between. Traveling around these metropoles reveals islands of prosperity surrounded by seas of poverty. The rich live in penthouses behind barricades and layers of security, enjoying living standards that a minority in the developed world match. The poor survive in dramatically different conditions in slums next door. Making matters even worse, those in the favelas have far better choices than their relatives in the rural locations their families had occupied for millennia.

Most of the poor of these exploding cities have neither the skills nor the land to cultivate their own food. Instead, they subsist either by doing jobs in the informal sector (e.g., as domestic servants on the estates or in the houses and apartments of the rich) or in low-skill jobs in emerging industrial sectors (e.g., as workers or cleaners in factories, hotels, or offices or as servers in retail establishments). Many are unemployed and work in marginal occupations (e.g., prostitution, drug trafficking, or other criminal activities). Under such conditions, living standards are low and survival is marginal; such are the limited choices of urban subsistence.

Why massive urbanization across the developing world is now occurring is covered in Chapter 3. This trend is not a sign of failure but rather a harbinger of success. Though presenting stresses and challenges, urbanized populations are far easier to reach, educate, and serve than remote rural populations are. Moving the marginalized residents of crowded, exploding cities from urban subsistence to middle-class lives is one of the main twenty-first-century development challenges. Global stability, as well as sustaining the ongoing human struggle for productivity, largely rests on accomplishing this task.

Having outlined the starting conditions currently facing most developing countries today, it is important to understand how those already industrialized achieved this status. Once the process of industrialization is better appreciated, how developing countries might embark upon their efforts to modernize is revealed. Chapter 3 deals with the Industrial Era and explains the models followed to industrialize from the 1800s until the end of the twentieth century.

Conclusion and Synthesis

That subsistence agriculture dominated human production from around 10,000 years ago until the Industrial Revolution benchmarks the lack of productivity characterizing the Pre-Industrial Era. Moreover, this peasant farmer cultivation of small land holdings produced little tradable surplus, meaning that in addition to working the land for food to survive, families also had to hunt for animal protein, build their homes, and make their clothes. Meeting the basic needs of food, clothing, and shelter was always the priority, and given this fact, life for many remained "solitary, poor, nasty, brutish, and short" over the hundreds of generations that societies reproduced themselves under these conditions.

Many factors contributed to this cumulative circle of scarcity, foremost among them the lack of usable economic capital. Had better farming tools or manufacturing equipment existed, productivity might not have remained so low for so long. Further, and again indicative of the paucity of economic capital, humans were also treated as capital assets. Slavery, the low-water mark in the human struggle for productivity, confirms how man's inhumanity to man so widely pervaded the Pre-Industrial Era and has plagued humanity for all of recorded history.

The strict control of land access and the lack of freedom associated with feudalism meant peasants worked mostly as indentured servants, enjoying a status not far removed from slavery. Moreover, and congruent with political economies that relied on harsh instruments of control to maintain the living standards of a mostly plundering elite, entrepreneurship during the Pre-Industrial Era also reflected a negative hue.

Possessing the most impressive form of economic capital available at the time—the sailing ship—Christopher Columbus embodies the plundering nature of pre-industrial entrepreneurship. Considered by some a brave explorer who risked his life to open sea routes to the Americas and the New World's indigenous inhabitants, he was a looter and plunderer who used harsh power to obtain dominion over lands and peoples through conquest. Though a true visionary with a valid entrepreneurial goal, Columbus's venture is consistent with the notion that in pre-industrial times, wealth was best acquired by taking from those unable to defend themselves. Columbus expanded the geographies where the weak could be reached and plundered.

In the quest for resources, initially to comply with the dictates of mercantile capitalism and later for commodities to sustain the material intensity of industrialization, European colonialists and settlers destroyed or destabilized many communities in Africa, the Americas, and Asia. Columbus's arrival in the Americas and the European scramble for Africa made life for local inhabitants brutal and short across three continents.

The study of the Pre-Industrial Era is not only necessary because it reveals the difficult conditions under which mankind struggled over most of human history. Around half of the world's 8 billion people still subsist in starting conditions similar to those encountered over the era, and understanding the contexts faced as Failures start their early struggles for productivity is essential. Pre-industrial survival for some in the twenty-first century will differ from the conditions faced by their ancestors over history. With 57.5 percent of the world's inhabitants urbanized,[88] survival is moving from rural to urban subsistence.

It is in the favelas and slums of the exploding cities that appear as Failures start industrializing that urban subsistence is now the modern equivalent of the subsistence existence led by most in pre-industrial times. Maintaining stability in these fast-growing poor urban enclaves, where residents neither have land to grow their food nor skills to obtain high-value employment, is now a key challenge, and moving these humans from urban subsistence to middle-class lives is among the major tasks faced over the rest of the twenty-first century.

We now turn to the Industrial Era and to the world of the present. Chapter 3 reveals how those who pioneered industrialization achieved this unprecedented revolution in productivity (the First Movers) and how some (the Fast Followers) achieved industrialization in the twentieth century at a rate not seen by the early movers into the era.

---

88 *The World Factbook*, "Explore All Countries." The estimate is for 2023.

CHAPTER 3

THE INDUSTRIAL ERA

Follower Abundance from Input Mobilization and Economic Diversification

Though Chapter 1 sets 1800 as the start of the Industrial Era, the precise time of commencement of the age is disputed. To Kuznets, the 1971 Nobel Prize winner in Economics for pioneering work on identifying the economic and social structural changes experienced as societies industrialize and modernize, modern economic growth started around 1760, after being preceded by European merchant capitalism from the 1500s.[89] To Maddison, the process began around 1820, following work of economic historians such as Crafts and Harley, who alleged British industrial growth increased noticeably only in the early nineteenth century.[90] This debate is not settled here; 1800 was selected as the starting point of the Industrial Era because it falls around the midpoint of credible estimates of the start time.

Neither is arguing about specific starting points necessary, as structural (i.e., permanent) change of this nature does not occur at single

89 Simon Kuznets, *Modern Economic Growth: Rate, Structure, and Spread* (New Haven, CT: Yale University Press, 1966).

90 Maddison, *The World Economy: A Millennial Perspective*, 45; and N. F. R Crafts and C. K. Harley, "Output Growth and the British Industrial Revolution: A Restatement of the Crafts-Harley View," *The Economic History Review* 45, no. 4 (November 1992): 703–30.

points but takes place over decades. What's important is economic historians agree that a discontinuous, substantial structural shift in human productivity began around the beginning of the nineteenth century and propelled mankind onto a radically different economic path.

This chapter describes what industrialization is and how it is accomplished. It reveals the difficulties faced as societies start the struggle for productivity and, through industrialization, move from Failures to Followers. The process is complex and multidimensional, is multigenerational in length, and requires resources, organization, good economic governance, hard work, and deferred gratification to attain. Moving from Failure to Follower is not easy or quick.

Industrialization as Transformer of Nations and Peoples

Industrialization is one of many terms used to describe mankind's recent economic advance. Rostow referred to "stages of economic growth" through which societies proceed in the transition from underdeveloped to developed but implied economic growth is the engine that propels societies from traditional subsistence (pre-industrial) to mass consumption (industrial) economies.[91] Organski used national development, national growth, and modernization interchangeably to describe "national development," which he characterized as increasing economic production, increasing geographic and social mobility, and increasing political efficiency in mobilizing national human and material resources to achieve national goals.[92] All these terms—*economic growth, national development and growth,* and *modernization*—incorporate industrialization.

Kuznets defined a country's economic growth as "a long-term rise in capacity to supply increasingly diverse economic goods to its population, this growing capacity based on advancing technology and the

91 W. W. Rostow, "The Stages of Economic Growth: A Non-Communist Manifesto," *The Economic History Review* 12, no. 1 (1959): 1–16.
92 A. K. F. Organski, *The Stages of Political Development* (New York: Alfred A. Knopf, 1965), 65.

institutional and ideological adjustments that it demands."[93] Along these lines, Table 2 describes some characteristics of industrial versus pre-industrial societies across three dimensions: principal factors of production, productivity levels, and economic structure.

Table 2 indicates pre-industrial societies are those where land and labor are the principal factors of production and where economic capital is so limited that it does not noticeably contribute to production. A majority of the economic output is produced in small-scale subsistence agriculture, using primitive, labor-intensive production. With an ability to produce surplus to trade equally constrained, entrepreneurs are not major factors of production either. Most live hand-to-mouth, producing only to meet basic needs. Agrarian subsistence is the dominant lifestyle; productivity is low and scarcity reigns. These are all Failure characteristics that Chapter 2 identifies.

Table 2: Industrial versus Pre-Industrial Societies

Dimension	Pre-Industrial	Industrial
Major factors of production	Land Labor	Land Labor Capital Entrepreneurship
Productivity levels	Low: unskilled labor using little economic capital in production.	High: based on capital- and labor-intensive, technology-based production in mostly urban areas. Mass production and consumption.
Economic structure	Undiversified: small-scale agrarian subsistence; trade of goods limited. Output mostly agriculture based.	Diversified: based on capital-intensive mass production and consumption of agriculture, manufactures, and services. Agriculture smallest percentage of total output; manufacturing largest.

93 Simon Kuznets, "Modern Economic Growth: Findings and Reflections," *American Economic Review* 63, no. 3 (June 1973): 247.

Industrialized societies, by contrast, display economic output that includes agriculture, manufactures, and services (primary, secondary, and tertiary), produced by more-skilled and specialized labor working alongside sophisticated economic capital (in Kuznets's terminology, "advancing capital"). Industrializing elites playing entrepreneurial roles are also needed. Moreover, agriculture, produced using capital-intensive production methods, employs substantially less labor than does manufacturing—the majority of people work in factories and not on the land as in pre-industrial times. Finally, self-sustained economic growth is fueled by mass production and consumption. Industrialization is accordingly defined as follows:

> *Industrialization is the process that transforms societies from primary product producers using land and unskilled labor as factors of production to producers of primary, secondary, and tertiary goods and services, utilizing capital-intensive production on a scale that self-sustaining mass production and consumption occurs in that society.*[94]

Industrialization's Voracious Demand for Capital, Labor, Energy, and Materials

Industrialization has four elements. First, it is capital intensive, meaning investible surplus must be available to build the infrastructure and economic capital is needed to initiate and sustain the transformation; second, it is labor intensive, meaning human capital is required to work alongside the economic capital in production; third, it is energy intensive, meaning energy to power factories, extract and transport raw materials, and operate goods that are produced is needed; and fourth, it is materials intensive, meaning raw materials to convert into the diverse range of goods and services industrialization offers must also be available.

94 Collins defines *primary products* as "a product consisting of a natural raw material; an unmanufactured product," *Collins Online English Dictionary*, s. v. "primary product," accessed May 1, 2023, https://www.collinsdictionary.com/us/dictionary/english/primary-product.

Capital, labor, energy, and materials are the four ingredients of the industrialization cake, and that all must be present underscores the complexity of industrialization: much must be in place to accomplish the transformation. Regretfully, a fifth characteristic, and more a consequence or effect of industrialization than an element of itself has recently appeared: pollution. The four core elements are discussed next. Chapter 5 covers the impact of this negative consequence when climate change/global warming is considered.

Recent research supports conceptualizing industrialization as a diversification process, though with one important caveat: the relationship between economic diversification and time at the nation-state level appears curvilinear and is best captured in an inverted U. Data from the 1960s until the 1990s from 99 countries—a wide sample of both industrialized and developing countries—shows developing countries first diversify, but as industrialization proceeds and economic maturity is reached, the benefits of diversification wane and focus and specialization become imperative.[95] Why this curvilinear trend is noted is considered at this chapter's end and also in Chapters 4 and 5 when post-industrial competitiveness is covered. Focus is more imperative as societies move into post-industrial production.

Industrialization's Capital Intensity: Deferring Gratification as Productive Bases Are Built

Though economists have long argued about what fosters economic takeoff and growth, one element is unanimously supported: accumulating surplus (i.e., savings) and investing these appropriately is essential to promote and sustain economic growth. Moreover, in early industrialization substantial saving and investment are needed; only once the industrial base is established can saving and investment decrease propor-

95 Jean Imbs and Romain Wacziarg, "Stages of Diversification," *American Economic Review* 93, no. 1 (March 2003): 63–86.

tionally as consumption grows and the richer society begins to enjoy the fruits of its early labor.

That considerable investment is needed early on is because resources are not only needed to build the economic capital that will be used directly in production. Substantial supporting infrastructure (hard and soft) is also needed. Hard infrastructure includes transport links (roads, airports, harbors, ports, rail); energy sources (electricity, oil, gas, and in the post-industrial world, clean renewable energy); communications capabilities (telegraph, telephone, and in the post-industrial world, the internet); industrial parks and offices for factories and offices; and housing and related physical community facilities to prepare and house workers (schools, hospitals, healthcare, housing, water, sewer).

Soft infrastructure includes education (primary, secondary, and tertiary); laws for the conduct of business, the raising of financial capital, and the protection of property rights (company law, law of contract, law of purchase and sale, tax law, labor law, civil and criminal law); and a regulatory infrastructure that controls market participants and clarifies state and private sector roles in industrialization (constitutional law, trade, economic and industrial policy, foreign investment regulation, and monetary and fiscal policy).

The first question facing any society wishing to industrialize is where will the surplus come from to build its supporting infrastructure and economic capital? America's early surplus came from three sources: free land taken by European settlers; voluntary immigrant labor who traveled to the New World mostly from Europe looking for opportunity (initially in agrarian communities growing across the continent, and later in factories of the Northeast and the Midwest); and slavery, mostly in the antebellum South. These early sources were augmented in the late nineteenth century by tariffs and domestic savings.

Similar to America, China sparked its early industrialization off land owned by China and made available for factories at either no or low cost and from hard-working labor similar to American immigrants in the late

1800s and early 1900s. China also extracted some surplus from foreign MNCs assisting factories in the country, but it was the high savings in the country itself that provided much of the surplus.

> China has had by far the highest overall saving rate in the world since at least 2000, and her saving rate has increased even further since 2000—to nearly 50% of GDP. Gross capital formation (investment) is also high in China, but because saving exceeds investment, China has been running a net saving surplus, which translates into a current account surplus, and that surplus has been growing sharply—from 1.9% of GDP in 2000 to 3.6% in 2004 and a remarkable 7.2% in 2005—even though China is investing at a staggering rate of 43–46% of GDP and even though China is still relatively poor.[96]

The Chinese government and entrepreneurial bureaucrats in state-owned enterprises invested the surplus to build the hard and soft infrastructures and the economic capital to produce the multitude of products that turned China into the world's factory. "Made in China" is attached to goods sold across the globe, and manufacturers who wish to enter global markets today must operate in infrastructures and factories that compete with those in China. Most recently, and in search of energy and raw materials for industrialization, China is also using its surplus to access commodities from around the world. One reason for the country's Belt and Road Initiative is to facilitate raw material flow back to China. This initiative is covered in Chapter 5 when China's engagement with the world moving forward is considered.

As the hard and soft infrastructures are built, and as foundational economic capital is established, little increase in personal consumption is noted: hard work and deferred gratification is mostly the lot of workers. For the first two generations at a minimum, long hours of work in difficult conditions are the norm, causing wealthy consumers of more

---

96 Charles Yuji Horioka and Junmin Wan, "The Determinants of Household Saving in China: A Dynamic Panel Analysis of Provincial Data" (working paper 2007-28, Federal Reserve Bank of San Francisco, 2007), 2, accessed May 1, 2023, http://www.frbsf.org/publications/economics/papers/2007/wp07-28bk.pdf.

advanced economies to worry about worker exploitation in countries struggling through the pressures of early industrialization.

Those expressing outrage at the sweatshops operating across newly industrializing societies must recognize an important historical fact: similar conditions existed in London and New York factories when Britain and America went through their early industrializations in the late nineteenth and early twentieth centuries. They were even observed by Marx in the plight of workers in the London factories of the 1870s and gave rise to a cornerstone of Marxian theory: labor was being so poorly treated (exploited) that only a revolution leading to workers owning the means of production would reverse the situation. Capitalism's collapse was needed to remedy the exploitation.

Testimony to the early exploitation of workers as surplus was extracted in the American Northeast, is seen in an excerpt from the *Voice of Industry* describing conditions in Lowell, Massachusetts, in the mid-nineteenth century:

> Observing a singular looking, "long, low, *black*," wagon passing along the street, we made inquiries respecting it, and were informed that it was what we term a "slaver." She makes regular trips to the north of the state, cruising around in Vermont and New Hampshire, with a "commander" whose heart must be as black as his craft, who is paid a dollar a head, for all he brings to the market, and more in proportion to the distance—if they bring them from such a distance that they cannot easily get back. This is done by "hoisting false colors," and representing to the girls, that they can tend more machinery than is possible, and that the work is so very neat, and the wages such, that they can dress in silks, and spend half their time in reading. Now, is this true? Let those girls who have been thus deceived, answer. . . . Is there any humanity in this? Philanthropists may talk of negro slavery, but it would be well first to endeavor to emancipate the slaves at home. Let us not stretch our ears to catch the sound of the lash on the flesh of the oppressed black

> while the oppressed in our very midst are crying out in thunder tones, and calling upon us for assistance.[97]

In the 1850s exploitation was present in the United States, and not only in the South.

Fortunately, Marx's prediction of class warfare and revolution turned out to be wrong not because his analysis of the status quo in the factories of the time was incorrect, but because he had no idea of what was to come. Though capitalists were certainly living well off exploited labor, the surplus was not only being consumed by industrialists living in hedonistic delight; it was also being reinvested in the infrastructure and economic capital of the day to upgrade the productivity across the system.

The absence of alternatives and the hope for better lives for the next generation motivated millions and millions of first- and second-generation industrial workers to toil their lives away in factories, in conditions unpalatable to residents of industrialized nations today. The climb out of poverty to a diverse productive society is long and arduous and is not without cost or struggle.

Returns in the form of higher wages and widespread improved living standards only came much later—in the British and American cases, almost two generations (50 years) later. Ford's moving assembly line and mass production were required before a widespread increase in living standards became possible. Until this point, deferred gratification and hard work were the order of the day. How these innovations circumvented Marx's prophecy of class warfare is explained later in this chapter when Ford's contribution is covered.

Industrialization's capital intensity and the associated need for an investable surplus are key components required to industrialize. Where the surplus will come from, where it will it be invested, and which products and services will be produced must be determined. Only with

---

97 "Factory Mode of Obtaining Operatives," *Voice of Industry* 1, no. 29, ed. W. F. Young, (Lowell, MA: January 2, 1846), 4, accessed May 1, 2023, https://www.marxists.org/history/usa/pubs/voice-of-industry/1846/v1n29-w029-jan-02-1846-voi.pdf.

the hard and soft infrastructures in place and with factories and offices built will the broad-based diversification and widespread productivity upgrading occur. More importantly, no infrastructure will be built and no products and services will be produced without human capital to establish and work in the factories. We turn now to industrialization's second element: its labor intensity.

Industrialization's Labor Intensity: Leaders Building Infrastructure and Businesses to Employ Workers on the Assembly Line

Two core groups provide the human capital needed to accomplish the industrialization task: a smaller leadership cadre to form and manage the economic capital that builds the infrastructure and industrial businesses needed; and a larger group employed in the companies, factories, offices, and institutions that provide the infrastructure and produce the goods and services that industrialization requires and offers. Not without irony, these groups somewhat align with Marx's capital versus labor class distinction, but they are referred to here in less loaded terms: *industrial leadership* and *industrial workforce*. To understand their composition and characteristics, it is again helpful to observe the early American industrialization experience.

America's Early Industrial Leadership: Robber Barons or Visionary Icons Enabling a World of Plenty

Chandler noted that early American business emerged in two phases: from 1840 to 1880 when the transportation and communications infrastructures were built off innovation in steam-powered railroads, the electric telegraph, and anthracite coal; and from 1880 to 1920 after railroad and telegraph networks had provided conditions for the establishment of industrial product/service enterprises.[98] These phases permit early Amer-

98 Alfred D. Chandler Jr., *The Visible Hand: The Managerial Revolution in American Business* (Cambridge, MA: Harvard University Press, 1977).

ican industrial leaders to be labeled as infrastructure builders and business entrepreneurs.

Chandler named his Pulitzer Prize–winning book *The Visible Hand* to contrast this work with Smith's *Invisible Hand* after concluding that the capital-intensive, technologically complex, large-scale enterprise that characterized American business in the twentieth century was not coordinated by the invisible hand of market forces Smith identified, but rather by the visible hand in the structure and coordination of manager-led hierarchies.

Chandler's data also provides insight into timing, and broadly speaking, the sequencing of business emergence in America was infrastructure first, product-oriented businesses second. This generalization, though possessing face validity, must be applied cautiously. Products are also needed to build infrastructure (steel to build rails, trains for railroads, etc.), and to this extent the phasing is less helpful. In addition, some industries can be established before or while portions of the industrial infrastructure are being built.

Textiles is a notable example. Typically, because of the industry's relatively low-skilled labor intensity and because of its valuable, utilitarian, light-to-transport output—second to food, humans need clothing—this is among the first industries entered as industrialization begins; the economic capital for textiles is often established before the core industrial infrastructure is fully in place.

For example, in the 1860s the American South's economy was based on tobacco and cotton, and by the end of the nineteenth century, textiles were an important export from the region, mostly to factories in the US Northeast.[99] Textiles was also among the first industries targeted by South Korea in its drive to industrialize in the 1960s, and Nike was among the first to enter China in the early 1980s, seeking shoemaking and apparel and textiles competence based on low-cost, high-quality Chinese labor.

---

99 Alex Gray and Peter Brews, *Dan River, Inc.: Reorganizing for the 21st Century* (Chapel Hill, NC: UNC Kenan-Flagler Business School Case Study, 2007).

China also started in textiles, before most of its industrial infrastructure had been built.

Despite the caution that must be applied to the infrastructure first, product businesses second hypothesis, it is clear that in America infrastructure builders were the first to attain notable wealth. Denoted "robber barons" who built wealth through questionable, anticompetitive business practices, regulation was eventually introduced to curb the cartels and monopolies formed by America's early industrialists. The Sherman Antitrust Act of 1890 was the first federal legislation to curb anticompetitive behavior in America; interstate restraint of trade and monopolization of interstate trade or commerce were outlawed. The Clayton Act of 1914 followed, prohibiting price discrimination, exclusive dealings, and mergers that substantially lessened competition. Both are now codified under Title 15 of the United States Code.

Whether early American infrastructure builders were robber barons remains in dispute. Nevin's "industrial statesmen" hypothesis suggested that while the early industrialists behaved unethically, their contribution to building American infrastructure should be recognized and valued.[100] DiLorenzo differentiated market entrepreneurs offering superior goods to consumers free of government subsidy or interference from political entrepreneurs thriving from government subsidy or legislation and argued calling all early industrialists robber barons was incorrect. He even suggests Rockefeller's Standard Oil Trust breakup was prompted by less efficient producers disenabling a better competitor and was an instance of political entrepreneurs using federal antitrust regulation to further their own self-interested ends.[101]

Notwithstanding the merits—or otherwise—of the early industrialists' behaviors, infrastructure that facilitated production and distribution across America was built by their collective efforts, and leveraging this

---

100 Allan Nevins, *John D. Rockefeller: The Heroic Age of American Enterprise*, 2 vols. (New York: Charles Scribner's Sons, 1940).

101 Thomas DiLorenzo, *How Capitalism Saved America: The Untold History of Our Country, from the Pilgrims to the Present* (New York: Three Rivers Press, 2004).

platform, business entrepreneurs pioneered the goods and services that became the middle-class staples of an industrialized America. Similar infrastructure icons are encountered in western Europe: for example, Werner von Siemens (Siemens AG, inventor of the pointer telegraph in the 1840s) and Sir Henry Bessemer (Henry Bessemer & Co., inventor of the Bessemer process that produced steel more efficiently in the 1850s).

Roads, airports, harbors and ports, electricity generation and transmission, and water reticulation are all elements of industrial infrastructure, and Followers wishing to industrialize must allocate surplus to construct these physical infrastructures. In the United States, the roads, airports, ports, and electrical generation and transmission were mostly built through public investment, funded by the federal government and by state authorities.

America's first federally financed interstate road, the National Road or Route 40, was built by the federal government between 1811 and 1834 and ran from Cumberland, Maryland, to the Ohio River.[102] The country's interstate highway road system (connecting the 48 contiguous states and constructed between the mid-1950s and the 1980s with over 46,000 miles of highway), the Dwight D. Eisenhower System of Interstate and Defense Highways, was labeled the largest engineering and construction project in the world.[103]

Included in the pioneering group of American business entrepreneurs are names such as Alexander Graham Bell (AT&T), Richard Warren Sears and Alvah Roebuck (Sears, Roebuck), Thomas Edison (General Electric), William E. Boeing (Boeing), James S. McDonnell (McDonnell Douglas), Alfred P. Sloan Jr. (General Motors), and Henry Ford (Ford Motor Company). These and many others like them provided the industrial leadership that built the world's most diverse, productive, and powerful industrial economy by the mid-twentieth century. Similar European names

---

102 Rickie Longfellow, "The National Road," US Department of Transportation Federal Highway Administration, accessed May 1, 2023, http://www.fhwa.dot.gov/infrastructure/back0103.cfm.
103 Dan McNichol, *The Roads That Built America: The Incredible Story of the U.S. Interstate System* (New York: Sterling Publishing, 2006).

would be Karl Benz and Gottlieb Daimler (founders of Daimler AG, owner of Mercedes-Benz), Ferdinand Porsche (involved in establishment of Germany's Volkswagen AG and Porsche automobiles after World War II), and Gerard and Anton Philips (founders of Koninklijke Philips Electronics N. V./Royal Philips Electronics in the Netherlands).

Aspirant Followers wishing to industrialize must have access to similar leadership talent to envision and build the industrial infrastructure and businesses that eventually attain the economic diversification and abundance that industrialization offers.

Industrialization's Workforce: Labor for Routine Assembly Line Work

Industrial leadership is not the only human capital needed to propel nations to industrialized status. Trained people that build the industrial infrastructure and who work alongside the economic capital are also required, and these differ from the industrial leadership in two major ways: first, there are considerably more of them; second, their role in the industrial firm differs. The need to develop a pool of industrial labor presented industrializing societies with two significant challenges: urbanization and education.

Because many workers were needed to staff factories, and because industrial production is best done in urban areas, migration from rural to urban settings occurred as industrialization proceeded. Urbanization had an additional benefit: the provision of services (e.g., education) is immeasurably easier when people live in close proximity. Urbanization greatly reduces the physical difficulties faced when serving geographically dispersed populations. The exploding cities of the developing world referred to in Chapter 2 are mostly explained by rural residents urbanizing en masse in search of the economic opportunity that industrialization promises.

That the living conditions of these new urban residents remains poor for a protracted period of time—in some cases for generations—flows from the fact that after they arrive, they do not quickly or easily acquire the skills to become productive. In addition, it takes time to build the infrastructure and businesses that eventually provide sufficient employment opportunities to absorb workers seeking employment.

Today it is accepted that educational enrollment and literacy rates are vital indicators of life quality and expectancy as well as of output per capita.[104] Education also means parents face an additional challenge: children need support while obtaining the skills needed to enter the world of industrial work. The on-the-job training provided by parents in pre-industrial times no longer works, and for the first time in history, mass education became important. Faced with this need to invest in and educate children, parents reacted predictably: they had fewer children. No longer employable in the fields from an early age, the costs of raising children rose, and their numbers dropped precipitously. The fertility transition noted in all industrializing societies is explained by this fact.[105]

Though the level of education required in the late eighteenth century was nowhere close to that required by the end of the Industrial Era in the 1950s, it was apparent by the 1870s that education was required to prepare humans for work. Regarding early British education:

> The Liberal victory in the general election of 1868 began a new period in British political history. Among the major reforms in Gladstone's first government (1868–1874) was the Education Act of 1870, which created the nucleus of the modern state system of education.[106]

---

104 M. R. Hagerty et al., "Quality of Life Indexes for National Policy: Review and Agenda for Research," *Social Indicators Research* 55 (July 2001): 1–96; and M. D. Morris, *Measuring the Condition of the World's Poor: The Physical Quality of Life Index*, (Oxford: Pergamon, 1979).

105 The cost of raising children increased significantly over the last century. In 2015 the US Department of Agriculture estimated that "middle-income, married-couple parents of a child born in 2015 may expect to spend $233,610 ($284,570 if projected inflation costs are factored in) for food, shelter, and other necessities to raise a child through age 17." This excludes the cost of a college education (Mark Lino, "The Cost of Raising a Child," US Department of Agriculture, January 13, 2017, accessed May 1, 2023, https://www.usda.gov/media/blog/2017/01/13/cost-raising-child). In 1960 the cost in 2011 dollars was estimated at US$191,720.

106 John Roach, *Secondary Education in England 1870–1902: Public Activity and Private Enterprise* (New York: Routledge, 1991), 3.

At the time, three categories of secondary schools were envisioned in Britain: classical schools for boys to ages of 18 or 19; professional and business schools for boys until they were 16; and schools to educate children up to the age of 14. Schooling for girls and free schooling for all until age 18 had to wait until later. By the end of the nineteenth century, Britain had endowed, public, and private schools, each for specific tasks and niches. For example, public schools were mostly elite boarding schools devoted to preparing the next generation of British leaders; curricula were more concerned with sports than academics.

Given its size, history, and political culture, American primary and secondary education followed a different path. Thomas Jefferson argued in 1818 that local schools were vital democratic institutions to teach correct political principles and encourage responsible citizenship from young ages. He also asserted local schools would offer closer control, a cornerstone of American education until today. Jefferson wrote:

> Schools should be established to provide tuition—free education for three years for all male and female children. In these schools, children were to be taught 'reading, writing, and common arithmetick' [sic], and the books shall be used therein for instructing the children to read shall be such as will at the same time make them acquainted with Grecian, Roman, English, and American history.[107]

Based on these ideals, Jefferson designed an elaborate elementary and secondary public education system for all white males in Virginia, subsidized for those who could not afford it. Consequently, though private schools remained at the forefront, publicly financed local schools became the dominant institution that provided the educational foundation to obtain employment in the factories and offices of industrializing America.

The nineteenth century in America is called the common school period, and the drive for public schooling commenced in the country in the 1820s when formal common school reforms were introduced by

---

107 Joel Spring, *The American School: 1642–2004* (Boston: McGraw-Hill, 2004), 52.

Massachusetts Secretary of Education Horace Mann.[108] By 1918, laws requiring compulsory school education for elementary-age children had been passed by every state, and by 2000 compulsory school age attendance ranged between 16 and 18 years, though states still determined the age levels at which their students were to remain in school.[109]

Though not without fault, the decentralized model has survived:

> Despite the fact that participation in school elections is very low and information on which to base a vote is often scarce, Americans will not surrender local control without a fight. They simply will not permit distant politicians or experts in a centralized civil service to make educational decisions. The reasons for this preference are complicated, including the incredible diversity of the population and the huge size of the country. Not least important, however, is the fact that local districts mirror and reinforce separation by class and race. . . . Public schools are essential to make the American dream work, but schools are also the arena in which many Americans first fail.[110]

The public school legacy in the United States is both positive and negative and raises concerns about their ability to prepare Americans for the rigor and intellectual challenge of twenty-first-century work. Nonetheless, this survey of primary and secondary education in the United States underscores two important points for Followers wishing to industrialize: first, education is vital; second, it takes time to build educational institutions. In America, this is still a work in progress after six generations of effort.

The labor intensity of industrial production not only required a cohort of appropriately educated workers to present themselves for work at the factory gate. Innovations in the organization of work and employ-

108 Carl F. Kaestle, *Pillars of the Republic: Common Schools and American Society, 1780–1860* (New York: Hill and Wang, 1983).

109 "Ages for Compulsory School Attendance, Special Education Services for Students, Policies for Year-Round Schools and Kindergarten Programs, by State: 1997 and 2000," *Digest of Education Statistics*, National Center for Education Statistics, US Department of Education, table 150, accessed May 1, 2023, http://nces.ed.gov/programs/digest/d02/dt150.asp.

110 Jennifer L. Hochschild and Nathan Scovronick, *The American Dream and the Public Schools* (New York: Oxford University Press, 2003), 4-5.

ment practices also contributed, seen in specialization and the division of labor, in the standardization of human work on the assembly line through "scientific management," and in better employment conditions industrial workers negotiated on the factory floor. Human resources management in the Industrial Era now considers the employment innovation that emerged in the first 50 years of the twentieth century and explains how labor contributed to production in the industrial firm.

Industrialization's Human Resources Management: Specialization and Scientific Management, Thinkers, and Doers

Considerably more attention was paid to organizing work and workers in the Industrial than in the Pre-Industrial Era. Workers were divided into managers/thinkers and assembly line workers/doers, and the ideas of Adam Smith and Frederick Winslow Taylor provided the logic for work in the emerging industrial corporation. Smith's much fabled division of labor was described in the mundane task of pin making. After doubting whether one worker doing all activities could make even 20 pins a day, Smith described the more specialized pin production he had observed:

> One man draws out the wire; another straights it; a third cuts it; a fourth points it; a fifth grinds it at the top for receiving the head; to make the head requires two or three distinct operations . . . and the important business of making a pin is, in this manner, divided into about eighteen distinct operations, which, in some manufactories, are all performed by distinct hands, though in others the same man will sometimes perform two or three of them.[111]

According to Smith, 10 men working together in a specialized manner made over 48,000 pins in a day. Taylor added the need to capture routines embedded in each specialization in a practice termed *scientific management,* and like Smith, underscored the need for specialization, with factory floor workers also needing different skills from the planners

111 Smith, "Of the Division of Labour," Book 1, chap. 1, para. 3, *The Wealth of Nations.*

in management. Smith's division of labor persisted even until the end of the twentieth century:

> Today's airlines, steel mills, accounting firms, and computer chip makers have all been built around Smith's central idea—the division or specialization of labor and the consequent fragmentation of work. The larger the organization, the more specialized is the worker and the more separate steps into which the work is fragmented. This rule applies not only to manufacturing jobs. Insurance companies, for instance, typically assign separate clerks to process each line of a standardized form.[112]

In Taylor's scientific management, production was standardized into repetitive routines that humans performed efficiently. Instead of master craftsmen or apprentices requiring years to master a craft as in the Pre-Industrial Era, previously less-skilled workers (now armed with *science* that replaced arbitrary, idiosyncratic *rules of thumb* with tried and tested scientific routines) joined the world of productive work. Their manual dexterity, coupled with basic education and on-the-job training, permitted millions to join assembly lines across the industrializing world. Though greatly increasing productivity and delivering a better material existence compared with the pre-industrial subsistence that Failures had endured, the work was often physically demanding, repetitive, and dehumanizing.

Workers did not think and did only what instructed to do. To commentators they were nothing more than biological cogs keeping pace with relentless, unforgiving machines. Charlie Chaplin's *Modern Times* provided a 1930s sociological and cultural commentary on assembly lines. Pressure for efficiency and continuous innovation and the monotonous inhumanity of the assembly line drove Chaplin's Little Tramp mad. Lucille Ball in her *I Love Lucy* TV series later turned this drive for speed into comedy in episode 1 of season 2, "Job Switching," broadcast September 15, 1952.

---

112 Michael Hammer and James Champy, *Reengineering the Corporation: A Manifesto for Business Revolution* (New York: HarperBusiness, 1993), 14–15.

Even in the twenty-first century, automobile assembly line work remains unattractive. Reporting on assembly line work at Toyota in 2006 in Japan, Ihara observed:

> The other casual workers who started at the same time as I did, told me that they had also gradually achieved a level of fusion of body and mind that enabled them to work more efficiently. In all their cases too, this process took something over a month. Young Naganuma (18 years old), who was in the same group as me, said after two months that he could do his job in his sleep.[113]

Ihara also noted that by then the assembly line had been redesigned to make humans central to the production process rather than subservient to the dictates of an automated plant. This was the twenty-first century's improved, more human-friendly production line, but the work remained repetitive and routine. Concluded Ihara:

> Assembly line work is fundamentally a standardized, repetitive operation. Regardless of whether you are on sub-assembly or cleaning, as a production line worker you are obliged to repeat the same fixed motion over and over again.[114]

Although appearing almost inhuman to those in advanced industrial or post-industrial nations, to residents of aspirant Followers in early industrialization, assembly line work remains life-changing, just as it was in the early twentieth century when workers entered the Highland Park Plant in Michigan to assemble the Model T. But one change is important to note. As Chapter 4 indicates when the Post-Industrial Era is covered, assembly lines now have far more machines and robots and far fewer humans than they did a generation ago. That twenty-first-century production is far less labor intensive is one reason why Chapter 2's

---

113 Ryoji Ihara, *Toyota's Assembly Line: A View from the Factory Floor*, trans. Hugh Clarke (Melbourne, Australia: Trans Pacific Press, 2007), 58.
114 Ihara, *Toyota's Assembly Line*, 21.

exploding cities have so many trapped in urban subsistence in the slums that dot their landscapes.

Why organized labor emerged and the vital role it played in industrialization is now considered.

Organized Labor and the Sharing of Abundance

In the Pre-Industrial Era, workers were mostly employed under duress, with harsh instruments of power extracting productivity out of people. In the Industrial Era, rather than forcing unwilling workers to submit to serfdom or slavery, more balanced employment institutions emerged to structure employment. By the mid-twentieth century, labor in the industrial world was typically hired through contracts of service, many collectively negotiated by trade unions on behalf of their membership. These rights were won after centuries of struggle, and organized labor reached the peak of its power in the United States in the 1950s, when almost 40 percent of private sector workers were unionized.

Industrialization's capital intensity resulted in the emergence of big capital, and the presence of this powerful vested interest placed individual workers at a serious disadvantage. Since they lacked the resources to develop the economic capital being formed, labor's bargaining positions relative to big capital was weak, and the existence of these two groups with different and often conflicting interests provided new fuel to a fire that had smoldered for centuries. As far back as 1349, a group of bakers' servants were indicted in London for refusing to work unless their wages were doubled or tripled.[115] This early assertion of labor rights reflected a conflict that plagued labor relations for much of the Pre-Industrial Era, first between slaves and masters, then between serfs and lords, and finally between guild masters and journeymen. In the Industrial Era, the conflict materialized in the struggle between industrial leadership/capital and industrial workers/labor.

115 Philip S. Foner, *History of the Labor Movement in the United States, Vol. 1: From Colonial Times to the Founding of the American Federation of Labor* (New York: International Publishers, 1972).

Early American industrial relations mirrored the struggle. As was the case in England, the law initially sided with employers. Noted Smith: "We have no acts of parliament against combining to lower the price of work, but many against combining to raise it."[116] The first reported legal suppression of trade unions was in *Commonwealth v. Pullis*, decided in 1806. In 1794 Philadelphia shoemakers formed the Federal Society of Journeymen Cordwainers and turned the Philadelphia shoe industry into a closed shop, meaning union membership was obligatory to work in the industry. Until 1804 moderate wage increases were negotiated, but in 1805 higher wages were sought through a strike action. The strike was broken when the leaders were found guilty of raising wages, and unions were labeled illegal conspiracies. With organizing to seek higher wages turned into a criminal offense, employers had triumphed.

English law began supporting worker attempts to improve their status in the 1820s, and in 1842 the Massachusetts Supreme Court held trade unions were legal and had the right to organize and strike.[117] But it was only in the twentieth century that labor finally obtained widespread rights to organize and collectively bargain for improved work conditions. From the landmark Massachusetts Supreme Court decision, close to a century passed before these rights were perfected.

In 1914 the Clayton Act legalized peaceful strikes, picketing, and boycotts, and in 1935 the National Labor Relations Act affirmed American workers' rights to form and/or join unions. Finally, in 1938 the Fair Labor Standards Act established a minimum wage and time-and-a-half for work in excess of 40 hours a week.

Labor's right to organize and collectively bargain, coupled with a watchful, mediating government, contributed to the wage increases that became the backbone of the middle classes emerging across the industrialized world in the twentieth century. This applied as much in the United States as it did anywhere across the industrializing world: as productivity grew, organized labor captured gains for its members, and trade union

116 Smith, "Of The Wages of Labour," Book 1, chap. 8, para. 11, *The Wealth of Nations*.
117 *Commonwealth v. Hunt*, 45 Mass. 111, 4 Metcalf 111 (Mass. 1842).

power expanded accordingly. But this power eventually reached its limits in America.

Table 3 reports private sector trade union membership in the United States from 1900 to 2014.

Table 3: Private Sector Trade Union Membership in the United States: 1900–2014

Year	Private Sector Trade Union Membership	Percent of Private Sector Employees
1900	917,000	6.5
1905	1,923,000	11.1
1910	2,109,000	10.5
1915	2,508,000	12.2
1920	4,664,000	19.2
1925	3,495,000	13.2
1930	3,482,000	13.3
1935	3,337,000	14.2
1940	6,848,000	24.3
1945	11,674,000	33.9
1950	13,550,000	34.6
1955*	15,341,000	35.1
1960	14,613,000	31.9
1965	15,638,000	30.8
1970	16,978,000	29.1
1975	16,397,000	26.3
1980	15,273,000	20.6
1985	11,226,000	14.6
1990	10,247,000	12.1
1995	9,400,000	10.4
2000	9,148,000	9.0
2005	8,255,000	7.8
2010	7,092,000	6.9
2014	7,359,000	6.6

*1953 was the peak for private sector trade union membership: 35.7 percent of US private sector employees were unionized. After 1954, for every year data was reported, membership declined, except in 2007 and 2008, when numbers increased to 7.5 and 7.6 percent, respectively.

Source: "Labor Market Reporter," The Public Purse, updated February 2015, accessed January 19, 2023, http://www.publicpurpose.com/lm-unn2003.htm.

Private sector employee trade union membership in America was strongest in the mid-twentieth century; corresponding with these numbers and using union density (membership) and the relative union–nonunion wage gap to measure union strength, union success peaked in the 1950s and 1960s.[118] Since then this power has declined uniformly, and organized labor's representation of private sector workers in the United States is now below that of 1900. In 2023, 6 percent of private sector workers and 32.5 percent of public sector workers were unionized; combining public and private sector workers, 10 percent of American wage and salary workers were unionized.[119]

Organized labor's role in the United States was important in the last three decades of the Industrial Era. Labor, capital, and government formed a triumvirate that ensured industrialization's gains were well spread among the respective stakeholders. To amend a well-known phrase: what was good for General Motors *and its industrial workers* was good for America. The lesson for Followers industrializing is that a balancing of competing interests is required to ensure productivity gains are fairly distributed. This was accomplished in America and Europe by trade unions, though American unions did not reach the strength those in Europe attained.

A 12-nation study of union density—union membership as a percentage of paid employment—based on data gathered from 1955 to 1990 confirmed the United States remained a country of low union density compared with Australia, Canada, Great Britain, Japan, and most of western Europe.[120] These density differences reflect how capitalism practiced around the world varies. In American/Anglo-Saxon capitalism,

---

118 John Pencavel, "How Successful Have Trade Unions Been? A Utility-Based Indicator of Union Well-Being" (discussion paper no. 08-02, Stanford Institute for Economic Policy Research, 2008).
119 US Bureau of Labor Statistics, "Union Members Summary," January 23, 2024, accessed May 3, 2023, http://www.bls.gov/news.release/union2.nr0.htm.
120 Clara Chang and Constance Sorrentino, "Union Membership Statistics in 12 Countries," *Monthly Labor Review*, US Bureau of Labor Statistics, December 1991, 46–53, accessed May 3, 2023, https://www.bls.gov/opub/mlr/1991/12/ressum.pdf.

efficiency is more valued over equity, while in European communitarian capitalism, the opposite is true.

Following two world wars and a generation of instability, equity and equality were more needed and more prominent in postwar Europe. As is indicated in Chapter 4, where the various forms of capitalism are compared in the context of twenty-first-century global capitalism, America may benefit from more equity, while Europe might require more efficiency. Regardless, the challenge of balancing the distribution of gains and resources among stakeholders continues.

Surplus to convert into infrastructure and economic capital and human capital to build infrastructure and work in the factories and offices of the Industrial Era are not the only resources industrialization needs. Industrialization is also energy and materials intensive, and it is to these that we now turn. Here, rather than being treated as two, energy and raw materials are considered under the single moniker of industrialization's materials intensity. Notwithstanding this treatment, they nevertheless remain two distinct industrialization characteristics.

Industrialization's Materials Intensity: Endless Search for Energy and Raw Materials

Industrial manufacturing involves the conversion of raw materials into products sold to consumers. By the 1950s, when the American and European economies emerged from the blight of two world wars and finally perfected widespread mass production, middle-class consumers across the industrialized world had at their disposal an impressive array of goods and services, including housing, household appliances and furniture, food and clothing, pharmaceuticals, transport, healthcare, education, good government, security, and entertainment. Producing, operating, and maintaining these required a diverse set of physical inputs, accounting for the energy and materials intensity that accompanies industrialization.

Aspirant Followers, as all did before them, face the challenge of acquiring the energy and raw materials needed to sustain their growth, and once found, these must deliver products in sufficient volumes to factories and consumers when and where required.

Industrialization's Energy: Fossil Fuels and Our Carbon-Based World

The wide availability, easy transportability, and energy efficiency of three natural resources (coal, crude oil, and natural gas) provided the energy upon which industrialization across the world has been based. Coal provided the energy for much of the electricity generated over the past century, and oil provided fuel to operate one of the century's most important inventions: the automobile. Oil emerged mostly to provide an easily transportable energy source to match automobile mobility and was also used for electrical generation, but after the oil price spike in the 1970s, natural gas replaced oil as an electrical generation source.

By 1950, renewable energy provided 8.6 percent of the energy consumed by Americans; fossil fuels supplied the balance. In addition, electricity accounted only for only 19 percent of coal use; residential and industrial use was responsible for the majority of coal consumption. Finally, in 2022, 79 percent of American energy consumption was fossil fuel–based, 8 percent was nuclear power, and 13 percent was renewable energy.[121] Natural gas made up 36 percent of the country's energy production, petroleum was 31 percent, and coal was 12 percent.[122]

The US National Academy of Engineering concluded the electricity grid was the most significant invention of the twentieth century—ahead of oil, coal, motor vehicles, trains, computers, etc.—underscoring the vital role electricity plays in the industrialized world. Nonetheless, coal-fired power stations produced 45 percent of American electricity in 2010 and were the country's biggest single source of greenhouse gases at the time.[123] This can be contrasted with France's 70 percent of electricity

121 US Energy Information Administration, "U.S. Energy Facts Explained," last updated August 16, 2023, accessed December 19, 2023, https://www.eia.gov/energyexplained/us-energy-facts/.
122 US Energy Information Administration, "U.S. Energy Facts Explained."
123 US Energy Information Administration, *Annual Energy Review 2010*, October 2011, 236, accessed August 16, 2023, https://www.eia.gov/totalenergy/data/annual/archive/038410.pdf.

from nuclear power; today, France is the world's largest net exporter of electricity because of its low-cost nuclear power.[124]

The widespread nature of energy consumption once industrialized is easily seen by end-use consumption in the United States in 2022: transportation consumed 36 percent of US energy; industrial use was 35 percent; residential use was 16 percent; and commercial use was 13 percent.[125] In early industrialization, industrial use accounts for more, but as the commercial and residential capital stock expands, so will consumption in these sectors. America's high transportation use is likely due to its geographic size.

Materials sustaining the fastest industrialization ever shows a similar pattern to those before. China's industrialization has been resource and energy intensive and also based primarily on fossil fuels. The country is today the world's biggest polluter, releasing 29.2 percent of worldwide greenhouse gases in 2022, over double the United States at 11.2 percent,[126] even though (based on GDP at official exchange rates [OERs]) China's economy is only about 66 percent of the US economy's size (using OERs to determine the Chinese economy's size denominated in US$).[127] China's energy use has been particularly poor. The country is at a similar stage that the polluted city of Pittsburgh was in the 1950s and will have to clean up its production as the Americans did before it.

> The coal that has powered China's economic growth, for example, is also choking its people. Coal provides about 70 percent of China's energy needs: the country consumed some 2.4 billion tons in 2006—more than the United States, Japan, and the United Kingdom combined. . . . Consumption in China is huge partly because it is inefficient: as

---

124 World Nuclear Association, "Nuclear Power in France," last updated March 2024, accessed February 23, 2023. https://world-nuclear.org/information-library/country-profiles/countries-a-f/france.aspx.

125 US Energy Information Administration, "U.S. Energy Facts Explained."

126 Statista Research, "Distribution of Greenhouse Gas Emissions Worldwide in 2022, by Major Emitter," September 12, 2023, accessed October 15, 2023, https://www.statista.com/statistics/500524/worldwide-annual-carbon-dioxide-emissions-by-select-country/.

127 *The World Factbook,* "GDP (Official Exchange Rate)," *Central Intelligence Agency*, accessed February 23, 2023, https://www.cia.gov/the-world-factbook/field/gdp-official-exchange-rate.

> one Chinese official told *Der Spiegel* in early 2006, "To produce goods worth $10,000 we need seven times the resources used by Japan, almost six times the resources used by the U.S. and—a particular source of embarrassment—almost three times the resources used by India."[128]

That the first centuries of our industrial struggle for productivity was sustained by fossil fuels means current economic output worldwide is primarily carbon-based. Concludes Bradford in 2006:

> Harnessing ever greater quantities of fossil fuels over the last three centuries for industry, transportation, and electricity has allowed for unprecedented growth in the world economy, extended life, and improved livelihoods for billions of people, though not equally around the globe.[129]

A chapter entitled "An Unsustainable Status Quo" follows this quote, in which the greatest long-term threat now facing our collective prosperity is identified: unless less environmentally damaging sources of energy are found quickly, catastrophe awaits. Clean renewable sources are urgently required to sustain humanity's onward economic march. And it is not really a climate crisis all face. It is an energy crisis given the impact existing energy uses are having on our climate.

Industrialization's energy intensity presents Failures and aspirant Followers with several challenges: first, do they have access to the energy so fundamental to industrialization? Second, and presuming such access, are they able to build the infrastructure to support the generation and distribution of energy to producers and consumers alike, when and where it is needed? Third, how will their energy choices impact the environment? Industrializing societies over the past two centuries did not face this challenge, but our warming world means all must use energy

---

128 Elizabeth Economy, "The Great Leap Backward? The Costs of China's Environment Crisis," *Foreign Affairs*, September/October 2007, 39, accessed February 23, 2023, https://www.foreignaffairs.com/articles/asia/2007-09-01/great-leap-backward/.

129 Travis Bradford, *Solar Revolution: The Economic Transformation of the Global Energy Industry* (Cambridge, MA: MIT Press, 2006), 43.

sources that do not impose the environmental costs fossil fuels have so far. Chapter 5 considers this challenge in more depth.

The provision of electricity in particular requires considerable infrastructure investment, provided mostly in industrializing societies by state-owned, vertically integrated electrical utilities. Recently, and based upon a neoclassical economic doctrine that suggests market-based utilities would operate more efficiently than state-owned entities, the deregulation and privatization of electrical unities in some industrialized countries pioneered new vehicles to build energy infrastructure in developing countries. These reforms in the last decade of the twentieth century resulted in the emergence of independent power projects (IPPs), essentially privately financed utilities funded off the cash flows expected from the projects themselves. It remains unclear, however, to what degree IPPs might solve the electrical generation deficits of newly industrializing societies.[130]

Industrialization's Insatiable Demand for Raw Materials

Industrialization's demand for raw materials casts a wider net than did the search for energy; considerably more than three natural resources have been used. Given they were the core inputs for infrastructure and product businesses such as railroads, skyscrapers, and automobiles, iron and steel were early raw material measures of industrialization and industrial capacity. The importance of iron and steel—and energy—to industrial capacity formation is underscored in Kennedy's analysis of the rise and fall of the great powers from 1500 to 2000. Considering the period from 1885 to 1918, Kennedy noted the following:

130 A study of forty IPPs in Africa—where only 25 percent of the population had access to electricity—indicated North African IPPs produced better outcomes than those operated in sub-Saharan Africa (Katharine Gratwick and Anton Eberhard, "An Analysis of Independent Power Projects in Africa: Understanding Development and Investment Outcomes," *Development Policy Review* 26, no. 3 [May 2008]: 309–38, accessed February 24 2023, https://doi.org/10.1111/j.1467-7679.2008.00412.x). However, no clear indication of the IPPs' success or otherwise across the continent was provided.

> The important *differences* between the Great Powers emerge yet more clearly when one examines detailed data about industrial productivity. Since iron and steel output has often been taken as an indicator of potential military strength in this period, as well as of industrialization *per se*. . . .
>
> But perhaps the best measure of a nation's industrialization is its energy consumption from modern forms (that is, coal, petroleum, natural gas, and hydroelectricity, but not wood), since it is an indication both of a country's technical capacity to exploit inanimate forms of energy and of its economic pulse rate.[131]

The broader array of raw materials needed for industrialization became apparent as industrialization deepened, and the metals and minerals mined in South Africa offer glimpses into this diversity. South Africa is chosen because it possesses a treasure chest of raw materials Leaders and Followers rely upon for their industrializations.

Tables published by the Mineral Economics Directorate of the South African Department of Mineral Resources list the 38 metals and minerals mined in the country in the late twentieth century and early twenty-first century.[132] These are divided into three categories: precious metals and minerals (4), metallic minerals (10), and nonmetallic minerals (24). Precious metals mined are gold, diamonds, platinum, and silver, all of which have both industrial and retail uses. Metallic minerals are antimony, chromite, cobalt, copper, iron ore, lead concentrate, manganese ore, nickel, uranium oxide, and zinc; nonmetallic minerals include andalusite, asbestos, barytes, coal, feldspar, granite, limestone, silica, sulfur, and vermiculite.

Not all are as fortunate as South Africa; natural advantage in the form of minerals or other valuable raw materials is unequally distributed across the world. Some countries are rich in natural resources; others are not.

---

131 Paul Kennedy, *The Rise and Fall of the Great Powers*, 199–201.
132 Department of Mineral Resources, Republic of South Africa, *Minerals Statistical Tables 1994–2015*, Bulletin B1/2016, i–ii: accessed February 23, 2023, https://www.dmr.gov.za/LinkClick.aspx?fileticket=mLk4MgQH9pY%3D&portalid=0.

Further, it was not random that America's industrialization progressed as well as it did: the country is blessed with a combination of natural endowments few possess in such diversity and abundance.

> Here the United States came out best: large expanses of fertile, virgin land; a fine climate for growing a crucial industrial-entry raw material, namely, cotton; rich deposits of the key ingredients for ferrous metallurgy; plenty of wood and coal for fuel, plus generous waterpower all along the east coast; an abundance of petroleum, valuable from the mid-nineteenth century for light, as lubricant, and above all as fuel for internal combustion motors; copper ores in quantity, ready by the end of the nineteenth century for the burgeoning demands of electrical power, motors, and transmission.[133]

Yet a lack of raw materials does not disqualify a nation from industrializing. Japan is an early example of industrialization while obtaining raw materials mostly from elsewhere. A very small landmass left Japan with few raw materials, and only around 25 percent of its land is suitable for agriculture. In the twentieth century, Japan became a massive importer of commodities and energy, and despite these natural disadvantages, it was the first in Asia to industrialize and is now the world's fourth largest economy.[134] With its scramble for raw materials and energy sourced from Russia, the Middle East, Africa, and South America, China is replicating this strategy.

The major question facing Followers and Leaders wishing to import raw materials is what to export to pay for them? This was not, however, always the case. From the fifteenth century to the early twentieth century, colonies provided raw materials to European home markets and industries. These were not willing buyer–seller exchanges but unequal exchanges strongly in favor of colonial powers. Moreover, a shortage of raw materials has often been shown to be less a hindrance than a help;

---

133 David S. Landes, *The Wealth and Poverty of Nations*, 295.

134 *The World Factbook*, "GDP (Official Exchange Rate)." Japan's GDP (on a PPP basis) in 2021 was US$5.126 trillion, placing it behind China, the United States, and India. Its US$5.079 trillion GPD (on an OER basis) placed it third, behind the United States and China.

a common characteristic of the Fast Followers considered below is a shortage of raw materials. Paradoxically, an overabundance of natural resources may impede industrialization:

> Natural resources, especially mineral wealth, seem to be an obstacle, not a spur, to economic development. This "resource curse" has many dimensions: resources tend to corrupt politics, turning it into a race to seize the incomes produced by resources, often generating debilitating civil wars; they generate unstable terms of trade because prices of natural resources or agricultural commodities fluctuate widely; and they produce a high real exchange rate that, among other things, hinders development of internationally competitive manufacturing.[135]

At the heart of industrialization is economic diversification, which forces capability development previously beyond the society involved. Followers whose living standards quickly improve as a result of windfalls from raw material exports typically fail to use their good fortune to diversify. Instead, consumption levels not commensurate with the productivity levels attained are supported, and living standards remain high for as long as the raw materials attract high market prices (and if diversification is not accomplished, only for as long as reserves last). Here, the diversification pain and deferred gratification typically seen in early industrialization is avoided.

The resource curse explains the lack of economic diversification noted in oil-exporting nations today. Kuznets even argued undiversified, resource-rich nations should not be counted as industrialized:

> Some small countries can provide increasing income to their populations because they happen to possess a resource (minerals, location, etc.) exploitable by more developed nations, that yields a large and increasing rent. Despite intriguing analytical problems that these few fortunate countries raise, we are interested here only in the nations

135 Martin Wolf, *Why Globalization Works* (New Haven, CT: Yale University Press, 2004), 147.

> that derive abundance by using advanced contemporary technology—not by selling fortuitous gifts of nature to others.[136]

Kuznets's line of reasoning adds to our understanding of the resource curse and how it affects incentives, and it is perfectly in line with the essence of industrialization as described in these pages. Many oil exporters and their citizenry enjoy living standards close to the very rich around the world but without the skills necessary to produce the output needed to sustain their high living standards as others have done through industrialization.

Readers should now be convinced of industrialization's capital, labor, energy, and materials intensity. Any Failure or aspirant Follower wishing to industrialize must recognize the process's capital intensity, its need for qualified labor—both leaders and workers—and its demand for energy and raw materials. To complete coverage of the key enablers of the Industrial Era, two additional factors require attention. First, entrepreneurship in the era must be considered; as seen in this chapter, industrial entrepreneurs enjoyed considerably more capacity with which to build their entrepreneurial ventures than those in the Pre-Industrial Era. Second, the organizational innovation that emerged to structure and control these industrial ventures must also be recognized. These two factors are described through the progress of two iconoclastic organizations—Ford Motor Company and General Motors Company—in the quintessential industrial enterprise: automobile manufacturing.

Ford's development and manufacture of the Model T provides the context through which entrepreneurship in the Industrial Era is described, while Sloan at General Motors offers a lens through which to view the emergence of the multidivisional, professionally managed, hierarchically controlled industrial firm. Leaders and Followers around the world copied these industrial icons as they built their industrial economies.

---

136 Kuznets, "Modern Economic Growth: Findings and Reflections," 247.

Industrial Era Entrepreneurship: Henry Ford and a Car for the Everyman

Three reasons qualify Henry Ford to represent Industrial Era entrepreneurship. First and foremost, he exemplifies many of the productive capabilities that characterized entrepreneurship in the era. Unlike Columbus, Ford did not amass wealth through plunder or application of harsh instruments of power. Instead, he did so by offering a product with immeasurable utility that changed our prospects forever. At his core Ford was an engineer and tinkerer, an innovator and mechanical genius with a specific interest in machines and what made them work.

Second, Ford perfected the moving assembly line that was replicated across the industrializing world. Ford's factory model, pioneered in the Highland Park plant that produced the Model T, proved that humans and machines could combine to increase productivity so that not only basic human needs were met. The productivity gains were so significant that material living standards improved notably and broadly in industrializing societies. Ford's Rouge plant then showed how vertically integrated capital- and labor-intensive production operated together in the context of modern industrial capitalism.

Third, some astonishing economic insights were displayed as Ford Motor Company was built. The increase in minimum wage to US$5 a day in January 1914 provided practical enactment of an economic principal enunciated by French economist Jean-Baptiste Say a century earlier. Loosely articulated as supply creates its own demand, Say's law emphasized a core principle of modern classical economics: in order to demand in an economy, you must supply something of value to that economy. This principle still applies today, whether for Leader, Follower, or Failure.

Economic insight was also shown in the experience curve pricing Ford used to set the market price for the Model T. Unlike competitors at the time who were building luxury vehicles for the rich, Ford's goal was a car to be bought by all. Noting that cost per unit dropped as volume grew and fixed costs remained fixed—the benefit of the experience curve—

Ford assumed a high volume would be produced and set a low market price accordingly and ensured those on the assembly line making the Model T could buy the product they were producing. This astonishing insight led to a middle class emerging across America.

Ford's Early Years: Farmer to Mechanic/Engineer

Henry Ford was born on July 30, 1863, in Springfield Township, now part of Dearborn, Michigan. His early years were typical of those living on a successful family farm: attending a one-room schoolhouse while completing farm chores. Ford displayed an early penchant for things mechanical, and his autobiography noted his mother said he was born a mechanic. He credited his sighting of a steam-powered thresher in July 1876 as the moment he decided he would devote his life to building moving machines.

Ford disliked farming, as it seemed too much hard, physical work for too little return, and at the age of 15, he quit school and went to Detroit to pursue his mechanical passions. His schooling did not provide much: "He learned little in his years in a one-room schoolhouse in Dearborn beyond simple arithmetic. He was a poor reader and his scattershot spelling rivaled Sam Colt's."[137] Ford possibly began work life functionally illiterate and never supported the idea of a college education. One of his early heroes and later lifelong friends, Thomas Edison, was also self-taught.

Ford's early work life involved a variety of experiences, and his father's connections were responsible for apprenticeships he obtained in Detroit. His first job at Michigan Car Company (a streetcar producer) lasted a week, and after apprenticing at James Flower & Brothers Machine Shop (a manufacturer of a wide range of machine parts), he joined Detroit Dry Dock Company, where he worked from 1880 to 1882. Detroit Dry Dock built steam engines to propel ships, these eventually transporting

137 Harold Evans, Gail Buckland, and David Lefer, *They Made America: From the Steam Engine to the Search Engine: Two Centuries of Innovators* (Boston: Little, Brown and Company, 2004), 237.

ore up the River Rouge to Ford's Rouge plant. This was probably Ford's first exposure to combustion engines.

In 1882 Ford returned to the family farm but continued experimenting. He set up a small workshop with the tools needed and turned to developing a farm tractor. This work preceded his focus on automobiles:

> I thought it more important first to develop the tractor. To lift farm drudgery off flesh and blood and lay it on steel and motors has been my most constant ambition. It was circumstances that took me first into the actual manufacture of road cars.[138]

To earn money, Ford serviced Westinghouse Company portable horse-drawn steam engines on farms across the region, and seeing Westinghouse's new gasoline-fired, four-stroke internal combustion engine named "silent Otto" provided new motivation to build a gasoline-fired engine for a vehicle. But after struggling to determine how Otto's ignition operated, Ford returned to Detroit in 1892 to join Edison Illuminating Company and learn more about electricity. He was promoted to chief engineer at Edison's main Detroit plant, prompting a move to a house closer to his workplace. The house was among the first in Detroit to be electrified. The dwelling also had a backyard shed perfect for a workshop, and out of this small structure, Ford's first gasoline-powered vehicle emerged in 1895.

Finally, after years of work, trial, and error, on June 4, 1896, Ford unveiled his gasoline-powered horseless carriage. Named the Quadricycle, the vehicle was built on a rectangular steel chassis with a two-cylinder, four-horsepower engine behind and below the driver's seat. Making a distinctive *pop* sound soon known across Detroit, the internal combustion engine transmitted power to the back wheels by leather belt and chain to produce a top speed of around 20 miles per hour. He was 32 years old; his first prototype had taken 15 years.

---

138 Henry Ford with Samuel Crowther, *My Life and Work* (Garden City, NY: Doubleday, 1922), 26, accessed December 23, 2023, https://www.loc.gov/item/22026971/.

In the three years after the Quadricycle's debut, Ford built two more prototypes, and in August 1899 he left Edison Illuminating Company to become chief engineer at the newly formed Detroit Automobile Company, the first automobile manufacturer in Detroit. The company's backers, which included the mayor of Detroit and other prominent city businessmen, expected Ford to commercialize his third prototype but to no avail.

Detroit Automobile produced an unimpressive gasoline-powered delivery vehicle and manufactured fewer than 20 vehicles and was dissolved in February 1901, though it briefly reappeared as Henry Ford Company later that year following Ford's racetrack success. Some Detroit Automobile funds had apparently been used to build a racer that beat famed driver and automobile manufacturer Alexander Winton in a 10-lap race at Grosse Pointe, Michigan, on October 10, 1901.

Ford's racing victory brought national acclaim and publicity, prompting Detroit Automobile's backers to support him again. Yet, the renamed company failed a few months later, and Ford was fired, leaving him associated with two failed ventures. Most observers, including Ford's close associates, attributed Detroit Automobile's failure to Ford. His inexperience in directing manufacturing operations and dissatisfaction with his car and its need for further work were suggested as the primary causes.[139]

Ford Motor Company at Full Stride: The Model T, Highland Park and Rouge, and Enlightened Capitalist Henry Ford

After building two more race cars, Ford turned to developing a vehicle for the average man. Alexander Malcomson, a Detroit coal man keenly interested in racing, provided the initial capital. James Couzens, Malcomson's 30-year-old clerk, managed Malcomson's business interests with Ford, proving fortuitous as Couzens became the practical, business-oriented counterweight to the somewhat unpredictable, less disciplined, often

139 Willis F. Dunbar and George S. May, *Michigan: A History of the Wolverine State*, 3rd ed. (Grand Rapids, MI: William B. Eerdmans Publishing Co., 1995), 430.

capricious Ford. Eventually, 11 men and Henry Ford became founding stockholders of Ford Motor Company, formed in Detroit in June 1903. Ford was responsible for engineering and production; Couzens took care of the business side. Malcomson was treasurer.

In July 1903 Ford Motor Company took the first order for its Model A (not to be confused with the later Model A that succeeded the Model T), and 1,750 of these two-seater vehicles were sold. Though mechanically defective as most early automobiles were, the product made the company profitable quickly and ensured its survival when dozens failed.[140] Yet it would only be in 1908 when the company's stride was finally reached with the Model T. Through it Ford finally realized his vision of a car for every man. Notably, the Model T was later given the Car of the Century award.[141]

High demand from introduction in 1908 necessitated a change in production methods and culminated in the first mass production automobile assembly line ever. The 12-acre factory in Highland Park, Michigan, opened on January 1, 1910, and introduced a new model of production that became known as Fordism, "a term widely used to describe (1) the system of mass production that was pioneered in the early twentieth century by the Ford Motor Company or (2) the typical postwar mode of economic growth and its associated political and social order in advanced capitalism."[142]

Highland Park's first line was only 150 feet long, employed 140 workers, and was stationary. The introduction of a mechanized moving line in January 1914, where workers remained stationary and vehicles moved by attaching each chassis to a chain weaving through the plant,

---

140 Eighty-eight US firms were producing automobiles in 1903, 15 in Detroit alone. Sixty-four failed by the end of 1904 (Douglas Brinkley, *Wheels for the World: Henry Ford, His Company, and a Century of Progress, 1903–2003* [New York: Viking Penguin, 2003], 68). Failure is an inevitable and unavoidable companion of innovation.

141 James G. Cobb, "This Just In: Model T Gets Award," *The New York Times*, December 24, 1999, Section F, Page 1, accessed February 23, 2023, https://www.nytimes.com/1999/12/24/automobiles/this-just-in-model-t-gets-award.html.

142 Bob Jessop, s. v. "Fordism" *Encyclopaedia Britannica Online*, posted May 15, 2020, accessed February 23, 2023, https://www.britannica.com/money/topic/Fordism.

added to the impressive productivity gains made in the final years of stationary operations. On the stationary line, chassis assembly took 748 minutes; on the mechanized line it immediately dropped to 350 minutes, and a month later it reached 99 minutes.[143]

Despite the impressive gains in productivity enjoyed, not all was positive at Highland Park. Product, part, and task standardization combined with special-purpose machinery left labor subservient to machines; the work, which was mostly done by low-skilled immigrants who had left Europe in search of better opportunities, was routine, repetitive, and grindingly monotonous. These unattractive work conditions, combined with poorly disciplined, unhappy workers, caused turnover and absenteeism to explode. Alarming statistics surfaced by 1913: 10 percent worker absenteeism per week and 360 percent annual turnover, prompting the annual hiring of 54,000 workers to maintain a workforce of 15,000.[144]

The Highland Park labor problem was resolved with an innovation that stunned the business community and changed the nature of industrial capitalism forever. Though framed as a profit-sharing scheme and with conditions and fine print, Ford Motor Company announced on January 5, 1914, that a minimum wage of US$5 per day would be paid to qualifying workers, and daily work time also decreased from nine to eight hours.

Almost double average automobile worker's pay at the time, the move instantly turned Ford from isolated extractive capitalist into workingman hero. More importantly, after the scheme's introduction, the labor difficulties that had plagued Highland Park decreased so much that in time labor turnover was no longer measured.

The five-dollar day wage was not introduced because Ford became socially responsible and felt the need to compensate workers more equi-

---

143 Wayne Lewchuk, *American Technology and the British Vehicle Industry* (Cambridge, UK: Cambridge University Press, CUP Archive: 1987), 49.
144 Eric Arnesen, ed., *Encyclopedia of U.S. Labor and Working-Class History* (New York: Routledge, 2006), 457.

tably. The increase was a smart and informed business decision, based on a profound understanding of the business economics emerging at the time. Surrounding workers with well-calibrated machines and employing them on mechanized moving assembly lines doing standardized, specialized, repetitive tasks increased the output of each worker significantly. Matched with the drop in vehicle per unit cost as volume increased—as fixed costs are amortized over the growing output—gains were almost exponential.

Ford quickly realized workers could safely be paid more: they were producing more, and as volume increased, fixed cost per unit of output dropped. The growing surplus could be allocated in multiple ways: reinvested in the business; used to reduce market prices; allocated to increased wages; applied to pay greater dividends; or any combination thereof. In the case of the five-dollar day, workers were a main beneficiary.

As output grew, the profits from Highland Park were so substantial that there was enough to reward both capital and labor. Even customers gained along the way: in 1909 the Model T's base price was US$850, considerably less than the more luxurious vehicles available. By 1913 this had dropped to US$550, and by the 1920s to US$300. Model T prices were continually reduced so more and more Americans could afford their own, heralding birth of the virtuous cycle of twentieth-century industrial capitalism. Choices surrounding options on the Model T were also restricted to keep manufacturing as simple as possible and to guarantee costs declined as volume grew:

> Therefore in 1909 I announced one morning, without any previous warning, that in the future we were going to build only one model, that the model was going to be "Model T," and that the chassis would be exactly the same for all cars, and I remarked: "Any customer can have a car painted any color that he wants so long as it is black."[145]

145 Henry Ford, *My Life and Work*, 72.

Black was chosen because it dried fastest and minimized inventory time.

Restricting product variability and choices of the Model T did not prevent Ford from applying the principle of continuous improvement. He always insisted engineers cut costs, recycled and reused waste, and found better ways to perform processes to do more with less. This was done to keep focus on one of Ford's main goals: to build quality vehicles that the average man earning a good salary could buy. A simple, robust product; economies of scale; and continuous production improvement were key levers to attain this goal. Sorensen, a long-time close associate of Ford, concluded:

> Ford mass production made it available to everyone. Ford wages enabled everyone to afford it. The Ford $5 day rejected the theory that labor, like other commodities, must be bought in the cheapest market. It recognized that mass producers are also mass consumers, they cannot consume unless they are able to buy.[146]

This is an example of Say's law in practice, using a production model that was finally scalable. In addition, Ford's restriction of choice and color on the Model T is an early indication of the strategy industrialists followed as industrialization commenced. High-volume production of low-variety products would yield high quality at low cost. These principles, together with mass production and mass distribution, became the dominant rules of engagement in the Industrial Era.

Despite its vital role in the early history of the company, Highland Park's notoriety was soon eclipsed by a new complex seven miles southwest in Dearborn, Michigan. Highland Park was the opening act; the Rouge plant was the main event. Taking over a decade to construct, and compared to the Taj Mahal and Chartres Cathedral, Ford's Rouge plant eventually became the standard that early-twentieth-century industrialists visited and aspired to match or exceed.

146 Charles E. Sorensen with Samuel T. Williamson; introduction by David L. Lewis, *My Forty Years with Ford* (Detroit, MI: Wayne State University Press, 2006), 136.

Rouge was the result of many factors converging at the time: World War I caused raw material shortages and commodity price volatility; in addition, as Highland Park volume grew, external suppliers became increasingly difficult to coordinate—some proved unable to organize their subassembly lines to match Ford Motor Company's ever-increasing precision and speed, resulting in inventory bottlenecks and holding costs. To attenuate these, Ford concluded that self-sufficiency was desirable. Construction of a massive, vertically integrated complex was commissioned, designed to ensure Ford Motor Company controlled most aspects of automobile production, from raw materials sourcing to production of steel and parts to assembly and finishing of products. A cradle-to-grave facility, Rouge embodied the full extent of Ford's industrial vision.

Transaction cost economics (TCE) focuses on why firms exist in the form they do.[147] An important question asked is why some activities are performed internally while others are done outside in the open market, and recourse to TCE explains why Ford Motor Company performed so many activities inside rather than obtaining them from outside suppliers. TCE holds that firms exist to minimize production and transaction costs, and where the costs of activities are higher in the open market, they will remain inside the firm.

At Ford Motor Company circa 1915, raw material scarcity and price volatility increased the potential for transaction uncertainty with external contractors, and supplier inability to manage subassemblies imposed avoidable costs if done internally. Further, as the company was a First Mover into many of the activities it pioneered, more often than not, it could do these better than outsiders, thus the decision to perform them internally. This explains the extent of the company's vertical integration.

---

147 For explanations of TCE: Ronald H. Coase, "The Nature of the Firm," *Economica* 4, no. 16 (1937): 386–405; and Oliver E. Williamson, *Markets and Hierarchies: Analysis and Antitrust Implications* (New York: Free Press, 1975). Williamson received the 2009 Nobel Prize in Economics "for his analysis of economic governance, especially the boundaries of the firm." The Nobel committee noted Williamson provided "a theory of why some economic transactions take place within firms and other similar transactions take place between firms, that is, in the marketplace."

But despite extensive vertical integration, Rouge never operated with fewer than 6,000 outside suppliers.[148]

Located on the banks of the Rouge River so that raw materials could easily be transported to the complex, the Rouge plant was constructed as much for logistics as for production—even oceangoing ships reached the plant via the Great Lakes. Ford Motor Company's backward vertical integration—acquiring control of suppliers of inputs used in production—was extensive. The company owned and operated a regional railroad and a fleet of lake freighters to transport iron ore, coal, and limestone to the plant. To safeguard raw material supply (and underscoring the raw material and energy needs of industrialization), 700,000 acres of forests, iron mines, and limestone quarries in Michigan, Wisconsin, and Minnesota were acquired, in addition to coal mines in West Virginia, Kentucky, and Pennsylvania. The plant generated its own electricity; produced its own steel; made its own paint, tires, and glass; and produced almost every Model T component, though assembly remained at the Highland Park plant:

> It was a city without residents. At its peak in the 1930s, more than 100,000 people worked at the Rouge. To accommodate it required a multi-station fire department, a modern police force, a fully staffed hospital and a maintenance crew 5,000 strong. One new car rolled off the line every 49 seconds. Each day, workers smelted more than 1,500 tons of iron and made 500 tons of glass, and every month 3,500 mop heads had to be replaced to keep the complex clean.[149]

Industrial capitalism was finally in full bloom: vertically integrated; capital, labor, energy, and materials intensive; massive; and immensely productive. Industrialists from around the world visited Rouge and then applied what they had seen in factories worldwide, producing goods that became the staples of modern industrial life, from automobiles, to

148 The Henry Ford, "Henry Ford's Rouge," accessed February 23, 2023, https://www.thehenryford.org/visit/ford-rouge-factory-tour/history-and-timeline/fords-rouge.
149 The Henry Ford, "Ford Rouge Factory Tour—History and Timeline," accessed February 23, 2023, https://www.thehenryford.org/visit/ford-rouge-factory-tour/history-and-timeline/.

aircraft, to ships, to shoes, to shirts, to refrigerators and ranges, to radios and TVs, to most products that enriched the lives of middle-class twentieth-century industrial consumers.

Industrial Organization at Its Best: The Multidivisional, Professionally Managed, Hierarchically Controlled Firm

Ford's mechanical genius did not extend into the wider managerial realm, and while Ford Motor Company pioneered the Industrial Era's factory model, crosstown rival General Motors Company developed the organizational model. Ironically, the foundation of General Motors's pioneering and pathbreaking operating structure was established in the early 1920s by four executives with no direct responsibility for automobile production, among them Alfred P. Sloan Jr., who became president of the company in 1923 and board chair in 1937.

Rather than focusing on the mechanics of automobiles and their production, Sloan was more interested in how twentieth-century industrial organizations should be structured, managed, and controlled, and his response was the multidivisional, professionally managed, hierarchically controlled industrial firm.

> The Sloan approach, which used Fayol's functional organizations for the subunits, the individual "divisions," but organized the businesses itself on the basis of "federal decentralization," that is, on the basis of decentralized authority and centralized control, became after World War II the organization model worldwide, especially for larger organizations.[150]

General Motors initiated many structural innovations, the most important being its multidivisional character, later called the M-form firm. U-form firms—single businesses organized by functions such as sales, finance, and production—were compared to M-form firms by Williamson, who initially described M-form firms as collections of smaller

150 Peter F. Drucker, *Management: Tasks, Responsibilities, Practices* (New York: Harper & Row, 1974), 520.

U-form firms, though he later acknowledged operating divisions could be further subdivided by geography, brand, or product. Williamson considered M-form firms autonomous profit centers (i.e., divisions) operating at arm's length from corporate officers, competing independently for capital based on performance. He concluded M-form firms were more efficient than traditional U-form structures, as they operated as internal capital markets that "[favor] goal pursuit and least-cost behavior more nearly associated with the neoclassical profit maximization hypotheses than [do] the U-form organizational alternative."[151]

Unlike Ford Motor Company, which mostly maintained a single brand and marketed products one at a time, General Motors sold multiple brands and models initially in a ladder of six price levels from US$450 to US$600 for the cheapest vehicle to US$2,500 to US$3,500 for the most expensive. The multibrand, multiproduct M-form firm was explained in the company's 1924 annual report as "a car for every purse and purpose."[152]

GM's base brand Chevrolet competed with the Model T. The others on offer in order of increasing price were Oldsmobile, Oakland, Buick, and Cadillac. Pontiac was added in 1926, filling a gap between Chevrolet and Oldsmobile. Ford Motor Company's absorption of Lincoln Motor Company in 1922 remained its only brand extension until Edsel Ford's introduction of the Mercury in 1939. Mercury was to match the Buick and Oldsmobile marques, and though Lincolns became known as the "car of presidents," the brand did not make steady profits until after World War II.[153]

General Motors also surpassed Ford Motor Company administratively. While Ford Motor Company control mostly remained in its founder's hands, General Motors's multidivisional makeup and Sloan's

---

151 Oliver E. Williamson, *Corporate Control and Business Behavior: An Inquiry into the Effects of Organization Form on Enterprise Behavior* (Englewood Cliffs, NJ: Prentice Hall, 1970), 134.
152 The Henry Ford, "Advertisement for General Motors, 'A Car for Every Purse and Purpose,'" accessed February 24, 2023, https://www.thehenryford.org/collections-and-research/digital-collections/artifact/192114/.
153 Douglas Brinkley, *Wheels for the World*, 308.

early decentralization of authority and centralization of control necessitated introduction of a multiplicity of offices and institutions to manage the common and disparate issues facing the multiproduct, multidivisional firm.

General Motors showed it was not only the divisional structure that mattered: how power was allocated between the center and the periphery and how authority was distributed between divisional and corporate officers did too. Based on a balanced and judicious allocation of power, a hierarchy of committees with clearly defined roles and responsibilities (populated by corporate and divisional managers) governed and controlled the company.

General Motors also differentiated line from staff organizations and underscored the importance of control structures (policy committees) and control mechanisms to accomplish the complex tasks of management. Moreover, how large, diverse industrial organizations should be managed was also specified: decentralization offered flexibility, speedy decision-making, and motivated personnel close to the ground while coordination and centralized control delivered efficiency, reduced redundancy, and ensured divisions did not act too much in their own interests at the expense of the corporation. A continuous and rich information flow between divisions and the corporation was the oil to keep organizational engines functioning smoothly.

Perhaps the most valuable lesson learned by General Motors was that good management was not static but involved complex, ongoing balancing to ensure the reconciliation of centralization and decentralization, which "varies according to what is being decided, the circumstances of the time, past experience, and the temperaments and skills of the executives involved."[154] Moreover, based on these insights, the responsibilities of professional managers—acting in the best interests of the corporation (and not shareholders or employees) and making ethical, informed deci-

---

154 Alfred P. Sloan Jr., *My Years with General Motors* (Garden City, New York: Doubleday, 1963), 504.

sions based on facts and performance (and not on opinions or personal biases)—emerged.

Ford in the factory and Sloan in the executive suite provided benchmarks for all to follow as industrial enterprises were built across the industrializing world. Followers around the world adopted the innovations pioneered at Ford Motor Company and General Motors, and now, a century later, their legacies are still present in factories and organizations on every continent. These impressive legacies, like any legacy, also have their downsides, revealed in Chapter 4. We now turn to comparing Columbus with Ford as entrepreneurs. Each represent the entrepreneurship of their era, and insight is gained from comparing the experiences and contributions of each.

Comparing Columbus and Ford: Plundering Pre-Industrial Pioneer versus Enlightened Industrial Capitalist

There are many similarities between Ford and Columbus. First, at the heart of entrepreneurship is an idea to do something not yet done. Both were visionaries that set out to change the world, and both did. Second, both spent many years working to get their ventures off the ground. Columbus took from 1484 to 1492 to raise the finance to support his first expedition. Ford needed even longer: 15 years to build his first prototype and another 12 before his first notable success, the Model T, was produced. By then Ford was 44 years old. Ford's early years, like Columbus's, were a scramble to survive while developing prototypes or promoting a nascent enterprise. Third, both died wealthy men and enjoyed considerable rewards from their entrepreneurial endeavors. High returns are also independent of the era in which they are earned.

The differences between the two ventures are possibly better material for comparisons. That Ford took longer to establish his business is explained mostly by the difference in the basis of his enterprise. Ford's entrepreneurship was not transport-based and plundering in nature but focused on developing a complex machine and then producing it reliably and cheaply. This was a far more complex engineering and production task than constructing and sailing small vessels from Europe to the Americas and establishing trade routes to connect these continents.

Moreover, the value created by Ford's first mass-produced vehicle provided sufficient funds to pay for the resources required in its manufacture. Ford covered his input and production costs while paying workers a wage that permitted them to afford the product they were making. Columbus did not cover his costs: neither the lands he took nor the resources he obtained were paid for, and slaves worked the plantations of the New World.

A third difference is the way the two ventures were financed and the amount of money that was required to fund each: because Columbus conquered lands and took sovereignty over locations, state involvement was imperative. Further, the amassing of men and armies to subdue and subjugate acquired lands was also better left to sovereigns to organize and finance. At the very least, a private sector/public sector partnership was necessary.

Ford, in contrast, raised capital independent of government involvement, though the amount of financial capital required to fund the establishment of Ford Motor Company was far greater than the funds needed for Columbus's three expeditions. Such is the nature of capital-intensive industrial versus capital *light* pre-industrial productive operations. Comparing Columbus's *Santa Maria* to Ford's Rouge plant is an apple-to-orange match. Finally, capital markets were far more liquid and deeper in the twentieth than fifteenth century, facilitating formation of large sums of financial capital that were converted into economic capital and yielded sufficient returns given the risk.

Surrounding workers with machines and requiring them to perform standardized, repetitive manual tasks on moving assembly lines in factories that converted raw materials into reliable affordable products was the innovation that released mankind from the pre-industrial scourge of scarcity. Through his mechanical, engineering, and production genius,

Ford increased the marginal productivity of average workers considerably; once this was followed in other industries, the grinding material shortages plaguing humanity from the beginning of time were finally vanquished. Abundance had finally arrived for those lucky enough to reap industrialization's full benefits.

The model pioneered by Ford spread fast across America and Europe and then to all corners of the industrializing world. By the twentieth century's end, factories in fast-developing China adopted Ford's methods as meeting the China Price became the challenge all industrial manufacturers faced. Industrialization by then had been perfected and many Followers were moving to expand its reach. We now turn to the political economy of industrialization.

Industrialization Era Political Economy: Generations of Sacrifice and Deferred Gratification

The political economy of industrialization is best revealed by studying two groups: those industrializing first (Great Britain, the United States, and some nations in western Europe: the First Movers) and those mostly industrializing in the twentieth century (Japan, followed by nations such as South Korea, Hong Kong, Singapore, and Taiwan: the Fast Followers). Comparing these two groups provides insight into the models used to industrialize and reveals the range of policy choices implemented as nations industrialized. But before analyzing the approaches followed by these two groups, some initial thoughts on industrialization's challenges are warranted.

Readers are already aware that industrialization is a complex process and that industrial societies, like Rome, are not built in a day. Industrialization is a lengthy, capital-intensive process best measured in generations and not in years or even decades. Using 1800 as the start of the Industrial Era, almost 130 years passed before industrialization's factory and organizational models were perfected, and America's middle class only emerged after World War II.

That the United States took six generations to industrialize (1800–1950) is the upper limit of the time needed now. Pioneers inevitably take longer than those who follow, which explains why Japan et al. are labeled Fast Followers. As they had the luxury of following and learning from others, their progress was more rapid. But regardless of increases in the pace of industrialization, building the hard and soft infrastructures and achieving economic diversification will still take generations, especially for nations with large populations. Despite China's impressive rapid economic growth since the late 1970s (i.e., around two generations), a minority of the Chinese population is fully industrialized. At least two more generations will be required to lift all Chinese out of poverty to middle-class lives.

Industrialization's capital intensity means substantial surplus is required to build the infrastructure and capabilities that industrialization demands. In pre-industrial societies where not even basic needs are being met, every dollar invested in infrastructure or economic capital means a dollar less to feed a hungry child or house a marginalized slum dweller. This harsh trade-off is especially acute in early industrialization. The first one or two generations of industrialization do not produce noticeable improvements in living standards; as surplus is converted into infrastructure and other functioning operations, hard work, deferred gratification, and sacrifice are its principal companions.

Finally, the need for policy linearity (i.e., the long time to implement the policy) and the pressure to allocate surplus for investment and capacity building at the expense of consumption or welfare raises questions about the government best suited for the conditions of early industrialization. Three hypotheses concerning modern democracy as a form of government and its suitability to early industrialization have been proposed: the complementary, the conflicting, and the sequential. Which is correct is key to understanding the political economy of industrialization.

CHAPTER 3

Modern Democracy and Early Industrialization: Complementary or in Conflict?

The complementary hypothesis holds that modern democracy and industrialization are mutually supportive and suggests those wishing to industrialize should rely on democratic regimes (DRs) to guide the process. According to this hypothesis, economic growth reduces inequality and extremist politics while promoting stability and democracy; industrialization makes democracy viable, and vice versa. Support for this hypothesis is mostly found in the capitals of the industrialized world, based on the presumption that modern democracy is the best model to govern nations, regardless of development stage. The governments installed in Iraq following Saddam Hussein's removal and in Afghanistan following the Taliban's ouster was based on the complementary hypothesis. Americans bet Iraq and Afghanistan would democratize and industrialize simultaneously.

The conflicting hypothesis, in contrast, proposes modern democracy and early industrialization are in conflict: every increase in political freedom comes at the expense of industrial development, and every gain in industrial development takes place at the expense of political freedom. After reviewing the twentieth-century industrialization efforts of developing countries, Organski noted:

> Industrial take-off in the mid-twentieth century has some supremely painful consequences. In concrete terms, the impressive economic performance of Brazil (Turkey or the Philippines) in the modern period has depended upon massive poverty and political repression, and it would not have been possible under democratic governments pursuing egalitarian economic policies.[155]

The conflicting hypothesis has also been called the Lipset hypothesis, following the work of Lipset:[156]

---

155 Organski, *The Stages of Political Development*, 65.

156 Seymour M. Lipset, "Some Social Requisites of Democracy: Economic Development and Political Legitimacy," *American Political Science Review* 53, no. 1 (March 1959): 69–105.

> From Aristotle down to the present, men have argued that only in a wealthy society in which relatively few citizens lived in real poverty could a situation exist in which the mass of the population could intelligently participate in politics and could develop the self-restraint necessary to avoid succumbing to the appeals of irresponsible demagogues.[157]

The conflicting hypothesis was almost accepted wisdom in the mid-twentieth century:

> This theme is so pervasive in the literature that it is generally accepted as fact. . . . Recently a group of college students was asked, toward the end of a seminar course on economic and political development in which they had been exposed to an extensive range of literature in the field, whether they thought an authoritarian or a competitive form of government was more conducive to economic development. The reply was virtually unanimous—authoritarian.[158]

The conflicting hypothesis accounts for the difficult trade-off faced in early industrialization. Deferring consumption to establish industrial capacity means welfare needs remain unmet, whereas using savings for immediate consumption or welfare means productive capacity remains underdeveloped. Further, promising welfare without the wealth to honor the promise is as irresponsible; festive macroeconomic populism in poor societies will not foster industrialization. Democracy should only be offered once the wealth base to sustain it exists; hence, early on, modern democracy and industrialization are in conflict.

The sequential hypothesis accepts the conflicting hypothesis and offers a third: if early industrialization and modern democracy conflict, industrialize first, democratize later. Supporters of this hypothesis, after considering nineteenth-century Western democracies, point out that prior to evolving to mass democracies, these countries were ruled by bourgeois industrial elites to the exclusion of the masses:

157 Lipset, "Some Social Requisites of Democracy," 75.

158 G. William Dick, "Authoritarian versus Nonauthoritarian Approaches to Economic Development," *Journal of Political Economy* 82, no. 4 (July–August 1974): 818.

> The importance of this exclusion cannot be overstressed. It was as crucial an aspect of bourgeois politics as the placing of the bourgeoisie in control of the national government, for the function of the middle classes to create capital for industrialization could not have been carried out under existing conditions if the working class had been given governmental protection against economic expansion at its expense.[159]

Empirical Evidence: Contradictions in Poorly Designed Studies

Studies testing which hypothesis best explains the democracy/industrialization relationship have not resolved the controversy; results contradict. For example, Dick investigated Gross National Product (GNP)[160] increases and per capita growth rates over a nine-year period for 27 authoritarian, 19 semi-competitive, and 13 competitive (i.e., democratic) regimes in the developing world and concluded:

> LDCs with authoritarian forms of government perform either very well or very poorly. Though, in general, competitive governments may not be able to achieve the high growth rates attained by authoritarian countries, neither are their chances of failure so high; and the overall performance of semi-competitive governments generally surpasses that of either of the other two forms of government.[161]

Berg-Schlosser categorized 45 African regimes into four types—polyarchic (democratic), socialist, authoritarian, and military/praetorian—and measured how each performed across GNP growth and the Physical Quality of Life Index (the PQLI, a noneconomic measure that

159 Organski, *The Stages of Political Development*, 65.

160 The US Department of Commerce Bureau of Economic Analysis defines GNP as the "market value of goods and services produced by labor and property supplied by U.S. residents, regardless of where they are located. It was used as the primary measure of U.S. production prior to 1991, when it was replaced by gross domestic product (GDP)," https://www.bea.gov/help/glossary/gross-national-product-gnp, accessed February 25, 2023.

161 Dick, "Authoritarian versus Nonauthoritarian Approaches," 819–20.

approximates human quality of life).[162] Findings over a 15-year period revealed authoritarian regimes displayed strong positive effects on GNP growth but showed little association with PQLI improvement (providing support for the conflicting hypothesis), while socialist regime GNP growth rates were considerably lower but better for PQLI (again in line with the conflicting hypothesis).[163] Praetorian systems performed poorly against both indices, while polyarchic regimes performed relatively well on both. Moreover, polyarchies fared best in maintenance of civil liberties and freedoms, praetorian regimes fared worst, and socialist and authoritarian regimes were located somewhere in between.

Sørensen studied two authoritarian developmentalist regimes (ADRs) and two DRs and found DRs do not automatically increase welfare and tend to respect elites to such a degree that their ability to mobilize resources for economic growth is impeded. DRs were also found to implement little reform against elite vested interests, decreasing their capacity to promote economic development too.[164] In contrast, ADRs curbed consumption to promote economic growth but not necessarily at a rate below previous levels. Moreover, while not concerned with the provision of tangible benefits to an electorate, ADRs may promote welfare through combining economic restructuring and specific welfare measures. Finally, Siegle et al. compared the 40-year economic growth rates (from 1960 to 2000) of 14 low-income democracies and 38 low-income autocracies and found democracies grew as fast as autocracies, while life expectancy was nine years longer and infant deaths were 20 percent lower in democracies. Children in poor democracies were also found to have a 40 percent greater chance of attending secondary school.[165]

---

162 The PQLI was developed in the mid-1970s to provide a measure that better evaluates the lives of the poor than did traditional economic measures such as GNP. The PQLI is an index of three variables: infant mortality, life expectancy at age one, and basic literacy.
163 Dirk Berg-Schlosser, "African Political Systems: Typology and Performance," *Comparative Political Studies* 17, no. 1 (April 1984): 121–51.
164 G. Sørensen, *Democracy, Dictatorship and Development: Economic Development in Selected Regimes of the Third World* (London: Macmillan, 1991).
165 Joseph T. Siegle, Michael M. Weinstein, and Morton H. Halperin, "Why Democracies Excel," *Foreign Affairs* 83, no. 5 (September–October 2004): 57–71.

These findings support two conclusions. First, though democracies on average produce more balanced outcomes, they do not always outperform authoritarian regimes. Second, all authoritarian regimes are not equal. Authoritarian regimes can be divided into two categories: authoritarian developmentalists and authoritarian plunderers. Important here is that authoritarian developmentalists provide superior outcomes to other types of authoritarian regimes (e.g., praetorian/militarist regimes) and at times have outperformed democracies.

Power can be used to empower or plunder, and the twofold authoritarian categorization makes this distinction overt. Further, though autocracies may exhibit both developmental and plundering tendencies at the same time, it is usually possible to differentiate those that are more developmental from those that have mostly plundered. Autocratic developmentalist regimes include those led by President Park of South Korea and Prime Minister Lee Kuan Yew of Singapore as well as the current Chinese leadership; autocratic plunderers include governments led by President Mobutu Sese Seko of Zaire, President Saddam Hussein of Iraq, and President Muammar Gaddafi of Libya. Autocrats also seem to be more plundering than developmental in nature, meaning *good* dictators are scarce.

Regardless of the more fine-grained classification of authoritarian regimes into plunderers versus developmentalists, none of the studies directly tested which of the complementary, conflicting, or sequential hypotheses best explains the democracy/industrialization nexus. Few, if any, of the nations in any sample were fully industrialized, and in the Siegle et al. sample, no regime was even close to industrialized; all were very-low-income countries still operating pre-industrial economies. As no industrialized countries were present in any study, these studies cannot reliably determine if democracy complements, conflicts with, or best follows industrialization. Stumbling democracies are compared with stumbling autocracies, and all that the findings show is that between these two, stumbling democracies may perform marginally better.

To test which hypothesis best explains the democracy/industrialization relationship, only industrialized countries should be in the sample, meaning progress should be measured over generations. This is done in this chapter by comparing First Mover and Fast Follower industrializations, and we will see that the sequential hypothesis better explains both the First Mover and Fast Follower successes. Also, democracy at the time First Movers industrialized differed significantly from the democracy now in place in the advanced industrial world. In addition, none of the early dashes for growth by Fast Followers in the twentieth century were done under DRs. No support for the complementary hypothesis is found among any industrialized nations if the modern (i.e., mid-twentieth-century) form of democracy is relied upon.

Empirical support for the conflicting and sequential hypotheses is also noted in one of the few studies that sampled industrialized and less developed countries. After studying data from over 100 countries over a 35-year period (1960 to 1995), Barro noted:

> Despite the lack of clear predictions from theoretical models, the cross-country evidence examined in the present study confirms that the Lipset/Aristotle hypothesis is a strong empirical regularity. In particular, increases in various measures of the standard of living forecast a gradual rise in democracy. . . . In contrast, democracies that arise without prior economic development—sometimes because they are imposed by former colonial powers or international organizations—tend not to last.[166]

This vexing question of regime type and industrialization is returned to after First Mover and Fast Follower industrializations are explained and compared. The coverage of the First Movers relies mostly on data from Great Britain and the United States, though aspects of the industrialization of other European powers are mentioned when helpful.

---

166 Robert J. Barro, "Determinants of Democracy," *Journal of Political Economy* 107, no. S6 (December 1999): S160. Democracy was measured by a subjective indicator of electoral rights, and living standards were measured by changes in per capita GDP.

First Mover Industrialization: Generations of Toil Starting in Great Britain, Perfected in the United States

Economic historians divide British and American industrializations into two separate revolutions: in Great Britain, the first lasting a century from around 1750, and the second starting in 1850 and eventually being eclipsed by the more successful American experiment in the second half of the nineteenth century. Toynbee popularized the term Industrial Revolution to describe changes in Great Britain between 1760 and 1830; to him, the country's first revolution was driven by power looms, steam engines, and workers urbanizing to enjoy the benefits the new economic capital offered.[167] Later research showed Great Britain's early transition to be more complex:

> During the Industrial Revolution in numerous occupations the ratio of capital to labour, and the tools and technologies used to perform manual and skilled work, were similar to what they had been in Tudor times. Modes of production such as small-scale and family firms continued to thrive in symbiosis with factories, large-scale enterprises, and corporations.[168]

Moreover, many protoindustries existed in Europe in 1750; in England, mostly rural-domestic cottage industries centered on textiles (cotton weavers, framework knitters, and wool producers) and metallurgical finishing.[169] Labor in these industries also participated in agriculture, confirming industrialization and agrarian subsistence coexisted for a time. Prior to industrialization, rural specialization acceleration was already underway in Great Britain such that "at the eve of the Industrial

---

167 Arnold Toynbee, *Lectures on the Industrial Revolution in England* (London: Rivington's, 1884), 15–16.

168 Giorgio Riello and Patrick K. O'Brien, "Reconstructing the Industrial Revolution: Analyses, Perceptions and Conceptions of Britain's Precocious Transition to Europe's First Industrial Society" (working paper no. 84/04, Department of Economic History, London School of Economics, 2004), 6–7, https://www.lse.ac.uk/Economic-History/Assets/Documents/WorkingPapers/Economic-History/2004/WP8404.pdf.

169 Joel Mokyr, "Growing-Up and the Industrial Revolution in Europe," *Explorations in Economic History* 13, no. 4 (November 1976): 371–96.

Revolution rural-domestic industries had become a central feature of European economic life."[170]

Similar conditions were noted prior to the start of America's second industrial revolution in the mid-nineteenth century. Driven by British demand for agricultural commodities such as cotton and grain, American specialization had also increased notably by the 1840s but remained dominated by activities similar to those that had flourished since the Middle Ages in Europe. Between 1821 and 1850, America supplied over 75 percent of Great Britain's raw cotton, spreading commercial agriculture to the southern United States and encouraging commercial specialization in the Northeast around New York City.[171] With exports to Europe and the American Northeast growing, specialized importers of finished consumer goods soon appeared such that the American economy provided "a believable illustration of the working of the untrammeled market economy so eloquently described by Adam Smith."[172]

To underscore the economic diversity and specialization already achieved in the United States, Chandler summarized America's economy around 1850 in a section entitled "The Traditional Process of Production and Distribution," where under the subheading "The Traditional Enterprise in Commerce," specializations in finance, transportation, and commerce were detailed, and under the subheading of "The Traditional Enterprise in Production," the expansion of prefactory production, managing traditional production, the plantation, the integrated textile mill, and the Springfield Armory were presented as exemplars.[173]

Chandler also noted that the American economy at the time was dominated by small, traditional businesses with general—and later commission—merchants, linchpins from whom traditional firms obtained raw materials and tools, and to whom finished goods were sold at wholesale prices for distribution to nearby markets.[174]

---

170 Mokyr, "Growing Up," 374.
171 Chandler, *The Visible Hand*, 20.
172 Chandler, *The Visible Hand*, 28.
173 Chandler, *The Visible Hand*, ix–x.
174 Chandler, *The Visible Hand*, 17.

To discover the dimensions of the second industrial revolution, developments in the United States best instruct. Chandler annotated America's second industrial revolution through the emergence of large American enterprises in the latter part of the nineteenth century and the first quarter of the twentieth century, and in so doing, differentiated the second from the first industrial revolution while offering insight into the sequencing that followed.

> The enormous increase in the volume of output and transactions was not an inevitable consequence of the First Industrial Revolution, which began in Britain at the end of the eighteenth century. . . . A much more important cause was the coming of modern transportation and communication. The railroad, telegraph, steamship, and cable made possible the modern mass production and distribution that were the hallmarks of the Second Industrial Revolution of the late nineteenth and early twentieth centuries. These new high-volume technologies could not be effectively exploited unless the massive flows of materials were guided through the process of both production and distribution by teams of salaried managers.[175]

As noted in the coverage of America's industrializing leadership, industrial businesses in the country emerged in two phases: first, when the transport and communications infrastructures were built between 1840 and 1880, and second, when product-oriented businesses were established between 1880 and 1920. Page 87 also underscored that the *infrastructure first, product-oriented businesses second* hypothesis be applied with care, as certain products (e.g., steel) build infrastructure, and some products can be made while infrastructure is being built (e.g., textiles). Nevertheless, Chandler broadly outlines the sequencing through America's second revolution.

Further, given industrialization's materials intensity, it is not surprising that the transport infrastructure was among the first built. Raw mate-

175 Alfred D. Chandler Jr., "The Emergence of Managerial Capitalism," *Business History Review* 58, no. 4 (Winter 1984): 474.

rials transported to factories and goods transported to consumers need physical infrastructure. Rail, steamships, and communications (post, telegraph, and telephone) came first, followed by early mass distribution (commodity dealers, wholesale jobbers, and mass retailers) and mass production (the refining and distilling industries, the metal making and metalworking industries, and the beginning of scientific management), and finally by goods mass production and distribution that led to the twentieth-century visible hand of managerial capitalism and the M-form industrial corporation.

The massive Ford Motor Company and its equally impressive multi-divisional, crosstown competitor General Motors were only perfected by the 1930s. Both were key members of Chandler's second revolution, and he supported his thesis by listing the 200 largest American corporations by assets in 1930, indicative of the American economy's diversity and size by this time. Table 4 reports these, together with similar data for the United Kingdom, Germany, and Japan, confirming that although differences existed between the four, all were well on the way to being industrialized by the 1930s.

Table 4 shows that the four nations' placement and specializations were already visible in the 1930s. First, as a Fast Follower that began industrializing later than the other three, Japan had 62 of its largest 200 firms in textiles, while America had only 3; the United Kingdom and Germany had 24 and 15, respectively. Second, given its munificent natural resources, America had significantly more large firms in petroleum (26); the other three nations, being poor in raw materials, possessed 3 to 5. Third, the idiosyncratic capabilities of some countries are already apparent: Germany's technical and manufacturing affinity is reflected in firms in primary metal (47) and machinery (19), compared with the United Kingdom (18 and 7) and Japan (22 and 4); the United Kingdom's predominance in printing and publishing likely relates to the English language's predominance across the empire combined with the country's impressive literary heritage.

Table 4: Distribution of the 200 Largest Manufacturing Firms in the United States, United Kingdom, Germany, and Japan by Industry, Circa 1930

SIC Number and Industry	US	UK	Germany*	Japan
20 Food	32	64	28	30
21 Tobacco	5	4	0	1
22 Textiles	3	24	15	62
23 Apparel	0	3	0	2
24 Lumber	4	0	1	1
25 Furniture	1	0	0	0
26 Paper	7	5	2	6
27 Printing and publishing	3	10	1	1
28 Chemicals	18	9	27	22
29 Petroleum	26	3	5	5
30 Rubber	5	3	1	1
31 Leather	2	0	3	1
32 Stone, clay, and glass	9	6	9	14
33 Primary metal	25	18	47	22
34 Fabricated metal	10	7	7	3
35 Machinery	22	7	19	4
36 Electrical machinery	5	18	16	12
37 Transportation equipment	21	14	16	11
38 Instruments	2	1	2	1
39 Miscellaneous	1	4	1	1
	200**	**200**	**200**	**200**

* All data is for 1930 except Germany, which is for 1928.
** The United States data adds up to 201 in the original text, where the total is stated at 200 as is done here.
Source: Chandler, "The Emergence of Managerial Capitalism," 480–83.

Finally, all were well represented in food (with which all want self-reliance) and transportation equipment (another important basic infrastructure industry), while all were equally underrepresented in apparel, furniture, leather, and instruments.

Though providing the substance of First Mover second industrializations in some detail, missing in Chandler's analysis are the small and medium firms that added to the mix, along with how they coexisted with their larger neighbors. For example, men's clothing in the United States in the 1920s was a product of two groups: a few large, technologically and organizationally sophisticated firms in the Chandlerian mold and a greater number of widely dispersed, smaller, primitive firms. Larger firms manufactured the more expensive, higher-quality merchandise to meet more stable demand, while smaller firms competed in more volatile segments and niches, making lower-quality garments sold at lower prices.[176]

Indicative of the complex structures existing at the time, large and small firms both cooperated and competed with each other. As noted previously, possibly the world's most vertically integrated firm ever, Ford Motor Company still engaged 6,000 external suppliers at its Rouge plant in the 1930s. Cooperation between large automobile manufacturers and their suppliers persisted over the twentieth century even to the point that supplier tiers were established (e.g., Tier 1, 2, or 3) to facilitate control and stability. Having clarified the industrial organizations common in First Mover industrialization, we now turn to the political economy employed to accomplish the task.

First Mover Industrialization: Triumph of the Visible Invisible Hand

First Mover governments mostly followed a laissez-faire economic approach to industrialization, and two factors explain this policy. First, economic wisdom at the time held that markets (not governments) were

176 Steven Fraser, "Combined and Uneven Development in the Men's Clothing Industry," *Business History Review* 57, no. 4 (1983): 522–47.

the best mechanisms to answer the five fundamental economic questions (what to produce, where, how, for whom, and for how long?). Second, because they were pioneers, First Movers invented as they went along. Even if governments wanted to intervene, they had little idea of what to do. Direction is possible only when you know where you are going or have someone to follow.

Classical economics, built on two beliefs and the first modern school of economic thought, prevailed as First Mover industrialization began:

> Classical economists, who included Adam Smith, David Ricardo and John Stuart Mill, believed that the pursuit of individual self-interest produced the greatest possible economic benefits for society as a whole through the power of the invisible hand. They also believed that an economy is always in equilibrium or moving towards it.[177]

The first belief ensured government intervention was kept to a minimum, and the second meant governments took few steps to rectify imbalances that appeared. As this was the economic philosophy that informed governments as industrialization gathered pace in Great Britain, Europe, and the United States, the governments of the day felt no responsibility to actively engage in or facilitate the process. Their main brief was to stay out of the way to let the invisible hand and markets do their work. America's early industrial growth was led by private agents operating in more or less free markets as they built the M-form firms that became the backbone of America's industrial economy, and in so doing they validated the view that the private sector's *visible* invisible hand was the best mechanism to promote industrialization.

But limited government did not mean no government. Three policies critical to America's second industrial revolution were implemented: adherence to the international gold standard, development of an unregu-

---

177 "The A to Z of economics," *The Economist*, accessed February 25, 2023, https://www.economist.com/economics-a-to-z/.

lated national market, and extensive local tariff protection.[178] Adherence to the gold standard provided currency stability and removed a source of risk for emerging industrialists.

The formation of an open national market ensured American states could not protect local champions through regulation of interstate commerce; mass production and distribution required scale, and where national champions serving the growing American national market emerged, size and scale enabled them to prevail. The national market was mostly accomplished by decisions of the American Supreme Court. As the political institution most removed from day-to-day politics—Supreme Court justices are appointed for life, and local or state politics have little influence on the court's decisions—it is no surprise that the court was the vehicle that ensured the internal opening of the American market. From a local perspective, the move to an internal open market is possibly the most controversial of the three policy initiatives; America was fortunate to have the separation of powers its founders imposed. The justices who ensured the market remained open internally could not be voted out of office.

Finally, tariffs provided protection from foreign competition while American industrial capacity was built and transferred wealth to industrialists at the expense of agrarian interests in the South and West, facilitating formation of the surplus needed for industrialization. Most of the surplus for American industrialization was generated internally, aided in no small measure by high tariffs.

American tariffs in the latter part of the nineteenth century and the first quarter of the twentieth century were among the world's highest. Though British, French, and German tariffs remained around 6 to 7 percent from the mid-nineteenth century through the 1920s, average American tariffs were around 30 percent in 1900, after declining from

---

178 Richard Franklin Bensel, *The Political Economy of American Industrialization, 1877–1900*, (New York: Cambridge University Press, 2000).

more than 40 percent in 1865; they were still three times higher than the three European countries in 1915.[179]

> In protecting their industries, the Americans were going against the advice of such prominent economists as Adam Smith and Jean Baptiste Say, who saw the country's future in agriculture. However, the Americans knew exactly what the game was. They knew that Britain reached the top through protection and subsidies and therefore that they need to do the same if they were going to get anywhere.[180]

British average tariffs were also above 30 percent in the 1820s and 1830s and only declined below 20 percent in the 1850s. Average tariff rates globally from 1870 to 1914 were around 15 percent.

Though industrialization policy was mostly laissez-faire, the gains from infant industry protection and extensive tariffs were not ignored early on by First Mover governments. Calls for free trade by any of these nations, including the United States, were only made after a period of protection and internal nurturing readied their economies for global competition. Free traders are not born—they are built. Building international competitiveness takes time, investment, and hard work and does not happen easily in open free markets.

A final indication of government involvement in First Mover industrialization relates to a state responsibility that has existed since governments were first created: defense. The nineteenth-century capital goods industry in Great Britain was "for all practical purposes no more than a subordinate branch of the British army and navy, and military demand contributed to many technical advances, including improvement of

---

179 Timothy J. Hatton and Jeffrey G. Williamson, "A Dual Policy Paradox: Why Have Trade and Immigration Policies Always Differed in Labor-Scarce Economies?" in *The new comparative economic history: essays in honor of Jeffrey G. Williamson*, ed. Jeffrey G. Williamson, T. J. Hatton, Kevin H. O'Rourke, and Alan M. Taylor (Boston: MIT Press, 2007), 219.

180 Ha-Joon Chang, "Kicking Away the Ladder: How the Economic and Intellectual Histories of Capitalism Have Been Re-Written to Justify Neo-Liberal Capitalism," *Post-Autistic Economics Review* 15, September 4, 2002, accessed February 25, 2023, http://www.paecon.net/PAEtexts/Chang1.htm.

steam engines and innovations such as iron railways and iron ships."[181] This is expected, given Great Britain's use of seafaring and military power to build and control its far-flung empire. Germany and France followed with arms races starting in the 1880s, and as technological innovations revolutionized military weaponry, transport, and communications, European powers perfected the scourge of twentieth-century Europe: the conduct of total war using the techniques of industrialization.[182] Industrialization had its downside, none more damaging and catastrophic than mass production's recruitment for military service.

Ultimately, Great Britain was exhausted by the military struggle of two world wars, while many American enterprises cut their mass production teeth under wartime production. American GNP increased by more than 50 percent during World War II, while Europe's declined by around 25 percent.[183] Arguably, the war was the final push needed to get the United States out of the Great Depression. By the end of World War II, America was the dominant economic power, and global leadership had passed to America. In defeating the Axis powers, the United States became democracy's policeman of last resort, and after peace was restored, it set out to become the world's consumer of last resort, a capacity that all Fast Followers relied upon in their search for scale to industrialize.

One issue regarding First Mover industrialization remains: given the portents of the conflicting hypothesis noted earlier, how did the British, other Europeans, and Americans avoid the pitfall of industrializing under DRs? We now turn to this important question.

Regime Type in First Mover Early Industrializations: Democracy Light

How First Movers negotiated early industrialization under DRs is explained by an often-ignored fact: institutions evolve. Democracy in

181 Giovanni Arrighi, *The Long Twentieth Century: Money, Power and the Origins of Our Times* (London: Verso, 1994), 259.
182 Arden Bucholz, "Militarism," in *Encyclopedia of Violence, Peace, & Conflict*, ed. Lester R. Kurtz and Jennifer E. Turpin, (St. Louis, MO: Academic Press, 1999), 2:429.
183 Paul Kennedy, *The Rise and Fall of the Great Powers*, 368.

the nineteenth and early twentieth centuries differed vastly from that of advanced industrialized nations in the mid-twentieth century. The American republic did not live up to one of its founding principles for at least its first 180 years: that "all men are created equal."[184] The Fifteenth Amendment's ratification in 1870 gave African Americans the right to vote, and it took until the 1960s and the Civil Rights era to remove all legal racial restrictions against African Americans in the country. Further, women obtained voting rights in most modern Western European democracies only in the twentieth century; state and federal agencies were prohibited from including gender-based voting restrictions in America in 1920, and British women gained the same voting rights as men only in 1928.

Moreover, just as democracy's political boundaries expanded in the first half of the twentieth century, so did the role and responsibility of government in economic affairs. The Great Depression led Keynes to conclude that markets did reach states of rest below full employment, and instead of being self-correcting—as classical economists held—markets could persistently operate at high levels of unemployment unless governments intervened to stimulate demand.

Keynes's advice helped nations deal with the Great Depression, and as countercyclical economic management became an important government responsibility, tax cuts and increased government borrowing or expenditure became widely employed to guide, manage, and stimulate economic activity. These evolved into the fiscal and monetary policy alternatives modern democratic governments now routinely employ to manage economies, and active, more interventionist governments became the norm by midcentury in the industrialized world.

Most importantly, electorates began to judge governments on how well they managed the economy and to what degree policies maintained full employment and delivered acceptable living standards. These policies

---

184 "Declaration of Independence: A Transcription," National Archives, accessed February 20, 2023, https://www.archives.gov/founding-docs/declaration-transcript. An opening phrase of the American Declaration of Independence, ratified by the Continental Congress on July 4, 1776.

were not high on the political agenda in any western European country facing the challenges of early industrialization in the 1800s or early 1900s.

First Mover governments really only felt pressures to improve their citizenry's economic lot after World War I, by which time they were well on their way to industrialized status and had the wealth to meet the demands made of them. Prior to this time, other economic interests were served. For example, a developmental coalition in the Republican Party supported the protective tariffs and the creation of a national market that facilitated the formation of the American industrial base in the late nineteenth century, even though tariffs favored industrialists in the northern manufacturing belt at the expense of agricultural interests in the South and West.[185] This development coalition was America's version of Organski's "bourgeois politics" that placed the bourgeoisie in control of the national government. Capital formation was possible, free of the pressure the conflicting hypothesis fears under modern democracy.

Most importantly, from the start of their industrializations until the early twentieth century, First Mover governments were not encumbered by the redistributive pressures consistent with concerns noted in the conflicting hypothesis. Compared with twentieth-century democracy, the nineteenth-century version was democracy "light." As broader social demands surfaced only after the stresses of early industrialization had been traversed, First Mover industrializations correspond more to the sequential hypothesis; they industrialize first, and become modern distributive democracies second.

The minimal taxes gathered by First Mover governments support the assertion that the early stages of First Mover industrializations align with the sequential hypothesis. Lincoln was the first American president to impose an individual income tax at a very low rate, which only lasted for 11 years. The Revenue Act of 1861 imposed a 3 percent tax on income earned by individual Americans in excess of US$800 per annum, though any national, state, or local taxes assessed on the property from which the taxes

185 Bensel, *The Political Economy of American Industrialization*, 8.

were derived were first deducted. This income tax was abolished in 1872, as the need for federal revenue dropped dramatically after the Civil War. Federal receipts remained below 3 percent of economic output from 1900 to 1916, and what Americans most expected from their government was low taxes. Without resources to meet welfare or social needs, the trade-off that proponents of the conflicting hypothesis feared did not arise.

The tradition of low taxes and limited central government goes back to the foundation of the American republic. The imposition of taxes to fund England's war against France was one cause of the American Revolution, and the colonists' cry of "taxation without representation is tyranny" captures this fact. The desire to evade an overbearing central government meant the American Articles of Confederation adopted in 1781 ensured individual states kept much power at the expense of the new federal authority.

Americans to this day are less trusting of government than Europeans are, and they still expect less from their federal government than do Europeans from their national governments. As Adam Smith concluded, "the prince must provide three categories of public goods to his subjects: defense, justice, and public works, plus a private good subject to externalities: primary education."[186] This notion, consistent with the idea of limited government, still persists today in the minds of many Americans.

The effect of the Sixteenth Amendment, ratified in early 1913 and providing the constitutional foundation for federal fiscal expansion, was profound and underscores how governance in America changed compared with conditions before World War I:

> It is almost impossible to see how most of the social legislation passed since 1912 could have been financed without the income tax. Lack of the tax must also have meant the almost complete frustration of any government seeking to redistribute income in an orderly fashion. The

186 Bernard Salanié, *The Economics of Taxation* (Boston: MIT Press, 2003), 9.

> modern democratic social service state, in fact, probably rests more upon the income tax than upon any other single legislative act.[187]

Though the modern welfare state first appeared in Prussia under Bismarck with the creation of compulsory health insurance in 1883 and a pension system in 1889, most First Movers only followed in the twentieth century. The United Kingdom, Germany, France, and the United States created unemployment benefits in 1911, 1927, 1931, and 1936, respectively, and pension systems were first introduced in the United Kingdom and the United States in 1909 and 1935, respectively.[188] Social services expenditure—including education, welfare, housing, and social insurance—in the United Kingdom, Germany, and the United States were 2.1, 4.1, and 5.1 percent of GNP in 1913, and by 1932 these had increased to 6.3, 12.9, and 19.3 percent, respectively.[189] In 1965 tax revenues were 25 percent of American, 30.4 percent of British, and 34.5 percent of French GDP, and by 1997 these had increased to 27.6, 37.2, and 45.1 percent, respectively.[190]

The combination of two world wars and the emergence of the modern welfare state had led to substantial increases in government-mediated expenditures across the industrialized world. Governments were expected to do far more than was the case only two generations earlier. Requiring pre-industrial countries to operate at these levels at commencement of industrialization presents challenges no First Movers faced; in the context of democracy light, little early scarce surplus was allocated to social or community needs.

---

187 George E. Mowry, *The Era of Theodore Roosevelt, 1900–1912* (New York: Harper & Row, 1958), 263.

188 Bernard Salanié, *The Economics of Taxation*, 4.

189 W. W. Rostow, *Theorists of Economic Growth from David Hume to the Present: With a Perspective on the Next Century*, 3rd ed. (New York: Oxford University Press, 1990), 157.

190 OECD Statistics, "Revenue Statistics–OECD Countries: Comparative Tables," Organisation for Economic Co-operation and Development, last updated Q3 2023, https://stats.oecd.org/index.aspx?DataSetCode=REV.

We now turn to Fast Follower industrialization, the notion of which emerged from the impressive industrializations of five countries in the mid-to-late twentieth century, starting with Japan, followed by South Korea, Singapore, Taiwan, and finally Hong Kong. All five are industrialized, and the routes they followed yield additional insights into industrialization and its political economy.

Japan differs from the other four, as it was well on its way to being industrialized by the mid-twentieth century when the other four began ascending. Like Germany, Japan faced rebuilding more than industrialization in 1945, and the model used to achieve the "Japanese Miracle"[191] provided a template others followed when commencing industrializations after World War II. For this reason, Japan is categorized as the first Fast Follower, though it could legitimately be included as the last First Mover instead.

Fast Follower Industrialization: Triumph of Interventionist Governments, Markets, and Deferred Gratification

First Mover and Fast Follower industrializations are distinguishable for one obvious reason—the second group had others to follow, learn from, and rely on: "Whereas industrialization in the eighteenth and nineteenth centuries was propelled by new products and processes, late industrialization is being driven by borrowing technology or 'learning.'"[192] But imitation neither signifies a second class industrialization (there are no pure First Movers—the Americans learned from the British, the British learned from the Dutch, etc.), nor does it detract from the Fast Followers' impressive achievements. In addition, even following has its challenges.

191 Chalmers Johnson, *MITI and the Japanese Miracle: The Growth of Industrial Policy, 1925–1975* (Stanford, CA: Stanford University Press, 1982).
192 Alice H. Amsden, "Diffusion of Development: The Late-Industrializing Model and Greater East Asia," *American Economic Review* 81, no. 2 (1991): 285.

A World Bank study on seven high-performing Asian economies (Japan, South Korea, Taiwan, Singapore, Indonesia, Thailand, and Malaysia, collectively the HPAEs) concluded that their growth was achieved by "getting the basics right. . . . There is little that is 'miraculous' about the HPAEs' superior record of growth; it is largely due to superior accumulation of physical and human capital."[193] Yet despite a lack of or need for miracles, Japan, South Korea, Taiwan, Hong Kong, and Singapore remain more exceptions than the rule: "getting the basics right" appears more difficult than it first may seem. If this were not the case, the notable successes of the Fast Followers would have been replicated more widely. So far only China has stepped into this void.

To fully appreciate Fast Follower industrialization, more fine-grained analysis is required. For complex endeavors, the devil is always in the detail, and Tables 5 and 6 hint at this detail under four headings: *Public Institutions Guiding Industrialization*, *Industrial Policy Overall Orientation*, *Supporting Trade and Economic Policies*, and *Private Sector Agents Used to Industrialize*. Table 5 includes Japan and its colonies, Taiwan (colonized in 1895) and Korea (colonized in 1910). Table 6 includes Hong Kong and Singapore, city-states that were formerly British colonies (Singapore until 1959 and Hong Kong until 1997).

Tables 5 and 6 underscore how industrialization's terminology had advanced by the mid-twentieth century. Armed with concepts such as industrial policy, export promotion, import substitution, industry targeting, and managed competition, Fast Followers entertained questions not on the radar screen when the First Movers started industrializing. These include: Should governments play more pervasive roles in fostering industrialization, and if so, what is this role? Should the primary development agents be public or private sector entities, or both? Should foreign investment be encouraged, or not? What supporting economic and trade policies should assist in the effort? As the tables indicate, answers to these questions varied.

---

193 Nancy Birdsall et al., *The East Asian Miracle: Economic Growth and Public Policy*, World Bank Policy Research Report (New York: Oxford University Press, 1993), 5.

The tables reflect four areas of congruence: (1) export-led growth of labor-intensive manufactures promoted early industrialization in all, though because of its domestic economy and more established markets, Japan's export reliance was less pronounced than the others; (2) all used private sector organizations as primary development agents, though the specific types varied; (3) all discouraged private consumption at home and encouraged high savings in producer-oriented (as opposed to consumer-oriented) societies; and finally, (4) all governments provided little social welfare as their industrial economies were built.

For aspirant Followers the message is clear: world-class production validated through exports is the license to operate; to achieve this, high savings and the creation of robust private sectors are required, and local consumption and welfare must be limited. Though useful, such a summary is reminiscent of the World Bank's "getting the basics right"—no acts of God yet. It is perhaps in the detail and where Fast Followers' miracles are revealed.

Table 5: Fast Follower Industrialization: Japan, South Korea, and Taiwan

Japan	
Public Institutions Guiding Industrialization	Ministry of International Trade and Industry (MITI); Ministry of Finance (MOF); Ministry of Agriculture and Forestry; Ministry of Construction; Ministry of Transport; Economic Planning Agency; Bank of Japan; Development Bank of Japan; Export-Import Bank of Japan
Industrial Policy Overall Orientation	Mostly domestic-led growth, though export promotion facilitated by administrative guidance, industry targeting, import/foreign investment controls, licensing of foreign technology, infant industry protection, and domestic competition management also present
Supporting Trade and Economic Policies	Low-interest loans to targeted industries; exchange rate manipulation and government control of foreign exchange; tariffs, subsidies, and quotas; direct subsidies to research and development; extensive government control of financial markets and credit direction to strategic industries; weak labor unions; low rates of return on savings and limited consumer credit; low welfare expenditure
Private Sector Agents Used to Industrialize	Large keiretsu, supported by small- and medium-sized subcontractors

South Korea	
Public Institutions Guiding Industrialization	Economic Planning Board; state-owned commercial banks; state-owned corporations
Industrial Policy Overall Orientation	Import substitution initially, followed by export-led, labor-intensive industrialization; industry targeting; tax incentives; import protection; export promotion devices; credit preferences offered in successive five-year government plans
Supporting Trade and Economic Policies	Tariff-free access to imported inputs processed for export; exchange rate manipulation and government control of foreign exchange; extensive government control of financial markets and credit direction to strategic industries; import substitution to promote local scale and export promotion; state corporatist control of labor; little welfare or social expenditure; limited consumer credit; prohibition of luxury imports
Private Sector Agents Used to Industrialize	Relatively few large, family-based chaebol

Taiwan	
Public Institutions Guiding Industrialization	Council for International Economic Cooperation and Development; Economic Planning Council; Economic Planning and Development Council; state-owned banks and corporations
Industrial Policy Overall Orientation	Import substitution in protected domestic market from 1950 to 1958, followed by export-led, labor-intensive industrialization
Supporting Trade and Economic Policies	Exchange rate manipulation and government control of foreign exchange; extension of low-interest loans and income tax holidays to strategic industries; high real interest rates on deposits and government control of financial markets and credit direction to strategic industries; little welfare expenditure; weak labor unions; limited consumer credit
Private Sector Agents Used to Industrialize	Small- and medium-sized businesses supported by state-owned petroleum, power, steel, and transport infrastructures (rail, road, harbors)
Sources: Paul W. Kuznets, "An East Asian Model of Economic Development: Japan, Taiwan, and South Korea," *Economic Development and Cultural Change*, 36, no. 3 (April 1988): S11–43; Larry E. Westphal, "The Republic of Korea's Experience with Export-Led Industrial Development," *World Development* 6, no. 3 (March 1978): 347–82; Gary G. Hamilton and Nicole Woolsey Biggart, "The Organization of Business in Taiwan: Reply to Numazaki," *American Journal of Sociology* 96, no. 4 (January 1991): 999–1006; William V. Rapp, "Japan: Its Industrial Policies and Corporate Behaviors," *Columbia Journal of World Business* 12, no. 1 (1977): 38–48; Richard Beason and David E. Weinstein, "Growth, Economies of Scale, and Targeting in Japan (1955–1990)," *The Review of Economics and Statistics* 78, no. 2 (May 1996): 286–95; Robert Wade, "East Asian Financial Systems as a Challenge to Economics: Lessons from Taiwan," *California Management Review* 27, no. 4 (1985): 106–27; Johnson, *MITI and the Japanese Miracle*.	

Table 6: Fast Follower Industrialization: Hong Kong and Singapore

Hong Kong	
Public Institutions Guiding Industrialization	None: positive nonintervention
Industrial Policy Overall Orientation	No explicit industrial policy; export-led, labor-intensive industrialization based on laissez-faire economic policy
Supporting Trade and Economic Policies	Nil; free entry to port; no credit preferences; no exchange or investment controls, though HK$ pegged to US$ from 1983; limited regulation of financial, trade, and labor market activities; limited welfare beyond public housing; absence of high taxes, tariffs, or duties; fiscally minimalist
Private Sector Agents Used to Industrialize	Few large, non-Chinese hongs (banking, telecommunications, and transport) and thousands of small Chinese family businesses providing small-scale subcontracting as merchant manufacturers
Singapore	
Public Institutions Guiding Industrialization	Economic Development Board; National Wages Council; statutory boards (e.g., Post Office Savings Bank, Singapore Broadcasting Corporation, Housing and Development Board, Jurong Town Corporation, Public Utilities Board, Port of Singapore Authority, Telecommunication Authority of Singapore, Urban Redevelopment Authority, and Sentosa Development Corporation); and wholly owned government holding companies and joint ventures with domestic and foreign partners
Industrial Policy Overall Orientation	Import substitution from 1960 to 1966, followed by export-led, labor-intensive industrialization supported by foreign direct investment, shifting later to more capital-intensive, higher-value-added products and services
Supporting Trade and Economic Policies	Modest initial infant industry protection; few tariffs and import controls; superb local infrastructure; no foreign exchange controls; weak labor unions and close labor market regulation; targeting of specific activities with tax and other fiscal incentives; high domestic savings and limited local consumption; little welfare beyond the provision of public housing; population control; care of parents and elderly relatives via compulsory saving for old age

Private Sector Agents Used to Industrialize	Multinational corporations (MNCs)
Sources: Lawrence B. Krause, "Hong Kong and Singapore: Twins or Kissing Cousins?," *Economic Development and Cultural Change* 36, no. 3, (1988): S45–66; Jan Selmer and Corinna de Leon, "Culture and Management in Hong Kong SAR," chap. 3 in *Culture and Management in Asia*, ed. Malcolm Warner (New York: Routledge, 2003); Mick Carney and Howard Davies, "From Entrepôt to Entrepôt via Merchant Manufacturing: Adaptive Mechanisms, Organizational Capabilities and the Structure of the Hong Kong Economy," chap. 2 in *Managed in Hong Kong: Adaptive Systems, Entrepreneurship, and Human Resources*, ed. Chris Rowley and Robert Fitzgerald (New York: Routledge, 2000), 13–32; Ow Chin Hock, "Development Strategies, Economic Performance, and Relations with the United States: Singapore's Experience," *Journal of Asian Economics* 1, no. 1 (Spring 1990): 61–85; W. G. Huff, "The Developmental State, Government, and Singapore's Economic Development Since 1960," *World Development* 23, no. 8 (August 1995): 1421–38; Steven C. Chow and Gustav F. Papanek, "Laissez-Faire, Growth and Equity—Hong Kong," *The Economic Journal* 91, no. 362 (June 1981): 466–85.	

Governments guiding and managing industrialization is the arena where Fast Followers diverged most from First Movers:

> In states that were late to industrialize, the state itself led the industrialization drive, that is, it took on developmental functions. These two differing orientations toward private economic activities, the regulatory orientation and the developmental orientation, produced two different kinds of government-business relationships. The United States is a good example of a state in which the regulatory orientation predominates, whereas Japan is a good example of a state in which the developmental orientation predominates.[194]

Fast Followers were unwilling to let private agents in mostly free markets determine what should be produced. Directive government policy, and even direct government support implemented by *plan-rational* (as opposed to *market-rational*) states was preferred; four of the five Fast Followers relied on active *developmental states* to guide progress. In these states, explicit industrial policies were implemented, defined as "deliberate efforts by governments to guide the market by coordinating and

194 Johnson, *MITI and the Japanese Miracle*, 19.

planning industrial activities,"[195] or "a summary term for the activities of governments that are intended to develop or retrench various industries in a national economy in order to maintain global competitiveness."[196] Only Hong Kong followed a laissez-faire approach reminiscent of First Movers and did not adopt a specific industrial policy, indicated in the nil responses in much of the Hong Kong data in Table 6.

Japan was the first to adopt an explicit industrial policy, and though explanations for the country's twentieth-century successes are many, "state-led capitalism"[197] was a major contributor to economic growth from the early 1950s until the mid-1980s. Staffed by bureaucrats operating mostly free of political interference, the Ministry of International Trade and Industry (MITI) and Ministry of Finance (MOF) were the primary institutions that directed financial capital to promote formation of world-class capabilities in select targeted industries. A myriad of trade and economic policies (including administrative guidance, industry targeting, managed domestic competition, import and foreign investment controls, and foreign technology licensing) were implemented to build the then second largest industrial economy in the world. The Japanese economy increased 55-fold from 1946 to 1976, by which time the country accounted for around 10 percent of GWP with only 3 percent of the world's population.[198] The Japanese search for imported technology was relentless:

> Under strict government supervision, technology worth US$281 million was imported between 1956 and 1960. Most of this money came from the large banks, which were able to recycle Japan's historically high rate of personal savings into investment capital, and "over-loans" . . . guaranteed ultimately by the government meant that unusually large amounts of money could be loaned. . . . Between 1964 and 1971,

195 Todaro and Smith, *Economic Development*, 816.

196 Chalmers A. Johnson, "The Industrial Policy Debate Re-examined," *California Management Review* 27, no. 1 (1984): 74.

197 Pan A. Yotopoulos, "Exchange Rates and State-Led Capitalism: What Can the NIC's Learn from Japan?," *Asian Economic Journal* 5, no. 1, (March 1991): 76–99.

198 Johnson, *MITI and the Japanese Miracle*, 6.

> Japan paid more for foreign know-how than any other major industrial country.[199]

Keiretsu, the private sector agents that guided the diversification of the Japanese economy, eventually coalesced into two major forms: horizontal, comprising a large bank, insurance companies, several mostly unrelated manufacturing firms, and a general trading company (also known as *sogo shosha*—for example, Mitsubishi and Mitsui) and vertical, comprising suppliers, distributors, and capital providers of a focused, industry-specific manufacturer (for example, Toyota and Honda). In horizontal keiretsu, a core bank held equity positions in affiliates and funded their business operations, and a trading company assisted in the international sales of these affiliate company goods. In vertical keiretsu, tiered suppliers typically contracted only with their manufacturer: Toyota suppliers did not supply Honda. Cross shareholdings were also part of vertical keiretsu structures.

Japan's market protection and technology imports reflect the advantage of being more developed than other Fast Followers were when beginning industrialization. Japan's large domestic market—relative to other Fast Follower domestic markets at commencement of their industrializations—provided the base on which scale could be built, and the Japanese economy, accordingly, remained more closed than the other four.

> Japan's growth did not depend nearly so much on exports as it did on the development of the domestic market (a market half the size of the United States in terms of population). . . . By the late 1960s Japan's exports were only 9.6 percent of GNP, compared for example with Canada's 19.8 percent. From 1953 to 1972 Japan had consistently lower dependency on exports and imports as a percentage of GNP at constant prices than France, Germany, Italy, Britain, or OECD Europe

199 Dennis B. Smith, "The Japanese Economy Since 1945," chap. 1 in *The Japan Handbook*, ed. Patrick Heenan (Chicago: Fitzroy Dearborn Publishers, 1998), 8, 10.

> as a whole. . . . Home demand led Japan's growth for the twenty years after 1955.[200]

Given its size and sophistication, *by Japan, of Japan, for Japan* was feasible. After World War II Japan rebuilt its economy by pulling itself up by its own bootstraps. Singapore, South Korea, and Taiwan's bargaining power was far more limited, and their ability to license and import technology was constrained by a lack of resources and purchasing power.

South Korea under President Park implemented a series of five-year plans, under which large, family-based chaebol (e.g., Samsung, Hyundai, Lucky Goldstar, and Daewoo) emerged under government protection:

> Daewoo's history reflected that of the Korean economy. As the Korean economy had grown explosively in the late 1960s and the early 1970s propelled by exports, Daewoo became one of the nation's front-running exporters. When Korea began in mid-1970 to shift its focus from light to heavy industries, Daewoo also extended its domain from exporting textiles and other light goods to manufacturing heavy industrial goods. In the early 1980s, Daewoo further extended its business activities to home appliances, telecommunications and other electronic equipment, in line with the government's economic plan to emphasize electronics.[201]

The South Korean government also exercised corporatist control over labor, spent little in the way of welfare or social expenditures, and limited consumer credit. To further restrict local consumption, luxury imports were prohibited for a time too.

---

200 Johnson, *MITI and the Japanese Miracle*, 15–16. According to the US Department of State: "The Organization for Economic Co-operation and Development (OECD) is a unique forum where the governments of 37 democracies with market-based economies collaborate to develop policy standards to promote sustainable economic growth. . . . Today, OECD member countries account for three-fifths of world GDP, three-quarters of world trade, over 90 percent of global official development assistance, half of the world's energy consumption, and 18 percent of the world's population" (US Department of State, "The Organization for Economic Cooperation and Development (OECD)," accessed February 28, 2023, https://www.state.gov/the-organization-for-economic-co-operation-and-development-oecd/).

201 Francis J. Aguilar, *Daewoo Group*, Harvard Business School Case 9-385-014 (Boston: Harvard Business School Publishing, July 1984, revised September 1986), 2.

South Korea by the 1980s boasted manufacturing costs 25 percent lower than Americans and 10 percent lower than Japanese, accounting for joint ventures between its chaebol[202] and American MNCs such as Caterpillar and General Motors.[203] South Korea offered high-quality, low-cost manufacturing while MNCs provided technology and access to their large home markets. Because of its limited domestic market and lack of foreign exchange, this production was not by and for the Koreans, but by Koreans for Americans.

Singapore used an array of statutory boards, state-owned enterprises, and joint ventures with domestic and foreign partners to drive its industrialization. The country offered MNCs a business-friendly, English-speaking, low-cost manufacturing location, attracting investment with low-cost labor, clean government, and world-class infrastructure. Unlike other Fast Followers, Singapore actively courted foreign direct investment, and the country's Economic Development Board "provided a kind of one stop shopping for foreign companies."[204]

Underscoring the importance of state-owned corporations to Singapore, by the end of the 1980s, state-owned corporations "controlled between 44% and 69% of the assets and 75% of the profits of all Singapore-controlled companies,"[205] and by the late 1990s, around 5,000 MNCs operated in the city-state.[206]

In addition, led from 1959 to 1990 by Prime Minister Lee Kuan Yew and the People's Action Party, which for much of the time won all

---

202 Chaebol were large, diverse, hierarchically controlled family businesses. In 1980–81 the South Korean government recognized 26 chaebol that controlled 456 firms (Larry E. Westphal et al., "Republic of Korea," *World Development* 12, no. 5–6 [May–June 1984]: 505–33). By 1985, 50 chaebol controlled 552 firms and around 80 percent of the Korean GNP (Gary G. Hamilton and Nicole Woolsey Biggart, "Market, Culture, and Authority: A Comparative Analysis of Management and Organization in the Far East," *American Journal of Sociology* 94 [1988]: S59).

203 Aguilar, *Daewoo Group*, 8.

204 Joseph L. Badaracco Jr., *AT&T Consumer Products*, Harvard Business School Case 9-392-108 (Boston: Harvard Business School Publishing, March 1992, revised October 1994), 8.

205 Kulwant Singh and Hwee Ang Siah, "The Strategies and Success of Government-Linked Corporations in Singapore" (research paper 98-06, National University of Singapore, Faculty of Business Administration, 1998), 9.

206 Kenneth Hall and Stanley Petzell, "The Making of Technicians for a High-Technology Future: The Singapore Apprentice," *Journal of Asian Business* 16, no. 4 (2000): 39–56.

parliamentary seats in elections, Singapore's developmental—as opposed to distributive—democracy had little patience for social welfare apart from providing public housing, also offered in laissez-faire Hong Kong. Singaporean authorities also controlled the labor market to ensure labor costs remained low, and to maintain foreign investor confidence, foreign exchange controls were never imposed.

Hong Kong hongs were large trading companies established in the mid-nineteenth century. Run initially by tai-pans well connected to Hong Kong colonial authorities, these originally mostly British trade and warehousing companies evolved into widely diversified conglomerates by the late twentieth century, with interests in cargo handling, manufacturing, real estate, and retailing. Remnants of the original British hongs include Jardine Matheson Holdings, Hutchison Whampoa, and the Swire Group. Unlike chaebol and keiretsu, hongs were not formed to aid Hong Kong's industrialization. In fact, the opposite pertained until the mid-twentieth century:

> The reason why entrepôt trade continued to be defined as the *raison d'être* of Hong Kong, even though the manufacturing industry had gradually become the largest employment sector, was that the latter developed totally outside the imperial plan and the *hongs's* activities. In the first place, the British Government believed that any economic investment other than in trade was politically risky, given the turbulent situation in mainland China. Hong Kong was deemed unsuitable for developing long-term projects, especially industrial investment. Thus, most economic activities in the colony, such as banking, shipping and insurance, were seen as related exclusively to trading.[207]

In Taiwan, unlike in Singapore, MNCs were not relied upon much to provide the private sector contribution to its industrialization. Instead, small- and medium-sized domestic family firms dominated, resulting in

207 Tak-Wing Ngo, "Industrial History and the Artifice of *Laissez-Faire* Colonialism," chap. 7 in *Hong Kong's History: State and Society Under Colonial Rule*, ed. Tak-Wing Ngo (New York: Routledge, 1999), 129. James Clavell's novels *Tai-Pan* (set in Hong Kong in the 1840s) and *Noble House* (set in Hong Kong in the 1960s) captured the lore of the hongs.

"low levels of vertical and horizontal integration and a relative absence of oligarchic concentration."[208] Taiwan's industrialization was more bottom up than top down, as in the more centralized South Korea. Moreover, and unlike Japan's or South Korea's, Taiwan's industrial policy mostly remained agnostic to targeting and to selecting winners, though the country did have its big companies, some even formed by the government.

Most prominent of Taiwan's bigger companies is Taiwan Semiconductor Manufacturing Company (TSMC), organized by the Taiwanese government in 1987 in a joint venture with Netherlands-based Philips Electronics NV to promote chip manufacture. The company provided state-of-the-art chip manufacturing to complement Taiwan's strength in chip design, and today the company boasts that "TSMC has the broadest range of technologies and services in the Dedicated IC Foundry segment of the semiconductor manufacturing industry."[209] TSMC went public in 1994 and is currently listed on the Taiwanese and New York stock exchanges.

TSMC's symbiotic role in promoting the state-owned upstream and family-based downstream business ecology in Taiwan is confirmed by observers:

> The development of government-sponsored initiatives in the computer industry to finance factories, such as Taiwan Semiconductor Manufacturing Corporation, to supply intermediate inputs for smaller firms downstream was not only tremendously successful in helping Taiwan build a viable high technology sector, but also purposefully built on existing patterns: allowing exports manufactured by smaller firms to drive the demand for the intermediate inputs manufactured by larger upstream firms.[210]

---

208 Hamilton and Biggart, "Market, Culture, and Authority," S60.

209 TSMC, "Unleash Innovation: Technology Is Our Cornerstone. Innovation Is Our Passion," accessed February 25, 2023, https://www.tsmc.com/english/dedicatedFoundry/technology.

210 Robert C. Feenstra and Gary G. Hamilton, *Emergent Economies, Divergent Paths: Economic Organization and International Trade in South Korea and Taiwan* (New York: Cambridge University Press, 2006), 349.

Government policy and developmental states are not the only elements warranting attention in Fast Follower industrialization. The private sector agents listed in Tables 5 and 6 do too, primarily because they underscore that Fast Follower industrialization was not the result of governments or markets acting alone or independently. The keiretsu, chaebol, hongs, and state-owned enterprises listed in the tables are Asian equivalents of the Chandlerian large business enterprises established in the United States. In addition, how smaller businesses contributed is more clearly articulated in some Fast Follower industrializations.

The variety of Asia's private business models reflects conditions in each country. Keiretsu emerged from the ashes of the zaibatsu in postwar Japan and were the embodiment of Japan Inc.'s cooperative capitalism, while hongs resulted from Hong Kong's colonial legacy. Chaebol emerged directly from South Korean industrial policy, and why large, vertically integrated groups emerged in South Korea while small- and medium-sized family businesses dominated in Taiwan may be due to cultural and other institutional differences.

In South Korea, traditionally the eldest son inherited all or a majority of his father's assets, giving him power over his brothers and contributing to power centralization. He was also expected to remain in the family home, look after his elderly parents, and be responsible for the whole family. In Taiwan, family patrimony was typically divided equally among sons, distributing power and promoting networks of family businesses as opposed to larger centralized organizations controlled by the oldest son. Though both nations' assets were passed down the male line, this difference likely contributed to the business structures that emerged in each society.

That the two former British entrepôts adopted different industrialization approaches involves both timing and legacy. Granted self-government in 1959 and full independence in 1965, Singapore inherited, according to newly installed Prime Minister Yew, "an administration in good working order . . . effective both in improving the lives of the people and in dealing with the communists. It made a difference to the history of Singapore."[211] Hong Kong, in contrast, was handed back to China in 1997, and as noted previously, the colonial government had no interest in long-term industrial investment in the territory.

Moreover, Singapore, South Korea, and Taiwan faced security crises just before commencing industrialization (South Korea, a civil war, and Taiwan, absorbing fleeing immigrants with the flight of General Chiang Kai-shek), and these crises also help explain why they adopted more autocratic regimes. Hong Kong faced only an inevitable return to the mainland, adding to British unwillingness to invest in the territory. That a hands-off administration resulted in Hong Kong is both predictable and understandable; administering colonies for finite periods differs from building nations.

Regardless of its initial laissez-faire emphasis, internal developments in China combined with demographic changes in Hong Kong and the territory's pending return to the mainland eventually forced "the once uncaring and aloof colonial regime to cater more to grassroots needs."[212] Involvement in people's everyday lives increased steadily from the 1960s onward, such that by the 1990s the Hong Kong government was the monopoly owner of land, was the largest landlord in the territory (over 40 percent of the population live in public housing), and also imposed rent controls on private land. Public corporations operated the territory's three railways, and other major transport services and public utilities were regulated as monopoly franchises.[213] Hong Kong taxes still remained low.

To complete coverage of Fast Follower industrialization, Table 7 presents details of the industries and products that the four less developed Fast Followers competed in as they industrialized. When industries were entered, which products were offered, and the competitive advantage relied upon by each country are included. Details on the South Korean five-year plans are also provided. The range of industries entered and how

---

211 Lee Kuan Yew, letter to the *Times*, (London), September 27, 1986; reprinted in the *Straits Times*, October 3, 1986.
212 Ming K. Chan, "The Legacy of the British Administration of Hong Kong: A View from Hong Kong," *The China Quarterly* 151 (September 1997): 574.
213 Chan, "The Legacy," 574–75.

quickly these changed underscore the adaptability required as industrialization progresses.

Table 7: Major Industries, Products, and Competitive Advantages of Hong Kong, Singapore, South Korea, and Taiwan

	Major Industries, Products, Timelines
Hong Kong	1953–70s: Textiles/clothing, progressing to consumer electronics, watches, clocks, and plastics goods 1970s: Calculators, computer parts, digital watches, video games 1980s: Manufacturing declines from mid-decade; financial services, regional trade services, tourism expand 1990s: Consumer and industrial electronics design (fax machine, cordless telephone, small-screen color TV design, liquid crystal display production); manufacturing 9.3 percent of GDP in 1994
Singapore	1950s–60s: Transistor radios and black-and-white TVs, semiconductors, mostly with MNC investment 1980s: Electronics development, process capabilities, and limited design skills, mostly in MNC subsidiaries: hi-fi audio equipment, color TVs, compact disc players, new tuners and precision tools 1990s: Hard disk drives
South Korea	1962–66: First five-year plan: import substitution in cement, oil refining, fertilizers 1967–71: Second five-year plan: export-oriented light industries such as textiles, plywood, other consumer goods, and strengthening of industrial/scientific infrastructure 1972–81: Third and fourth five-year plans: heavy and chemical industries, technological and skilled, labor-intensive industries: shipbuilding, electronics, machinery, petrochemicals 1980s: Innovation and product differentiation in capital- and technology-intensive industries: microelectronics and telecommunications
Taiwan	1950s: Import substitution in infrastructure businesses 1960s: Air conditioners and audio electronics for MNCs 1970s: Color TVs and state-of-the-art, low-cost computer subassemblies and components 1980s: Computing and related goods exceed consumer goods production; semiconductor design and fabrication

Stated and *Aspirant* Competitive Advantages	
Hong Kong	1953–80: High-quality, low-cost, labor-intensive manufacture in flexible, small-scale operations 1980s: Shipping, banking; high value added entrepôt services 1990s: *Knowledge-intensive business and design services*
Singapore	1950s–60s: High-quality, low-cost labor 1980s: High-quality, low-cost manufacture
South Korea	1960–70s: High-quality, low-cost labor in light industries 1980s: High-quality, low-cost manufacture for US MNCs facing Japanese competition 1990s: *State-of-the-art electronics and semiconductor manufacture*
Taiwan	1960s–70s: High-quality, low-cost, labor-intensive manufacturing in capital- and R&D-light industries Post-1980s: *Development of local technology to offer higher-value-added manufactures*
Sources: Jan Selmer and Corinna de Leon, "Culture and Management"; Carney and Davies, "From Entrepôt to Entrepôt," 13–32; Michael M. Crow and Shrilata A. Nath, "Technology Strategy Development in Korean Industry: An Assessment of Market and Government Influences," *Technovation* 12, no. 2 (March 1992): 119–36; Hamilton and Biggart, "Market, Culture, and Authority," S52–94; Mike Hobday, "East Asian Latecomer Firms: Learning the Technology of Electronics," *World Development* 23, no. 7 (July 1995): 1171–93; Aguilar, *Daewoo Group*; Liu Shuyong, "Hong Kong: A Survey of Its Political and Economic Development over the Past 150 Years," *The China Quarterly* 151 (September 1997): 583–92.	

Table 7 reveals that not only do industries and products evolve as industrialization progresses, the underlying competitive advantage to support industrialization does too. Typical for the Fast Followers, Japan was the first to perfect the pattern embedded in the *Stated and Aspirant Competitive Advantages* in the table: "During the period 1967–1983, Japan's pattern of specialization in manufactures is found to have changed dramatically with Japan shifting from specialization in unskilled labor-intensive goods to human capital and research and development intensive products."[214]

214 Bela Balassa and Marcus Noland, "The Changing Comparative Advantage of Japan and the United States," *Journal of the Japanese and International Economies* 3, no. 2 (June 1989): 175.

Fast Followers in Table 7 also initially relied on low-cost, unskilled labor to drive early industrialization, then upgraded to low-cost manufacturing, and by the last decade of the twentieth century, all understood the need to move to higher-value-added, technology-intensive manufactures and services. These are captured in the aspirant competitive advantages in italics. In the world of shifting competitive advantage, global competitiveness is captured in the notion of up or out. You can start as a Follower, but as industrialization and catch-up is achieved, moving from Follower to Leader is optimal. This would mean up and not out!

Though the ambition of the four less developed Fast Followers to upgrade their competitive advantages is reflected in Table 7, evidence in the mid-1980s indicated this was yet to be accomplished. Exports from the four countries from 1966 to 1986 still resembled those of Japan in the 1970s:

> Presumably, much of their export expansion in the 1960s and 1970s resulted from their relatively low-cost of unskilled labor. Facing the rising momentum of labor movements in Korea and Taiwan, and the policy of deliberately high wages in Singapore, all these countries have embarked on a major drive to shift their exports to technology intensive and brain-intensive industries. However, by 1986, the structural shifts of their export industries, if any, were still not significantly reflected in the U.S. market.[215]

Though no proof shows the competitive advantages of South Korea, Hong Kong, Taiwan, or Singapore matched those of the advanced industrial nations by the late 1980s, evidence of the transfer of advantage from Japan to these and to other third-tier Asian developing countries succes-

215 Peter C. Y. Chow, "The Revealed Comparative Advantage of the East Asian NICs," *The International Trade Journal* 5, no. 2 (1990): 260.

sively is reported.[216] Denoted the "flying geese" theory of development, Asian countries exhibited:

> a multi-layered "catching up" process of industrialization. . . . As the lead economy, Japan supplied the rest of Asia with capital and technological know-how through the expansion of trade and FDI. In return, the Newly Industrialized Economies (NIEs) exported to Japan commodities that she no longer has comparative advantage in, and the follower economies, the ASEAN4, supplied Japan with raw materials.[217]

This data confirms the regional effects of Fast Follower industrialization and shows how competitive advantage was parceled out among the four industrializing Asian nations. Japan was the regional hegemon in a dynamic process; the others followed as their competitive advantage allowed.

Fast Follower Political Economy: Authoritarian Developmentalists Getting the Growth Job Done

As industrialization mechanics did not change much as First Movers and Fast Followers industrialized, Fast Followers faced the same challenges that First Movers did. The overall steps taken by Fast Followers were similar to those taken by First Movers. But, as already noted, Fast Followers had one important advantage—they had paths to follow and learn from. This advantage contributed to the two most notable differences in Fast Follower industrializations: the speed at which they were done and the role governments played to facilitate the industrialization process.

---

216 For example, Pradumna B. Rana, "Shifting Comparative Advantage Among Asian and Pacific Countries," *The International Trade Journal* 4, no. 3 (1990): 243–58; and I. Yamazawa, A. Hirata, and K. Yokota, "Evolving Pattern of Comparative Advantage in the Pacific Economies," in *The Pacific Economy: Growth and External Stability*, ed. M. Ariff (Sydney, Australia: Allen and Unwin Press, 1991).

217 Malcolm Dowling and Chia Tien Cheang, "Shifting Comparative Advantage in Asia: New Tests of the 'Flying Geese' Model," *Journal of Asian Economics* 11, no. 4 (Autumn 2000): 444.

The impressive pace at which Fast Followers industrialized is chiefly the result of willingness to save and invest at higher rates than First Movers did, and the resultant resource-intensive input-led growth enjoyed by Fast Followers is highlighted in the next section. As external demand (i.e., export-led growth) absorbed the goods produced (especially for Fast Followers except Japan), in Fast Followers production was favored over consumption, and production-oriented social contracts were imposed. Some even restricted local consumption to promote savings that were reinvested, a step not taken by any First Mover. Political economies oriented toward getting the growth job done resulted, and national effort was directed toward this end. Policies were implemented to maximize savings, promote production, and minimize local consumption.

Concomitant with getting the production job done meant Fast Followers were not societies where social equity or welfare were of primary concern. Economic catch-up was, and in four of the five Fast Followers, active, interventionist states used all the political and economic tools at their disposal to accomplish this end. Fast Followers add to the evidence that the conflicting and sequential hypotheses better explain the regime type industrialization nexus. Three of the five Fast Followers were governed by ADRs, and the fourth was governed by a nondemocratic colonial administration.

Taiwan and South Korea were ruled by authoritarian regimes for most of their early industrializations, one by a military dictator—President Park in South Korea—and the other by the one-party Kuomintang, led by General Chiang Kai-shek. Martial law was only lifted in Taiwan in 1987. Hong Kong was governed by a disengaged colonial administration and a governor appointed in London, supported by a cabinet whose members were almost exclusively drawn from a big business. Singapore, though holding elections every four or five years, was more authoritarian than democratic in governance, a situation that persisted until at least 2001:

> In Singapore, political representation is more than ever a procedural pretense since the power is irreversibly held by the bureaucratic and administrative apparatus. And it is the tip of this governmental iceberg that regulates the rest of society and that defines the duties of the individual citizens. Some features are missing which are considered the fundamental requirements for a political regime to be called democratic.[218]

Only one nation among the Fast Followers, Japan, was in any way democratic, and even there, Japan's democracy was possibly closer to First Movers' democracy light than to the redistributive democracy implemented in western European countries in the mid-twentieth century.

This data provides additional support for the conflicting and sequential hypotheses; no support for the complementary hypothesis incorporating mid-twentieth-century redistributive democracy is even remotely seen in any Fast Follower. Hong Kong does show, however, that industrialization can be accomplished with the state playing a smaller role. But no other developing society has industrialized in the fashion Hong Kong did in the twentieth century, and the city-state could be considered an exception that proves the rule. It was not a democracy, and none of the redistributive pressures facing early democracies were encountered as it industrialized.

Hong Kong's unique geographic location, history, and the human capital it attracted over the past 150 years produced an outcome yet to be replicated. Following the revolution in China, much of the Shanghai capitalist class fled to Hong Kong, taking with them the entrepreneurial skills and machines needed to set up textile and apparel businesses. These skills combined with willing Hong Kong workers formed the core of the merchant manufacturing class that emerged. In addition, Hong Kong's established businesses also acted as development agents. For example, the Hong Kong and Shanghai Banking Company was the territory's

---

218 Danilo Zolo, "The 'Singapore Model': Democracy, Communication, and Globalization," chap. 38 in *The Blackwell Companion to Political Sociology*, ed. Kate Nash and Alan Scott (Malden, MA: Blackwell Publishing, 2001), 412.

implicit central banker and made extensive loans to assist in the colony's reconstruction after the Japanese World War II occupation. Hong Kong established trading companies also facilitated the colony's transition from entrepôt or transshipment trade—where goods are imported, stored, and traded with no or little additional processing and no customs duties—to local manufacturing and exports.[219]

Established Hong Kong hongs and entrepreneurial local capitalists diversified the Hong Kong economy together and industrialized the colony without the overt support from a developmentally oriented state. What the state mostly did was levy minimal taxes and stay out of the way. This private capital and local entrepreneurial capability were not present in the same abundance in the other four Fast Followers. In each, a more directive state facilitated the early industrialization process. Early on, the establishment of world-class economic capacity typically requires the attention of a growth-oriented state primarily focused on helping its economic agents find their place in the global productive order. Given the learning and resources required, this is unlikely to occur if left to the market alone.

This is the same logic that precipitated the imposition of high tariffs in the United States in the latter part of the nineteenth and early twentieth centuries. Though protection in a closed market was provided for industry in America's early industrialization, the level of assistance was not nearly as comprehensive as that offered by Fast Follower development states to their private sector agents. Moreover, Fast Followers also relied upon open access to the American and European markets; protected home markets with access to open foreign markets—where their production could be absorbed—were core to Fast Follower export-led successes. Having rich consumers of last resort in the United States and elsewhere buying products as fast as they could produce them is another reason why Fast Followers industrialized so much faster than the First Movers did.

---

219 Siu-kai Lau and Hsin-chi Kuan, *The Ethos of the Hong Kong Chinese*, (Sha Tin N.T., Hong Kong: Chinese University Press, 1988), 25.

First Mover and Fast Follower industrializations have now been described. Their respective successes leave a last important question: How did the quality of the economic growth attained by each group differ? This question was answered when economists discovered that the nature of economic growth changes as economies mature. That following or catch-up differs from leading is no surprise; what is surprising is how clearly the macroeconomic data shows this to be so.

Fast Follower Economic Success: Growth Begets Growth as Inputs Accumulate

Malthusian versus Solow technologies were coined to account for the unprecedented growth in living standards enjoyed by industrialized nations. Malthusian technology anchored in the diminishing returns and negative feedback that prevailed in the Pre-Industrial Era, and Solow technology explained the economic growth that achieved continual technological progress as well as the concept of "growth begets growth" in the Industrial Era.[220]

Solow technologies developed from the work of Robert M. Solow, 1987 Economics Nobel laureate for his work on economic growth. Solow suggested economic growth emerged from two sources: either from adding inputs (by increasing the number of workers employed through adding labor or adding to the capital stock with buildings, factories, roads, etc.) or from increases in output per unit of input, which Solow called technical progress (not the result of adding inputs, but from improving efficiency by applying new methods, better organization, or new ways to organize, etc.).

Economic performance data gathered by Solow showed 87.5 percent of the increase in gross output per man-hour in America from 1909 to 1949 was attributable to technological progress; changes in capital and labor (inputs) explained only 12.5 percent of the increase. Solow's tech-

220 Gary D. Hansen and Edward C. Prescott, "Malthus to Solow," *American Economic Review* 92, no. 4 (September 2002): 1205.

nological change was popularized as Solow's residual because it represented the portion of change in economic output not explained by the input variables measured.

In social science, when models set out to explain changes in an independent variable (e.g., economic output) based on changes in a set of measured dependent variables (e.g., additions of capital and labor), the dependent variables typically do not explain all the variance seen in the independent variable, meaning that a portion of the variance remains unexplained or unaccounted for. Solow discovered that knowing how capital and labor inputs changed over 40 years in the United States explained little of its change in output. He concluded that in the United States, most output growth was not explained by additions of capital and labor alone (i.e., inputs), but by an unmeasured residual (i.e., technical progress).[221]

Growth economists now call this "missing" residual total factor productivity (TFP), though it has also been called multifactor productivity, or less favorably, the measure of our ignorance (i.e., the measure of latent variables yet to be specified). In Chapters 4 and 5, TFP is referred to as innovation. As is explained especially in Chapter 5, the only way Leaders remain leading is by doing what others have not yet done (i.e., by innovating).

Important is when economists applied Solow's methods to explain the impressive Fast Follower growth in the mid-to-late twentieth century, radically different results emerged. Early growth in Singapore, Hong Kong, South Korea, and Taiwan was explained by increases in capital and labor (i.e., by increases in measured inputs) and not by any latent variable captured in technical progress (Solow's residual or TFP). Young, among the first to report this unexpected finding, summarized the Fast Follower dashes for growth as follows:

---

221 Robert M. Solow, "Technical Change and the Aggregate Production Function," *The Review of Economics and Statistics* 39, no. 3 (August 1957): 312–20. Solow's thinking was also presented in an earlier paper: Robert M. Solow, "A Contribution to the Theory of Economic Growth," *The Quarterly Journal of Economics* 70, no. 1 (February 1956): 65–94.

> This paper documents the fundamental role played by factor accumulation in explaining the extraordinary postwar growth of Hong Kong, Singapore, South Korea, and Taiwan. Participation rates, educational levels, and (excepting Hong Kong) investment rates have risen rapidly in all four economies. In addition, in most cases there has been a large intersectoral transfer of labor into manufacturing, which has helped fuel growth in that sector. Once one accounts for the dramatic rise in factor inputs, one arrives at estimated total factor productivity growth rates that are closely approximated by the historical performance of many of the OECD and Latin American economies. While the growth of output and manufacturing exports in the newly industrializing countries of East Asia is virtually unprecedented, the growth of total factor productivity in these economies is not.[222]

Other findings supported Young's. Nobel laureate Paul Krugman even compared the growth achieved by the four Fast Followers to the early growth of the Soviet Union:

> Asian growth, like that of the Soviet Union in its high-growth era, seems to be driven by extraordinary growth in inputs like labor and capital rather than by gains in efficiency. Consider, in particular, the case of Singapore. Between 1966 and 1990, the Singaporean economy grew a remarkable 8.5 percent per annum, three times faster than the United States; per capita income grew at a 6.6 percent rate, roughly doubling every decade. This achievement seems to be a kind of economic miracle. But the miracle turns out to have been based on perspiration rather than inspiration: Singapore grew through a mobilization of resources that would have done Stalin proud.[223]

Decomposing economic growth sources into measurable, input-based factors versus harder-to-measure latent variables and pointing out that growth in the four Fast Followers is mostly explained by input accumulation may seem arcane and pedantic, but this result aligns squarely

222 Alwyn Young, "The Tyranny of Numbers: Confronting the Statistical Realities of the East Asian Growth Experience," *The Quarterly Journal of Economics* 110, no. 3 (August 1995): 641.
223 Paul Krugman, "The Myth of Asia's Miracle," *Foreign Affairs* 73, no. 6 (November–December 1994): 70.

with the characteristics of industrialization detailed in this book. As this chapter points out, industrialization is capital and labor intensive. Further, as Fast Follower industrialization was driven principally by "borrowing technology or 'learning,'" most Fast Follower accomplishments were based on the replication of what had already been done and not on new technological innovation. That the growth was input-led simply confirms this and so provides additional proof that Fast Followers were in fact following.

Catch-up is accomplished by mobilizing resources and copying, and for as long as it takes to accomplish this task (somewhere between one to three generations), high input-led growth and minimal innovation-led growth drive progress. Because diminishing returns are eventually encountered, however, once catch-up is accomplished, the balance shifts, and growth becomes more dependent on gains in efficiency than on additional input accumulation alone. In Krugman's words, "inspiration" (innovation) and not "perspiration" is needed.

For a clearer explanation of this logic, consider the following: compared with its neighbor Mexico, America has more roads, airports, and ports constructed; more businesses established; and the majority of its population housed, educated, and employed. Houses also have sufficient TVs, refrigerators, and ranges, with new housing formation needing population growth, which is low. Sustained long-term growth from adding infrastructure, building new houses, establishing new businesses using existing technologies, or adding to the education of an already well-educated workforce is unlikely. Growth in America's fully employed competitive economy will only emerge from innovation and the development of new ways to offer better products and services (more output per unit of input) or through offering new products unavailable in the market.

By contrast, in Mexico, growth can still be sustained by constructing infrastructure not yet in place; by building houses for those without them; by supplying TVs, refrigerators, and automobiles to those yet to possess them; and by educating the undereducated so they find jobs and add to economic output, and so forth. Under such conditions Mexico's growth will remain mostly input-led and driven by capital and labor accumulation, while American growth will rely on gains in efficiency and innovation. Mexico has years to follow before catching up. For America to grow and continue leading, however, inspiration rather than perspiration is required.

How the sources of growth evolve as economies mature is shown in Table 8, which reports on the sources explaining the economic growth of the East Asian newly industrializing countries (NICs) and the G5 industrialized countries over three time periods: pre-1973, 1974 to 1985, and post-1985. To underscore its unique position, Japan's results are reported separately from the other non-Asian G5 countries, reducing the remaining group to the G4 (United States, Great Britain, France, and West Germany). Results for China are included for comparative purposes.

The data in Table 8 is from a study that relied upon three measurable dependent variables to predict changes in real GDP output growth, two being the familiar tangible capital and labor, and the third, human capital (a new input variable), included to determine if changes in the years of formal education explained changes in the independent variable.[224] These three dependent variables reflect input-led growth, and as in all the other growth-accounting studies, technical progress (i.e., TFP, or Solow's residual) was the fourth missing variable accounted for in the study.

---

224 Lawrence J. Lau, "The Sources of East Asian Economic Growth Revisited" (mimeograph, Department of Economics, Stanford University, California, 2004). In an earlier paper, Lau and Kim compared the growth in the United States, Great Britain, West Germany, Japan, and France (the G5 countries) with the economic growth in Singapore, Hong Kong, Taiwan, and South Korea (the East Asian NICs) from after World War II until 1990. They found that input-led capital accumulation was by far the greatest driver of growth for East Asian NICs, accounting for between 48 and 72 percent of their economic growth, while for G5 industrialized countries, technical progress or innovation-led growth played the bigger role, accounting for 46–71 percent of their economic growth (Jong Il-Kim and Lawrence J. Lau, "The Sources of Economic Growth of the East Asian Newly Industrialized Countries," *Journal of the Japanese and International Economies* 8, no. 3 [September 1994]: 235–71). These findings display a similar pattern to that seen in Table 8 and corroborate Young's findings discussed earlier.

Table 8: Sources of Economic Growth: Hong Kong, Singapore, South Korea, Taiwan, China, Japan, and Non-Asian G5 Industrialized Countries

	Sample Period	Tangible Capital	Labor	Human Capital	Technical Progress/ TFP
Pre-1973					
Hong Kong	1966–73	68.37	28.50	3.13	00.00
Singapore	1964–73	55.59	40.18	4.22	00.00
South Korea	1960–73	72.60	21.87	5.53	00.00
Taiwan	1953–73	80.63	15.45	3.91	00.00
China	1965–73	85.29	10.36	4.35	00.00
Japan	1957–73	55.01	4.85	1.06	39.09
Non-Asian G5	1957–73	41.50	6.00	1.43	51.07
1974–1985					
Hong Kong	-	64.31	32.73	2.96	00.00
Singapore	-	64.68	31.72	3.60	00.00
South Korea	-	78.08	18.10	3.81	00.00
Taiwan	-	78.91	18.12	2.97	00.00
China	-	80.46	14.64	4.90	00.00
Japan	-	40.65	10.22	0.96	48.17
Non-Asian G5	-	36.29	–14.55	2.53	75.73
Post-1985					
Hong Kong	1986–95	41.81	6.46	1.58	50.14
Singapore	1986–95	37.01	31.30	1.52	30.17
South Korea	1986–95	44.54	14.98	1.75	38.73
Taiwan	1986–95	43.00	10.46	1.38	45.16
China	1986–95	86.39	10.34	3.27	00.00
Japan	1986–94	38.21	2.47	1.17	58.14
Non-Asian G5	1986–94	27.14	13.83	1.58	57.45

Source: Lau, "The Sources of East Asian Economic Growth Revisited."

Table 8 shows that in the first two periods, input accumulation alone explains growth in the four Fast Followers. The multiple 00.00 values for technical progress in the last column for these two periods confirm this. Post-1985, however, for these four Fast Followers, between 30.17 to 50.14 percent of their growth's variance is explained by TFP. For four of the five developing economies as time passes—and especially between the second and third periods—the contribution of input-led growth declines and TFP increases, though in the third period (excluding Hong Kong), input-led growth still explains more of the growth variance than does TFP. For non-Asian G5 countries, TFP always explains more growth than do the three (measured) input variables, regardless of the period controlled for.

Table 8 also provides important insights into the positioning of Japan. As a more developed than developing country caught between the First Movers ahead of it and the other Fast Followers behind it, that technical progress accounts for some Japanese growth in every time period is unsurprising. Moreover, as the last of the G5 to fully industrialize, that input-led growth contributes more than technical progress in the first two time periods is also to be expected. During these times, Japan was still more catching up than leading. This data confirms Japan's earlier placement in these pages as either the first Fast Follower or the last First Mover. Over the second half of the twentieth century, economically it has characteristics that matched both groups of industrializers, and it was only post-1985 that its economic growth from TFP finally exceeded the non-Asian G5.

Note, too, that in each successive period, the contribution of input-led growth for Japan decreased proportionately, while growth due to TFP increased. In the post-1985 period, 58.14 percent of Japanese growth is explained by TFP, a proportion greater than the average of the G5 countries (57.45 percent). By this time Japan was a fully-fledged member of the world's leading economies, and its proportional TFP contribution confirms this to be so. Japan was no longer following and relying on input-led growth; it was leading. Commensurate with this status is the ability to drive growth through TFP or innovation-led growth rather than from adding inputs only.

Corresponding with its status as a newly industrializing country in the earlier stage of its fast dash for growth, China's growth being accounted for by input accumulation alone repeats the pattern followed by the East Asian

NICs Fast Followers before it. China, with at times the highest savings rate in the world (and controlled by an ADR pursuing export-led growth on a basis similar to the East Asian NICs), can attribute over 80 percent of its growth to the addition of tangible capital. None of the country's growth is associated with TFP. In addition, because of China's relatively low-level development (like Mexico, as explained previously), this input-led growth will likely suffice for the foreseeable future. It will take at least one if not two more generations for Chinese infrastructure to be fully formed, for all Chinese to be educated, for the Chinese housing stock to be fully built, and for all Chinese consumers to acquire the goods and services middle-class life allows.

Distinguishing input-led growth from innovation-led growth and identifying the patterns reflected in Table 8 also reconcile how First Movers continue growing while Fast Followers catch up. Though achieving lower economic growth rates than Fast Followers did (to be expected as First Mover economies matured), First Movers nevertheless continued innovating while Fast Followers replicated their steps, and the relatively high proportion of TFP enjoyed by First Movers avoided the specter of diminishing returns and kept their economies growing. Technical progress remained the dominant driver of First Mover growth after World War II and underscores from an economic growth perspective that Leading quantitatively and qualitatively differs from Following.

Industrialization's core characteristics and the challenges facing societies as they industrialize are now more clearly articulated, and the paths nations have followed to industrialize have been described. In this analysis the First Movers and later Leaders have been differentiated from the Fast Followers/Followers, and why the imperative of continuing to lead while others follow is suggested as the basis of the ongoing human struggle for productivity is justified.

Yet, industrialization is only one element of a more widespread process negotiated in the ascent to a stable, productive, economically diversified nation. This process of nation-building and industrialization's role in it concludes this chapter, drawing again from lessons that First Mover and Fast Follower experiences offer. In the twenty-first century, Failures or Followers will only complete the task if they fully understand nation-building.

A comment on nation-building as a concept is first warranted. The construct is most often applied to the resuscitation of failed states, often through foreign intervention:

> Nation-building, as it is commonly referred to in the United States, involves the use of armed force as part of a broader effort to promote political and economic reforms with the objective of transforming a society emerging from conflict into one at peace with itself and its neighbors.[225]

Nation-building is not as narrowly construed in these pages. Built nations in these pages are those that have joined the community of prosperous, stable nation-states through their building of modern industrialized economies. Peace within and without are only starting conditions that must be in place before the longer-term process of economic nation-building can commence and be accomplished. Based on this broader conceptualization, the American interventions in Iraq and Afghanistan in the first two decades of the twenty-first century were not concerned about nation-building as explained here. They were concerned about establishing stability (as defined in the next section) so that nation-building might begin in earnest in either nation.

Further, no nation has ever been built by foreigners or by foreign intervention. As the coverage of Fast Follower industrializations shows, foreign engagement may assist at the margin as a nation industrializes and diversifies its economy. But if Iraq is to be industrialized and built, this effort must be driven by Iraqis for Iraqis in Iraq. Iraqi leadership is required to establish how its country is able to engage economically with the world and, on the basis of this engagement, start to sell to the world.

---

225 James Dobbins et al., *The Beginner's Guide to Nation-Building* (Santa Monica, CA: RAND Corporation, 2007), xvii.

From there, it may buy from the world and begin the task of forming and investing surplus in input-led growth that will permit it to follow and begin the generations-long task of catching up.

The decisions needed to implement this process should not be made by outsiders, as well intentioned as they may be. These will likely face mistrust if they come from foreigners, and in the anvil of the harsh trade-offs inevitably faced as a nation moves from Failure to Follower, they may be abandoned or ignored as foreign conspiracies as the heat increases. More importantly, outsiders especially from the industrialized world may not know what is best for a failing nation. They may be biased toward what works for them and may even be in the country to promote interests other than those of the country itself. Years spent learning of the resources available and a country's cultural heritage are usually required. Temporary sojourners parachuted in will likely be insufficient.

The Economic Nation-Building Virtual Cycle: Maintaining Stability and Achieving Growth, Then Fostering Development

The interaction among three factors captures the long-term economic nation-building process. These factors are stability, growth, and development, depicted in the economic nation-building triangle in Figure 8.

Figure 8: The Economic Nation-Building Triangle

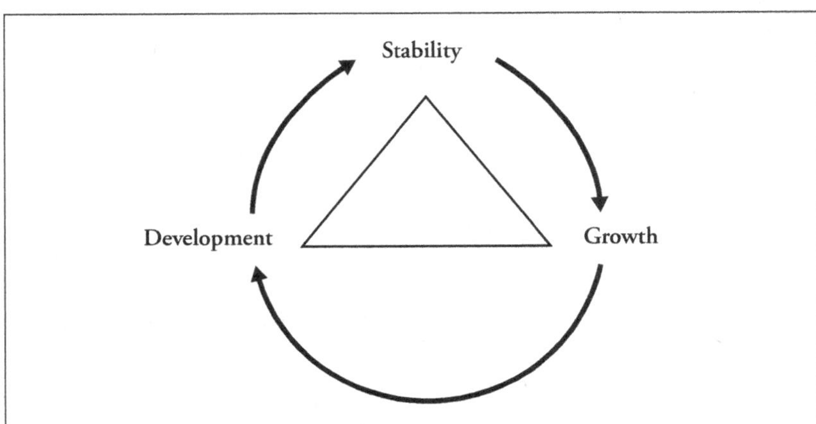

Stability refers to a variety of subconstructs: from political stability that enables laws to be passed and enforced; to physical and personal stability so industrial leaders can form capital and build businesses and industrial workers can work within them without fear of persecution, physical threat, or harm; to legal stability that permits contracts to be honored without capricious intervention from corrupt interests demanding payment for little or no value in exchange. Growth captures the subject of this chapter: economic growth and industrial diversification as industrialization proceeds. As a central component of economic nation-building, industrialization builds diverse, productive economies; lifts labor productivity and offers gainful employment; and generates the wealth to fund public expenditures. Development refers to how those excluded from economic participation are treated and invested in so that their marginalization is eliminated or kept at tolerable levels.

Early on, the rising industrial tide does not lift all ships; how have-nots that remain at the periphery as industrialization occurs are dealt with is an important part of the economic nation-building challenge. When inequality gets too wide, instability and/or revolution is possible; development prevents such outcomes by keeping the marginalized off the streets so that stability and growth continue.

A rise in inequality and a gap between haves and have-nots is inevitable in early industrialization, and the exact time of when development must be earnestly focused on is unclear. Politics on the ground and the wealth of a society indicate when this step is feasible. What is clear is that making promises to redistribute wealth before knowing how to bake the industrial cake is irresponsible. Wealth must be created to be redistributed, and if this is not done, what likely will occur is hyperinflation as too much money chases too few goods. Regardless, the impoverished will remain marginalized and angry.

Until recently, theorists held that economic growth automatically trickled down so unequal living standards across societies over time diminished on their own. This is incorrect:

> The experience of the 1950s and 1960s, when many developing nations did reach their economic growth targets but the levels of living of the masses of people remained for the most part unchanged, signaled that something was very wrong with this narrow definition of development. . . . In short, during the 1970s, economic development came to be redefined in terms of the reduction or elimination of poverty, inequality, and unemployment within the context of a growing economy.[226]

Should economic growth not noticeably improve the living standards of a large proportion of a society, policy to redress the situation is required. Development focuses on this need.

Readers must recognize that the use of the word *development* here differs from the earlier use of the word to describe ADRs. ADRs are not chiefly concerned about the welfare needs of the poor or economically marginalized in early industrialization. They are concerned more about the development of modern, diversified, high-growth economies. *Development* in this context relates to accomplishing economic growth. The concern for welfare and meeting basic needs is subordinated to the imperative of building a sustainable modern economy and getting the growth job done. Another metaphor for authoritarian developmentalists could be benevolent dictators or those who use autocratic power to build sustainable modern economies.

The placement of stability, growth, and development and the directional arrows in Figure 8 indicate the influence and interaction among the three variables. Stability is at the top, as without it little else occurs. American so-called nation-building efforts in Iraq and Afghanistan in the early 2000s underscore this placement. After the deposition of Saddam Hussein, civil conflict persisted in Iraq, meaning that from their arrival in 2003 and until the end of the decade, American military forces mostly focused on helping the country gain stability. Though steps to improve the country's infrastructure and economic conditions were taken, because of the instability on the ground, little growth occurred.

---

226 Todaro and Smith, *Economic Development*, 16.

In Afghanistan, the struggle for stability was even more tenuous. A corrupt and inept government combined with a Taliban insurgency that returned to power in 2022 after the Americans withdrew has kept Afghanis insecure and worried about their future. Afghanistan still awaits stability, and until this condition is reached, growth will remain in the wings. For these reasons, stability is placed at the top of the triangle, with the directional arrow first flowing from stability to growth.

With stability in place, economic growth begins in earnest, explained by growth's location at the triangle's bottom-right corner. Moreover, if the First Mover and Fast Follower experiences are instructive, at least two generations (50 years) but often more are needed to build fully diversified industrial economies. Much of this time early on is characterized by deferred gratification and hard work as surplus is invested in infrastructure and economic capital and as the ability to produce is learned and the production task is mastered. Following, even if fast, takes decades, if not generations.

Further, if the lessons of the Fast Followers are indicative, plan-rational states with the prime objective to assist and guide the industrialization process are optimal initially. Ideally, these plan-rational states should implement industrial strategies that take into account their country's starting conditions and productive resources. The earlier coverage of the industrial policies adopted by Fast Followers provides insights into the industrial policy approaches followed by these nations in their industrialization efforts.

Development is placed on the bottom-left corner of the triangle to indicate the directionality from stability to growth to development. Recall that the sequential hypothesis best explains both the First Mover and the Fast Follower industrializations, and implicit in this is that an initial period of stability and growth is required before any redistribution (development in Figure 8's terms) at the levels of twentieth-century First Mover democracies is feasible. Redistributing too much too soon places industrialization in jeopardy, as instead of being invested in productive capacity, the surplus is consumed to meet immediate basic needs. Further, promising to redistribute the cake before possessing its ingredients or knowing how to bake it may result in unsustainable festive macroeconomic populism followed by inevitable economic collapse and enduring political instability.

The causal relationship in Figure 8 captures the reinforcing virtuous cycle among the factors: stability that for a time permits growth, followed by development as have-nots are included and provided for, which ensures more stability so that growth continues and development is sustained, and so on. Both the First Mover modern democracies and the Fast Follower political economies were built and stabilized over generations following this cycle.

A small but important clarification is, however, necessary. Though the cycle is presented as a sequence from stability to growth to development, in practice growth and development do not occur completely sequentially. Even the most growth-oriented, plan-rational states provide some development early on. Balancing the two is the important calibration. Figure 8 indicates that for industrialization to occur, stability and growth must be emphasized early on and that development is only earnestly focused on once stability and growth have dominated for a while. Given the scarcity of resources faced in early industrialization, the stark choice is to either invest the seed corn—and enjoyment arrives later—or eat the seed corn, in which case, though current food shortages are alleviated, resources next year will be diminished and growth constrained.

In new democracies where redistribution (development) is offered too soon, the longer-term opportunity cost may be too little growth, meaning development itself is eventually placed in jeopardy. This is the outcome the conflicting hypothesis predicts if industrialization and democratization—with redistributive pressures—are attempted simultaneously. Democracy of the modern distributive kind should only occur once the wealth base to support the developments costs imposed is in place.

Testing how well it describes the phenomenon it purports to explain is the best validation of a model. To this end, the economic nation-building efforts of six nations—China, Brazil, South Africa, South Korea, Singapore, and India—conclude this chapter. These six nations are at different stages of the nation-building process. China started most recently after Deng Xiaoping assumed leadership in the late 1970s, while the Brazilian and South African efforts began earlier in the mid-twentieth century. South Korea and Singapore also began their efforts around this time, but unlike South Africa and Brazil, both are now industrialized and can be considered built. India's nation-building efforts, which also began in earnest in the 1950s, show a path that the model does not recommend. Though a proud democracy, compared with the other five, India is the least economically diversified. Where India's path differed and why the country is where it is relative to the others are explained using the model's terms.

Economic Nation-Building in Practice: Six Nations and the Stability, Growth, Development Framework

China: Authoritarian Developmentalists at Work

Governed by an authoritarian regime with an objective to industrialize the country, China is the textbook example of a state that has imposed autocratic stability while encouraging the growth required during early industrialization. The fastest industrialization on record, this achievement has taken place as Figure 8 predicts. Political freedom and democracy have been suppressed, and little redistribution of the development form has been promised or offered. As all Fast Followers did before it, China is industrializing first; if democracy follows, it will occur later. Authorities in China have mostly been concerned about two imperatives: maintaining stability and ensuring economic growth.

Moreover, as long as the Communist Party creates jobs and improves material choices, the Chinese people will likely stay off the streets awaiting their chance to join the human struggle for productivity and lift their living standards. The Chinese government's hold on power mostly depends on whether it keeps economic growth high enough to create jobs that employ Chinese workers. Bureaucrats across the country are promoted according to how efficiently they create jobs. Development is not a priority. Commensurate with the sequential hypothesis and in line with Figure 8, at this time, keeping stability and maintaining growth is.

> China has no choice but to retain economic growth as its top priority—in order to provide employment, particularly for surplus farmers and laid off workers; if the country cannot sustain employment, social disintegration looms.[227]

Moreover, Chinese authoritarians are also conscious of the Mandate of Heaven, an age-old Chinese philosophy that holds rulers may lose their mandate if ruling irresponsibly:

> An emperor's ability to rule was said to reflect the cosmic sanction bestowed on his reign by tianming, or the "mandate of heaven," which Chinese believed was signified by peace and harmony within his realm. Traditional political philosophers held that moral legitimacy was a vital component of tianming and that if the moral bonds between ruler and ruled were irrevocably violated, the all-embracing forces of "heaven" from which an emperor drew his "mandate" to rule as "the son of heaven" would be withheld and his dynasty would collapse. Before such a fall, it was believed that "heaven" would signal its displeasure with such portents as natural disasters and popular rebellions.[228]

The Chinese people do have ways to express discontent with autocratic leaders.

---

227 Robert L. Kuhn, *How China's Leaders Think: The Inside Story of China's Past, Current and Future Leaders*, rev. ed. (Singapore: John Wiley & Sons [Asia], 2011), 125.
228 Orville Schell, *Mandate of Heaven: The Legacy of Tiananmen Square and the Next Generation of China's Leaders* (New York: Simon & Schuster 1995), 21.

CHAPTER 3

Brazil and South Africa: After Stability and Growth, Transitions to Democracy Underway

Both Brazil and South Africa are beyond the authoritarian regimes that governed their early stability and growth, and their nascent democracies show how development increases after stability and growth have been traversed and the transition to democracy begins. Their data, like those of the Fast Followers and First Movers before them, supports the sequential hypothesis.

Between 1950 and 1980, Brazil was among the world's fastest-growing economies, all under military dictatorship. Growth was most impressive under President Médici.

> If repression was the Médici government's gravest liability in international opinion, the economic boom was its greatest asset. Observers both in Brazil and abroad agreed that rapid growth was "legitimizing" the regime, especially in the eyes of the middle class. . . . Economic growth under Médici was the highest sustained rate since the 1950s. GDP rose at an annual average of 10.9 percent from 1968 through 1974.[229]

Similar to the Chinese authoritarian developmentalist state, Brazil's dictatorship gained legitimacy by presiding over strong economic growth. Brazil was chided, however, by World Bank President McNamara in 1972 for ignoring its least privileged in favor of a small, emerging middle class, and by the early 1990s Brazil had the unfortunate distinction of being among the world's most unequal societies. The 1950s to the 1980s was Brazil's time of stability and growth; little development occurred over this time.

Following a return to democracy in the late 1980s, but only after economic stabilization in the 1990s and the election of President Luiz Inácio Lula da Silva in 2002 (known locally as Lula), the move toward

---

229 Thomas E. Skidmore, *The Politics of Military Rule in Brazil, 1964–85* (New York: Oxford University Press, 1988), 138.

development began. Introduction of the Bolsa Família Program was the most powerful early evidence of this shift.

> The Bolsa Família Program (BFP) was created in October 2003, through the merger of four preexisting cash transfer programs in an effort to improve efficiency and coherence of the social safety net and to scale up assistance to provide universal coverage of Brazil's poor. The program provides transfers ranging from R$15 to R$95 (US$7–45) per month to poor families. Like other conditional cash transfers (CCTs), the BFP seeks to help (a) reduce current poverty and inequality, by providing a minimum level of income for extremely poor families and (b) break the inter-generational transmission of poverty by conditioning these transfers on beneficiary compliance with human capital requirements (school attendance, vaccines, pre-natal visits).[230]

By 2006 the program reached over 11.2 million families and increased public social investment from 1.1 to 2.5 percent of government expenditure, about 0.5 percent of Brazilian GDP.[231]

South Africa's pattern is similar. The country's highest economic growth was over the 1960s when apartheid was at its worst.

> The 1960s proved to be "one the most prosperous decades in South Africa's history," with the economy growing at 5.5% per annum, among the highest growth rates in the world. . . . Fixed direct investment (FDI) more than doubled between 1960 and 1972 to benefit from protectionism, and accounted for nearly 30% of investment in manufacturing. Government and the private sector also invested in the manufacturing input sectors and, for the period between 1946 and 1975, annual growth in manufacturing output grew from 4.5% to

230 Kathy Lindert et al., "The Nuts and Bolts of Brazil's Bolsa Família Program: Implementing Conditional Cash Transfers in a Decentralized Context" (Social Protection Discussion Paper 0709, World Bank, Washington, DC, 2007), 6.

231 Kathy Lindert, "Brazil: Bolsa Familia Program—Scaling-up Cash Transfers for the Poor," in *MfDR Principles in Action: Sourcebook on Emerging Good Practices* (Washington, DC: World Bank, 2005), 67.

> 10%, while employment grew by between 3.2% and 6.6% in most of those years.[232]

But employment growth related mostly to white South Africans; black South Africans remained unskilled and unemployed, forced to settle and exercise their political rights in the homelands that formed apartheid's cornerstone.

South Africa's so-called separate development policy was a race-based democracy: white South Africans elected a government to govern white South Africa, and black residents of South Africa elected leaders to govern 10 geographically fragmented tribal homelands, formed out of less than 15 percent of South Africa's land. Black South Africans were treated as guest workers in white South Africa and provided unskilled labor:

> Apartheid's planners determined blacks were "born to be the hewers of wood and the drawers of water," in the words of Hendrik Verwoerd, father of Apartheid. In line with this philosophy, black children were denied good education; the Apartheid government spent between four and seven times more on white pupils than it did on black.[233]

Though over the apartheid years (1948 to 1994) substantial investment in security sustained an increasingly tenuous stability, investment in road, rail, electricity, telecommunications, white education, and the building of a mostly private modern economy occurred. In addition, the isolation of the country as external anti-apartheid pressures grew resulted in projects that might otherwise not have happened (e.g., a project to convert South Africa's extensive coal reserves into oil to remedy the country's lack of oil reserves). By the early 1980s, South Africa had a functioning industrial economy envied across Africa, though it competed with Brazil for the distinction of being the most unequal society on Earth.

232 Tessa Murray and John Luiz, "South Africa: The Battle for Social and Economic Policy" (Wits Business School Case Study WBS-2008-1, Graduate School of Business Administration, University of the Witwatersrand, Johannesburg, South Africa, 2007), 2–3.

233 "Education for All," EFA Media Training Resource Kit (United Nations Educational, Scientific and Cultural Organization, 2005): 148, accessed 25 February 2023, https://unesdoc.unesco.org/ark:/48223/pf0000265988.

Nonetheless, its time of stability and growth under autocracy established the wealth base that the African National Congress (the ANC), elected in 1994 under the astute leadership of Nelson Mandela, could rely upon to sustain the transition to democracy. Not having to deal with the black majority's development needs allowed avoidance of the trade-off the conflicting hypothesis fears, and as white South Africans made up less than 20 percent of the population, their development needs did not divert enough funds to restrict early growth significantly.

Like the Fast Followers before it, and again in congruence with the sequential hypothesis, South Africa industrialized first and democratized second. In addition, and as Figure 8 predicts, after its period of stability and early growth, the transition to democracy has been accompanied by increased emphasis on development.

The post-apartheid constitution contains a bill of rights obligating the state to ensure progressive realization of every South African's right to housing, healthcare, food, water, social security, and education. Programs launched by post-apartheid governments include the Reconstruction and Development Programme in early 1994; the Growth, Employment and Redistribution Strategy in mid-1996; and Black Economic Empowerment in the early twenty-first century. Yet imbalances created over generations will not be remedied quickly:

> South Africa has in recent years passed legislation instituting the world's most rigorous form of affirmative action. The Broad-Based Black Economic Empowerment Bill strives for the "effective participation of black people in the economy" in order to achieve the "economic unity of the nation." Although the professed aims of Black Economic Empowerment (BEE) are noble, the program has achieved little success in eradicating poverty, increasing employment, or fostering overall economic growth.[234]

234 Natasa Kovacevic, "Righting Wrongs: Affirmative Action in South Africa," *Harvard International Review* 29, no. 1 (2007): 6.

The virtuous cycle of nation-building (i.e., from stability to growth to development to ensure ongoing stability so growth is maintained and development deepens) is underway in both Brazil and South Africa. But transitions to democracy are not of a flag-down, flag-up type that occurs overnight. It usually takes decades to fully consolidate democracy. Moreover, many Brazilians and South Africans will likely remain economically excluded for decades, and some may never acquire the skills needed to compete in the demanding world of twenty-first-century post-industrial capitalism and may rely on state aid for life. Keeping stability and maintaining the tenuous balance between encouraging growth while meeting the legitimate but at times overwhelming development needs of those economically marginalized is likely to dominate political discourse in both countries for at least the next generation.

Lula, in office from 2003 to 2010, presided over solid economic growth as Brazil became among the strongest and largest emerging markets. The awards of the 2014 FIFA World Cup and the 2016 Summer Olympics are testimony to its rising standing. But the economy lagged under successor Dilma Rousseff, impeached by the Brazilian Congress in 2016 after being in power since 2011. Conservative president Jair Bolsonaro became Brazil's thirty-eighth president in 2019 and was narrowly defeated by Lula, who returned to office in January 2023. But indicative of the political turmoil, Lula was convicted of accepting bribes and was jailed in 2018–19, though his conviction was overturned in 2021. Bolsonaro represented a force more for growth than development, while Lula is the opposite.

South Africa's progress since democratizing has been even more tumultuous. As in Brazil, imbalances in resource allocation, opportunities, and public services continue to plague the country with corruption and poor political leadership, meaning those at the bottom of the ladder have seen little progress since the ANC gained power in 1994. After improving conditions in its first two decades in power, in the past decade progress has stagnated. The South African 2021 unemployment rate reached 35.3 percent; 66.5 percent of youths between 15 and 24 were unemployed.[235]

Of more concern, South Africa is now the most unequal nation in the world,[236] and in the 2021 local municipal elections, ANC support fell below 50 percent for the first time ever. Political instability and complicated coalition politics are likely over the coming years. Regardless, South Africa is failing in both growth and development and faces an uncertain and possibly even more unstable future when even its stability might again be in jeopardy.

South Korea and Singapore: Stability to Growth to Development to Stability and So On, but Singapore Differs

Like Brazil and South Africa, the initial dashes for growth in South Korea and Singapore were accomplished under authoritarian states that maintained stability and promoted growth as early industrialization was accomplished, and their experiences offer additional detail to enrich Figure 8's nation-building model. For example, the decades-long South Korean industrial policy exposed the country to moral hazard, and the unintended consequences of years of misdirected policy came home to roost in the late 1990s. The difficulties faced by South Korea should warn every authoritarian developmentalist state. Just as good government policy enriches all, poor policy costs are borne by all too. Regardless of these mistakes, South Korea was immeasurably better off after its period of authoritarian growth than it was before, and after a period of restructuring, the country's economy continued to grow under a consolidating democracy.

While South Korea's lessons might be extracted from its failure, Singapore's lessons are derived from its success. Unlike Brazil, South Africa, and South Korea, the country did not face a transition from

---

235 World Bank, "The World Bank in South Africa," accessed February 26, 2023, https://www.worldbank.org/en/country/southafrica/overview.

236 *The World Factbook*, "Gini Index Coefficient—Distribution of Family Income," Central Intelligence Agency, accessed February 28, 2023, https://www.cia.gov/the-world-factbook/field/gini-index-coefficient-distribution-of-family-income/country-comparison.

autocracy to democracy after its initial period of stability and growth. The city-state provides one of the few examples of a seamless transition from stability to growth to development under a mostly authoritarian developmentalist regime and offers insights into maintaining the balance between growth and development in early industrialization. Singapore also provides an alternative perspective on how democracy may consolidate in Asia; its template may be more instructive for China than any in the West or other developed nations.

To support its industrialization efforts, Singapore's leadership took steps to ensure "good" government was institutionalized across every level of government and that the best and the brightest were recruited to staff important government positions:

> Lee Kuan Yew's opinions on bribery and corruption are unambiguous. He is appalled by some Third World leaders' acquisition on a vast scale of wealth for their families and themselves. . . . After the PAP became the government, it stiffened the rules in corruption cases in the prosecution's favor; for instance, it allowed the courts to treat proof that accused persons were living beyond their means, or were unable to explain the possession of property, as evidence that bribery had occurred. . . . The primary reason for Singapore having the highest salaries for ministers and top civil servants is to attract and retain meritocratic candidates. However, a subsidiary reason is to eliminate the smallest temptation to be corrupt.[237]

This is opposite to the outcomes in South Africa and Brazil.

The industries, products, and competitive advantages upon which South Korean industrial policy was based are reported in Tables 5 and 7. At the core of the policy was an implicit contract between the state and the chaebol: the government provided low-cost loans, bank guarantees, suppressed labor unions to keep wages down, and allowed the exchange rate to depreciate to maintain favorable terms of trade, and the chaebol

---

237 Diane K. Mauzy and R. S. Milne, *Singapore Politics Under the People's Action Party* (New York: Routledge, 2002), 6.

produced exportable goods in alignment with the industries targeted. Protected internal markets provided safe harbor for catch-up, and access to American and European markets provided the purchasing power and scale to amortize the setup cost. But chaebol's unfocused, debt-driven expansion eventually became unsustainable, and by the late 1980s moral hazard was endemic:

> With little chance of bankruptcy, the chaebols were given strong incentives to keep expanding without carefully considering their investment returns and risks. They could easily borrow as much as they wanted from financial institutions, often using cross guarantees. . . . As a result, a few chaebols with very high financial leverage began governing huge portions of the country's resources, operating under the "too big to fail" doctrine.[238]

Further, by this time America was demanding South Korea open its market to foreign competition, and the perfect storm was completed by pressures added in the transition to democracy underway in the country. The assassination of President Park in 1979 after 17 years of military dictatorship initiated a move toward democracy, and consistent with a predictable shift in emphasis from growth to development, the *Wall Street Journal* reported in 1989:

> The democratically elected government doesn't want to coddle chaebol any longer because it is confronted with new demands. Voters want a better standard of living, and the government is responding by spending less on supporting the chaebol and more on social-welfare programs, housing and highways. It also has allowed labor to organize.[239]

No longer favored children of an authoritarian regime, the chaebol needed restructuring. That they could operate under state support and

238 Dong-Se Cha, "The Korean Economy in the New Millennium: Reform or Revival?," chap. 3 in *Korea's Economic Prospects: From Financial Crisis to Prosperity*, ed. O. Yul Kwon and William Shepherd (Northhampton, MA: Edward Elgar Publishing, 2001), 41.
239 Damon Darlin, "Tougher Times: Korea's Goldstar Faces a Harsh New World Under Democracy," *Wall Street Journal*, November 8, 1989.

protection was clear; competing under their own steam in a world of innovation, specialization, dispersed value chains, and open global competition was less clear. Unfortunately, most could not, but change still proved difficult; a cat-and-mouse battle between the chaebol and the South Korean government persisted until the 1997 Asian crisis intervened. The crisis provided the opportunity for deeper reform, though costs were high. By December 1997, South Korea's external debt had reached US$159 billion and economic growth had plummeted to –7 percent, and in early 1998 unemployment exceeded 8 percent, up from less than 3 percent in the early 1990s.[240]

Explanations for South Korea's difficulties vary. Conventional wisdom held a corrupt, state-directed economy that needed opening and deregulation caused the failure. Here, creation of an open and market-based economy through the liberalization of finance, international trade, and labor markets was the favored prescription. A counter explanation asserted underregulation—not overregulation—was the culprit and that poorly managed financial deregulation, abandonment of investment coordination, and poor exchange rate management were the primary causes.[241] A third placed blame on the Asian crisis that ultimately infected South Korea,[242] while a fourth, though accepting early economic development in South Korea was mainly rooted in the South Korean government's aggressive role, placed blame on "heavily indebted Chaebol (conglomerates), labor- and capital-market rigidities, high concentration on a few industries, inefficient financial systems, inadequate infrastructure, and corruption."[243] This study also noted "carefully sequenced 'target shifting' and 'constant upgrading' by government were the ultimate sources of Korea's outstanding economic performance in

240 Jai S. Mah, "Economic Restructuring in Post-crisis Korea," *The Journal of Socio-Economics* 35, no. 4 (2006): 682–90.

241 Ha-Joon Chang, "Korea: The Misunderstood Crisis," *World Development* 26, no. 8 (August 1998): 1555–61.

242 Frederick I. Nixson and Bernard Walters, "The Asian Crisis: Causes and Consequences," *The Manchester School* 67, no. 5 (September 1999), 496–523.

243 Yoon Heo, "Development Strategy in Korea Reexamined: An Interventionist Perspective," *Social Science Journal* 38, no. 2 (Summer 2001): 217–31.

the early stages of development,"[244] underscoring that government policy started on the right path but later lost its way. A lesson from South Korea is that as a nation's people stand up, the government should put in place measures for it to stand down.

The contradiction in explanations for South Korea's failures reveal the deep ideological divide between supporters of state-led versus market-led industrializations, a division captured in the distinction between market-rational versus plan-rational states noted previously. Proponents of market-based initiatives, most in advanced industrial countries, typically favor the Washington Consensus as the ideal model.[245] Proponents of state-led initiatives argue directed government assistance is required to facilitate industrialization.

Debating which ideology is correct is neither helpful nor necessary; events over the past 50 years across the Fast Followers—and including China—have shown that both good government and market-based agents and institutions play important roles in industrialization. Both are necessary; neither is sufficient.

In four of the five Fast Followers (Hong Kong excepted), plans and markets fostered industrialization, though even in these exemplary cases, some plans were flawed. A central challenge of early industrialization is to know which plans to follow and to what degree markets should be relied upon:

---

244 Heo, "Development Strategy," 217.

245 Economist John Williamson originated the Washington Consensus to note reforms Latin American regimes needed at a time of economic disarray in the region. Notably, no role for a plan-rational state was envisaged. Market opening and liberalization was preferred instead. Williamson's initial 1989 list contained 10 reforms: (1) fiscal discipline, to reign in the large budget deficits that caused balance of payment crisis and high inflation; (2) reordering of public expenditure priorities toward public goods such as education, basic healthcare, and infrastructure; (3) tax reform to encourage a broadening of the tax base and moderate marginal tax rates; (4) liberalizing interest rates and encouraging financial liberalization; (5) establishing competitive exchange rates; (6) trade liberalization, though how fast the process should be achieved was not specified; (7) liberalization of inward foreign direct investment, though comprehensive capital account liberalization was not included; (8) privatization of state-owned assets; (9) deregulation to lower barriers to entry and exit from countries; and (10) property rights encouragement, especially for those in informal sectors (John Williamson, "A Short History of the Washington Consensus," *Law and Business Review of the Americas* 15, no. 1 [2009]: 9-10, accessed 27 February 2023, https://scholar.smu.edu/cgi/viewcontent.cgi?article=1381&context=lbra).

> Once upon a time, economists believed the developing world was full of market failures, and the only way in which poor countries could escape from their poverty traps was through forceful government interventions. Then there came a time when economists started to believe government failure was by far the bigger evil, and that the best thing that government could do was to give up any pretense of steering the economy. Reality has not been kind to either set of expectations. Import substitution, planning, and state ownership did produce some successes, but where they got entrenched and ossified over time, they led to colossal failures and crises. Economic liberalization and opening up benefited export activities, financial interests, and skilled workers, but more often than not, they resulted in economy-wide growth rates (in labor and total factor productivity) that fell far short of those experienced under the bad old policies of the past.[246]

The first challenge in early industrialization is determining which plans should be followed. A second is determining when markets left to their own devices will result in sustainable economic diversification. Market failure advocates must ensure their interventions remedy the market failure and do not create new problems faced later. A third aspect of industrialization flowing from both plans and markets relates to the balance between the two as industrialization proceeds. In early industrialization, surplus is scarcest and capacities are weakest, and it is at this time that the need for an informed directive state is highest. As Figure 8 holds, the dominant concern at this time is maintaining stability and facilitating growth to diversify economically.

As economic capabilities are built and businesses are established, state influence should decline, based on the premise that as private businesses stand up, the state stands down. Any developmentalist state's ultimate measure of success is the degree to which the economic agents it empowers—be they corporations or individuals—compete on their own without need for state support or assistance. To reduce moral hazard,

246 Dani Rodrik, "Industrial Policy for the Twenty-First Century," prepared for the United Nations Industrial Development Organization (UNIDO), 2004, 1, accessed February 26, 2023, https://drodrik.scholar.harvard.edu/files/dani-rodrik/files/industrial-policy-twenty-first-century.pdf.

recipients must be aware no support is forever and that at some time they will be expected to operate without it. This was the ultimate triumph of Yew's Singapore. A sustainable industrial economy was built without much moral hazard arising, and the success also meant little change was needed to the more autocratic regime that had ruled the city-state since independence.

A final lesson from Fast Followers and First Movers is that the balance between growth and development differs across nations. At the end of the twentieth century, social welfare expenditure (a proxy for development) in Western democracies was far higher than in any Fast Follower. Using public social welfare expenditure as a percentage of GDP, four groups were noted: Hong Kong and Singapore, which spent just above 5 percent of GDP; South Korea and Taiwan, which spent about 10 percent; Japan, which allocated about 16 percent; and the remaining Western democracies, which devoted between 20 to 45 percent of GDP.[247]

In Asia, only public expenditures on education are equivalent to those in the West, and the region's lower public social welfare expenditures on the aged may be attributed to the fact that this is considered a family responsibility. Another reason for the differentials among social welfare expenditures could be that Fast Followers operate under different social contracts than the Western European democracies do; Asians may expect less from their governments. Other explanations have been presented, including a higher reliance in Fast Followers on private sector full employment so that public social welfare transfer payments are minimized or privatized. Differences in demographics also provide an explanation: younger populations face lower social welfare costs than do societies with aging populations.[248] A final explanation is based on how many remain excluded from productive work. If all in a society are

247 Didier Jacobs, "Social Welfare Systems in East Asia: A Comparative Analysis Including Private Welfare" (CASE Paper 10, Centre for Analysis of Social Exclusion, London School of Economics, London, 1998, 92).
248 Jacobs, "Social Welfare Systems in East Asia."

educated and equipped to produce and manage their resources appropriately, they should not need public benefits after retirement.

Arguably, one goal societies should strive for is to minimize the need for welfare payments as they modernize. The more independent and self-sustaining citizens are, the lower welfare support will need to be. With global competition increasing in the twenty-first century, nations with the most productive workers and the lowest carrying costs for those unable to support themselves will prevail.

India: Democratic Stability with Growth and Development Lacking, but Policy Shifts Offer Hope

India is the final example to test the validity of Figure 8's nation-building model. India differs in two key ways from Fast Followers: distributive democracy was adopted as the country's post-independence regime type; and the economic policy implemented after independence was unlike any Fast Follower. That India became a democracy is as much a result of its history and makeup as a conscious choice. At independence, the country was not a cohesive, established nation. British India as late as 1931 was made up of British territory, princely states, and French and Portuguese enclaves.[249]

Combining India into a single nation was not unlike formation of the European Union, and to accommodate its diversity, democracy was the only feasible choice. Unlike homogenous China with its long tradition of authoritarians ruling under the Mandate of Heaven (see page 184), diverse, argumentative, fragmented India could not accept an authoritarian regime at independence from the British Raj in August 1947. Instead, twentieth-century modern social democracy was chosen. With distributive democracy and industrialization wedded, India bet the complementary hypothesis held true.

As a result, economic policy in the country's first four decades of independence differed widely from Fast Follower choices: instead of

249 Niall Ferguson, *Empire*, 173.

investing surplus in input-led growth based on exports to the advanced industrial world, import substitution and local production in a protected, closed economy was chosen. The Indian government took control of the economy and followed a policy closer to the Soviet Union than to any others. And again, a result of its recent history, an independent India was deeply mistrustful of capitalism and foreign corporations; its policy became anything opposite to what Britain supported when controlling the country. Since Britain was pro capitalism and economic openness, India became closed and pro communism/socialism.

The results were disastrous—poor economic growth and "poverty, hunger, and illiteracy persisted amid abundant food stocks; much of industry remained internationally noncompetitive and required import of technology; and the public sector did not generate significant surplus and remained inefficient."[250] And failed economic policy was not the only yoke carried by India. In a social democracy facing reelection every five years, considerable effort was directed toward poverty reduction but with no success. After 40 years of independence, poverty actually increased.

> The most disappointing aspect of India's performance relates to its main objective of poverty removal. Almost every plan has had a target of removing poverty within fifteen years. And yet poverty persisted and still persists in abundant measures. Over the years a large number of antipoverty programs have been initiated, and sizeable resources have been allocated to these measures. To a great extent, these programs had not reached the poor and the money spent had largely leaked out to the not-so-poor.[251]

This was not the democracy light of Europeans and Americans in their early industrializations; instead, precious surplus for poverty reduction ended up either in the hands of corrupt democrats or was invested in small giveaways to retain political power. Choices to eat rather than invest

250 Kirit S. Parikh, "Economy," chap. 2 in *India Briefing: A Transformative Fifty Years*, ed. Marshall Bouton and Philip Oldenburg (Armonk, NY: M. E. Sharpe, 1999), 61.
251 Parikh, "Economy," 62.

the seed corn were made, even though this limited sustenance did not always reach those needing it most. The result was decades of stagnation and lost productivity in a policy regime where regulation was preferred over economic development, and the wishes of a fragmented, vested-interest-driven, economically illiterate polity dominated the overall needs of the country.

> The conventional narrative of India's post-World War II economic history begins with a disastrous wrong turn by India's first prime minister, Jawaharlal Nehru, toward Fabian socialism, central planning, and an unbelievable quantity of bureaucratic red tape. This "license raj" strangled the private sector and led to rampant corruption and massive inefficiency. As a result, India stagnated until bold neoliberal economic reforms triggered by the currency crisis of 1991.[252]

That India after three generations of democracy is far poorer than China after two of authoritarian developmentalism is further evidence to accept the conflicting hypothesis. Figure 9 shows nominal GDP per capita at OERs for each country from 1970 to 2020.[253]

---

252 J. Bradford DeLong, "India Since Independence: An Analytic Growth Narrative," chap. 7 in *In Search of Prosperity: Analytical Narratives on Economic Growth*, ed. Dani Rodrik (Princeton, NJ: Princeton University Press, 2003), 184.

253 "Comparing China and India by Economy," Statistics Times, May 16, 2021, accessed February 27, 2023, https://statisticstimes.com/economy/china-vs-india-economy.php. Source data is from the World Bank.

Figure 9: GDP per Capita (US$ OER), China versus India: 1970–2020

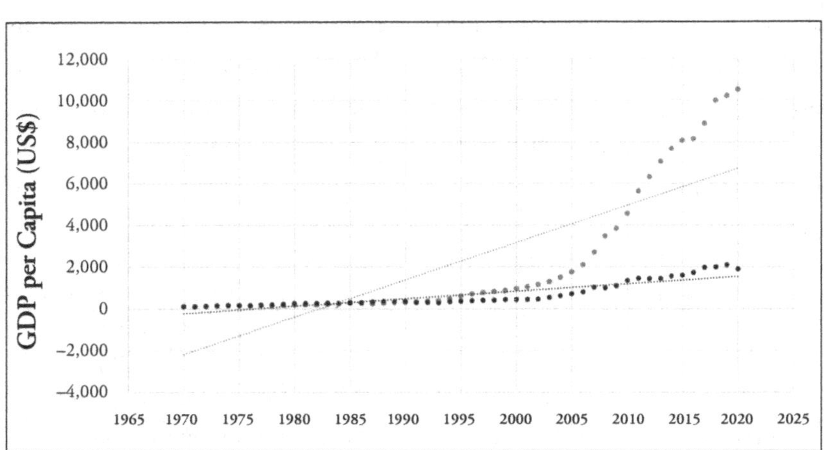

China's annual average economic growth of 8.38 percent (gray dots) compared with India's 4.22 percent (black dots) shows the impact of high growth over 50 years. In 1970, China's and India's nominal GDP per capita were US$113 and US$112, respectively. China's increased 92.92 times to reach US$10,500 in 2020, while India's reached only US$1,901, a 16.97 increase. The slope of each line in Figure 9 (in gray and black lines) conveys the difference too. Also important is Chinese GDP, like India's, remained flat until the mid-1990s, and as is typical in early industrialization, the fruits of its deferred gratification are only seen in its mid-2000s takeoff. But Indian GDP remained constrained for the two generations depicted, and though higher growth is seen post-2000, no takeoff is noted. Table 9 provides additional comparative information on the two countries, in three categories: Economics, Population, and Infrastructure. American data provides further comparison.

Table 9: India versus China: Comparative Data

	China****	India	US
Economics			
GDP (PPP)	US$24.86 tn (1)	US$9.28 tn (3)	US$21.13 tn (2)
GDP (OER)	US$14.33 tn (2)	US$2.84 tn (5)	US$21.43 tn (1)
GDP/capita (PPP)	US$17,600 (100)	US$6,600 (160)	US$63,700 (15)
Private consumption (% GDP)	39.1	59.1	68.4
Government consumption (% GDP)	14.5	11.5	17.3
Investment in capital/inventory (% GDP)	44.4	32.4	17.3
Exports (% GDP)	20.4	19.1	12.1
GDP in agriculture (%)	7.9	15.4	0.9
GDP in industry (%)	40.5	23.0	19.1
GDP in services (%)	51.6	61.5	80.0
Population			
Population	1.413 bn (1)***	1.399 bn (2)***	340 m (3)***
Population growth rate*	0.18 (181)	0.70 (128)	0.68 (130)
Urbanization: urban (% total pop.)	64.6	36.4	83.3
Life expectancy at birth (yrs.)	78.2 (77)	67.7 (192)	80.8 (48)
Literacy**	96.8	74.4	n/a
Median age	39.8 (62)	29.5 (139)	38.5 (68)
Infrastructure			
Airports	507 (13)	346 (21)	13,513 (1)
Railways (km)	150,000 (2)	65,554 (4)	293,564 (1)
Roadways (million km)	5.2 (3)	6.371 (2)	6.587 (1)
Energy consumption (m. Btu/person)	105.687 m (54)	23.231 m (132)	304.414 m (11)

Source: *The World Factbook,* "Guide to Country Comparisons," Central Intelligence Agency, accessed December 23, 2023, https://www.cia.gov/the-world-factbook/references/guide-to-country-comparisons/. Data differs from data in Table 14 given it covers different times and is from a different agency (CIA vs. IMF).

In the table, *m* indicates *millions, bn* indicates *billions,* and *tn* indicates *trillions.*

* % average annual change from births over deaths and migrants entering or leaving.

** % 15 years or over who read and write.

*** Early 2023 estimates for all three countries. India's population exceeded China's in mid-2023.

**** Dates of estimates differ; for example, China's GDP percentages in agriculture, manufacturing, and services are from 2016, while the GDP/capita estimates are from 2021. The data still remains useful for comparisons.

Table 9 provides additional evidence of China's progress relative to India. The numbers in parentheses indicate where each country is placed against all others. On a purchasing power parity (PPP) basis, China, India, and the United States are the world's three biggest economies. Using OERs, all are in the top five, with the United States reverting back to first and China to second. That China and India rank so high is because of population size and not because of widespread economic capability. With GDP/capita at US$17,600 and US$6,600 compared with America's $63,700, and with 7.9 and 15.4 percent of GDP still in agriculture compared with the American 0.9 percent, both are still developing. China will likely still take around 50 years to fully industrialize, and India may take 75 or more.

India remains far behind China in GDP/capita and urbanization, and the country's lag is also seen in infrastructure. India consumed only 23.231 million Btus/person in 2019, placing it at 132 of 212 nations. China at 54 consumed 105.687 million Btus/person in 2019, but both are still far behind the United States at 304.414 million Btus. Moreover, though Indian roadways exceed those of China in kilometers, their quality is questionable. Only 622,000 of China's 5.2 million kms of roadway are unpaved; in India, of the 6.371 million kms of roadway, only 312,000 are national highways/expressways or state highways. India also lags China in railways (65,554 versus 150,000 kms) and airports (346 versus 507). Indicative of their developing status, both are far behind America's 13,513 airports.

Many factors explain India's paucity of infrastructure investment, and primary among these is the complex, nonlinear Indian political economy and the lack of government attention paid historically to infrastructural investment.

> Beijing plows about 9% of its GDP into public works, compared with New Delhi's 4%. And because of its authoritarian government, China gets faster results. "If you have to build a road in China, just a handful of people need to make a decision," says Daniel Vasella, chief executive of pharmaceutical giant Novartis (NVS). "If you want to build a road in India, it'll take 10 years of discussion before you get a decision."
>
> Blame it partly on India's revolving-door democracy. Political parties typically hold power for just one five-year term before disgruntled

> voters, swayed by populist promises from the opposition, kick them out of office.[254]

India also lags China in life expectancy and literacy, and its median age is also 10 years younger than China's. The age and population growth rate differentials between India and China are not only a function of industrialization/urbanization differences. They also reflect policy/political economy differences. China's One Child Policy was an authoritarian solution ruthlessly imposed. Such a policy could not have been imposed in democratic India. Soon after independence, the Indian government tried to curb population growth:

> In 1952, the Indian government initiated what would become in the 1960s the largest government-sponsored family-planning program in the world. For 25 years, the government stressed the importance of family planning primarily as a way to reduce the rate of population growth. In the 1970s, however, government leaders came to realize that spending large sums of money on an elaborate family-planning program had not been effective in reducing the growth rate (still 1.8% to 2.2% as opposed to a world rate of 1.75%).[255]

Similar to its drive to reduce poverty, early government steps to curb population growth were unsuccessful too. Nonetheless (and as Table 9 shows), the population growth rate in India has since decreased to a level close to that in the United States but still exceeds China's by a wide margin.

The democratic discount feared by Conflict theorists is easily seen in India, and compared with China or other Fast Followers, its industrialization is unimpressive. ADRs with the ability and means to maintain stability and growth through an early, focused mobilization of people and capital have proved far more successful than the succession of DRs

254 Steve Hamm and Nandini Lakshman, "The Trouble with India," Bloomberg, March 19, 2007, accessed February 23, 2023, https://www.bloomberg.com/news/articles/2007-03-18/the-trouble-with-india.

255 Rosanna Ledbetter, "Thirty Years of Family Planning in India," *Asian Survey* 24, no. 7 (July 1984): 736.

that governed India after independence. Generations of Indians will be poor far longer than their Chinese counterparts. And because India has not enjoyed a time of stability and growth, its capacity to deliver development is also constrained.

Yet, all is not doom and gloom in India. A shift in economic policy starting in the late 1980s and refined in the 1990s under the government of Prime Minister P. V. Narasimha Roa and Finance Minister Manmohan Singh produced notable improvements in economic growth. From 1960 to 1980, India's growth rate of output per worker was 1.3 percent per annum, the lowest in the world except for sub-Saharan Africa. Over the 1980s and 1990s, its rate substantially exceeded all other regions but East Asia,[256] and by the 2000s, Indian GDP growth was among the highest in the world. Driven by a higher savings rate, government liberalization and deregulation, and the appearance of a globally competitive IT sector in the late 1990s and early 2000s, India recorded growth in the twenty-first century's first two decades not that far behind China's. Figure 10 provides Indian GDP growth rates from 1961 to 2021; the higher, more stable growth since the early 1990s—possibly indicative of the Great Moderation in India (pages 16–17)—is easily seen.

The reforms and liberalization started in the 1990s continued to pay off in the first two decades of the twenty-first century; under Prime Minister Narendra Modi from 2014 onward, India enjoyed impressive growth, with six of eight years exceeding 6 percent. The 2020 –6.60 percent was the COVID-19 pandemic impact; the last time a negative growth rate had been recorded was in 1979 at –5.24 percent.

256 Dani Rodrik and Arvind Subramanian, "From 'Hindu Growth' to Productivity Surge: The Mystery of the Indian Growth Transition" (working paper WP/04/77, International Monetary Fund, 2004), accessed February 23, 2023, https://www.imf.org/external/pubs/ft/wp/2004/wp0477.pdf.

Figure 10: Indian Annual GDP Growth: 1961–2021[257]

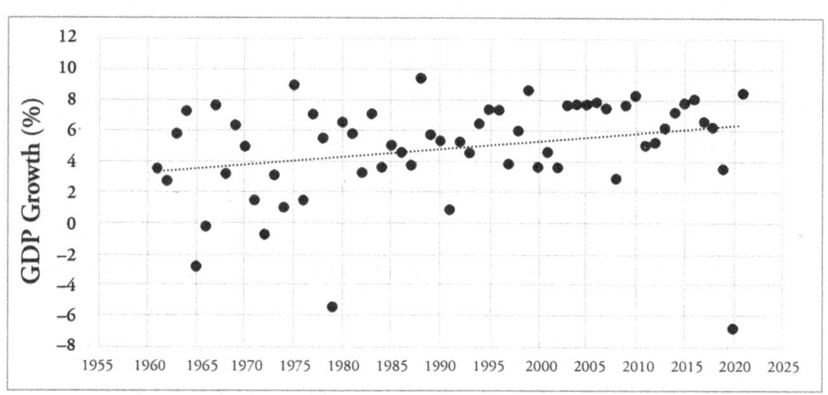

Explaining India's first 30 years of independence is uncontroversial. The conflicting hypothesis would argue the results are as to be expected from democratizing too soon. In the terms of stability, growth, and development, India had stability but too little growth and development; or to keep stability, too much development was required and the price was less growth.

Noting that in the second 30 years of independence democratic India performed closer to authoritarian China provides pause for reevaluation. In India post-independence, the regime type remained constant while economic policy changed, and it may be that economic policy is more important than regime type in early industrialization. Distributive democracy and early industrialization may have coexisted in India, provided the economic policy followed was more growth supportive.

Under such conditions, democracies with objectives to foster both development and growth—provided economic policy is followed that is supportive of both development and growth—may display slower economic growth than do authoritarian developmentalists with growth objectives alone. These democracies will still get the growth job done;

257 World Bank, "GDP Growth (Annual %)—India," accessed March 2, 2023, https://data.worldbank.org/indicator/NY.GDP.MKTP.KD.ZG?locations=IN. Annual GDP growth at market prices based on constant local currency at constant 2015 prices expressed in US dollars are provided.

the cost is a longer time to industrialize. The price of democracy may be that scarcity and poverty endure for longer. The counter to this rationale is that distributive democracy in itself may prevent the correct economic policy from being followed in early industrialization, mostly because scarce resources will always be devoted more to development than to growth as a result of the incentives that distributive democracy operates by.

Time will tell if this rationale better explains India. If over the coming decades the country's GDP growth matches China's early takeoff growth and its economy reaches world-class levels, at least one country will have shown balancing stability, growth, and development is possible under distributive democracy. But if Indian economic growth fails to take off and living standards do not improve to absorb the country's population, facts will continue to support the more conventional conflicting hypothesis explanation. India would still face the hypothesis's democratic discount; all its improved economic policy since 1990 will do is reduce the discount's extent. A 60-pound weakling would have become a 90-pound weakling, and the country would remain a struggling Follower governed by a regime unable to deliver the growth and wealth it needs.

What happens in India and China is not only important domestically: global economic growth will be deeply affected by their progress or lack thereof. In addition, because their paths were not the same, the challenges they each face differ too. While India must build infrastructure and educate more so they leave agriculture as their means of survival, China must stimulate local consumption and consume more and invest less. The choices facing these two economic giants are further considered in Chapter 5.

Prior to considering these, the emerging conditions of the post-industrial world must be revealed. As Chapter 4 describes, our struggle for productivity from the 1950s onward advanced to a new level with different rules of engagement and changed productive roles for capital and labor. For those more concerned about maintaining Leader post-industrial competitiveness in the face of rising Follower competition, the account of the Post-Industrial Era is more germane.

Conclusion and Synthesis

Industrialization is capital, labor, energy, and materials intensive and transforms Failures from agrarian subsistence to production of primary, secondary, and tertiary goods and services on a scale such that self-sustaining mass production and consumption occurs. The accumulation and investment of surplus to build the hard and soft infrastructures and the economic capital needed to resource industrialization is also essential to the process.

Deferred gratification and sacrifice are required in early industrialization, meaning that harsh trade-offs between investing for the future versus meeting immediate needs arise. As a result, modern distributive democracy is an unsuitable form of government, especially if regimes are judged by their ability to deliver immediate welfare benefits to voters every election cycle.

Ford Motor Company showed that in capital- and labor-intensive industrial factories, high volume and low variety led to high quality and low cost and that the gains to productivity enjoyed by workers doing repetitive manual work on moving assembly lines permitted employees to earn a wage to purchase the goods they were producing. Organizational innovation at crosstown rival General Motors then pioneered the professionally managed, hierarchically controlled M-form firm that emerged across the industrializing world.

Because of their availability, transportability, and efficiency, coal, oil, and natural gas provided the energy upon which industrialization is based, but clean sources of energy are now required. Facing our twenty-first-century warming world, energy that does not levy the environmental cost that fossil fuels are imposing must be found. Most importantly, and unlike those who are already industrialized, aspirant Followers must also use cleaner energy to power their industrializations.

Two groups, the First Movers and the Fast Followers, show the paths aspirant Followers may take to industrialize. Fast Followers are so named because unlike the First Movers who took six or more generations to industrialize, they industrialized in around two generations (50 years). They, and not the United States, Great Britain, or other European First Movers, are the examples Failures should study and learn from.

Not one Fast Follower negotiated its first two generations of industrialization under modern distributive democracy. Three had ADRs adopting explicit industrial policies to diversify their economies, while Hong Kong industrialized under a hands-off colonial administration following laissez-faire economic principles and relying on a cooperative business elite to build the island's economic capability.

Japan—like the Fast Followers after it—also supports the sequential hypothesis, meaning it industrialized before it democratized. Dealing with defeat and ready to defer gratification, the country pioneered the producer-oriented, export-led industrial policy that other Fast Followers adopted to industrialize.

Fast Followers also have some characteristics similar to those of the First Movers. Japanese vertical and horizontal keiretsu, South Korea chaebols, and Hong Kong hongs are the M-form firms Fast Followers relied upon. Taiwan also has TSMC and other M-form firms, and Singaporean industrial policy resulted in thousands of foreign multinational firms investing in the territory.

Four of five Fast Followers also showed that their early fast dashes for growth were input-led, confirming that mobilization of capital and labor explained their growth until after 1985, when technical progress, or TFP—or innovation—began explaining their progress too. China displayed only input-led growth from 1965 until the end of the century, showing its early industrialization was similar to those of the Fast Followers before it.

The economic nation-building triangle's virtuous cycle suggests that stability, growth, and development are continually balanced by nations, but maintaining stability and achieving growth is key in early industrialization. Only through growth is wealth created that may be redistributed to those unable to provide for themselves. Nonetheless, India over the past two decades shows early industrialization under distributive democracy may be feasible too, but only if economic policy closer to the Fast Follower developmental states is followed.

Accordingly, economic policy more than regime type may explain early industrialization, and as long as surplus is accumulated and invested for the longer term and not all absorbed to meet immediate welfare needs, an amended complementary hypothesis may hold. A less distributive, more growth-oriented democracy closer to America's pre-twentieth-century democracy light could avoid the jeopardy that the conflicting hypothesis predicts.

But regardless of the recent Indian success, the conflicting and sequential hypotheses still explain all Fast Followers and four of the other five nations analyzed in the chapter. Moreover, no Follower, fast or otherwise, has industrialized under a less distributive, more growth-oriented DR. In addition, India's low growth since its 1947 founding clearly hampered development and shows that the economic nation-building triangle still explains India, just as it explains the nation-building efforts of South Korea, Singapore, China, Brazil, and South Africa. Regardless of regime type, an early stability/growth focus remains essential for aspirant Followers wishing to become industrializers.

We turn now to the Post-Industrial Era and to the world of Leaders and the future.

Chapter 4

THE POST-INDUSTRIAL ERA

Leader Creative Core Innovation, Business in Tightly Controlled Networks, and Humans Doing What Smart Machines Cannot Do

Chapter 1 lists the Post-Industrial Era's start as 1950, and Chapter 3 notes that when considering such transitions, they occur over decades. Single years are only approximations. The twentieth century's midpoint is demarcated as the start of the Post-Industrial Era, as computers appeared at this time. The everyday uses that would come from personal computing were already apparent by 1950:

> Some day we may even have small computers in our homes, drawing their energy from electric-power lines like refrigerators or radios. . . . They may recall facts for us that we would have trouble remembering. They may calculate accounts and income taxes. Schoolboys with homework may seek their help. . . . We may find the future full of mechanical brains working about us.[258]

Computers and their application changed many aspects of our struggle for productivity, including the characteristics of the goods and services offered; how they are produced and supplied; how the organi-

258 Edmund C. Berkeley, "Simple Simon," *Scientific American*, November 1, 1950, 42.

zations that produce them are structured, operated, and controlled; and even the nature of organization and human work itself.

In this chapter, post-industrialization as a construct is evaluated, and five vignettes capture lessons from the front lines of business to reveal conditions now in the era. Then, how post-industrial economic capital and infrastructure differ from those in the Industrial Era and the human abilities needed for work in the era are covered. Third, the organizational model to operate and control post-industrial business and post-industrial entrepreneurship are explained. Finally, post-industrial political economy is contrasted with Industrial Era political economy, and how Leaders stay ahead is revealed.

Post-Industrialization: Mobilizing Knowledge and Information to Enhance the Human Condition

That structural (i.e., permanent) change was again underway as Western societies reached the third quarter of the twentieth century was apparent to many scholars, prominent among them sociologist Daniel Bell, who coined the phrase "post-industrial society" in 1973.

> A pre-industrial sector is primarily *extractive*, its economy based on agriculture, mining, fishing, timber, and other resources such as natural gas or oil. An industrial sector is primarily *fabricating*, using energy and machine technology for the manufacture of goods. A post-industrial sector is one of *processing* in which telecommunications and computers are strategic for the exchange of information and knowledge. . . . Broadly speaking, if industrial society is based on machine technology, post-industrial society is shaped by an intellectual technology. And if capital and labor are the major structural features of industrial society, information and knowledge are those of the post-industrial society.[259]

---

259 Daniel Bell, "The Coming of Post-Industrial Society," in *Modernity: Critical Concepts*, ed. Malcolm Waters, vol. 4, *After Modernity* (New York: Routledge, 1999), 216. The chapter in Water's book was sourced from the 1976 edition of Bell's work: *The Coming of Post-Industrial Society: A Venture in Social Forecasting* (New York: Basic Books, 1973), ix–xii.

Drucker also suggested a new "Age of Discontinuity" appeared in the mid-twentieth century and had four elements: the rapid emergence of new technologies and industries; the emergence of a global economy where conflict between developed and developing economies replaced class conflict in national economies; the emergence of new forms of government and societal interactions that obsolesced those in operation at the time; and the emergence of knowledge as the new capital and central resource in an economy.

Reflecting on Bell and Drucker's ideas, which Kumar noted focused on the move to a service economy and a "knowledge society" and the changes that accompany them. Kumar continued:

> Over the past quarter of a century there have been persistent claims that Western societies have entered a new era of their history. While still being undoubtedly industrial, they have undergone, it is suggested, such far-reaching changes that they can no longer be considered under the old names and by means of the old theories. Western societies are now in various ways "post-industrial": "post-Fordist," "post-modern," even "post-historical."[260]

Kumar highlighted two important facts. First, though Western societies by the twentieth century's end were indeed entering a new era, they still remained indisputably industrial. Even the most post-industrial societies have elements remaining industrial. Second, that new names and theories are required to deal with "far-reaching changes" facing societies underscores the breadth of the change in progress, and main elements of the changes characterizing the new era will now be described. As still a work in progress, describing the transition is more challenging than capturing the elements of the Industrial Era. What *has* happened is easier to identify than what *is* happening or *may* happen.

One way to reveal a phenomenon is to present data that exemplifies the condition under analysis and then based on this data identify its

260 Krishan Kumar, *From Post-Industrial to Post-Modern Society: New Theories of the Contemporary World* (Malden, MA: Blackwell Publishers, 1995), vi.

characteristics. Accordingly, five vignettes that capture different slices of emerging post-industrial contexts are first presented. Then, the characteristics of the Post-Industrial Era, focusing especially on where they differ from those in the Industrial Era, are described. Covering materials used in post-industrial times is unnecessary, as in both eras materials are used. Similarly, energy is also needed regardless of the era, and the challenge is no longer the need for energy but about finding cleaner, less pollutive energy. This issue is considered in Chapter 5.

Post-Industrial Lessons from the Front Lines: Automated Information, Stores, Vehicles, Factories, and Earthworks, and from Product to Service to Solution in a Networked World

Chapter 3 points out that industrialization was both capital and labor intensive and that Industrial Era productivity was built on a symbiotic man/machine relationship. Humans worked on assembly lines alongside machines, with our manual dexterity unmatched by machines. From the 1950s on, however, more dexterous machines began eroding the human manual advantage. Machines replacing humans went as far back as the 1960s. In its 1964 Labor Day message, the Canadian Catholic Hierarchy noted:

> Labor Day, 1964, finds us seriously involved in a technological world; the threat of the machine replacing man is with us . . .
>
> Automation, a method of improving human productivity through machines, finds application not only in industry but also in the business world where computers are beginning to replace clerical workers. Such widespread introduction of automatic processes has grave implications. Increasing numbers of persons are beginning to suffer unemployment and displacement by the application of these new processes.[261]

---

261 The Canadian Catholic Hierarchy, "Labor Day Message—1964 Automation," in *Do Justice! The Social Teaching of the Canadian Catholic Bishops*, ed. E. F. Sheridan (Toronto, ON: Jesuit Centre for Social Faith and Justice; Sherbrooke, QC: Édition Paulines, 1987), 104–5.

By 1964, automation was threatening manufacturing and services alike. Probably not realized was automation was to prove a greater threat to services than to manufacturing. Services jobs are mostly information-based, and information is imminently automatable. Once an information-based process is amenable to *if this, then that* statements so that the process can be modeled and reduced to routines, it is only a question of time before that process is automated. By the end of the century, it was clear humans in the Post-Industrial Era would do only what machines could not do.

The next vignettes widely reflect this development, and as is seen in the material that follows them, post-industrial economic capital and organization and even the role of humans in productive work are deeply affected by routines captured in formal models and routine statements. As they are machines that replace humans, post-industrial robotics is where lessons from the front lines begin.

Post-Industrial Robotics and the Pervasive Automation of Production

The first factory robot was a die-casting machine installed at a Trenton, New Jersey, General Motors plant in 1961: "This pioneering industrial robot lifted up hot pieces of metal from a die-casting machine and stacked the pieces up for processing by a trim press,"[262] focusing on either dull (i.e., monotonous), dirty, or dangerous activities, a mantra adopted by the machine's codeveloper and a father of robotics, Joseph F. Engelberger. Over the next 40 years, robot capabilities advanced, building on many fields and disciplines, including mechanical and electronic engineering, locomotion, miniaturization, and biomechanics. By the twentieth century's end, it was clear robotics had applications in more than automobile manufacture, where the technology first enjoyed wide application.

262 Joseph A. Angelo Jr., *Robotics: A Reference Guide to the New Technology* (Westport, CT: Greenwood Press, 2007), 104.

> Robotics, robots, and their peripheral equipment will respond well to the challenges of space construction, assembly, and communications; new applications in agriculture, agri-industries, and chemical industries; work in recycling, cleaning, and hazardous waste disposal to protect our environment and the quality of our air and water; safe, reliable, and fast transportation relying on robotics in flight and on intelligent highways. Robotics prospered in the 1990s; it will thrive and proliferate in the twenty-first century.[263]

Automation is machines working independently of humans, and such machines led to an "engineering discipline which focuses on the study of robots," which are "the embodiment of manipulative, locomotive, perceptive, communicative and cognitive abilities in an artificial body, which may or may not have a human shape."[264] These robots were initially categorized in two forms—humanoid and industrial—with humanoid robots resembling human forms and typically performing tasks with humans present (hence their humanoid appearance), while industrial robots possessed limbs of varying configurations designed to perform specific tasks (e.g., replacing hands on assembly lines, or transporting products in warehouses, or spray-painting automobiles), all free of human assistance.

More recently, industrial robots were differentiated from service robots, where an industrial robot is an "automatically controlled, reprogrammable, multipurpose manipulator, programmable in three or more axes, which can be either fixed in place or fixed to a mobile platform for use in automation applications in an industrial environment"[265] and a service robot is a "robot in personal use or professional use that performs useful tasks for humans or equipment" with "a degree of autonomy" and an "ability to perform intended tasks based on current state and sensing

263 Donald A. Vincent, "Guest Forward-Changing Our World," in *Handbook of Industrial Robotics*, 2nd ed., ed. Shimon Y. Nof, vol. 1 (New York: John Wiley & Sons, 1999), xv–xvi. Vincent was executive vice president of the Robotic Industries Association, based in Ann Arbor, Michigan.

264 Min Xie, *Fundamentals of Robotics: Linking Perception to Action* (Singapore: World Scientific , 2003), 1, 8.

265 International Federation of Robotics, "Standardization," accessed April 1, 2023, https://ifr.org/standardisation.

without human intervention."[266] ISO 8373:2021 added a third category, medical robots, and this includes robots assisting in surgery; rehabilitation or radiotherapy; those delivering medications, meals, and specimens and ensuring room sanitization in hospitals; and robots providing patients with cognitive support through an ability to interact with humans.[267]

With robots already assisting in surgery and (as shown in the following sections) being applied in industrial settings ranging from earthmoving to agriculture to assembly lines to retail to warehouse product movement (with potential application in autonomous vehicles), a more important question is which domain of productive life will robots not add value to?

Industrial robots also received a boost with arrival of a new technology, 3D printing, which permits machines to make products out of materials ranging from plastic to stainless steel, aluminum, graphene, composite materials, and even food (chocolate, cheese, flour, and sugar, among others). 3D printing, or additive manufacturing, uses computer-aided design (CAD) to convert molten or powdered materials into objects through the layering of the material to build the required form.

Offered in applications for hobbyists, professional and small businesses, product designers, and engineers, among others, and priced from US$180 for beginners to US$6,950 for pro-level large objects,[268] 3D-printed objects are found in many industries, ranging from eyewear, footwear, and furniture to medical, healthcare, and dental products; to automotive and aerospace prototypes and parts; to architectural scale models; to intricate edible food products.[269] Common to all is production free of human engagement once digital designs and materials are loaded onto the printer.

---

266 International Federation of Robotics, "Service Robots," International Federation of Robotics (IFR), referencing *International Organization for Standardization (ISO) 8373: 2021: Robotics–Vocabulary*, accessed April 1, 2023, https://ifr.org/service-robots.

267 Lauren Greenwood, "The Types of Medical Robots in Use Today and in the Future," Journal (Brainlab), updated November 22, 2021, accessed April 1, 2023, https://www.brainlab.com/journal/types-of-medical-robots-in-use-today-and-in-the-future/.

268 Tony Hoffman, "The Best 3D Printers for 2023," *PC Magazine*, updated March 20, 2023, accessed March 27, 2023, https://www.pcmag.com/picks/the-best-3d-printers.

269 HP, "What Can You Make with a 3D Printer?," accessed April 1, 2023, https://www.hp.com/us-en/printers/3d-printers/learning-center/what-can-you-make-with-3d-printer.html.

Post-Industrial Air Travel: Automated Travel and Aircraft Products to Services and Solutions

With airlines and hotels communicating directly with consumers, by the early twenty-first century, online services such as Expedia, Travelocity, and Priceline had replaced travel agencies. Travelers with internet access set up itineraries in their time, meeting their needs more efficiently and at lower cost than relying on human travel agents.

Itineraries are not the only automated segment of twenty-first-century air travel. Passengers check in online on smartphones or at airport kiosks, reducing airline agents at counters. Agents remain mostly for security to visually check accepted government-issued identifications and ensure passengers board appropriately. Automated information processing, from the scheduling of itineraries to flight check-in to the control and transfer of luggage in transit, now directly benefits travelers. Even digital trackers report in real time where checked bags are. Technology has eliminated many information-based air travel jobs done by humans in the twentieth century.

Another change in the transition to post-industrial air travel is not on the passenger side but on aircraft maintenance and support. On its 787 Dreamliner, first in service in 2011, aircraft manufacturer Boeing offers GoldCare.

> The GoldCare suite, which offers customers choices among materials management, engineering, planning and control, and maintenance services, is an excellent example of the evolution of logistics from being necessary functions required to sell parts to customers to a capability that is itself sold directly to customers. Customers buying the GoldCare package do not pay for individual parts or maintenance projects; rather they pay for scalable service contracts that guarantee availability of planes for given flight time hours. This service makes operating costs for Boeing's customers much more stable and predictable, lowering their overall risk.[270]

---

270 Charles C. Poirier, Francis J. Quinn, and Morgan L. Swink, *Diagnosing Greatness: Ten Traits of the Best Supply Chains* (Fort Lauderdale, FL: J. Ross Publishing, 2010), 149.

GoldCare enables carriers to focus on airline operations while Boeing maintains their fleets. Data-rich information systems provide fault codes that identify mechanical problems in real time, and problems developing in flight are repaired soon after planes land. Information flows through aircraft-based electronic flight bags and logbooks to the ground, and Boeing's engineering and maintenance systems determine the parts required, made ready for installation through the materials management system.

Boeing's supply base is also integrated into the information flow to report when and where maintenance is required and to ensure the right part is delivered to the right people at the right time. Operational benefits are many: more accurate and efficient troubleshooting of mechanical problems, repairs done right the first time and more quickly, less expensive maintenance costs, and most importantly, increased aircraft uptime for carriers. In 2016 Boeing extended GoldCare to its 737 MAX fleet and in 2017 began its largest-ever commercial services contract with Norwegian Air upon delivery of its first 737 MAX aircraft. Boeing had provided GoldCare service to Norwegian's 787 fleet from 2012; extension to the 737 MAX fleet was set to run until 2034.[271]

GoldCare provides services relating to aircraft maintenance, performing them for airlines previously doing them internally or through a maintenance partner. Those currently maintaining aircraft for others—for example, Lufthansa Technik,[272] owned by carrier Lufthansa—face a new competitor, while Boeing is effectively competing with an important customer. Key about such offerings is an airline may no longer have to purchase an aircraft to operate it. Instead, it might lease a maintained

271 "Boeing, Norwegian Agree to Record GoldCare Coverage," PR Newswire, July 11, 2016, accessed September 23, 2023, https://www.prnewswire.com/news-releases/boeing-norwegian-agree-to-record-goldcare-coverage-300296363.html.

272 In March 2023, Lufthansa Technik boasted having over 800 customers and supporting over 4,200 aircraft under exclusive contracts, with over 20,000 employees worldwide (Lufthansa Technik, "About Lufthansa Technik," accessed March 3, 2023, https://www.lufthansa-technik.com/company).

aircraft and pay for a solution that delivers more uptime and better reliability than enjoyed previously.

GoldCare shows a product generating and transmitting data while in operation, and by the second decade of the twenty-first century, a new network domain captured machines talking to machines:

> In what's called the Internet of Things, sensors and actuators embedded in physical objects—from roadways to pacemakers—are linked through wired and wireless networks, often using the same Internet Protocol (IP) that connects the internet. These networks churn out huge volumes of data that flow to computers for analysis. . . . What's revolutionary in all this is that these physical information systems are now beginning to be deployed, and some of them even work largely without human intervention.[273]

Estimates were that 55.7 billion connected devices would operate across the Internet of Things (IoT) by 2025,[274] and by 2023 these were working across homes (in security systems and appliances from doorbells to thermostats to washers and dryers to TVs and radios to light bulbs), in healthcare and fitness (in smartwatches and glasses, and in wearable wellness devices from pacemakers to continuous glucose and health monitors), in motor vehicles (in advanced driver-assistance systems ranging from Global Positioning System [GPS]–based navigation to systems enabling vehicle operation with little or no human involvement), and widely across operations in almost every industry in the post-industrial world.

---

273 Michael Chui, Markus Löffler, and Roger Roberts, "The Internet of Things," *McKinsey Quarterly*, March 1, 2010, 70.

274 Jeffrey Hojlo, "Future of Industry Ecosystems: Shared Data and Insights," *IDC Blog*, International Data Corporation, January 6, 2021, accessed March 10, 2023, https://blogs.idc.com/2021/01/06/future-of-industry-ecosystems-shared-data-and-insights/.

Post-Industrial Retailing: Automated Retail and the Retail Apocalypse

The automation and replacement of humans by machines in the airline industry is also seen in retailing. Today consumers across America and elsewhere routinely scan and bag goods at checkout kiosks or scan UPC barcodes with smartphone apps in real time while shopping. Should they so desire, human checkout lines are avoided completely.[275]

In 2017 Amazon introduced Amazon Go, where consumers shop with no store staff present.[276] As customers walk through the store, RFID tags record products placed in *smart* trolleys, and as they exit the store, the Amazon Go app activates automatic payment.[277] Amazon Fresh followed, adding Amazon Go's seamless experience to grocery purchases through "Just Walk Out" and "Dash Cart" shopping.[278] But customers can still use traditional checkout or online ordering with their choice of same-day delivery or store pickup. In these instances, two retail activities are in play: checkout/payment and managing last-mile delivery from store to consumer (via customers themselves or the store or its agents).

Retail in the post-industrial world differs from retail in the 1950s, the halcyon days of the Industrial Era. Instead of written lists presented to store clerks for advice and fulfillment, customers may enter and exit with little or even no contact with store personnel. Consumers with RFID readers can even learn where products are as they arrive at the mall.

275 Barcode US, "UPC Barcodes: The Basics," accessed March 11, 2023, https://www.barcode-us.info/upc-codes/. UPCs (universal product codes) are "standardized global identifiers, which enable products to be sold, reordered and tracked through supply chains." Accurate product identification is needed to sell through online marketplaces, and in the United States barcodes are typically graphical representations of a 12-digit number assigned to products; 8- and 13-digit numbers are used outside of North America, and 14-digit numbers also identify items at different packaging levels.

276 Uptin, "NO STAFF at Amazon Store! #shorts," September 8, 2021, YouTube video, accessed March 12, 2023, https://www.youtube.com/watch?v=D5F2xp-5lnc.

277 Doug, "Radio Frequency Identification," *RFID Journal*, accessed March 10, 2023, https://www.rfidjournal.com/glossary/radio-frequency-identification. RFID is "any method of identifying unique items using radio waves. Typically, a reader (also called an interrogator) communicates with a transponder, which holds digital information in a microchip. But there are chipless forms of RFID tags that use material to reflect back a portion of the radio waves beamed at them."

278 Amazon.com, "Amazon Fresh Groceries," accessed March 12, 2023, https://www.amazon.com/fmc/m/30003175?almBrandId=QW1hem9uIEZyZXNo.

As customers walk by stores, notifications and coupons for products on their app wish lists are received. Alternatively, and to avoid the need to visit stores at all, orders may be placed online and disintermediate the traditional retail supply chain.

The economic gains from arbitraging retail and wholesale margins down are substantial. A 2004 study found the average markups in wholesale and retail distribution in 12 OECD countries was 2, meaning if a supplier sells to a wholesaler or retailer for 50, the retail price would be around 100.[279] A large price decrease is possible if no intermediary takes the risk of carrying obsolete or unsold stock or faces stock shrinkage, though convenience—compared with going to a store and getting products immediately—is sacrificed. The direct-from-supplier-to-customer model also assumes products are transportable by logistics providers such as FedEx, UPS, or DHL. And even more specialized delivery services that provide the transport and labor to carry boxes too big for single drivers (e.g., furniture or large appliances) also now operate across America; where there is a need, markets nearly always respond.

The COVID-19 pandemic forced even more purchasing to move online and made retail disintermediation even more widespread. In early 2023, Dennis Dick, a trader at Las Vegas–based Bright Trading LLC, coined the phrase "retail apocalypse" to describe the sudden decline in the retail industry.

> While talking about the 25 percent fall in Walmart's quarterly profit back in May 2022, Dick said: "This is a little bit of a retail apocalypse, it was Walmart and everybody thought it was a one-off. Now that Target missed earnings [by] a lot more than Walmart even did, they're scared that the consumer is not as strong as everybody thinks," said

279 OECD, *OECD Economic Surveys: Netherlands 2004* (Paris: OECD Publishing, 2004), 144, accessed March, 15, 2023, https://doi.org/10.1787/eco_surveys-nld-2004-en's total cost is US$48.03 and its profit is US$4, placing the wholesale price at US$52.03. US$47.97 covers the costs and markup requirements of the retail chain. Thus, while Nike makes on average US$4 on a pair of shoes (8 percent), the retail chain's markup to cover costs and profits is almost 12 times greater (Katherine McIntyre et al., *Nike–Channel Conflict*, Case EC-9B [Stanford, CA: Graduate School of Business, Stanford University, 2000]: 13, accessed March 10, 2023, https://www.gsb.stanford.edu/faculty-research/case-studies/nike-channel-conflict).

> Dick. There has been a bit of a snowball effect since then as more retailers announce store closings. No specific type of store has been spared from the apocalypse, as everything from clothing to grocery stores has been affected.[280]

Ten retailers and the number of stores expected to close, were closing, or had closed were also listed: JCPenney reported over 800; Old Navy, 350; Bed Bath & Beyond, 150; and Macy's, over 120.

If direct from supplier dominates, traditional retailers will remain only if products have limited shelf lives and are purchased repetitively; if they must be seen, touched, tried on, or experienced before purchase; or if purchases are too small for disaggregated online purchase. For globally sourced products, logistics challenges and consumers wanting to transact with known entities means retailers like Wayfair will also remain despite its near lack of retail stores;[281] online platform marketing and supplier and warehouse logistics management (i.e., fulfillment) are the competencies Wayfair is built on.

A benchmark for fulfillment, Amazon's 100-foot-high, 2.9-million-square-foot Sioux Falls, South Dakota, fulfillment center opened in October 2022. Supported by thousands of roboticized drives and aisles, human packers remain in one place to pack products arriving automatically for fulfillment, reducing average shift walking to 2 miles from 16 to 20. At full operation, 1,500 associates will handle 8 million inbound and 12 million outbound units per week, providing same- and next-day shipping to customers in the Sioux Falls and tri-state area and across North

---

280 Josephine Fuller, "Full List of Stores Closing doors with 10 Retailers Out—as 'Retail Apocalypse' Shows No End," *U.S. Sun*, February 18, 2023, accessed 10 March 2023, https://www.the-sun.com/money/7431525/full-list-stores-closing-doors-retail-apocalypse/.

281 Wayfair, headquartered in Boston, MA, is a public e-commerce retailer formed in 2002 that employs over 14,000 people, operates 18 fulfillment and 38 delivery centers across the United States, Germany, Canada, and the United Kingdom, and describes itself as one of the world's largest home retailers. 2022 revenues were US$12.2 billion, serving 22.1 million customers with over 40 million products from over 20,000 suppliers, all shipped to customers free (Wayfair, "About Us," accessed April 4, 2023, https://www.aboutwayfair.com/who-we-are).

and South Dakota into eastern Montana and Wyoming.[282] Amazon also announced that new robots under testing could master the most common human fulfillment job: picking up and placing individual items. These tests followed the mid-2022 introduction of its first fully autonomous goods-moving warehouse robot that lifts and moves carts weighing up to 800 pounds while seamlessly navigating around human associates.[283]

Regardless of fulfilment improvements, big-box retailers will have to match competing online prices (including from suppliers directly), offer online purchasing with same-day delivery and pickup, and may have to offer additional value-added services or solutions, as in Boeing's Gold-Care. For example, Best Buy's Totaltech (costing US$199.99 annually and touted as "the plan you need to protect the tech you love") offers many benefits, including free Geek Squad technical support 24/7/365 (24 hours a day, 7 days a week, 365 days a year); free two-day shipping as standard delivery, installation, and haul away; VIP access to dedicated phone and chat teams; and 60-day returns and exchanges on most products.[284] Hopefully, these will keep consumers buying, either online or in Best Buy stores.

Absent the need for physical validation, retail aggregation, or a trusted party to contract with, consumers will likely search online for products and transact directly with suppliers. Most at risk are retailers/wholesalers in the traditional industrial retail supply chain, those providing wholesale/retail shopping space to them, and shop floor retail service workers. Just as industry structure evolved for airlines and travel agents, as post-industrial retailing matures, the same is happening in traditional retailing.

---

282 Jill Callison, "Inside Sioux Falls' New Amazon Fulfillment Center, High-Tech Robots Support Human Workers," SiouxFalls.Business, October 13, 2022, accessed April 5, 2023, https://www.siouxfalls.business/inside-sioux-falls-new-amazon-fulfillment-center-high-tech-robots-support-human-workers/.

283 Christopher Mims, "Amazon Takes Steps Toward Warehouse Automation," *Wall Street Journal*, December 13, 2022, accessed April 5, 2023, https://www.wsj.com/story/amazon-takes-steps-toward-warehouse-automation-14b7131d.

284 Best Buy, "About Best Buy," accessed April 7, 2023, https://corporate.bestbuy.com/about-best-buy/. Best Buy Co. Inc., a public multinational consumer electronics retailer based in Richfield, MN, with 2023 sales of US$46.3 billion, has over 1,000 stores and about 100,000 employees in the United States and Canada.

Automation and machines replacing humans is also apparent in retail financial services. Among the earliest machines to replace humans was the automated teller machine (ATM):

> This revolution sprang directly from the annoyance of Don Wetzel. He is the American engineer who thought up the ATM while waiting in a Dallas bank line in 1968. . . . Working with him were Tom Barnes, a mechanical engineer, and George Chastain, and electrical engineer. All their names appear on the 1973 patent. They built a prototype ATM in 1969 at a cost of $5 million, and the first one was installed in the Rockville Center branch of New York's Chemical Bank in 1973.[285]

Early ATMs were not connected to bank accounts; cards with magnetic strips that permitted the networking of account information were required before the invention reached its full potential. Banking now takes full advantage of the ability to network account information, and retail banking customers are able to bank online with little need to visit their bank, assuming the banks have physical presences at all. Similar to Wayfair, online banks with minimal or no retail brick-and-mortar presence operate across the United States, typically offering higher interest rates at lower costs than traditional banks with online presences and legacy branch networks.[286]

Post-Industrial Automobile Automation: From Factories to Highways

Automation and human disintermediation are also apparent in the quintessential industrial industry, automobile production. Here the substitution of humans with machines occurred long before computers and IT had the impact outlined previously. Union power and increasing labor

---

285 William H. Marling, *How "American" Is Globalization?* (Baltimore, MD: The Johns Hopkins University Press, 2006), 145.

286 Amber Murakami-Fester, "What Is Online Banking? Definition, Pros and Cons," NerdWallet, updated March 25, 2021, accessed March 13, 2023, https://www.nerdwallet.com/article/banking/pros-cons-online-only-banking.

costs in the 1940s forced Ford Motor Company management to search for ways to mitigate the threat, and automation was an early solution:

> Only a little more than a decade after the emergence of the UAW, in a period of tremendous labor strength, automation was a formidable tool for management. A manager in the newly automated Ford engine plant in Cleveland reminded UAW President Walter Reuther that "you are going to have trouble collecting union dues from all these machines."
>
> By 1953, the Cleveland and Dearborn plants were running parallel production. Where 950 workers made piston connecting rods at the Rouge, they were replaced by two units of 146 workers each at Cleveland and Dearborn, resulting in a net loss of 804 jobs in the Detroit area.[287]

Ironically, and only 20 years after creation, the most widely benchmarked Industrial Era manufacturing complex was among the first to feel the effect of more automated production. By the 1980s, European automobile manufacturers were following but with computers and robots added. Engine and gearbox plants opened by French automobile producer PSA in 1980 were described as follows:

> Each of the four factories utilized advanced technologies; all were automated and robotized. At Trémery output reached 1,000 engines per day during the first year of operation and 2,000 by the end of 1983. At Valenciennes, automated equipment reduced production times by 40 percent. The Charleville foundry, with only about a hundred workers, was completely automated and controlled by computer.[288]

In the twenty-first century, automobile assembly continues the trend: compared with two decades ago, today there are far more robots and computer-integrated machines on an average assembly line and far

---

287 Thomas J. Sugrue, *The Origins of the Urban Crisis: Race and Inequality in Postwar Detroit* (Princeton, NJ: Princeton University Press, 1996), 132–3.

288 Jean-Louis Loubet, "Peugeot Meets Ford, Sloan, and Toyota," in *One Best Way? Trajectories and Industrial Models of the World's Automobile Producers*, ed. Michel Freyssenet et. al., (New York: Oxford University Press, 1998), 348.

fewer humans. Honda had assembly lines operating with robots only in the early 2000s, and a 2010 Toyota Camry assembly line shows similar conditions there.[289] But full automation of automobile production remains unlikely according to some:

> More than three decades after Honda Motor Co. first built an Accord sedan at its Marysville, Ohio, factory in 1982, humans are still an integral part of the assembly process—and that's unlikely to change anytime soon.
>
> "We can't find anything to take the place of the human touch and of human senses like sight, hearing, and smell," Tom Shoupe, the chief operating officer of Honda's Ohio manufacturing unit, said in an interview.
>
> Japanese rival Toyota Motor Corp. uses just a handful of robots on the Camry final assembly line at its plant in Georgetown, Kentucky, and has no plans to add more, according to Mark Boire, chief production engineer. Markus Schaefer, production chief at Mercedes-Benz, in 2016 said the carmaker was de-automating and relying more on humans to install the endless array of options that luxury customers demand.[290]

Factory and assembly line automation is not the only arena where post-industrial automobile operations will differ from those in the Industrial Era. Services such as General Motors's OnStar turned vehicles into nodes on a network so they are permanently connected to receive and generate information. Relying on wireless and GPS-based satellite tech-

289 Gizmodo Social, "The Factory Robots Building the Toyota Camry Hybrid," August 30, 2009, YouTube video, accessed March 13, 2023, https://www.youtube.com/watch?v=82w_r2D1Ooo.
290 John Lippert, "Honda: Humans Still Build the Best Cars," *Detroit News*, January 23, 2018, accessed March 13, 2023, https://www.detroitnews.com/story/business/autos/foreign/2018/01/23/honda-humans-build-best-cars/109741724/.

nology,[291] OnStar offers many services, including online vehicle diagnostics, emergency services (with automatic calls from live OnStar operators if airbags deploy), location assistance for stolen vehicles, roadside/crisis assistance, remote door unlock, remote activation of the horn and lights if drivers cannot locate cars, navigation, and hands-free calling.[292]

Operated as a separate business unit from 1995, initially dealer-installed OnStar hardware proved expensive and inefficient. Factory installation remedied this problem, and by mid-2002 OnStar was available on 38 of GM's 52 new models. The company set out to establish OnStar as the standard for new in-vehicle communication services: by 2003, Lexus, Audi, Acura, Isuzu, and Subaru used the platform for their new in-vehicle service offerings.[293] More importantly, OnStar-enabled vehicles exceeded 2 million by 2002, up from 50,000 in 1999; 4 million vehicles were expected by 2003.[294] But the service only connected with consumers when safety and security were emphasized:

> Soon after its introduction, OnStar highlighted its ability to provide "remote diagnostics" on engine performance, and then tried a concierge service that offered to help drivers buy flowers and find restaurants. . . . Unfortunately, all of these additions were just various functional benefits, valued differently depending on the subscriber. When OnStar really started to connect with consumers is when it repositioned itself as synonymous with "security," providing help "out of the blue" whenever a driver needed it.[295]

---

291 Garmin Ltd., producer of GPS-based navigation and communication devices for a wide range of settings, defines GPS as follows: "The Global Positioning System (GPS) is a U.S. government satellite-based navigation system that currently consists of at least 24 operational satellites. GPS works in any weather conditions, anywhere in the world, 24 hours a day, with no subscription fees or setup charges. . . . Each satellite transmits a unique signal and orbital parameters that allow GPS devices to decode and compute the precise location of the satellite. GPS receivers use this information and trilateration to calculate a user's exact location" (Garmin, "What Is GPS?" accessed March 13, 2023, http://www8.garmin.com/aboutGPS/).

292 OnStar, "Get Your OnStar Trial," accessed March 13, 2023, https://www.onstar.com/content/onstar/na/us/en/index/plans/safety-security.html.

293 Adrian Slywotzky and Richard Wise, "Demand Innovation: GM's OnStar Case," *Strategy & Leadership* 31, no. 3 (2003): 21.

294 Slywotzky and Wise, "Demand Innovation," 21.

295 Steve Diller, Nathan Shedroff, and Darrel Rhea, *Making Meaning: How Successful Businesses Deliver Meaningful Customer Experiences* (Berkeley, CA: New Riders, 2006), 40.

Yet despite these benefits, adoption and renewal did not increase significantly. In 2007 OnStar had 4.7 million North American subscribers, but it remained under pressure to offer additional services to justify its value.[296] By 2017 over 7 million subscribers used the platform but by 2021 that number had declined to just over 5 million.[297] Moreover, OnStar did not become the industry standard: among others, BMW, Mercedes-Benz, Lexus, and Acura had telemetric services, all independent of GM.

The risk is OnStar will only be widely adopted if free, a situation often the case in internet-based services, but its future viability may be influenced by factors not yet fully apparent. In 2017 the US Department of Transportation National Highway Traffic Safety Administration (NHTSA) defined automated driving systems (ADSs) as "systems for which there is no human driver or for which the human driver can give control to the ADS and would not be expected to perform any driving-related tasks for a period of time."[298]

With self-driving automobiles on the horizon, NHTSA issued a guide to innovators and states focused on the safe deployment and appropriate regulation of ADSs. OnStar-like connectivity may eventually be as essential as engines, brakes, and tires—the IoT writ large connecting smart motor vehicles. And if fully automated self-driving automobiles arrive, they will join the countless industrial robots—or service robots—already in operation around the world.

---

296 Dale Buss, "Telematics: Can Great Tech Find an Encore?" Edmunds,March 15, 2007, accessed March 13, 2023, http://www.edmunds.com/ownership/audio/articles/120715/article.html.
297 Automoblog Staff, "The Truth About OnStar," Automoblog, updated March 21, 2022, accessed March 13, 2023, https://www.automoblog.net/the-truth-about-onstar/.
298 National Highway Traffic Safety Administration, "Advanced Driving Systems: A Vision for Safety," US Department of Transportation, September 2017, accessed March 13, 2023, https://www.nhtsa.gov/sites/nhtsa.gov/files/documents/13069a-ads2.0_090617_v9a_tag.pdf.

Post-Industrial Earthmoving: Dozer Solutions at Work

The Caterpillar Inc. and Nasdaq-listed Trimble Inc. partnership provides insight into how earthmoving evolved as the transition to the Post-Industrial Era gathered pace. Trimble's business is as follows:

> Trimble is transforming the way the world works by delivering products and services that connect the physical and digital worlds. Core technologies in positioning, modeling, connectivity and data analytics enable customers to improve productivity, quality, safety and sustainability. From purpose built products to enterprise lifecycle solutions, Trimble software, hardware and services are transforming industries such as agriculture, construction, geospatial and transportation and logistics.[299]

Building on a deep understanding of an industry's value chain, Trimble integrates its core technology into a solution that fits the conditions at hand. At its 2001 formation, the Caterpillar/Trimble partnership was described as follows:

> As part of the 50-50 jointly owned venture, both Trimble and Caterpillar intend to contribute selected existing electronic products that combine Global Positioning System, laser, wireless communications, computing and software technologies into on-board packages that improve productivity for both the construction and mining markets. . . . The joint venture will develop machine control products that use site design information combined with positioning technology to automatically control dozer blades and other machine tools.[300]

In 2003 the joint venture launched its AccuGrade range of products, and these systems are now available for Caterpillar bulldozers, motor graders, and excavators. In these machines, GPS satellites provide blade guidance to operators. Machines also automatically finish road or

299 Trimble, "Who We Are," accessed December 20, 2023, https://maps.trimble.com/company/.
300 "Caterpillar and Trimble to Form Joint Venture," Rental Equipment Register, October 1, 2001, accessed March 14, 2023, https://www.rermag.com/mag/article/20933462/caterpillar-and-trimble-to-form-joint-venture.

site grading; the automatic control capability provides direct inputs to hydraulic valves to control the lift and cross slope of blades, reducing site preparation time, minimizing operator fatigue, and decreasing operating costs, all while achieving higher accuracy.

A 2006 study compared identical access road construction on adjacent sites in Malaga, Spain, one constructed conventionally and one using the same machines but with AccuGrade systems added.[301] The same drivers operated Caterpillars on each job, done in similar weather using the same materials. The time taken for each operation, and the passes, buckets, truckloads, fuel consumption, and man-hours were compared. Results were impressive: a decline in surveying costs and finished design accuracy within tolerance—98 versus 45 percent—using conventional methods was noted, and completing the design in less time with significantly fewer passes produced a 43 percent fuel savings. AccuGrade also promoted a safer working environment, as less labor was needed. Other AccuGrade savings and efficiency improvements were reported by 2009:

> After only a few hours of working with the system we realised that it was the ideal solution. Surveying and grading work on the 22 degree slope that would take a day using conventional methods took just a couple of hours with AccuGrade—even with an operator who had never used the system before. So we extended the rental period for another month. Using AccuGrade meant that we could release three people and a motor grader to work on other tasks and still we saved time and money, finishing the grading and paving in just four months instead of the scheduled six.[302]

---

301 Caterpillar, "Caterpillar Road Construction Production Study," December 2006, accessed March 14, 2023, http://sitechsul.com/wp-content/uploads/MALAGA-PRODUCTION-STUDY.pdf.

302 "AccuGrade Saves Time and Money in Slovenia," *CAT Magazine* 1, 2009, 20, accessed March 27, 2023, https://www.teknoxgroup.com/fileadmin/user_upload/katalogi/en/CM_teknox_2009_01.pdf.

But few technologies are static. By 2017 competitors had bested first-generation Caterpillar AccuGrade solutions.[303] Topcon's mastless 3D-MC MAX system offered automated applications that increased operator speed and accuracy and delivered new efficiency levels and cost cuts.[304]

To retrofit bulldozers in early generations, hardware and antennas were bolted on and wired up to provide GPS-based machine control, and receiver and antenna installation and removal prevented theft of these valuable items. Mastless systems eradicated this need, saving workers from climbing onto blades often twice daily—a safety hazard—and eliminating equipment that obstructed operator view or needlessly tangled in site obstructions and/or broke off.[305]

As is the case in other industry settings, advanced computer-based systems and solutions reduced workers and significantly increased the productivity of those working with the better-equipped machines. Unclear is when these machines will become so adept that they are fully automated and will not need human operators at all. At this point, and similar to fully autonomous automobiles, they will become industrial robots that eliminate the need for humans to engage directly in earth-moving work.

Autonomous construction is already underway in more predictable settings. To automatically install solar farm piles, Built Robotics boasts

---

303 Topcon Positioning Systems, "Integrated 'Mastless' Dozer System | Topcon," February 10, 2016, YouTube video, accessed March 27, 2023, https://www.youtube.com/watch?v=ZMWUvc-G1jz8.

304 Tom Jackson, "Side-by-Side: Comparing Cat, Deere, Komatsu, and Topcon Mastless Dozer GPS Systems," Equipment World, April 7, 2017, accessed March 27, 2023, https://www.equipmentworld.com/equipment-controls/machine-control/article/14966889/side-by-side-comparing-cat-deere-komatsu-and-topcon-mast-less-dozer-gps-systems.

305 Jackson, "Side-by-Side."

the world's first robotic pile driver system, the RPD 35.[306] The company's Exosystem—with proximity radar, 360° cameras, GPS capability, and a liquid-cooled computer—controls the solution. Excavators with retrofitted baskets carrying over 200 piles and hammer assemblies automatically plucking and driving piles into the ground with subcentimeter accuracy claim an over 300-pile-per-day installation rate. Manual teams do around 100.[307] Remote bulldozing was also reported as far back as 2017 in a mining setting too dangerous for operators to work on in person,[308] just as Caterpillar bulldozers were being operated by remote-control joysticks in 2014.[309]

How far automation will change earthmoving is unclear; regardless, the ongoing drive for machines to replace humans will not cease soon. More predictable and easier-to-model construction applications will first succumb, and it is likely that machines will eventually be as adept operating autonomously as they are under human control. Again, at this point, these machines will become fully-fledged industrial robots, eliminating the need for humans to work directly on or under the land. Similar innovations are changing mining, just as they are transforming agriculture and farming:

> Farm automation, often associated with "smart farming," is technology that makes farms more efficient and automates the crop or livestock

306 Built Robotics, "About Built Robotics," accessed April 2, 2023, https://www.builtrobotics.com/about/company. Formed in 2016, Built Robotics's mission is "to build the robots that build the world." Coverage of the company's Series C US$64 million funding in 2022 stated the following: "'As a leader in autonomous construction technology, Built's focus on easy-to-install robotic upgrades for heavy equipment is generating significant demand,' Griffin Schroeder, partner at Tiger Global, said. 'We are excited to partner with them as their autonomous trenching solution helps transform the construction of solar farms, oil & gas projects, and other large and critical infrastructure projects around the world'" (Brianna Wessling, "Built Robotics Digs up $64M for Construction Vehicle Autonomy Kits," The Robot Report, April 6, 2022, accessed April 2, 2023, https://www.therobotreport.com/built-robotics-digs-up-64m-for-construction-vehicle-autonomy-kits/.)

307 Built Robotics, "Robots for the Solar Energy Revolution: The RPD 35 from Built Robotics," March 14, 2023, YouTube video, accessed April 2, 2023, https://www.youtube.com/watch?v=8Na6NF11iPc.

308 Teck Resources Limited, "Remote Control Dozer," November 16, 2017, YouTube video, accessed April 2, 2023, https://www.youtube.com/watch?v=K5ZSndS0gkE.

309 The Awesomer, "Remote-Controlled 900+ Horsepower Caterpillar Bulldozer," September 18, 2014, YouTube video, accessed April 2, 2023, https://www.youtube.com/watch?v=nri6wne8_yY.

> production cycle. An increasing number of companies are working on robotics innovation to develop drones, autonomous tractors, robotic harvesters, automatic watering, and seeding robots. Although these technologies are fairly new, the industry has seen an increasing number of traditional agriculture companies adopt farm automation into their processes.[310]

These vignettes and lessons from the front lines underscore that post-industrial economic capital and the quality of the products on offer are in most cases much improved. These and other data are now relied upon to reveal the characteristics of the Post-Industrial Era. First, the characteristics of post-industrial economic capital are described, followed by organization and infrastructure in the Post-Industrial Era. Human resources in the Post-Industrial Era conclude coverage of the characteristics typifying the Post-Industrial Era.

Post-Industrial Economic Capital: Computer Operated, Automated, and Networked

Distinguishing between three technology types helps track technological advances: transformational (producing revolutionary changes in society), extensions (offering additional scope for existing technologies), and niche (specialized applications of existing technologies for particular tasks).[311] Revealing the transformational technologies that enabled what is emerging before our eyes, much in the automated, computer-integrated post-industrial world and the smart products, services, and solutions now on offer would not have transpired without computers, GPS, and the internet.

Decades of gestation are typically required before a transformational technology's potential is fully realized. Invented in 1945, computers only became widespread in the United States in the 1970s and 1980s, and then

310 Linly Ku, "How Automation is Transforming the Farming Industry," Plug and Play, September 27, 2022, accessed April 3, 2023, https://www.plugandplaytechcenter.com/resources/how-automation-transforming-farming-industry/.

311 Daniel Bell, *The Coming of Post-Industrial Society* (1973), xliii.

only after technology had advanced from vacuum tubes to integrated circuits to microchips and computers had evolved from mainframes to personal computers. Similarly, it took from the 1960s to the 1990s before GPS became available for commercial use, and ideas sparked in the late 1960s only bore fruit 30 years later in the internet's deployment.

In addition, that all three technologies were initially funded by the US military continues a tradition going back at least as far as the nineteenth century when the British, German, and French militaries were significant sources of innovation in their industrializing economies (pages 141–142). But with participation from iconic American enterprises such as AT&T (Bell Laboratories), Xerox (Xerox PARC), IBM, Cisco, Intel, Microsoft, Apple, and Google, the private sector by far played the most significant role in the development of computers and the internet.

That GPS resulted from military/government investment is also predictable given the initial purpose of the system. Primarily built to enhance American national security and intended for precision weapons delivery and identifying nuclear explosions, as well as for use by military assets for location and navigation data (by land, sea, and/or air), these functions added pressure to keep GPS development under US military watch.

Moreover, ongoing innovation has significantly extended the impact of computers and the internet. Based on Intel founder Gordon Moore's 1965 observation—later a prediction—that computing power would double every two years, computing power has increased dramatically over the past 60 years. Data is the post-industrial oil, and lakes of this new oil are now being generated each minute around the world. More powerful computers and analytical tools will be needed to mine and turn this data from digital information into knowledge that improves decision-making, increases efficiency, enhances product offerings, and improves the human condition. Artificial intelligence (AI), machine learning, and quantum computing are now the latest tools being used to accomplish these purposes.

Among the earliest to perfect the automated, computer-integrated, and flexible production systems of the Post-Industrial Era was Fanuc Ltd., Japan's most innovative robotic company.

> [Fanuc] rose to a class by itself with the completion in 1980 of its Fuji Factory. . . . The Fuji plant is organized for totally automatic operations, and routinely works five days a week, three shifts per day. Human workers in their smart yellow uniforms come in to service the machines and use computer-aided design to program for new products just on the day shift. At night the entire factory works in darkness, unattended except for the one operator monitoring the displays at a control center.[312]

Japan's post-industrial manufacturing superiority was clear by the mid-1980s. By this time it had outspent the United States two to one in automation and had considerably more computer numerical controlled machines on factory floors (55 percent compared with 18 percent), and while in Japan 40 percent of the workforce in the study sample were college-educated engineers (all trained to use computer numerical controlled machines), in America only 8 percent were engineers, with less than 25 percent trained to operate computer numerical controlled machines.[313] At the twentieth century's end, Japan remained the dominant builder and user of industrial robots, accounting for between 60 and 70 percent of annual installations.[314]

Fanuc's pioneering work was prescient of what was to come: factories producing in darkness with humans not on the shop floor but instead building, programming, monitoring, and maintaining machines that do the manufacturing work. NC (numerical control) and then computer numerical control (CNC) and CAD were all mastered by Fanuc in its ascent to the world's top robotics company, and as computers in manu-

312 Gerard K. O'Neill, *The Technology Edge: Opportunities for America in World Competition* (New York: Simon & Schuster, 1983), 97.

313 Ramchandran Jaikumar, "Postindustrial Manufacturing," *Harvard Business Review*, November 1986, 69–76.

314 Joseph F. Engelberger, "Historical Perspective and Role in Automation," in *Handbook of Industrial Robotics*, 2nd ed., ed. Shimon Y. Nof, vol. 1 (New York: John Wiley & Sons, 1999), 10.

facturing and computer science matured, CNC, CAD/CAM, and CIM (computer-aided manufacturing and computer-integrated manufacturing) became techniques that built the automated, computer-integrated, flexible economic capital of the Post-Industrial Era. It is to their contribution that we now turn.

Post-Industrial Production: CNC to CAD/CAM and CIM, and the Rise of Automated Factory and Production Systems

NC goes back to the sixteenth and seventeenth centuries.[315] In 1725, English knitting machines had punch card controls, and self-playing pianos were developed between 1840 and the early 1860s. Perforated music sheets were patented in 1840; a US patent for a keyboard piano player was issued to E. D. Bootman in 1860, and in 1863 Frenchman Henri Fourneaux patented the first pneumatic keyboard piano player.[316] With these, pianos played autonomously—pianist no longer required.

To better control manually operated machines on twentieth-century factory floors (then guided by human-operated levers and hand wheels), NC, "an operation of machine tools by means of specifically coded instructions to the machine control system," was developed.[317] Composed of numbers, letters, and symbols that included decimal points, percent signs, and parentheses, the instructions were logical statements specifying the exact movements machines followed to perform. NC machines had three components: programs (of instruction), controllers (mechanisms to control machines), and machine tools (performing controlled tasks). Essential were human programmers visualizing movements machines made and converting these into instructions that machine tools interpreted.

---

315 William W. Luggen, *Computer Numerical Control: A First Look Primer* (Albany, NY: Delmar, 1997), 20.

316 Alfred J. Hipkins and Kathleen Schlesinger, "Pianoforte" in *The Encyclopedia Britannica: A Dictionary of Arts, Sciences, Literature and General Information*, 11th ed., vol. 21, PAYN to POLKA, (New York: The Encyclopedia Britannica Company, 1911), 573, accessed December 20, 2023, https://archive.org/details/encyclopaediabri21chisrich/page/572/mode/2up.

317 Peter Smid, *CNC Programming Handbook: A Comprehensive Guide to Practical CNC Programming*, 3rd ed. (New York: Industrial Press, 2008), 1.

NC had one important disadvantage compared with CNC: the machine control system could not easily be adjusted on the factory floor. The control logic determined how control system wires were connected, and these were hardwired to interpret instructions loaded onto machines by punched tapes. CNC changed this.

> The modern CNC system (but not the old NC system) uses an internal microprocessor (*i.e.,* a computer). This computer contains memory registers storing a variety of routines that are capable of manipulating logical functions. That means the part programmer or machine operator can change any program at the control unit (at the machine), with instantaneous results.[318]

Most prevalent in machine tool metalworking, which accounted for around 70 percent of production machines in 2007,[319] CNC offered many advantages over NC-based systems, including:

> . . . the elimination of (punched-) tape handling, the capability for on-line program revision, automatic correction of machine inaccuracies, the control of several machines from a single control center, and the capability for integration into a sophisticated total manufacturing control system.[320]

Further, now found in a variety of machines (such as lathes, mills, laser cutting machines, welding machines, and printing and punch presses) and also in inspection, drafting systems, and garment cutting, the fact that CNC machines worked with other manufacturing control systems led to the next enhancements that improved the performance of post-industrial economic capital: the development of CAD/CAM and, finally, CIM.

---

318 Peter Smid, *CNC Programming Handbook*, 1.

319 Hassan El-Hofy, *Fundamentals of Machining Processes: Conventional and Nonconventional Processes* (Boca Raton, FL: CRC Press, 2007), 2.

320 James Madison, *CNC Machining Handbook: Basic Theory, Production Data, and Machining Procedures* (New York: Industrial Press, 1996), 15.

NC and CNC focused on the calibration and control of machines working on the factory floor, dictating how they executed tasks. The computerization of individual or groups of production devices was the central task. CAD extended computer use into the design phase of production, and CAM expanded computing into manufacturing from the design phase. CIM used computers to integrate the entire production process, combining CNC, CAD/CAM, and other subprocesses into a single, tightly integrated production system.

Initial development of CAD is attributed to Massachusetts Institute of Technology (MIT)–trained scientist Ivan Sutherland, who developed Sketchpad, the world's first graphical user interface (GUI). Though producing only 2D drawings, "the early version of the SKETCHPAD system showed that the designer could, for the first time, interact with the computer graphically via the medium of display screen and light-pen."[321]

Other developments followed. Vector-related 2D/3D software packages appeared, based on the Cartesian coordinate system (x, y, z) that permitted graphical screen representation of objects in 2D and 3D form. Computing power also grew exponentially, with machines such as the IBM 7094 mainframe—a relatively large-scale computer—debuting in 1964, and better CAD software heralded CAD's transition from costly mainframe/minicomputer programs (costing tens of thousands of dollars) to less expensive, microcomputer-based systems costing only thousands of dollars. CAD's commercialization contributed to the widespread application of the technique, such that CAD eventually permitted the following:

> The designer, working with the CAD system rather than the traditional drafting board, creates the lines and surfaces that form the object (product, part, structure, etc.) and stores this model in the computer database. By invoking the appropriate CAD software, the designer can

321 Michael Phiri, *Information Technology in Construction Design* (London: Thomas Telford, 1999), 52.

> perform various analyses on the object. . . . Once the design procedure has been completed, the computer-aided design system can generate the detailed drawings required to make the object.[322]

Deployment of CAD in the twenty-first century ranges from the creation of detailed 2D or 3D models of physical objects (such as mechanical parts, buildings, or molecules), to software that permits both the development and testing of products without the need to build costly prototypes, to applications helping architects or designers create technical plans and visual depictions of ideas, the latter enhanced by 3D printing that produces physical models of designs.

CAM was a natural progression from CAD: once product/object digital depictions were available, it was only a matter of time before software permitted geometrical data to be communicated to CNC machines so that design and manufacture were better integrated. CAM software converted design data into production codes that could be interpreted by CNC machines on factory floors.

Software conceived by French aircraft manufacturer Avions Marcel Dassault in the late 1970s is among the most sophisticated CAD/CAM software suites. Called CATIA (computer-aided three-dimensional interactive application) and marketed by Dassault Systèmes, the software gained notoriety when Boeing used it to develop its 777 airliner.

> In the mid-1980s, The Boeing Company invested in three-dimensional CAD/CAM (computer-aided design/computer-aided manufacturing) technology. . . . CATIA—along with several Boeing-created applications—allowed Boeing engineers to simulate the geometry of an airplane design on the computer without the costly and time-consuming investment of using physical mock-ups. The opportunity to apply the new CAD/CAM approach as well as other new engineering

322 A. Alavudeen and N. Venkateshwaran, *Computer Integrated Manufacturing* (New Delhi, India: PHI Learning, 2008), 2.

> and manufacturing ideas came in 1990 with the launch of the Boeing 777 twinjet.[323]

By 2010, CATIA applications were available in over 12 sectors, from automobiles and transport to aerospace and defense to architecture, engineering, and construction to high tech/electronics to consumer packaged goods. Dassault Systèmes described its business model as product life cycle management (PLM), which:

> helps companies share product data, apply common processes, and leverage corporate knowledge for the development of products from conception to retirement, across the extended enterprise. By including all actors (company departments, business partners, suppliers, OEM, and customers), PLM enables this entire network to operate as a single entity to conceptualize, design, build, and support products.[324]

The range of CATIA's PLM business model heralded the arrival of CIM, which in the case of Dassault Systèmes reflected the computerization of the entire production value chain, from design to manufacture to maintenance and support to decommissioning and finally to recycling. Because of its potentially wide scope, CIM's definition initially ranged from narrow to wide.

> Some observers take a narrow view and regard CIM as the linking of computer-aided design (CAD) and computer-aided manufacturing (CAM). Others take a broader view and see it partly as a methodology involving a consistent systems-based approach to running a manufacturing business, and partly as the integration of information and the integration of business and manufacturing activities. The CIM concept therefore starts with integration of the various aspects of production (e.g., design, planning, manufacturing, warehousing, materials handling, and quality control), but may also incorporate business aims and objectives, sales

323 Boeing, "777 Catia Designers at Work," https://secure.boeingimages.com/asset-management/2F3XC54VREX, accessed April 6, 2023. For more information on how CATIA and CAD/CAM were utilized in the 777 project, see Bill Yenne, *Inside Boeing: Building the 777* (St. Paul, MN: MBI Publishing Company, 2002).
324 Dassault Systèmes, "PLM Glossary," webpage retired http://www.3ds.com/plm-glossary/plm/.

> and marketing, and financial management. In some cases it is concerned with the linking of geographically separate sites. It can also involve electronically linking the business with its customers and suppliers.[325]

Fostered by the internet's arrival, hindsight shows the broader conceptualization perfectly captures CIM's boundaries. We now turn to considering how the internet and networking changed organization in the Post-Industrial Era, and in so doing enabled businesses and far-flung supply chains to be networked and tightly integrated both internally with partners and externally with customers.

Post-Industrial Organization: Networked, Less Hierarchical, More Focused/Specialized, Global and Local, Big and Small, Centralized and Decentralized

By the early twenty-first century, computers and networks were not only controlling factories and product design and manufacture: they were also replacing human-based hierarchy in organization administration and control and connecting organizations with customers, suppliers, and partners in a manner unimaginable only a decade earlier. In this process the structure of organization changed and rendered the industrial model of organization obsolete.

Understanding this new model of organization and where it is superior to organization in the Industrial Era is fundamental to competitiveness in the Post-Industrial Era. This transition from industrial to post-industrial organization is challenging for many industrial organizations, necessitating a category of post-industrial work described below as *post-industrial transformative work*. What this category represents and why it is required is covered later in this chapter when human capital in the Post-Industrial Era is considered.

Recall that in Chapter 3, the formation of the vertically integrated, hierarchically controlled, multidivisional industrial firm—exemplified

325 Karl-H. Ebel, *Computer-Integrated Manufacturing: The Social Dimension* (Geneva, Switzerland: International Labour Office, 1990), 1–2.

by Ford Motor Company and General Motors Company—was due to transaction costs faced at the time.[326] Given these costs were high, it was more efficient to perform most activities within firms.

Automation and computer integration of business processes and supply chains, in combination with the evolution of the internet, dramatically reduced transaction costs, and with these lower costs (and as TCE predicts), the structure of organizations changed. With many activities formerly performed internally now more efficiently available in the open market, organizations had to inevitably adjust.

The vignettes described previously show evidence of these changing transaction costs. Faced with the need to automate road building, Caterpillar could have formed an internal business unit and hoped to build its capability internally. Instead, it partnered with Trimble. Further, that travel agents have been replaced by online network-based services shows transaction cost changes even alter industry structure: here, lower transaction costs—mostly in the form of reduced traveler search costs—have almost eliminated an entire industry sector (travel agents). Consumers ordering online directly from suppliers is a final example of lower transaction costs changing industry structure. In post-industrial retail, information-rich networks permitting consumers to search and buy online, combined with FedEx or UPS logistics, are eliminating retailers and wholesalers.

This changing nature of post-industrial organization is supported by more widespread data. A study of 465 firms found that deeply internet-enabled organizations are more focused and specialized than less deeply "internetworked" organizations. In addition, higher levels of external partnering are also associated with the internet-enabling of business operations; the more deeply internet-enabled an organization is, the more external partnering it does.[327]

---

326 For how TCE influenced the formation of industrial firms, see footnote 163.

327 Peter J. Brews and Christopher L. Tucci, "Exploring the Structural Effects of Internetworking," *Strategic Management Journal* 25, no. 5 (May 2004): 429–51.

Consistent with declining transaction costs, the internet-enabling of businesses and extended supply chains have altered the vertically integrated, hierarchically controlled industrial enterprise. A new organizational form has emerged, pioneered by Cisco Systems, Inc. (Cisco).

Post-Industrial Organization in Practice: Cisco and the Internet Generation Company

Responsible for most of the early technical innovations that commercialized the internet, that Cisco was among the first to realize the internet could structure and organize business operations is unsurprising. Like Fanuc did with robots—before selling in the open market, the company used them internally—Cisco first deployed an internet-based network to manage its own business operations, and from its "Cisco on Cisco" lessons, the fundamentals of internet-based organization emerged. As Ford and General Motors pioneered the industrial factory and organizational model, Cisco pioneered the networked post-industrial organizational model.

In 1984, Stanford University staff Leonard Bosack and Sandra Lerner invented the router, a device that directs *packets* of information to specific destinations on a network. The packet addressing system developed to accompany this router—known as IP, or Internet Protocol—proved superior to circuit switching, prompting the two to quit their jobs and found Cisco, which sold its first router in 1986.[328] Essential to Cisco's success was that IP was technologically neutral; its routers were designed to connect computer systems operating on any protocol, unlike competitors such as IBM that had developed proprietary network architecture to connect IBM mainframes to dedicated *dumb* terminals.

By 2000, Cisco products were the backbone of the internet, and the company employed over 40,000 people located in over 225 offices in 75

---

328 Unless otherwise stated, information on Cisco is from Peter J. Brews and Glenn E. Bugos, *Cisco Systems: Empowering the Internet Generation of Companies* (Chapel Hill, NC: UNC Kenan-Flagler Business School, 2000) and Peter J. Brews and Elise Carner, *Internetworking @Cisco.com* (Chapel Hill, NC: UNC Kenan-Flagler Business School, 2003).

countries. Revenues were US$18.9 billion, up from US$69 million at the company's IPO in 1990, and in 1999 Cisco achieved the distinction of being the third most valuable company in the world by market capitalization, surpassed only by Microsoft and General Electric.

But Cisco is not exemplified because it was once the world's third most valuable company. Its share price peaked around this time and then declined and did not show much advance over the first two decades of the twenty-first century; this fall from grace showed that even the most sophisticated internet-enabled infrastructures do not protect against poor competitive strategy or unexpected market contractions. Cisco is exemplified because of its use of internetworking to attain unmatched organizational efficiency. In 2000 Cisco was an unmistakable Leader, showing the way forward into the internetworked post-industrial organizational form that would eventually drive all competitive businesses around the world.

A large-scale failure of Cisco's pre-internet IT system in May 1994 prompted the company to turn to the internet to control its business operations. At the time, Cisco was growing so fast that senior managers feared that unless a better organizational model was found, growth would falter, possibly even leading to the failure of the company itself. Faced with this challenge, the company turned to technology it had pioneered—the internet—to provide the backbone over which its business operations could be controlled. Legacy IT systems were replaced, and US$15 million was invested to build an internet-based IT infrastructure across the company.

In January 1995 John Chambers was appointed president and CEO and immediately introduced a new vision for the company: the supply of end-to-end internet-based networks to customers. Chambers reasoned the best way to market his vision would be to develop such a network within Cisco itself. Accordingly, over the next five years the company built an internet-based system to integrate and control its exploding business operations, and by 2000 the information elements of most business processes were internet-enabled and performed online. With a global internet-based network that provided interactive, 24/7/365 access to users in multiple languages, and operating off three major portals linking over 10 million web pages,[329] Cisco was the world's most deeply internetworked company.

The internet-based infrastructure delivered unparalleled efficiency and speed to Cisco customers, employees, suppliers, and partners alike. By 1997 Cisco reported its global internet-based network had increased customer satisfaction from 3.4 to 4.2 on a 5-point scale; had permitted sales to quadruple while call center staff grew only 10 percent; had increased speed and accuracy of orders, shipping, and deployment; had dramatically increased supply chain efficiency; and had saved over US$350 million on an annual basis.[330]

By 2000, over 90 percent of Cisco's orders were placed online with no human involvement; suppliers and partners received orders when placed; customers tracked order progress online with access to Cisco supplier and partner websites where required; and over 80 percent of after-sale service inquiries were handled electronically, many through frequently-asked-question (FAQ) pages that guided users to information they sought without human assistance.

The 2000 dot-com crash and the economic contraction that followed gave Cisco further impetus to enhance its internet-based infrastructure. Refinements across all areas of the business were made over the following years, including improvements in how sales were managed across the internet, how technical assistance was provided across the network, how human resources management was performed, how finance was administered and controlled, and how supply chain management was conducted across Cisco's expanding network of customers, suppliers, and partners.

---

329 The three portals were Cisco Connection Online (CCO), which connected external stakeholders such as customers (existing or potential), potential employees seeking jobs, investors, or other persons seeking general information on Cisco; Cisco Supplier System (CSC), which connected partners and suppliers; and Cisco Employee Connection (CEC), which connected and enabled employees to conduct internal business over an intranet.

330 Andy Reinhardt, "Meet Cisco's Mr. Internet," Bloomberg, September 13, 1999, accessed April 6, 2023, https://www.bloomberg.com/news/articles/1999-09-12/meet-ciscos-mr-dot-internet.

How human resources management and administration changed as the internet-based infrastructure deepened illustrates the way internet-based IT moved from a cost center to a value generator at Cisco. To help manage the heavy demand for new recruits during the high-growth period in the mid-1990s, human resources posted vacant positions online and accepted job applications only over the internet, with these instantly routed to decision-makers.[331] These processes reduced job application administration costs and improved hiring efficiency.

The downsizing in 2000 after the dot-com crash most clearly illustrates where internet-based human resources delivered value. Needing to reduce the 44,000 employees by 8,000 as a result of the unexpected economic contraction, management sought a tool to assess employees for this purpose. A team of around 100, including personnel from human resources, IT, and employee relations—mainly to ensure that the process was legally defensible—worked closely with senior line management to develop a downsizing algorithm. Compiled in a few days, the algorithm scaled every employee's performance, from John Chambers down, and the 8,000 who would be asked to leave were identified.

The algorithm was the first of its kind in the world and saved considerable time, money, and other resources while producing a downsizing that was efficient, transparent, equitable, consistent, and legally defensible.[332] Face-to-face meetings complemented online tools and communications that provided outplacement assistance and information on the severance packages offered. Though organization in the Post-Industrial Era is high-tech and network-based, it is also high touch. The need for human engagement remains.

331 At one stage in the mid-1990s, Cisco was hiring over 3,000 people per quarter, and without internet-based tools, the volume may have overwhelmed the company. Cisco also stopped accepting mail-in resumes once the internet-based job application system was in operation. Not only was administering traditional applications more expensive and cumbersome, the fact that an applicant did not use the internet for submission indicated this person was unsuited to Cisco's internet-based business model (not to mention misaligned with its core business). If you communicated by such "snail-mail" you were from the wrong time and not ready for Cisco's operations or business model.

332 Customer satisfaction data in the algorithm had been gathered over preceding years at Cisco, providing trusted data to scale employee performance. Without such data, the algorithm would have been infeasible.

The internet-enabling of business processes is not the only factor exemplifying post-industrial organization at Cisco. Its macrostructure does too. Rather than manufacturing routers in company-owned factories on the vertically integrated basis typical of the Industrial Era, from early on Cisco sourced product from external contract manufacturers, most based in Southeast Asia. In addition, faced with a need for in-country partners to install network equipment around the world, rather than establishing Cisco operations in each country, local organizations were contracted to perform the task. For example, Dimension Data, based in Johannesburg and still a top-tier Cisco partner, was Cisco's first *boots on the ground* in South Africa.

Cisco even outsourced innovation: instead of engineers toiling away in Cisco laboratories under company-approved budgets, acquisitions became the dominant way new technology was obtained; to this day, Cisco R&D personnel spend far more time in acquisition discussions than they do in Cisco research labs. Similarly, when Cisco needed logistics capabilities to move product around the world, internal logistics were not used. The likes of FedEx or UPS supplied the products and services needed.

Cisco's Internet-Based Structure: Tightly Integrated Collectives of Specialized Businesses, Partners, and Suppliers

The nature of post-industrial organization is revealed by Cisco's actions. Unlike the vertically integrated industrial firm where most of the activities to produce, market, maintain, and innovate are done under a single hierarchy, post-industrial organization, because of the automation of business processes and the ease with which activities can now be coordinated across internet-based networks, is better described as a collection of specialized, interdependent partners combining to meet customer needs. Focused partners responsible for specific niches make up the post-industrial enterprise.

The internet-enabling of business operations does not only narrow firm scope. Instead of human-mediated hierarchy being the central coordinating device, the network is the dominant control mechanism, which also profoundly affects firm scope, structure, and operational performance. A multi-industry study of 550 firms based in 46 countries showed the following:

> Deeper internetworking associates with a narrowing of organisational focus because activities that had been performed internally can be outsourced. Moreover, hierarchy and the human intermediation of routine tasks are replaced by internet-mediated processes: with internet-enabling, operational precision and speed increase while operating costs, headcount and hierarchy decline.[333]

Simply put, with the internetworking of business operations, organizational scope narrows, hierarchy diminishes, head count and operational costs drop, and operational efficiency improves.

Unlike the human hierarchy and systems that controlled only what transpired within industrial firms, internal and external firm stakeholders are coordinated and controlled by the network. Internet-based networks tightly link customers, suppliers, and business partners (including managers and employees from each collective member) and control interactions and operations both within and among all involved. Four principles guide these interactions:

> First, stakeholders must have 24/7/365 access to the network—information is available to all with appropriate authentication and network security. Second, once any activity/process can be modeled (i.e., reduced to statements capturing the routines which the activity/process/transaction represents) and is amenable to standardization and automation, it can be coordinated over the Internet. Third, interaction is achieved mainly through user-driven self-service, supported by frequently-asked-question (FAQ) links/default boxes that prompt

333 Peter J. Brews and Christopher L. Tucci, "The Structural and Performance Effects of Internet-working," *Long Range Planning* 40, no. 2 (April 2007): 223–4.

> correct choices when improper selections are made. Fourth, control through rules intermediated by humans is rejected in favor of control through algorithms. Humans control only processes that cannot be standardized and automated.[334]

That internet-based control replaces human-mediated control indicates automation and computer integration not only impact factory operations. Just as factory jobs are eliminated by computer-integrated machines, jobs performed by humans in finance, marketing, operations, HR, and general administration are too. In post-industrial organization as in post-industrial factories, humans do only what machines cannot do, and this includes activities in all functions and business processes, whether in the factory or office, across the logistics supply chain, or with partners, suppliers, customers, or employees.

This combination of networks and focused partners and suppliers also provides opportunities for post-industrial organizations to move from being more *either–or* to becoming *both–and* in composition and capabilities. Traditional industrial organizations were either big or small, were either centralized or decentralized, or were either global or local, and so forth. Now, because of the enhanced capabilities that specialization and internet-based networking allow, organizations and their networks are more flexible and adept.

Cisco is big where it needs to be big and enjoys all the benefits that size and scale afford (fiscal year 2022 revenues were US$51.6 billion, and the company employed 83,300 worldwide).[335] But it is also small where it needs to be small: Cisco can fund a few entrepreneurial engineers in startups to go after innovative ideas, though this small group is still part of and controlled by its network. Cisco is also centralized where it needs to be centralized, providing tight cost control: if conditions demand travel expense reductions, all the CFO needs to do is adjust per diem rates, and

---

334 Peter J. Brews and Christopher L. Tucci, "Internetworking: Building Internet-generation Companies," *Academy of Management Executive* 17, no. 4 (November 2003): 9.
335 Cisco, *Reimagining the Future of Connectivity*, 2022 Annual Report, accessed April 7, 2023, https://www.cisco.com/c/dam/en_us/about/annual-report/cisco-annual-report-2022.pdf.

with a code change, no employee will receive more than the new sum allows. But Cisco is also decentralized when it needs to be decentralized; for example, when business units add capabilities to their web-based infrastructures that do not apply to other parts of Cisco, these are done—and funded—by units themselves. Finally, Cisco is global when global is needed and local when local is needed, seen in suppliers that are the best global sources available and its choice of partner Dimension Data to represent it in South Africa.

That post-industrial organizations are big where they need to be big, small where they need to be small, centralized where they need to be centralized, decentralized where they need to be decentralized, global where they need to be global, and local where they need to be local are not the only benefits networked post-industrial structures deliver. In post-industrial organizations, structure is not something they have; structuring is what they do. Industrial firms constructed palaces—HQ buildings—to indicate their stability, prestige, and success, and they relied on organizational charts and lines—dotted or otherwise—to demarcate where all belonged and how power was allocated. Post-industrial networked organizations build digital tents, easily erected and taken down depending on the specifications and conditions required and encountered.

Importantly, what Cisco pioneered now routinely takes place in the many thousands, if not millions, of orders placed around the world every minute, governed and covered by digital tents that structure and control them as they move from placement to completion. This data then remains available for use should a customer wish to access past orders, or should a company wish to mine past orders to establish customer buying patterns for future product offerings.

Innovations since Cisco's new organizational form was pioneered have led to even greater disaggregation and fragmentation of operations and supply chains as well as many new IT services and solutions for firms and individuals alike. Organizations migrating from traditional centralized legacy IT systems to the IT cloud (essentially remote servers: devices that store, send, and receive data connected across the internet) can now rent computing power on demand in the cloud. With owning IT assets no longer needed to use them, cloud computing offers outsourced IT infrastructure, software applications, and platforms, often on a pay-as-you-go basis.

Underscoring the cloud's widespread reach, leading cloud computing provider Amazon Web Services (AWS) offers—from startups to MNCs—a myriad of cloud services broadly divisible into software as a service (SaaS), platform as a service (PaaS), and infrastructure as a service (IaaS). An Amazon subsidiary offering cloud-based services alongside others such as Salesforce, Microsoft, and Google, AWS reported 2021 revenues of US$65.2 billion, and in 2022 it employed 136,000 and served 34 percent of the cloud market, alongside Microsoft Azure at 21 percent and Google Cloud at 11 percent.[336] AWS's IaaS was fundamental to the cloud's formation and rapid expansion after 2002, and the company's impact on cloud computing has been substantial.

> AWS has revolutionized the way companies utilize computing services. By offering a vast array of cloud-based solutions and services, Amazon Web Services has effectively democratized access to cutting-edge technology and infrastructure. The pay-as-you-go pricing structure, coupled with continuous innovation and unparalleled scalability, has allowed businesses of all sizes to remain competitive and agile in an ever-evolving landscape.[337]

AWS's best-known customers include Airbnb, Kellogg's, McDonald's, Twitter/X, Epic Games, and Nordstrom.[338] Netflix, which operates thousands of its own internal servers, is also an important AWS customer that goes back at least as far as 2016.

336 Ch Daniel, "Amazon Revenue and Growth Statistics 2023," *The SignHouse blog*, SignHouse, updated January 15, 2023, accessed April 11, 2023, https://www.usesignhouse.com/blog/aws-stats.
337 Gitnux, "AWS: Business Model, SWOT Analysis & Competitors 2023," *Gitnux* (blog), accessed April 11, 2023, https://blog.gitnux.com/companies/aws/.
338 Daniel, "Amazon Revenue and Growth Statistics 2023."

> Online content provider Netflix can support seamless global service by using Amazon Web Services (AWS). AWS enables Netflix to quickly deploy thousands of servers and terabytes of storage within minutes. Users can stream Netflix shows and movies from anywhere in the world, including on the web, on tablets, or on mobile devices such as iPhones.[339]

End-user expenditure on public cloud services was forecast to reach US$591 billion in 2023, almost US$200 billion higher than just two years prior,[340] and the substantial increase in cloud-based services in the twenty-first century means massive server farms—many thousands of servers in single locations, serving multiple computing and storage needs—now operate worldwide. The Citadel in Tahoe Reno, Nevada—allegedly the largest server farm ever built—serves eBay, Microsoft, Google, Amazon, and FedEx, among others; when additions to the Citadel campus are fully constructed, it's projected to reach 7.3 million square feet in size.[341]

Now that organization in the Post-Industrial Era has been explained, infrastructure in the Post-Industrial Era will be considered. Predictably, this focuses on building the capacity to handle the immense digital traffic post-industrial society generates and uses to guide and control the products, services, and solutions delivered to post-industrial consumers.

As the vignettes and coverage of economic capital and organization in the Post-Industrial Era underscore, information and its dissemination and analysis are core to post-industrial work and life. As a result, infrastructure provision shifts from a focus on non-network-related physical infrastructure to the provision of connectivity and to the seemingly continual increase in network bandwidth. Infrastructure in the Post-In-

---

339 Amazon Web Services, "Netflix Case Study," 2016, accessed April 9, 2023, https://aws.amazon.com/solutions/case-studies/netflix-case-study/.

340 Gartner, "Gartner Forecasts Worldwide Public Cloud End-User Spending to Reach Nearly $600 Billion in 2023," press release, October 31, 2022, accessed April 10, 2023, https://www.gartner.com/en/newsroom/press-releases/2022-10-31-gartner-forecasts-worldwide-public-cloud-end-user-spending-to-reach-nearly-600-billion-in-2023. .

341 Mary Zhang, "Inside the World's Largest Data Center," Dgtl Infra, December 24, 2020, accessed April 9, 2023, https://dgtlinfra.com/inside-the-worlds-largest-data-center/.

dustrial Era mostly involves ensuring bandwidth of sufficient size is available for networks to operate efficiently and securely.

Post-Industrial Infrastructure: Bandwidth for Far-Flung Networks

Chapter 3 captured construction of the infrastructure to industrialize America in the efforts of early infrastructure builders and in the road building, port and airport construction, and electricity generation and transmission, all mostly done by public sector entities over the first half of the twentieth century. High-quality roads, rail, ports, airports, electricity, and water services are still required, but in the post-industrial world, the focus shifts to the telecommunications needed to sustain the deeply networked world that is appearing.

Early telecommunication was by telegraph or telephone line using twisted pairs of copper wire, but by the twentieth century's end, wireless communication complemented the more powerful wired networks that had appeared. By 2020, both wired and wireless wide area networks with reaches across far-flung geographies and even continents worked alongside wired and wireless local area networks (LANs) that provided local last-mile connectivity. Not using the twisted copper wire that carried the traffic of *plain old telephone service*, the more reliable wired Ethernet LANs used coaxial or fiber-optic cable to connect to the internet.

These Ethernet-based LANs now operate at speeds unimaginable just a decade ago. In 2023, standard Ethernet supported speeds of up to 10 Mbps (megabits per second); fast Ethernet, 100 Mbps; gigabit Ethernet, 1 Gbps (gigabits per second); and 10-gigabit Ethernet, 10 Gbps.[342]

In addition, technological advance also means twenty-first-century telecommunications infrastructure at times bypasses the materials-intensive methods of the Industrial Era. Instead of laying down millions of miles of wires for telephone services, India and China are connecting their

---

342 Kiran Kumar Panigrahi, "Difference between Fast Ethernet and Gigabit Ethernet," Tutorials Point, updated January 6, 2023, accessed April 10, 2023, https://www.tutorialspoint.com/difference-between-fast-ethernet-and-gigabit-ethernet.

massive populations through wireless communications. Indian farmers conversing on cell phones atop donkey carts transporting crops to market perfectly captures this pre- to post-industrial infrastructure leapfrog, with cell phones being scaled far faster than landline phones ever were in the twentieth century. Being a Follower at times has its advantages.

As communication now almost everywhere depends on some form of network-based connection, connectivity and its cost are vital. Some contend global competitiveness depends on how well-connected countries, communities, individuals, and organizations are:

> A postindustrial city dependent on knowledge-based industries for economic survival must give due attention to the progressive deepening of IT skills in the workforce and complement those skills with a modern telecommunications system. Anything less risks being left out of the knowledge and production network.[343]

Well-priced, widespread, high-speed connectivity is essential for any post-industrial society, and OECD data indicates how countries are progressing. But before reporting this data, broadband as a concept warrants attention.

Permitting data, voice, and video to be transmitted at high speeds, broadband-based communication, like computing power before it, continues to expand and makes static definition difficult. At the time of writing this book, the US Federal Communications Commission (FCC) considered 25 Mbps download and 3 Mbps upload speeds as the minimum for consumer broadband internet, and these speeds are available over a variety of technologies;[344] 256 kilobits per second (kbps) was thought sufficient when OECD broadband research started in the

---

343 Shahid Yusuf and Kaoru Nabeshima, *Postindustrial East Asian Cities: Innovation for Growth* (Palo Alto, CA: Stanford University Press, 2006), 91.

344 BroadbandUSA, "How Fast Is Broadband?" National Telecommunications and Information Administration, US Department of Commerce, accessed April 10, 2023, https://broadbandusa.ntia.doc.gov/about-us/frequently-asked-questions/how-fast-broadband.

early 2000s.[345] By 2023, 4G (fourth-generation broadband cellular technology) surpassed 3G, and 5G was already superseding 4G.

Determining where a country or community falls in broadband adoption and how fast this broadband is expanded as it develops is useful. Figure 11 shows broadband subscriptions per 100 inhabitants (in gray columns) between OECD countries at two times: 2009 and 2022. To show how adoption associates with economic wealth, US$ GDP per capita on a PPP basis are also included (in black).[346] As expected, Figure 11 shows developed nations typically have higher broadband adoption than developing nations do. The correlation coefficient between broadband adoption and GDP per capita for 2009 data was 0.70, a very high r^2 for data such as this, and though declining to 0.54 in 2022, the association remained strong.

The figure also reveals adoption has increased over the 13 years. Switzerland, highest in 2022 with 49.9 percent of inhabitants with broadband subscriptions, is up from 35.6 percent in 2009. America, at 26.4 percent of inhabitants with subscriptions in 2009, increased to 38.3 percent by 2022 (though dropping from 15 to 16).[347] The increase is also seen in the broadband scale moving from 5 to 40 in 2009 to 5 to 55 in 2022, with 2009's lowest score (Turkey) being 9 percent of inhabitants with subscriptions versus 2022's lowest score (Colombia) being 17.1 percent.

345 OECD, "The Development of Broadband Access in the OECD Countries," *OECD Digital Economy Papers* 56 (Paris: OECD Publishing, October 2001), accessed April 10, 2023, https://doi.org/10.1787/233822327671.

346 OECD, "OECD Broadband statistics," 2009 data is no longer online, 2022 data accessed April 11, 2023, http://www.oecd.org/digital/broadband/broadband-statistics/.

347 The FCC—based on 25 Mbps download and 3 Mbps upload (25/3), the minimum speeds for consumer broadband—reported over 97 percent of Americans had access to fixed high-speed internet in 2021, far higher than the 38.3 percent OECD broadband subscription estimate in 2022. But access differs from subscription, which is a better measure. Further, the FCC measures access by minimum download/upload speeds (25/3), while the OECD measures fixed subscriptions in five tiers (from <1.5/2 Mbps to ≥1,000 Mbps) and reported that 70.2 percent of the 38.3 percent of 2022 US inhabitants who had access through subscriptions enjoyed speeds ≥100 Mbps. FCC estimates also may be more optimistic than data indicates. A 2018 study noted no Pennsylvania county had at least 50 percent of its population with broadband access at the 25/3 minimum speeds, while FCC data indicated 100 percent did (Sascha D. Meinrath et al., "Broadband Availability and Access in Rural Pennsylvania, "The Center for Rural Pennsylvania, June 2019, accessed April 15, 2023, https://www.rural.palegislature.us/broadband/Broadband_Availability_and_Access_in_Rural_Pennsylvania_2019_Report.pdf).

Finally, an increase in the average subscription score of the countries included in both samples is seen. In 2009, 24.3 percent of sample residents on average had broadband subscriptions, the range from Turkey at 9 percent to the Netherlands at 37.1 precent. In 2022 the sample average of 35.3 percent of inhabitants with subscriptions was close to the highest score in 2009 of 37.1, with the 2022 range being from lowest Columbia at 17.1 percent of inhabitants with subscriptions to highest Switzerland at 49.9 percent. This 49.9 percent will likely be among the low scores in 10 years' time.

There are other insights from Figure 11. South Korea at 5 in 2009 and 2022 shows a nation punching above its economic weight. The country's broadband penetration is far higher than its GDP per capita would predict, reflecting long-standing government policy to make the country among the world's most electronically connected. South Korea's 45 percent broadband subscription in 2022 compared with America's 38.3 percent may be due to policy differences.

Figure 11: OECD Broadband Subscriptions per 100 Inhabitants and GDP/Capita (US$ PPP), 2009 versus 2022

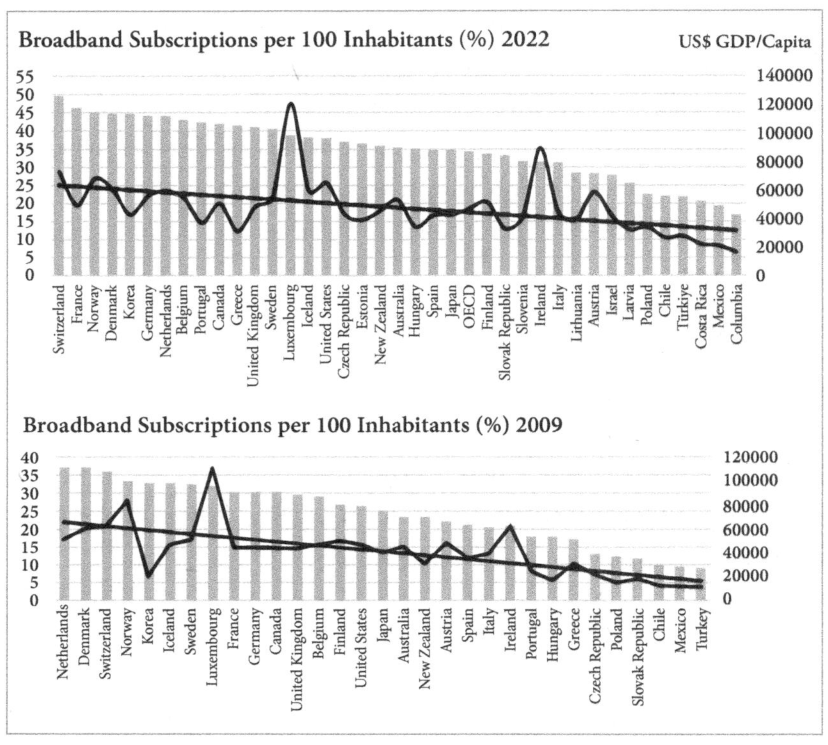

The U.S. Government has never adopted an aggressive broadband policy, despite rosy statements about the information superhighway by various politicians. In other nations, including South Korea, the government has accelerated and even subsidized broadband development with a goal of delivering the highest level of services possible to further such social goals as high-quality support for telemedicine, education, public services, and industrial development. Instead of building broadband systems on one seamless standard, U.S. cable companies and telephone companies are battling for dominance with their two separate systems.[348]

---

348 Jack W. Plunkett, *Plunkett's Infotech Industry Almanac 2009* (Houston, TX: Plunkett Research, 2009), 27.

Even in the Post-Industrial Era, the balance between infrastructure development led by the state versus the private sector differs across countries, reminiscent of the plans versus markets controversy noted in the First Mover versus Fast Follower industrialization models in Chapter 3. To build broadband infrastructure, America has relied more on markets, while South Korea has placed more faith in plans.

The relative position and rankings over time of each country in the OECD data seemingly show the South Korean approach has been more successful to date. Continuing this reasoning, the Greek and Portuguese 2022 rankings at 9 and 11, respectively, may also be an advantage of EU membership, another triumph of plans over markets given how low their GDPs are compared with others in the top 15.

Ireland is the second outlier in the table. Despite very high GDP per capita statistics, Ireland was 22 of 31 nations in broadband adoption in 2009 and fell to 27 of 38 nations in 2022 even though its GDP per capita increased from third- to second-highest in the sample. Ireland is a prosperous country but not as prosperous as is often thought because of the inappropriate use of misleading, albeit conventional, statistics. Ireland's broadband adoption may be more accurate than its GDP per capita statistic is.

> When we dig into the available data in the more relevant parts of per capita income and consumption, we find that Ireland's relative international position is somewhere between 8th and 12th in the European Union—a lot lower than is commonly presumed. The lower ranking comes not only from removing the distortions from multinationals but also from taking account of the fact that consumer prices in Ireland are relatively high.[349]

Figure 11 also supports the inference that American telecommunications infrastructure may not be at the level expected from the country

349 Patrick Honohan, "Is Ireland Really the Most Prosperous Country in Europe?," *Economic Letter*, Central Bank of Ireland, 2021, no. 1 (February 2001): 1–8, accessed April 15, 2023, https://www.centralbank.ie/docs/default-source/publications/economic-letters/vol-2021-no-1-is-ireland-really-the-most-prosperous-country-in-europe.pdf.

that pioneered the internet and the technology deployed in its operation. Out of the 31 countries included in the OECD data, America ranked fifteenth and sixteenth in broadband penetration in 2009 and 2022; however, it must be recognized that America is far bigger geographically than any sample country but Canada (though Canada's adoption was still higher than America at both times).

America's position over time has also deteriorated. When the OECD began gathering data in 2001, the United States ranked fourth, and by 2006 the country had regressed to twelfth. Despite OECD estimates that America accounted for 30 percent of broadband use worldwide, 2009 data revealed Americans still paid more for access than 24 of the countries in the OECD data. Only residents of the Czech Republic, the Slovak Republic, Mexico, Iceland, Hungary, Poland, and Norway paid more than Americans.

Different solutions to remedy the inadequacy of America's broadband infrastructure have been advanced. One that gained notoriety in 2005 was that the US federal government should push "the President's Information Technology Advisory Committee (PITAC), a group of private sector IT leaders and academics, to play a key leadership role in advancing broadband deployment."[350] This solution envisaged mostly a cheerleading role for government and primarily relied on private sector stakeholders to suggest and implement the steps needed to improve America's broadband services.

Other solutions demand more activist roles for government—for example, municipalities that offer broadband wireless service to reduce the digital divides in their communities, though these ideas invariably evoked protests from private operators.

> Private providers understandably express concern that cities providing a wireless broadband service have an unlimited base from which to raise capital, act as a regulator for local rights of way and tower permitting,

350 Thomas Bleha, "Down to the Wire," *Foreign Affairs* 84, no. 3 (May–June 2005): 122.

> own public infrastructure necessary for network deployment including street lights, and are tax-exempt organizations.[351]

A third blueprint called for a coordinated effort between federal, state, and local officials with guidance from an advisory committee of commercial and nonprofit institutions, including tax incentives to encourage private sector broadband investment and investment by municipalities and states. This solution alleged that to improve broadband penetration, America needed more government plans and less market involvement.

> The profit/loss statements of individual firms fail to take into account the positive externalities from a widely deployed broadband network, including economic growth, lower-cost health care, and higher-quality education. In contrast, most other nations treat broadband as necessary infrastructure; their governments adopted explicit broadband stimulus plans at the turn of the century, and their countries are now reaping the benefits.[352]

In May 2022 the Biden-Harris Administration announced its "Internet for All" initiative marshaling an investment of US$45 billion to provide affordable, reliable, high-speed internet for all by the end of 2030. US Secretary of Commerce Gina M. Raimondo noted:

> In the 21st century, you simply cannot participate in the economy if you don't have access to reliable, affordable high-speed internet. . . . Thanks to President Biden's Bipartisan Infrastructure Law, Americans across the country will no longer be held back by a lack of high-speed internet access. We are going to ensure every American will have access

351 Andrea Tapia, Julio Angel Ortiz, and Edgar Maldonado Rangel, "Making Good on Municipal Promises: Can Municipal Wireless Broadband Networks Reduce Information Inequality?," in *Emerging Trends and Challenges in Information Technology Management*, ed. Mehdi Khosrow-Pour, vol. 2 (Hershey, PA: Idea Group Publishing, 2006), 601.

352 John Windhausen Jr., "A Blueprint for Big Broadband" (EDUCAUSE White Paper, 2008), accessed April 15, 2023, 1, https://library.educause.edu/-/media/files/library/2008/1/epo0801-pdf.pdf.

to technologies that allow them to attend class, start a small business, visit with their doctor, and participate in the modern economy.[353]

Despite the press release announcing the initiative, few notable proactive steps have been taken by the US federal government to remedy the country's seemingly growing broadband deficit. However, the country's broadband access challenges may not be from infrastructure deficiencies themselves. A 2022 report from a respected nonpartisan independent research institute concluded:

> Claims that the United States stacks up generally poorly against other economies in its broadband performance are far off the mark, but there are still areas ripe for improvement. Despite populist rhetoric to the contrary, the U.S. broadband market is competitive, and private Internet service providers (ISPs)—fueled by their own investments and recent government funding for deployment to high-cost unserved areas—are continually improving the reach and quality of broadband service. The central remaining challenge for U.S. broadband policy is adoption, wherein the United States has a middling performance compared with international peers, but the United States also has a host of demographic factors that play into lower adoption rates.[354]

Key report takeaways included that mobile coverage was "ubiquitous," with 4G covering almost all the American population and 5G being competitive even with South Korea at 93 percent; that broadband access was widely available to most Americans and easily met the limit of 2 percent of monthly income used to determine affordability; that in 2019, 92 percent of the population had access to fixed broadband at speeds of 100 Mbps upload/10 Mbps download, and by 2020, 25

---

353 US Department of Commerce, "Biden-Harris Administration Launches $45 Billion 'Internet for All' Initiative to Bring Affordable, Reliable High-Speed Internet to Everyone in America," press release, May 13, 2022, accessed April 15, 2023, https://www.commerce.gov/news/press-releases/2022/05/biden-harris-administration-launches-45-billion-internet-all-initiative.

354 Jessica Dine and Joe Kane, "The State of US Broadband in 2022: Reassessing the Whole Picture," The Information Technology and Innovation Foundation: 3, December 5, 2022, accessed April 17, 2023, https://itif.org/publications/2022/12/05/state-of-us-broadband-in-2022-reassessing-the-whole-picture/.

percent had access to "highly superfluous" gigabit speeds (again on par with South Korea); and that though in 2019, 92 percent of the population had access to fixed broadband at 100/10 speeds, but despite this only 62 percent of households subscribed to fixed connections meeting the 25/3 FCC minimum benchmarks.

Possibly the report's most important conclusion was that subscription and adoption—impacted by many non-IT-based demographic factors—and neither access nor cost, were the country's greatest telecommunication challenges. This conclusion is similar to that regarding the lack of education in the United States being a result of poverty rather than factors in the delivery of education itself. Regardless, when broadband reaches the vast majority of Americans is still to be seen. Having covered economic capital, organization, and infrastructure in the Post-Industrial Era, we now turn to human resources in the Post-Industrial Era.

Post-Industrial Human Resources: Doing Only What Machines Cannot Do

With computers, machines, systems, and networks arbitraging them out of routine work, workers in leading-edge post-industrial contexts are left to contribute in three areas: creating new goods, services, or solutions (post-industrial creative work); finding better ways to organize, produce, and deliver existing goods, services, or solutions (post-industrial transformative work); or performing manual tasks machines cannot do, or manually assisting machines in the work they do (post-industrial manual work). Before considering these, however, observations regarding human capital in the Post-Industrial Era are warranted.

First, it must be recognized that the bar is rising for all factors of production, a fact already obvious from coverage of post-industrial economic capital. Applying this to human capital, recall that in the Industrial Era, manual dexterity, a high school education, and the discipline to arrive for work at 8:00 a.m. and work until 5:00 p.m. while following instructions represented the passport to a middle-class life. But as is pointed out often in this chapter, our manual dexterity no longer surpasses that of machines. Mental dexterity is now the license to higher living standards.

Second, and as is typical in structural change of this nature, both positive and negative effects are occurring as the transition progresses. Workers in fully industrialized (i.e., developed) societies with only manual industrial skills will experience downward mobility relative to those with skills better suited to post-industrial conditions. This was already apparent by the early 1990s in the United States:

> A distinguishing feature of the postindustrial order is that the economic fates of people in the same society disconnect, leading to greater income inequality. Well-paid, but relatively unskilled industrial jobs move from the first world to less-developed nations or disappear in the face of an expanding informal economy where sweatshops replace unionized factories. Meanwhile, those highly skilled workers who manage the global production process receive rich rewards. The postindustrial world is "divided into a prosperous technical, managerial, professional grouping on the one hand, and a poorly paid clerical and service proletariat on the other."[355]

How societies reduce the impact of such changes remains an important question: "prosperous technical, managerial, or professional" workers surrounded by "a poorly paid clerical or service proletariat" is a recipe for unrest and political instability. Further, income inequality has been increasing in America since the 1970s.

> The most commonly used measure of income inequality, the Gini index (also known as the index of income concentration), indicated a decline in family income inequality of 7.4 percent from 1947 to 1968. Since 1968, there has been an increase in income inequality, reaching its 1947 level in 1982 and increasing further since then. The increase

355 Keith Boeckelman, "The American States in the Postindustrial Economy," *State and Local Government Review* 27, no. 3 (Fall 1995): 182–3.

was 16.1 percent from 1968 to 1992 and 22.4 percent from 1968 to 1994.[356]

The US Gini index or coefficient, varying from 0 to 1 where 0 is perfect equality and 1 is maximal inequality among the variables measured, was 0.43 in 1990, 0.47 in 2010, and 0.49 in 2020.[357] This trend is explained by many factors in addition to the shift from industrial to post-industrial operations, including tax cuts for the wealthy, a move from welfare to workfare over the 1990s, a drop in the real minimum wage, intensifying global competition and the offshoring of low-value jobs, and a decline in union power.

Third, that mental rather than manual dexterity is required of humans in the Post-Industrial Era means education remains vital to prepare workers for post-industrial work, and given the intellectual demands of this work, education's role is even more paramount. The returns on education measured by income earned underscore this fact. Table 10 indicates the median weekly annual salaries and unemployment rates for full-time workers in the United States in 2022, controlling for educational attainment.

Table 10 shows education's importance in a country well on its way to post-industrial status. In 2022, high school graduates on average earned 60 percent of the income of bachelor's degree holders and only 41 percent of what professional degree holders earned. In addition, a master's or professional degree improved income compared with a bachelor's degree by 16 and 45 percent, respectively. Unemployment rates also drop noticeably

---

356 Daniel H. Weinberg, "A Brief Look at Postwar U.S. Income Inequality," *Current Population Reports* (Washington, DC: Bureau of the Census, US Department of Commerce, June 1996), 1, accessed April 17, 2023, http://academic.brooklyn.cuny.edu/soc/docs/Inequality(p60-191).pdf.
357 Statista Research, "Household Income Distribution According to the Gini Index of Income Inequality in the United States from 1990 to 2021," March 20, 2023, accessed April 17, 2023, https://www.statista.com/statistics/219643/gini-coefficient-for-us-individuals-families-and-households/.
At 0.63, South Africa has the world's highest Gini coefficient (Statista Research, "20 Countries with the Biggest Inequality in Income Distribution Worldwide in 2021, Based on the Gini Index," October 26, 2022, accessed April 17, 2023, https://www.statista.com/statistics/264627/ranking-of-the-20-countries-with-the-biggest-inequality-in-income-distribution/.

as educational attainment rises; unemployment for holders of doctoral or professional degrees in 2022 was 1.0 percent and 1.4 percent, respectively, increasing to 2.2 percent for bachelor's degree holders and almost doubling to 4.0 percent for high school graduates. Finally, in 2022 holders of less than a high school diploma not only earned far less than others, they also faced unemployment in excess of 5 percent.

Table 10: Educational Attainment, Earnings, and Unemployment in the United States: 2022

Educational Attainment	Median Weekly Earnings (US$)	Unemployment Rate (%)
Doctoral degree	2,083	1.0
Professional degree	2,080	1.4
Master's degree	1,661	1.9
Bachelor's degree	1,432	2.2
Associate degree	1,005	2.7
Some college, no degree	935	3.5
High school diploma	853	4.0
Less than high school diploma	682	5.5
All workers	1,123	3.0

Source: Current Population Survey, US Department of Labor, US Bureau of Labor Statistics, table 5.1, last modified September 6, 2023, accessed December 20, 2023, https://www.bls.gov/emp/tables/unemployment-earnings-education.htm, Data is for persons age 25 and older. Earnings are for full-time wage and salary workers.

Fourth, that mental—as opposed to manual—capability is now required underscores the knowledge dimension of post-industrial work and confirms knowledge as a capacity for humans to purposely accumulate. But knowledge as a contributor is not new. Every advance is based on a new insight, meaning that knowledge and knowledge workers have existed for most of human history. When humans started communicating—either by signal or symbol or verbally—the passing down of knowledge began; writing made transmission even easier. For most of this time, knowledge workers remained a small minority, charged mostly with communicating about God and man as their societies perceived these to be, or operating as scholars and scribes who educated and advised the elites who controlled the lives of all living in pre-industrial times.

In the Industrial Era, knowledge about the production task came to the fore, and computers and the internet with an increased ability to automate human activities and generate and disseminate massive amounts of information finally placed knowledge and its accumulation at the center of the human struggle for productivity.

Defining knowledge, more complicated than first meets the eye, has long challenged philosophers. Though he rejected each conceptualization after due deliberation, Plato considered knowledge as "perception," "true judgment," and "true judgment with an account,"[358] while to Confucius "to acknowledge what is known as known, and what is not known as not known is knowledge."[359] Drucker's late-twentieth-century definition is: "What we now mean by knowledge is information effective in action, information focused on results. Results are outside the person, in society and economy, or in the advancement of knowledge itself."[360]

Zen and Confucian conceptualizations focused on Chinese equivalents of self-knowledge, logic, and rhetoric. Grounded in the Western scientific method that requires theory to establish relationships among variables that are falsified or accepted until evidence shows otherwise, Drucker's conceptualization was criticized as narrow and culturally biased:

> When speaking of information- or knowledge-based economies, therefore, Western analysts implicitly refer to only a Western system of commercial values and practices and, within that system, only to a small, if currently privileged, fraction of it: the subsystem of utilitarian values. . . . Far from being universal instruments of knowledge, the new ICT and the new technosciences that support it are merely expressions

---

358 Timothy Chappell, "Plato on Knowledge in the *Theaetetus*," *The Stanford Encyclopedia of Philosophy* (Fall 2009 edition), ed. Edward N. Zalta, accessed April 23, 2023, http://plato.stanford.edu/archives/fall2009/entries/plato-theaetetus/

359 Baiyin Yang, "Toward a Holistic Theory of Knowledge and Adult Learning," *Human Resource Development Review* 2, no. 2 (June 2003): 106.

360 Peter F. Drucker, *Post-capitalist Society* (New York: HarperCollins Publisher, 1993), 42.

> of this economic subsystem that wishes to impose itself not only on Western culture as a whole, but on all other cultures, as well.[361]

Though correct in its two classifications (modern productive knowledge is mostly Western, and knowledge conceptualized as methods to produce more efficiently is utilitarian and narrow), the critique is misplaced in its assertion of cultural hegemony and wrong in objecting to the definition's lack of universality. That most production knowledge reflects a Western bias is expected; modern production was perfected in the West. What remains to be seen over the coming decades is if non-Western cultures develop better production knowledge, and if so, will it also be imposed on others. Japan illustrates this possibility.

By the 1980s, Japanese consumer electronics and automobile knowledge matched or exceeded the West's, heralding the rise of the Japanese consumer electronics and automobile industries. South Korea followed, indicated by successes such as Hyundai and Samsung in automobiles and consumer electronics. Whether other nations continue in this tradition and how others react will be part of the story of the human struggle for productivity over the twenty-first century. Given productivity's ongoing spread, production knowledge will likely emerge from all corners of the world, with dominance swapped back and forth as nations and their Leaders seek to remain ahead in an increasingly competitive global economy.

Finally, that the definition of knowledge only incorporates ideas of increasing production is also warranted. To understand the human struggle for productivity, knowledge that explains all things is not needed. Answering important questions unrelated to production and productivity—what is the meaning of life, why are we here, is there a God, what is happiness?—is not the intent in the economic realm. The focus is far less ambitious—how to increase productivity so that the

---

361 Mihai I. Spariosu, "Information and Communication Technology for Human Development," chap. 3 in *Remapping Knowledge: Intercultural Studies for a Global Age* (New York: Berghahn Books, 2006), 109.

scourge of economic scarcity is eliminated and the material choices of all are enhanced; defining knowledge in terms of production and productivity is appropriate.

We turn now to consider what capabilities human capital will require to perform the three categories of post-industrial jobs outlined earlier. The first two—post-industrial creative and transformative work—relate to knowledge work now being done by humans across the post-industrial world, and the third captures what manually dexterous humans are left to do as the transition proceeds. This is also a moving target, and knowledge is often required here too.

Post-Industrial Creative Work: New Products, Services, or Solutions from Creative Cores

Productive creativity requires the introduction of something not yet in existence and the conversion of an imaginary, hard-to-copy idea into a good, service, or solution produced and delivered at scale and consumed in sufficient volume to cover the costs of development. The human capital performing this creative task was placed among America's *creative class*, defined as:

> . . . people in science and engineering, architecture and design, education, arts, music and entertainment, whose economic function is to create new ideas, new technology and new creative content. Around this core, the Creative Class also includes a broader group of creative professionals in business and finance, law, health care and related fields.[362]

In 2004, the creative class was 23.6 percent of the US workforce, behind 10 other countries, led by Ireland at 33.5 percent.[363] By 2017, America's creative class was over 55 million strong and made up 35

---

362 Richard Florida, *The Rise of the Creative Class: And How it's Transforming Work, Leisure, Community, and Everyday Life* (New York: Basic Books, 2002), 8.
363 Richard Florida, "America's Looming Creativity Crisis," *Harvard Business Review*, October 2004, 4.

percent of the workforce; Washington, DC, was ranked first, with 61.1 percent of its workforce in the creative class. Seattle was second at 58.8 percent, and San Francisco was third at 54.8 percent.[364]

The capabilities required of those doing post-industrial creative work are best illustrated by example. Consider the Caterpillar/Trimble joint venture highlighted earlier that changed road building by automating earthmoving. To accomplish this innovation, scientific or technical expertise in many fields was required, ranging from how GPS technology operates to advanced hydraulics and the mechanics of moving dirt by bulldozer blades to how wireless and laser technology guide earthmoving equipment. Innovation no longer resides in a single mind as it did in Henry Ford's. Given its complexity, it comes from teams working together.

The technical creative core that developed the AccuGrade system likely included electrical, mechanical, civil, and network engineers, and even computer scientists. Underscoring that the know-how mobilized in business-based innovation goes beyond technical expertise alone, and building on the aforementioned *creative professionals*, knowledge of the earthmoving industry and its business operations would also have been needed. Answers to questions such as what was offered in the past, what competitors hoped to offer, and what was the risk of failure from customer rejection would have been invaluable. Thus, technical and business expertise from Caterpillar and Trimble formed the creative core that developed a solution neither would have introduced as effectively or efficiently on its own.

Post-industrial workers wishing to reach and maintain the status of Leaders in their industry segments should aspire to become members of the creative core of organizations they work for. Responsible for building the next product, service, or solution, these organizational creative cores are typically made up of scientific/technical members familiar with the scientific or technical aspects of the innovation involved and business-ori-

364 Richard L. Florida, "The Changing Geography of America's Creative Class," Bloomberg, August 27, 2019, accessed April 24, 2023, https://www.bloomberg.com/news/articles/2019-08-27/the-changing-geography-of-america-s-creative-class.

ented professionals familiar with the business or industry context where the innovation is to be offered.

Given this makeup, membership is possible by three routes: through understanding of an industry or business domain (the industry/business route); through possessing expertise about the scientific or technical aspects of an innovation (the scientific/technical route); or through creating a new industry from scratch (the visionary route).

Accumulating the scientific/technical expertise typically starts with acquiring mathematical or science-based skills at primary and secondary schools, followed by tertiary education so that at graduation, existing academic scientific/technical knowledge relating to a domain is mastered. Newly minted graduates armed with leading-edge domain knowledge are ready to join organizations where the translation of this academic knowledge into market-based applied innovation begins.

Leading-edge organizations that talented scientific/technical graduates join likely already have the technical experts who have the requisite knowledge to keep their organization at the frontier of innovation. The combination of seasoned and up-to-date scientific/technical knowledge coupled with deep industry/business expertise provides the human capital creative cores rely on to sustain productive creativity.

Creative core members joining through the industry/business route typically start as functional experts (e.g., in supply chain and operations, or in marketing, sales, or finance) and are likely to be employed after mastering the domain's latest thinking through tertiary business education. But from their first day at work, aspiring creative core members should seek to improve existing products, services, solutions, or business processes by first doing post-industrial transformative work, singling them out for creative core work later.

Further, while doing this transformative work, they acquire broader knowledge about the industry, company, products, customers, and competitors, all essential to filter ideas for new goods, services, or solutions. This building of industry/business contextual knowledge is as much a product of time as it is of academic training and can also be attained by moving among competitors in the same industry. Entering a new industry likely means starting again. A bachelor's or master's degree in business also may help screen business information and shorten the learning curve to acquire the broader industry/business contextual knowledge, but regardless, experience and seasoning of somewhere between 5 to 10 years is typically required.[365]

Organizational creative cores themselves form in many ways, the first from actions of organizations themselves. Popularized by Apple chairman Steve Jobs denoting "a group of people going in essence back to the garage, but in a large company"[366] as early creative cores, corporate intrapreneurship since then has been more formally defined as "a company-wide, internally oriented strategy designed to promote an entrepreneurial environment within the corporate organization," though this definition also separated intrapreneurship from internal corporate venturing, denoted as "the establishment of autonomous in-house new ventures."[367]

Regardless, all reflect organizational creative cores, whether autonomous in-house new ventures, intrapreneurial teams operating in garages, joint ventures such as the Caterpillar Trimble partnership, or teams purposely formed to bring new goods, services, or solutions to market. Creative cores also emerge serendipitously—for example, engineering and business students meeting while studying and then pursuing an idea, or entrepreneurs jolted into forming new businesses after job loss. Many entrepreneurs are displaced employees forced to found new enterprises after losing their jobs.

The third path to the creative core, the visionary route, requires founding an organization that leads its industry from inception. This is seen in the case of Bill Gates, who left Harvard to found Microsoft, despite not possessing much formal academic knowledge of any specific

365 Peter J. Brews, "Working at the Creative Core," *BizEd*, January/February 2016, 38.
366 Gerald C. Lubenow, "Jobs Talks About His Rise and Fall," *Newsweek*, September 29, 1985, accessed May 8, 2023, https://www.newsweek.com/jobs-talks-about-his-rise-and-fall-207016.
367 Kevin McNally, *Corporate Venture Capital: Bridging the Equity Gap in the Small Business Sector* (New York: Routledge, 1997), 32.

scientific/technical or industry/business domain. Zuckerberg did the same with Facebook.

Entrepreneurs smart enough to pioneer new industries where established knowledge is yet to be codified will be able to do so with little tertiary education. Yet Gates was in the top 1 percent of American high school students, hardly uneducated or unable to generate new knowledge. Facebook's Zuckerberg, also well-educated before admittance to Harvard, faced the same questions and like Gates dropped out to lead his company. The only difference was Gates left as a junior, while Zuckerberg was a sophomore.

Nonetheless, in most post-industrial entrepreneurial ventures today, founders typically follow the scientific/technical or industry/business routes to the creative core; only where the innovation is scaled differs. Rather than staying at established organizations, some leave to form their own creative cores to develop an idea. The question for those employing founders doing this is, why did they not form a creative core to include the defector instead?

These final examples provide additional insights to readers hoping to join or form organizational creative cores and lead in their industry segments. First, seeking to replicate the visionary action of a Gates or Zuckerberg is for the very brave: the success rate is minuscule. Second, with success rates still way below 5 percent, starting a business out of high school or college is almost as inadvisable. Before going where none have gone before (the heart of creativity), spending time learning about where others have already gone is invaluable seasoning in preparation for creative core work.

Acquiring leading-edge scientific/technical or industry/business skills at university and then joining an organization paying market rates for these skills is the best start to a professional career. Then, armed with practice-based scientific/technical or business/industry skills and supported by years of invaluable real-time learning, experience, and seasoning, you might bring a new good, service, or solution to market through a creative core you founded. Or you might be in an existing organization sustaining its competitiveness through your creative core work.

Finally, a word on organizations Leading but relinquishing this position to a more capable competitor and then Following for a time. Such jockeying represents the ordinary course of business in competitive markets and is usually not fatal, and for individuals in the Follower position it likely means engaging in creative core work to find ways to counter the better competitor. In the extreme, organizational failure will leave workers seeking employment elsewhere. We now turn to the second category of human work in the Post-Industrial Era, that of post-industrial transformative work.

Post-Industrial Transformative Work: Post-Industrial Operational Efficiency through Network-Based Business Process Restructuring

Understanding the difference between improving existing operations versus innovating from scratch through strategy formation clarifies the difference between post-industrial creative and transformative work. Table 11 highlights the differences.

Knowing strategy formation and the refinement of ongoing operations is not the same; high-performing firms use different methods to control the shorter-term precision and standardization of tightly coupled existing business operations compared with the creative, iterative, and often messy strategy-formation processes. They know that improving existing operations—which does not enhance competitiveness, as other firms also improve their operations—requires ongoing benchmarking and may be outsourced if more efficient external providers are found. Strategic activities relying on core competencies embodied in hard-to-copy new goods, services, or solutions are the heart of competitiveness and are never outsourced.

Table 11: Improving Existing Operations versus Forming Strategy

	Improving Existing Operations	Forming Strategy
Focus	Focuses on how efficiently existing goods, services, or solutions are being produced, sold, delivered, and maintained. Includes business process reengineering, Six Sigma–type activities, and benchmarking; may encompass downsizing/rightsizing; and involves improvement or enhancement of existing operations through tightly coupled plans and programs.	Focuses on the development of new goods, services, or solutions. Involves new idea creation, messy iterative experimentation, and learning from doing, combining new ideas/applications with new or existing technology.
Location	Done in-house or can be outsourced to best-in-class external vendors.	Done in-house and is never outsourced. Relies on unique, valuable, hard-to-copy, firm-based resources (a.k.a. core competencies).
Duration	Returns are immediate or soon after project completion; one year or shorter, sometimes one to three years.	Returns typically distant in time, usually around 3 to 10 years. Once a prototype is ready for production and for market, operational implementation begins and strategy formation ceases.
Impact	Reduces operating costs, enhances/improves customer experience as existing goods, services, or solutions are consumed. Because competitors perform similar processes and are able to copy them, improves operational efficiency but does not enhance competitiveness.	Provides valuable, hard-to-copy new goods, services, or solutions; attracts new or existing customers; and enhances competitiveness. Defines a firm's core business and delineates its core competencies.
Work Type	Post-Industrial transformative work	Post-Industrial creative work

Post-industrial creative work's strategic nature accounts for why it is more valuable than post-industrial transformative work and why more seasoned professionals are required for its execution compared with those doing operational work. Further, high-performing firms know both how to form strategy and how to execute efficient operations and recognize that once a new product is prototyped and ready for production, it leaves the strategy domain and becomes operational and conforms more to the precision of post-industrial transformative work than to post-industrial creative work.[368]

Post-industrial transformative work accordingly focuses on improving conditions in the known world, while post-industrial creative work creates the goods, services, or solutions of a world yet to be. Both require innovation; only the scope and impact of the innovation differs. Because of their leading-edge knowledge of a functional domain, business-oriented post-industrial transformative workers may find new ways to market goods or better ways to manage supply chains. Scientific/technical transformative workers, based on their mastery of a technical domain, may find ways to enhance technology used in an existing product, service, or solution.

Either way, innovation and improvement are required, and transformative workers should arrive at work every day seeking innovation or improvement in what they are doing. Rather than doing strategy formation's big-scale innovation, post-industrial transformative workers focus on the small-scale innovation required to improve existing operations.

Also, while performing work with innovation at its core, some post-industrial transformative workers assist firms with transitioning from a traditional industrial to a post-industrial organization, requiring them to move from being vertically integrated, hierarchically controlled industrial organizations to disaggregated, networked organizations like the kind pioneered by Cisco. Here, IT facilitating organizational transformation and change has a long and rich tradition: restructuring through electronic data interchange in the 1980s was succeeded by business process reengineering (BPR) in the early 1990s, introduced by Hammer

---

368 For more on how strategy formation differs from maintaining efficient operations and especially on how strategy is conceptualized, formed, and controlled, see Peter J. Brews, "Great Expectations: Strategy as Creative Fiction," *Business Strategy Review* 16, no. 3 (August 2005): 4–10.

and Champy with a proclamation that foretold a fundamental change in business procedures.

> For two hundred years people have founded and built companies around Adam Smith's brilliant discovery that industrial work should be broken down into the simplest and the most basic tasks. In the post-industrial business age we are now entering, corporations will be founded and built around the idea of reunifying those tasks into coherent business processes.[369]

Hammer and Champy also noted BPR involved "the fundamental rethinking and radical design of business processes to achieve dramatic improvements in critical, contemporary measures of performance, such as cost, quality, service, and speed,"[370] and the internet widened BPR's scope and impact by permitting it to go beyond the factory gate to reach external stakeholders. This widening added complexity: connecting customers, suppliers, business partners, and focal firms via tightly integrated networks is more complicated than reengineering and networking processes within a firm only.

To move to post-industrial organization, one capability needed is BPR, in many cases involving the redesign of business processes and moving departmentally or functionally based organizations to process-based structures while also ensuring any process adopted suits user-led, internet-based infrastructures:

> That business process re-engineering (BPR) may be required is not new, and some of the techniques learned in BPR over the 1990s will assist. However, to prepare for Internet enabling, process refinement/simplification—as well as understanding how moving to user-driven self-service changes processes—will most likely be required. We fear that poor process definition/re-definition is a greater problem than incorrect technology choices. Moreover, as supplier, customer, and

369 Hammer and Champy, *Reengineering the Corporation*, 2.
370 Hammer and Champy, *Reengineering the Corporation*, 32.

partner processes are enabled, representatives from these stakeholders must also be included in the development process.[371]

Typically done by organizations lacking the operational efficiency of competitors around them, BPR starts off with mind-numbing process mapping of the process to be acted upon. Only once a process is described with all its permutations revealed is development of a redesigned, user-led, online process possible.

Work done at the US-based operations of electronics conglomerate Siemens AG reveals BPR's complexity and shows how value is created in such activities.[372] Involving Siemens's US holding company, Siemens Corporation (Siemens Corp.), working with US-based operating companies (Westinghouse Electric Company, Siemens Medical Solutions, Siemens Information & Communication Networks, Siemens Energy & Automation, and Siemens Building Technologies, hereafter the SOCs), the eHR@Siemens project (eHR) charter was to "optimize Siemens Human Resources' processes and systems through the development and implementation of an eHR strategy that solidifies Siemens Human Resources as a key business partner within and across SOCs."[373]

Commensurate with its scope at the corporate level of a multidivisional firm, eHR involved many stakeholders, including the top Siemens AG corporate human resources executive and Siemens Corp. and SOC executives. Two internal groups governed the project: a steering committee (chaired by the director of human resources and development at Siemens Corp. and staffed by other Siemens Corp. and SOC human resources executives) and a design team, staffed mostly by SOC US-based employees. Stakeholders from all affected entities were included.

The design team did the on-the-ground project framing, led by a dedicated project manager and staffed by an employee from each SOC. Design team members were selected primarily on their knowledge of the

---

371 Brews and Tucci, "Internetworking," *Academy of Management Executive,* 15–6.
372 Unless otherwise stated, eHR@Siemens information is from Peter J. Brews and Valerie Cook, *eHR@Siemens* (Chapel Hill, NC: UNC Kenan-Flagler Business School, 2001).
373 Brews and Cook, *eHR@Siemens*, 2.

business and willingness to challenge the status quo. High detail orientation and an ability to think conceptually were also sought. Most design team members had human resources backgrounds; only the project manager had a technical/IT background. Hewitt Associates, who had worked extensively with transferring human resources functions to the internet, provided political and cultural mediation between the design team and the steering committee.[374] Design team activity mapping also followed a model Hewitt suggested.

The range of processes acted upon by the design team underscores the activities typically done in the transformative work of this nature. Among the first project tasks performed was benchmarking, where best-in-class companies in the eHR domain were compared. Dell, Honeywell, and IBM were considered leaders, and their internet-enabled human resources functions and how these were delivered were carefully studied. Why Siemens could expect no competitive advantage from this work also becomes clear; it was only matching what others had done before.

Benchmarking was followed by the development of an activity map to capture those suitable for conversion to an internet-based platform, divided into four phases: phase 1, the strike zone, being easy-to-execute activities of high importance that could be employee/manager initiated with minimal workflow adjustment; phases 2 and 3, activities less easily executed or lower in priority; and phase 4, activities low in priority and hard to execute. Figure 12 reports this analysis.

---

374 Hewitt Associates, Inc. (formerly NYSE: HEW) provided HR consulting and outsourcing solutions to solve complex benefits, talent, and related financial challenges. Hewitt merged with Aon Consulting in July 2010 to form Aon Hewitt, now an unlisted subsidiary of AON Corporation (NYSE: AON).

Figure 12: eHR Activity Mapping

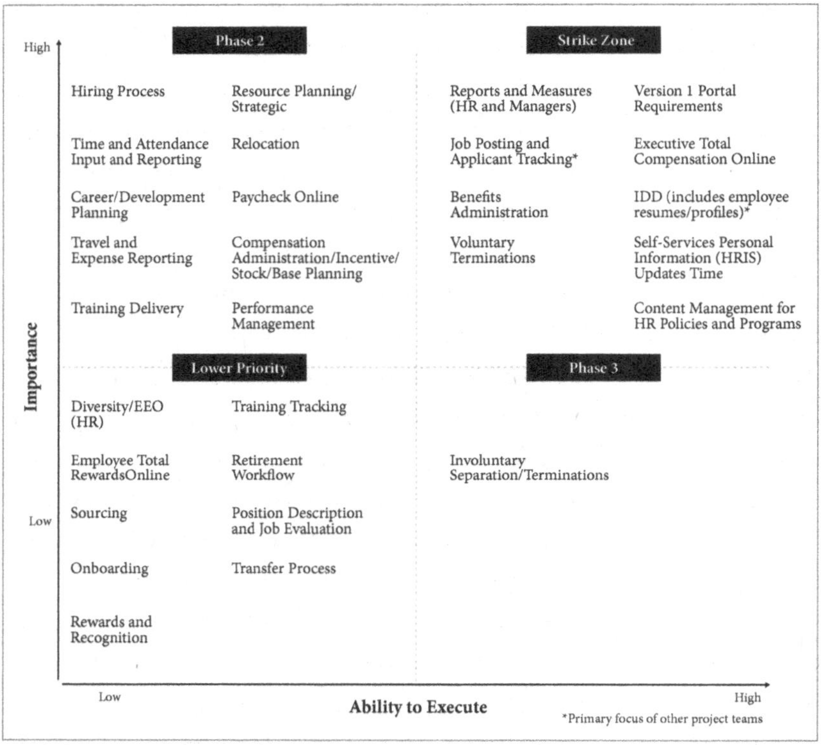

Importance (High – Low) / Ability to Execute (Low – High)

Phase 2

Hiring Process	Resource Planning/ Strategic
Time and Attendance Input and Reporting	Relocation
Career/Development Planning	Paycheck Online
Travel and Expense Reporting	Compensation Administration/Incentive/ Stock/Base Planning
Training Delivery	Performance Management

Strike Zone

Reports and Measures (HR and Managers)	Version 1 Portal Requirements
Job Posting and Applicant Tracking*	Executive Total Compensation Online
Benefits Administration	IDD (includes employee resumes/profiles)*
Voluntary Terminations	Self-Services Personal Information (HRIS) Updates Time
	Content Management for HR Policies and Programs

Lower Priority

Diversity/EEO (HR)	Training Tracking
Employee Total RewardsOnline	Retirement Workflow
Sourcing	Position Description and Job Evaluation
Onboarding	Transfer Process
Rewards and Recognition	

Phase 3

Involuntary Separation/Terminations

*Primary focus of other project teams

As Figure 12 indicates, the design team started with important but easy-to-execute processes, considered *low-hanging fruit*, to provide early wins crucial for those with little experience wishing to build confidence regarding their ability to perform. The map was also a template for overall execution: phase 2 (high in importance, but harder to execute) followed the strike zone activities, followed by phase 3 (lower in importance, but easy to execute) and ending with activities lowest in priority and hardest to execute (phase 4).

After identifying processes for conversion to a more efficient internet-based platform, the design team prepared business cases for each process. Essential were pre- and post-diagrams describing each process as executed followed by a redesigned process performed across an internet-based platform. Key questions asked to describe a process included who initiates a transaction, who completes a transaction, and what data is received from this transaction?

Figures 13 and 14 contain pre- and post-maps for a personal profile data change. The radical differences between the processes in the tables illustrates visually how value is derived from BPR.

Figure 13: Pre-eHR Employee Profile Change Map

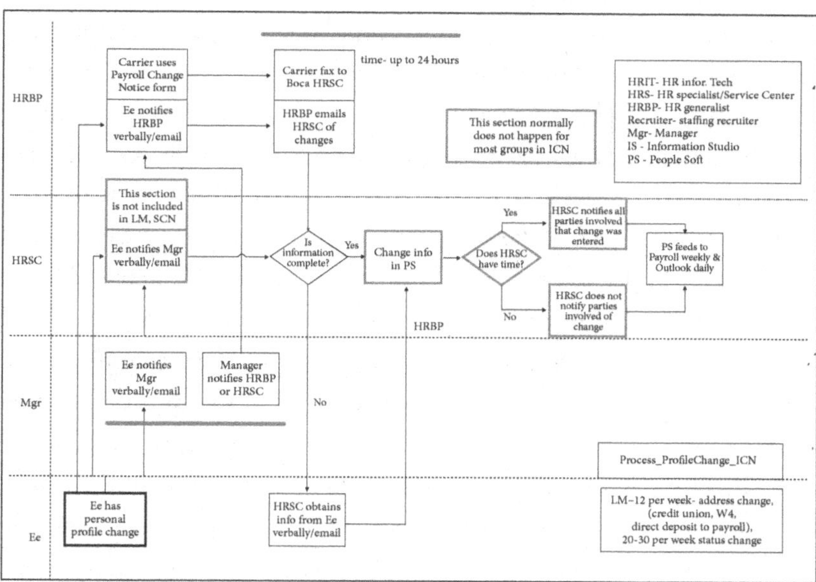

Figure 14: Post-eHR Employee Profile Change Map

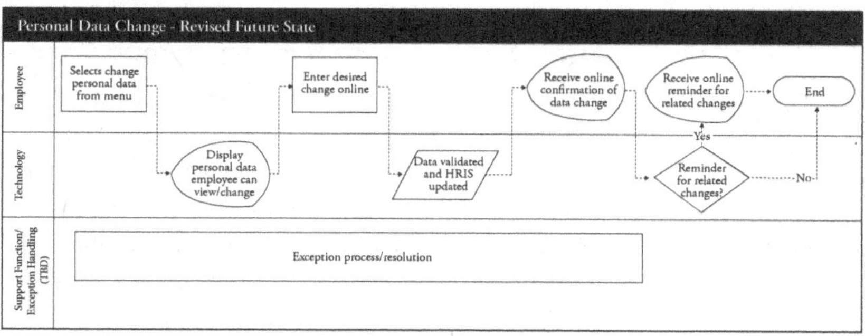

Figure 14 shows a simplified, redesigned process that will likely cost far less and be easier to execute, and the previous two figures also explain why business knowledge and not IT was the most important capability design team members needed. Though projects such as these encounter IT-based problems, most benefits derive from a reengineering of the processes themselves.

Standard capital budgeting compared redesigned process moving costs with expected savings generated. Phase 1 payback for the US$5.8 million invested was 2.75 years, delivering a five-year net present value of around US$3 million. Printing and distribution costs were forecast to decline by US$9.4 million over five years, and a 14 percent reduction in administrative head count was predicted. Outside research also supported these estimates. One survey reported after two years that eHR could result in a 50 percent increase in employee satisfaction, a 75 percent shift in personnel from administrative to strategic activities, and a 60 percent reduction in functional administrative cycle times.

eHR@Siemens shows steps taken by post-industrial transformative workers to upgrade a set of functional activities so that processes representative of a post-industrial organization were developed and implemented. Decades of operations across multiple divisions had resulted in multiple human resources processes performing the same function at varying levels of quality and cost. Redundant processes performing similar tasks across SOCs were optimized, standardized, and centralized, and by making them available on a user-led, self-service basis, operational efficiency was enhanced and administrative costs declined. By the end of the project, it was apparent that the potential for transformation went far beyond human resources alone. A steering committee member noted:

> We initially looked at this project as a way to improve and streamline some of our HR processes. But our vision has stretched into a much broader business portal. I firmly believe that this project could transform Siemens from an organizational capability standpoint. This

> could evolve into an employee desktop portal for all of the business functions, with HR just a component.[375]

If human resources processes are deliverable across internet-based platforms, so are finance, marketing, and sales processes, and so forth. Post-industrial organization applies not only to single functions or departments but across the entire enterprise.

The skills demanded of post-industrial transformative workers are also apparent from the project. They include high-level consultancy skills, change and project management capabilities, the ability to conduct BPR, business knowledge for developing new online processes, and capital-budgeting skills that evaluate the business cases presented to gain support for the project. Detailed knowledge of Siemens/SOC business processes and an ability to work in minute detail with confidence to confront the status quo were especially sought in design team members.

More important to note is that none of these roles are static. Business processes can always be improved as data expands and bandwidth increases, and new software solutions can offer better choices at lower cost. In the post-industrial world, software and systems will increasingly coordinate and control interactions between organizations and their stakeholders. The work for humans will be more and more about improving the software and systems that govern interactions than working with humans directly.

Finally, and as is noted in the description of post-industrial organization, the transition also involves the de-integration of traditional industrial supply chains. How to determine which parts of the supply chain remain internal and which should be outsourced are also skills required in post-industrial transformative work.

We now turn to the third category of post-industrial work for humans. Post-industrial manual work is where humans perform manual tasks machines cannot do or manually assist machines in the work they do.

---

375 Brews and Cook, *eHR@Siemens*, 11.

Post-Industrial Manual Work: Smarter Humans Working with Smart Machines

Despite automation and the appearance of adept machines, manual work remains for humans across many post-industrial settings, including performing surgery and dental work, working on assembly lines (though in more limited numbers than in the twentieth century), building/repairing houses, or working in food or hospitality services. Some of these occupations will involve working closely with machines, while others will be less aided by machines.

Those working with complex machinery will likely require training in the machine's use, obtained from a range of sources including tertiary-level technical training, vendor training, or apprentice-type training. University or community college preparation and licensure may also be required (for example, in medicine or dentistry). Post-industrial manual work is of both low and high value, depending on its sophistication and the training for proficiency in the domain concerned. Surgeons will earn more than their nurses and dentists more than their assistants, but those will all earn more than those cleaning hotel rooms or minding lawns.

Also of concern is how quickly machines automate the remaining manual tasks humans do, and this likelihood is already high in some contexts. Aspects of food service are already automated. In 2022 McDonald's opened a highly automated restaurant where customers picked up food delivered by conveyer belt in a dedicated drive-through express lane; with no place to order, the line is expected to move quicker than traditional lines. Further, customers placing orders in the restaurant do so at kiosks and do not interact with staff, who are left to produce food more accurately and quicker than before.[376]

Aramark claims to be the first in Germany to use fully automated robots to prepare pasta dishes and salads. Able to prepare 60 dishes an hour unaided, this system may free up preparers to work on dishes requiring

---

376 Kristin Houser, "McDonald's Opens Its First Automated Restaurant in Texas," Freethink, January 4, 2023, accessed May 8, 2023, https://www.freethink.com/robots-ai/automated-restaurant.

more culinary skill or creativity.[377] Even in the kitchen, machines may do routine work while humans focus on more creative endeavors.

Having clarified human work in the Post-Industrial Era, we now turn to entrepreneurship in the Post-Industrial Era, focusing on Bill Gates and likely the most successful software company ever. Political economy in the Post-Industrial Era then concludes the chapter.

Post-Industrial Entrepreneurship: Bill Gates and Microsoft Software Running Every Computer

Microsoft offers many insights into entrepreneurship in the Post-Industrial Era. Gates and Microsoft underscore the capabilities required of human capital in the era and offer an example of post-industrial *entrepreneurial* capitalism, where office workers become creative core members and reap entrepreneurial returns for the work they do. Their counterparts on the assembly line in the Industrial Era did not. In addition, while Ford Motor Company was about assembly line organization and combining mankind's manual dexterity with machines to produce a tangible item, post-industrial Leader Microsoft showed how to organize mental dexterity to produce carefully coded instructions that controlled and operated computers.

Commensurate with the *Information Age* descriptor applied to the Post-Industrial Era, Microsoft's business was the management of an intangible good: information. The company showed how to make money from providing information in carefully constructed templates called software, a "uniquely designed, highly structured set of assertions, instructions and decisions, all of which must be negotiated, codified, analysed for consistency and validated for effectiveness in a constantly

377 Industry Intelligence, Inc., "Aramark Says It Will Be First Foodservice Company in Germany to Use Fully Automated Kitchen . . .," December 6, 2022, accessed May 9, 2023, https://www.industryintel.com/transformation-and-innovation/news/aramark-says-it-will-be-first-foodservice-company-in-germany-to-use-fully-automated-kitchen-robots-in-corporate-restaurants-using-technology-from-berlin-based-startup-aitme-robots-prepare-dishes-such-as-pasta-salads-from-fresh-ingredients-to-order-158173370616.

changing environment."[378] Finally, those wishing to attract, motivate, and control high-value post-industrial *entrepreneurial* workers can learn from Microsoft's management of its most valuable asset: the software engineers and computer scientists that came to work every day to write code for the company.

Gates's vision to place computers on every desktop with Microsoft software running them was as profound as Ford's desire to provide a car for every man and Columbus's goal to find an alternative transport route to the East from Europe. Gates also had the foresight to recognize the importance of personal computers and knew where to position Microsoft to profit from their appearance. But Gates was more than a visionary. He also ensured from a business perspective that Microsoft flourished.

The company's outright acquisition of ownership of 86-DOS from Seattle Computer and its nonexclusive licensing of MS-DOS for use on IBM's new personal computer rank among the most impressive business deals negotiated. Finally, faced with a new intangible product (computer code/software), Gates recognized that the model to monetize such an asset required charging a fee for use or replication, priced low enough to ensure Microsoft's offering was chosen over others. Gates as businessman is as impressive as Gates as software entrepreneur.

Realizing the importance of standards also permitted Gates and Microsoft to perfect the competitive model for the hypercompetitive, complex world of operating system (OS) and applications development. Writing the best software is not the main task. Software that becomes widely adopted as a standard is, and this was accomplished by keeping Microsoft offerings more affordable than competitors.

Keeping prices low to generate sales was not new, however. Ford experience-curve priced the Model T to reach high sales volumes and drive down per unit costs so assemblers of the vehicle could afford the product they helped manufacture. Microsoft followed this logic too, but

---

378 Graham Samuel, Richard E. Thomas, and Herbert Weber, "Software Development Issues and Problems," in *The Software Factory Challenge*, ed. Herbert Weber (Amsterdam, Netherlands: IOS Press, 1997), 37.

for a different reason: not to drive volume up to cover costs, but to ensure its software became the standard used on personal computers around the world. The company has been spectacularly successful if measured by this criterion.

Gates's Formative Years and Amassing the World's Biggest Personal Fortune in Two Decades

William Henry "Bill" Gates III was born on October 28, 1955, second of three children in a family of professionals. His father, William Gates Jr., was a lawyer, and his mother, Mary, a schoolteacher. It was obvious from an early age he was intellectually gifted. Reverend Dale Turner, pastor of a church the family attended, recognized this when Gates responded to a challenge made to the confirmation class he was attending. Turner promised dinners for anyone memorizing the Sermon on the Mount.

> No one, in all his years in the ministry, had been able to make it through the entire passage without stumbling over at least a few words or lines. But Gates had recited the passage nonstop from the beginning, never missing a line. . . . "I couldn't imagine how an 11-year-old boy could have a mind like that. And my subsequent questioning of him revealed a deep understanding of the passage."[379]

In addition to being a voracious reader, Gates showed early math and science aptitude. In his second year at Lakeside School, an exclusive preparatory school for grades 7 through 12 that he attended to challenge his innate intellectual drive and curiosity,[380] Gates encountered a Teletype machine. Discovering communication with a General Electric mainframe computer close by was possible, he embarked upon a self-di-

---

379 James Wallace and Jim Erickson, *Hard Drive: Bill Gates and the Making of the Microsoft Empire* (New York: John Wiley & Sons, 1992), 7.

380 *Encyclopedia of World Biography*, "Bill Gates Biography," accessed May 11, 2023, http://www.notablebiographies.com/Fi-Gi/Gates-Bill.html. At the time, Lakeside's tuition was higher than Harvard's.

rected journey of learning about computers and how to write software for them.[381]

Gates proved adept at programming, and though often accused of hogging school equipment, fellow students frequently approached him for help with programs they were writing. He wrote software programs for a variety of Seattle-based organizations, at times for free access to computer time and at times for payment. Gates also met Paul Allen, two years his senior, at Lakeside School in Seattle. The motivation sustaining these emerging computer enthusiasts in general, and Gates and Allen in particular, was described as follows:

> Computers became an obsession, for games, for code-breaking, for sending messages, for sending anything. Gates and Allen and the other young pioneers of the new industry were all typical—bright, intense, remote young people utterly seduced by the lure of the blinking consoles.[382]

Less than a decade after meeting (and after both had dropped out of college), Gates and Allen founded Microsoft.

Armed with solid high school grades and excellent SAT scores (800 math; 790 verbal) and a National Merit Scholarship, Gates applied to Harvard, Princeton, and Yale. Accepted by all three, he chose Harvard, entering in September 1973. Significantly, down the hall from him was another person destined to play an important role at Microsoft, Steve Ballmer. Gates lasted until his junior year.

> A *Popular Mechanics* cover story about an early personal computer called the Altair was what doomed Gates' career at Harvard. "The thing that Paul and I had been talking about happening was happening," he says, "and we're sitting there going, Oh, no, it's happening without us!" Gates had realized that there was a future in writing and selling

381 Jeanne M. Lesinski, *Bill Gates: Entrepreneur and Philanthropist* (Minneapolis, MN: Twenty-First Century Books, 2009), 16.
382 Charles H. Ferguson and Charles R. Morris, *Computer Wars: How the West Can Win in a Post-IBM World* (New York: Times Books, 1993), 19.

> software for personal computers. It was one of the great technology and business insights of the century.
>
> Harvard wasn't impressed. When Gates and Allen sold the Altair folks a version of BASIC—which they wrote without ever having seen an Altair—the school brought him up on disciplinary charges for running a business out of his dorm room. So Gates turned on, booted up, and dropped out.[383]

Gates moved to Albuquerque, New Mexico, to be near Allen, who had become director of software development at Altair's manufacturer, Micro Instrumentation and Telemetry Systems. All that the Altair needed was a programming language to make it perform useful computing tasks, and Gates and Allen provided this. Important events in 1975—the year Microsoft started as an informal partnership, with Gates owning 60 percent and Allen 40 percent, reflective of Gates's greater share in the development of BASIC[384]—included revenues of US$16,005, three employees, and the licensing to the company's launch customer of the first language program written for a personal computer.[385]

Realizing the Altair was only the start of the personal computer revolution, instead of focusing on computer hardware, Gates and Allen concentrated on software, initially for the Intel 8080 microprocessors, the chip the Altair was built around. In 1977 Microsoft developed BASIC for Tandy's TRS-80 computer and licensed a version for a new personal computer, the Apple II.[386]

In 1979, by then the leading distributor of software development tools, Microsoft reported revenues of US$2,390,145 and employed 28. The company reorganized into a privately held corporation in June 1981 with Gates as president and chairman of the board and Allen as executive

---

383 Lev Grossman, "Bill Gates Goes Back to School," *Time*, June 7, 2007, accessed May 11, 2023, https://content.time.com/time/subscriber/article/0,33009,1630564,00.html.

384 Philip M. Rosenzweig, *Bill Gates and the Management of Microsoft*, Harvard Business School Case 9-392-019 (Boston: Harvard Business School Publishing, October 1991, revised July 1993), 2.

385 Microsoft, "Microsoft Fast Facts: 1975," May 9, 2000, accessed May 11, 2023, https://news.microsoft.com/2000/05/09/microsoft-fast-facts-1975/.

386 Rosenzweig, *Bill Gates*, 2.

vice president. Though already setting industry standards and licensing software to a variety of customers, developments with an East Coast–based company propelled Microsoft to icon status and made Gates the world's richest man 15 years later. The IBM partnership significantly contributed to achieving Gates's vision for Microsoft: "A computer on every desktop, and Microsoft software in every computer."[387]

Microsoft's Rise to Prominence: IBM's PC and MS-DOS, and Windows, Excel, Word, and Office

A historic August 1981 IBM press release heralded the arrival of IBM's Personal Computer, its smallest, lowest-priced computer.[388] Designed for first-time and advanced users and with an enhanced version of Microsoft's BASIC programming language, the machine was an inflection point to the realization that computers would be used by all. Not foreseen in the press release was the jostling to follow between IBM, the world's most powerful computer company, and a small software company that within a decade would usurp its might and power. While IBM was the quintessential industrial organization focused on hardware and manufacturing, Microsoft focused on writing software to make the IBM PC accessible to all who used it.

The PC's development happened at warp speed relative to usual IBM product development, and the development team relied on vendors for most parts and on outside software developers for the OS and application software.[389] This speed opened the door for partners like Microsoft, and that it developed the OS that would be most widely used on the IBM PC and become an industry standard resulted from many factors—some from Gates's and Allen's smart decisions, some from actions or mistakes of others, and some from sheer luck.

---

387 Wallace and Erickson, *Hard Drive*, 153.

388 "IBM PC Announcement 1981," bricklin.com, Daniel S. Bricklin, accessed May 11, 2023, http://www.bricklin.com/ibmpcannouncement1981.htm.

389 "The Birth of the IBM PC," IBM Archives, accessed May 12, 2023, http://www-03.ibm.com/ibm/history/exhibits/pc25/pc25_birth.html.

Entering the OS business was probably the most important decision Gates and Allen ever made.[390] Personal computers needed three software layers to operate at full potential: an OS, programming languages offering tools to develop software, and applications, which users executed to do tasks.[391] Microsoft's bread and butter was programming languages; entering the OS business opened it up to a far bigger niche. Microsoft Excel later trumping Lotus 1-2-3 and Microsoft Word obsolescing WordPerfect meant it eventually dominated application niches too.

That entrepreneurship involves both mistakes and luck is seen in Microsoft's entry into the OS business. IBM's initial preference was an OS developed by California-based Digital Research called CP/M for Control Program for Microcomputers. IBM chose Microsoft's BASIC because it was the standard among microcomputer users, and adding CP/M may have elevated this software to a standard too and given the IBM PC the best of both worlds. Its first two layers of software would be standards adopted by most users.

Though accounts of what occurred at the Digital Research/IBM meetings vary, IBM executives meeting with Digital Research were not treated in the fashion Microsoft had accorded them. But for the failure to reach an agreement around CP/M, Microsoft might have followed a different path, and the world today would be vastly different. After unsuccessfully courting Digital Research, IBM asked Microsoft to develop an OS for its PC. Facing a tight deadline, Microsoft encountered its second dose of good luck: an OS for the PC's Intel 8088 chips had been devel-

---

390 An operating system is defined as follows: "Every computer has an operating system, which is a sort of master program that runs automatically when you switch the computer on, and continues running till you switch off. It is responsible for the many routine tasks required to keep a computer running: moving the pointer when you move the mouse, providing icons and menus, running other programs such as a word processor or a game which you may request, controlling the various disk drives, the screen and so on. The most widely used PC operating system is Microsoft Windows." (The Computer Jargon Dictionary, InmoMundo S.A., accessed May 12, 2023, http://www.netmeg.net/mr.htm).

391 Graeme Philipson, "A Short History of Software," in *Management, Labour Process and Software Development*, ed. Rowena Barret (New York: Routledge, 2005), 13. By the early twenty-first century, software that combined the three layers had emerged—for example, database management systems, which combine applications, systems, and applications development software.

oped by Tim Paterson of Seattle Computer Products, just down the road. Later named 86-DOS, Allen learned of the development when Paterson asked Microsoft to amend its software to work with his new OS.

How the deals with IBM and Seattle Computer were brokered rank among the most impressive business negotiations ever. Carefully keeping the two parties apart, Allen negotiated with Seattle Computer and Gates with IBM. Testimony to the negotiating capabilities of the small software company, the terms of the deals finally agreed to were very favorable to Microsoft. In the case of 86-DOS, Microsoft first negotiated the nonexclusive right to market the system to IBM; Seattle Computer was free to license the software to others. As Microsoft sublicensed the OS to a single customer, Seattle Computer received US$25,000 in its initial Microsoft agreement, signed on January 6, 1981. Then, on July 27, 1981, weeks before IBM announced its new PC, Microsoft acquired full ownership of 86-DOS, paying an additional US$50,000 to avoid the cost of ongoing licensing fees. For a US$75,000 investment, Microsoft had acquired the intellectual property that would make Gates the world's richest man.

IBM faced a similar oversight on the negotiation's other side. But not demanding outright ownership of or exclusivity for use of 86-DOS was not only due to mistake or oversight. US Department of Justice antitrust action following IBM's successes in the 1960s and 1970s also contributed. "Many of IBM's actions in the 1970s and 1980s, particularly its supine attitude towards small suppliers of PC components and software, can be explained as the reflexes ingrained by a decade in the courtroom's harsh glare."[392]

Microsoft eventually received US$430,000 from IBM for developing MS-DOS[393] and that other OSs were also available for the IBM PC materially influenced Microsoft's pricing strategy. Gates recalled:

392 Ferguson and Morris, *Computer Wars*, 11.
393 Paul Allen, *Idea Man: A Memoir by the Cofounder of Microsoft* (New York: Penguin Group, 2011), 136.

> We gave IBM a fabulous deal—a low, one-time fee that granted the company the right to use Microsoft's operating system on as many computers as it could sell. This offered IBM an incentive to push MS-DOS, and to sell it inexpensively. Our strategy worked. IBM sold the UCSD Pascal P-System for about $450, CP/M-86 for about $175, and MS-DOS for about $60.[394]

Like Ford's Model T experience-curve pricing to drive volume so capital costs were recovered through scale, Microsoft realized some Industrial Era rules still applied. The model of volume that produces cash flow to sustain ongoing investment was repeated in the development of Windows, Microsoft's GUI OS, which started in 1982 but was only perfected 10 years later with the release of Windows 3.1 in 1992. Gates confirmed the importance of scale here too: "When you're shipping a million units of Windows software a month, you can afford to spend $300 million a year improving it and still sell it at a low price."[395]

Microsoft grew by leaps and bounds over the 1980s. Sales of US$7,520,720 in 1980 grew to US$804,530,000 in 1989, and employment expanded from 40 to 4,037. In the 1990s progress continued, with Windows and a move into applications leading the way. Microsoft was not the first to enter and then dominate related markets but is among the best executors of such a strategy.

How Microsoft dominated spreadsheet and word processing applications reveals its approach there; before Microsoft Excel and Word, Lotus 1-2-3 and WordPerfect were the dominant incumbents. Lotus 1-2-3 was released by Boston-based Lotus Development Corporation, and as an application that PCs would much utilize, initial sales were fast and furious.

> In the first few days after its official release in November 1982, 1-2-3 received more than $1 million in orders. . . . By the end of 1983, 1-2-

394 Bill Gates with Nathan Myhrvold and Peter Rinearson, *The Road Ahead* (New York: Viking Penguin, 1995), 48–9.
395 Michael A. Cusumano and Richard W. Selby, *Microsoft Secrets: How the World's Most Powerful Software Company Creates Technology, Shapes Markets, and Manages People* (New York: Free Press, 1995), 157–8.

3 was so popular that Lotus had become the second largest software company, just behind Microsoft, with sales of $53 million.[396]

Ironically, a Microsoft offer to acquire Lotus was rejected in 1984; underestimating Lotus's notoriety at the time was hard to do. Microsoft's revenues only again exceeded Lotus's in 1987,[397] and in the early years of personal computing, it was unclear which software layer would be more important: the OS or the application programs that opened computing to users.

But chinks in Lotus's armor soon appeared. Lotus Symphony, a bundled software package including word processing, data management, and a spreadsheet application, failed in 1984, and Lotus Jazz, a similar bundled package for Apple's Macintosh, did not meet expectations and was later "criticized both for being slow and for being difficult to learn, the same complaint that had been leveled at Symphony."[398] Microsoft Excel eventually proved superior to Lotus 1-2-3 on IBM's PC.

Microsoft Excel emerged chiefly out of an Apple/Microsoft partnership, the details of which are as intriguing as Microsoft's IBM dealings were. After learning of Microsoft's intent to enter the applications business, Steve Jobs and then Apple CEO John Sculley asked Microsoft to develop applications for Macintosh's new GUI. Realizing that having Macintosh applications provided leverage, Gates agreed to the request but with an astounding condition:

> In return for releasing the sparkling new Microsoft apps, he wanted the right to use the Mac OS, and particularly those elements that defined its graphic user interface (GUI), in Microsoft's PC-oriented products. If Apple didn't give Microsoft the necessary permissions, Gates would

---

396 Funding Universe, "Lotus Development Corporation History," accessed May 12, 2023, http://www.fundinguniverse.com/company-histories/lotus-development-corporation-history/.

397 Janet Lowe, *Bill Gates Speaks: Insight from the World's Greatest Entrepreneur* (New York: John Wiley & Sons, 1998), 233.

398 Funding Universe, "Lotus Development Corporation History."

> simply sit on his apps. Facing an untenable situation, Apple caved, and agreed that Microsoft could dip into the family jewels.[399]

Apple was forced to reveal the inner workings of a vital asset, while Microsoft obtained a prominent launch customer for its nascent applications business and access to knowledge about Apple's then stellar OS business. Microsoft Windows 1.0 emerged in 1985, and though not as functional or user friendly as the Macintosh OS, it looked so similar that Apple sued for copyright infringement but to no avail. The court concluded Microsoft software similarities were within the license.[400] Like IBM, Apple learned that partnering with Microsoft had its risks.

Because Microsoft Excel initially only operated on the Macintosh, Lotus held its spreadsheet position for a few more years. While Lotus 1-2-3 had over 90 percent market share in 1991, by 1997 Microsoft Excel held over 70 percent.[401] Lotus 1-2-3's dominance had ended forever.

The WordPerfect demise was similar. Introduced in 1982, the word processing package had 50 percent of the market by 1990, followed by Microsoft Word, which by 1988 was the second-most popular word processing package.[402] Unlike Microsoft Excel initially, Microsoft Word operated on DOS, and PC users could use the software, though adoption rates were initially unimpressive.

The final coup de grâce solidifying Microsoft's application dominance was the release of the Microsoft Office suite in 1990. Combining Microsoft Word, Excel, and PowerPoint proved more attractive—Microsoft Office 1.0 contained all three—such that Microsoft Office 4.0, offered in 1993, became a low-priced product that Microsoft sold separately in its own right. Gates noted:

---

399 Jeffrey L. Cruikshank, *The Apple Way: 12 Management Lessons from the World's Most Innovative Company* (New York: McGraw-Hill, 2006), 63.

400 *Apple Computer, Inc. v. Microsoft Corp.*, 35 F.3d 1435 (9th Cir. 1994), accessed May 12, 2023, https://casetext.com/case/apple-computer-inc-v-microsoft-corp.

401 Edward E. Lawler III and Christopher G. Worley, with David Creelman, *Management Reset: Organizing for Sustainable Effectiveness* (San Francisco, CA: Jossey-Bass, 2011), 51–2.

402 Don E. Waldman and Rochelle Ruffer, "Microsoft: Who Is Microsoft Today?" in *Industry and Firm Studies*, 4th ed., eds. Victor J. Tremblay and Carol Horton Tremblay (Armonk, NY: M. E. Sharpe, 2007), 303.

> For the first time, we're positioning our primary application as being Office as opposed to the individual applications. . . . Now this is not to say that the individual applications are not important. They are. But already today we sell over half the units of Excel and Word as part of our office package. And so we've turned Office into far more than simply a way of marketing a group of applications at a discount and rather into an individual product.[403]

To complete coverage of Microsoft's high-growth years, we now turn to the organizational model the company used over this time.

Microsoft's Organizational Model: Managing the Best and Brightest, with Millionaires Galore

Central to Microsoft's success in its first 25 years is how talented software engineers and computer scientists were put to work writing software that became standards in the markets it was offered. As is highlighted later in Microsoft's battles with antitrust regulators, part of the company's success, however, is also attributable to the brutal—and at times illegal—way competitors were treated.

Essential for any high-value-added post-industrial worker is strong intellectual ability, and this was (and likely remains) the dominant selector for those wishing to do important work at Microsoft. Gates, described with cofounder Allen as "super smart Einsteins,"[404] ensured human capital hired met this moniker: "At Microsoft the 'interview rounds' involve a grueling ritual in which candidates are grilled for hours. . . . The company prides itself on attracting, hiring, and retaining super smart people."[405]

403 Cusumano and Selby, *Microsoft Secrets*, 141.
404 John M. Ivancevich and Thomas N. Duening, *Managing Einsteins: Leading High-Tech Workers in the Digital Age* (New York: McGraw-Hill, 2002), 15.
405 Ivancevich and Duening, *Managing Einsteins.*

As evidence of the premium on intelligence, "one of the few ways to impress Bill Gates is to outthink him on an issue."[406] In the mid-1990s, only 2 to 3 percent of interviewees were hired, and once on board the work ethic was demanding. Only those willing to work 14-hour days and over weekends survived, and vacations were short and rare.[407] Hiring very smart people and working them hard was central to Microsoft's success.

Along with respect for outstanding intellect and hard work and alignment with Gates's combative personality, tenacious individual contribution was also highly valued:

> Gates and his lieutenants built a culture that prized the work of an individual. Employees hired by Microsoft knew that their efforts would make a difference. Inexperience was no obstacle, provided the person had the spunk and energy to move an idea ahead. Fierce arguments could be won by the most junior person on a team if that person presented the right data.[408]

Underscoring his commitment and work ethic between 1978 and 1984, Gates took only 15 days off work.[409] Structures to harness the company's collective intelligence were put in place too. All were pressed to use their minds to learn.

> What most struck me about Microsoft as I examined its operations at close range was not the company's market share but the intense, pragmatic thoughtfulness that informed its decisions. I observed no scolding "THINK!" signs on the wall as in the IBM of yore, but "THINK!" permeated Microsoft's bloodstream through and through. This was a company of smart people, managed well, constantly learning as it went . . . the extent to which the company has, we might

---

406 David Thielen with Shirley Thielen, *The 12 Simple Secrets of Microsoft Management: How to Think and Act Like a Microsoft Manager and Take Your Company to the Top* (New York: McGraw-Hill, 1999), 27.
407 Cusumano and Selby, *Microsoft Secrets*, 92–93.
408 Elizabeth Corcoran, "For Gates, Fight May Prove Costly," *Washington Post*, May 19, 1998, A01
409 Lowe, *Bill Gates Speaks*, 37.

say, learned how to learn, is not visible from afar, nor is it visible in a snapshot taken at a given moment.[410]

How Microsoft harnessed its "smarts" and "learned how to learn" is captured in a short phrase that frames important dimensions of the organization's culture: "Improve through continuous self-critiquing, feedback, and sharing."[411] Four subprinciples were embodied at the company: learn systematically from past and present projects and products, encourage feedback and improvement using quantitative measures and benchmarks, consider customer support as part of the product and as data for improvement, and promote linkages and sharing across product groups.[412]

Three other rules managed the company's workforce: organize small teams of overlapping functional specialists, focus creativity by evolving features and fixing resources, and do everything in parallel with frequent synchronization.[413] Microsoft's attention to forming and managing small groups of talented engineers and programmers was an important element explaining its success. These were the creative cores of post-industrial creative workers or teams of post-industrial transformative workers that kept the company dominant and ahead of competition, both strategically and operationally.

Microsoft provided its programmers both the structure and the freedom to write the complex code that built the systems and applications that eventually dominated the markets they served. How Microsoft found that elusive balance between control and creativity; between software development as art versus science; between individual work motivated by feistiness, ambition, and a willingness to challenge everything

410 Randall E. Stross, *The Microsoft Way: The Real Story of How the Company Outsmarts Its Competitors* (New York: Basic Books, 1996), 3.
411 Cusumano and Selby, *Microsoft Secrets*, 327.
412 Cusumano and Selby, *Microsoft Secrets*, 327.
413 Cusumano and Selby, *Microsoft Secrets*. Those interested in learning more about Microsoft's detailed efforts to manage its human capital should consult this work.

versus working in teams to accomplish corporate goals—all account for the coding capabilities developed.

Because of its diversity and complexity, there is "no one best way" to develop software,[414] and Microsoft's ability to set deadlines for project completion while development teams had autonomy to accomplish goals set for them created the "adhocracy based on teams, the decentralized decision-making, professionalism, and shared organizational values that is the prototype for organizing creative knowledge work."[415]

Rewarding those working at Microsoft also received attention. An employee stock ownership plan was introduced in 1981, adding to the company's ability to attract and retain talented workers and sustain their work ethic while earning lower than average monthly pay.

> Although there had been some grumbling about the lack of a company stock plan, most of the technical people working for Gates would probably have remained with Microsoft without one. But stock participation in the company made it easier to attract good people. Employees could buy stock for about $1 a share. Owning stock in the company made up for a lot of hard work at low pay. Microsoft did not pay very well in comparison with the rest of the industry, but it was very generous with its stock options.[416]

Blessed with strong cash flows, Microsoft did not need resources to fund its growth. The company's 1986 IPO was done to provide a market for the stock that employees owned.[417] Going public made many employees millionaires on paper, and by the end of the 1990s, Microsoft's wealth-creation capacity was manifest.

---

414 Rowena Barret, "Managing the Software Development Labour Process: Direct Control, Time and Technical Autonomy," in *Management, Labour Process and Software Development*, ed. Rowena Barret (New York: Routledge, 2005), 81.

415 Bente Rasmussen and Birgitte Johansen, "Trick or Treat: Autonomy as Control in Knowledge Work," in *Management, Labour Process and Software Development*, ed. Rowena Barret (New York: Routledge, 2005), 101.

416 Wallace and Erickson, *Hard Drive*, 210.

417 Richard Koch, *The 80/20 Individual: How to Build on the 20% of What You Do Best* (New York: Random House, 2005), 220.

> At $452 billion Microsoft had the largest market capitalization of any stock on a U.S. stock exchange as of March 31 of 1999. Incredibly, $10,000 invested at the IPO in March of 1986 would have been worth nearly $4.7 million. Microsoft turned even humble investors into millionaires. Employees, who received extensive compensation in stock options, had also benefited immensely from the stock's appreciation. . . . Perhaps even more amazingly, an estimated 3,000 Microsoft employees had become millionaires.[418]

Other estimates reported Microsoft created around 10,000 millionaires by 2000.[419] At the end of 1999, the company employed over 31,000; a large percent was independently wealthy.

The post-industrial entrepreneurial organization had arrived. Unlike the classic industrial organization where workers as *doers* didn't participate in entrepreneurial returns, at Microsoft, knowledge workers as *thinkers* received generous equity-based compensation for the output they produced. Many members of Microsoft's creative core, instead of only earning salaries that covered living expenses through their sweat equity, built individual wealth by equity accumulation en masse. In industrial organizations, only founders, senior managers, and early financiers typically enjoyed entrepreneurial returns.

The final dimensions of the Microsoft business model warranting attention are negative in import. Not all explanations of the company's success are attributable to positive characteristics like hard work, top leadership's mental and business acuity, the *smarts* of workers, a respect for individual contribution, good development team management, or generous equity-based remuneration. By the end of the twentieth century, it was clear some success had flowed from unsavory competitive behaviors. Microsoft faced the wrath of antitrust regulators from both

---

418 Mary E. Barth and Carlos Schonfeld, *Microsoft Corporation*, Graduate School of Business, Stanford University Case A-174 (Stanford, CA: Board of Trustees of the Leland Stanford Junior University, 2000), 1.

419 Julie Bick, "The Microsoft Millionaires Come of Age," *New York Times*, May 29, 2005, accessed May 14, 2023, http://www.nytimes.com/2005/05/29/business/yourmoney/29millionaire.html.

the United States and Europe, and its actions were found wanting. Part of Microsoft's success was from using its market power inappropriately. Microsoft, like IBM before it, was found to be monopolistic and was constrained.

Like Microsoft, Gates was also depicted in terms of good and evil:

> Consider attempts to describe the rise of Microsoft and its human symbol, Bill Gates. In version 1 of the Microsoft story, Gates is pictured as a brilliant innovator and tactician with extraordinary insight and managerial ability. . . . In version 2 of the Microsoft story, Gates is depicted as a lucky bully who never had an original idea in his life but has been ruthless in stealing and promoting the ideas of others. It is a variation on the robber baron stories of the nineteenth century.[420]

Some argue, however, that perceptions of Gates were produced from misunderstandings of the values that sustained him:

> The prevailing belief held that he was a devious, greedy, power-hungry businessman who disguised himself as a harmless eccentric in order to trick naïve technologists into signing away their crown jewels to him.
>
> But it was less a matter of Gates's intentionally assuming a disguise than it was a matter of people misreading his Seattleness. All those associations with the name "Seattle" that Howard Schultz had invoked—softness, sensitivity, laid-back attitudes, low ambition, tolerance, and so on—had contributed the first impression Gates made among his peers. That impression, which lulled partners and competitors alike, was deepened by Gates's Seattle-born lack of pretension: his casual wardrobe, insistence on flying coach rather than first class, disinterest in drawing attention to himself, distaste for limousines and other perks of corporate power.[421]

Where observers fall in the spectrum of Gates and Microsoft as saints or sinners probably depends on their interactions with the company.

---

420 James G. March, *The Ambiguities of Experience* (Ithaca, NY: Cornell University Press, 2010), 53.
421 Fred Moody, *Seattle and the Demons of Ambition: From Boom to Bust in the Number One City of the Future* (New York: Macmillan, 2003), 145.

Competitors at the sharp end of Microsoft's or Gates's actions would call them sinners. Supporters would argue they were victims of unnecessary government intervention.[422] Regardless, customers voted with their pocketbooks, and their support for the company's products indicates a bias more toward saints than sinners. The truth probably lies somewhere in between.

Microsoft's progress in the first two decades of the twenty-first century, though less impressive than its performance over the twentieth century, remains strong and robust. Though constrained by regulators, the company's core OS and applications businesses remain entrenched. The company continued investing in its Windows OS franchise, boasting on its website in October 2021 that Windows 11 was "the best Windows yet."[423] Microsoft Windows 12 was announced in March 2023. Other major steps include entry into the gaming market in 2001 through its Xbox gaming console, its Skype acquisition in 2011 for US$8.5 billion (at the time its largest acquisition), and its US$26.2 billion purchase of LinkedIn in 2016.

Microsoft is also in the cloud. Microsoft 365 is a SaaS product, offering access to office productivity apps for email, communication, file storage, and other processes through subscriptions to programs such as Microsoft Word, Excel, PowerPoint, OneNote, Outlook, and Skype, making online cloud computing as powerful as desktop computing. In addition, Microsoft Azure is Microsoft's public cloud platform that provides access to cloud-based services for networking, storage, analytics, and other activities, offering organizations cloud services that include PaaS and IaaS and complement the SaaS capability of Microsoft 365.

---

422 For among the most spirited defenses of Gates as *saint*, see Andrew Greta, "The Persecuted Titan: Bill Gates as Henry Rearden, the Businessman Who Created Revolutionary Technologies and Was Criminalized for His Success," chap. 5 in Donald L. Luskin and Andrew Greta, *I Am John Galt: Today's Heroic Innovators Building the World and the Villainous Parasites Destroying It* (Hoboken, NJ: John Wiley & Sons, 2011), 131–62.

423 Microsoft, "Meet Windows 11," accessed May 15, 2023, https://www.microsoft.com/en-us/windows/windows-11.

Microsoft Azure is offered on a pay-as-you-go basis, meaning users are charged only for what they use.

In addition, Steve Ballmer was appointed CEO in January 2000, having served as president since 1998, and Bill Gates, then appointed chief software architect, began a staged withdrawal from the company. In mid-2006 Microsoft announced Gates would relinquish his role as chief software architect in July 2008, after which he would continue to serve as board chair and advisor on key development projects. Gates remained chair until 2014 and stepped down from the board in March 2020, yet still holding an estimated 1.3 percent of the company's stock.

Though more constrained than it was in the early 2000s, the most successful software company in history still thrives. With a mission "to empower every person and every organization on the planet to achieve more,"[424] Microsoft does business in over 100 countries and in June 2022 employed 122,000 in the United States and 99,000 internationally. Of these, 85,000 were in operations (including manufacturing, distribution, product support, and consulting services); 73,000 were in product research and development; 47,000 were in sales and marketing; and 16,000 were in general and administration.[425]

In 2022, Microsoft was boasting revenues of US$198.27 billion (up 18 percent from 2021) and a net income of US$72.738 billion (up 19 percent from 2021);[426] also, on June 30, 2022, the company reported US$104.757 billion in cash, cash equivalents, or short-term investments.[427] More importantly, in FY 2022, US$24.512 billion was invested in R&D, supporting the 33 percent of its 221,000-strong workforce in this functional area.[428] The company remains as much a Leader now as it was in the twentieth century.

---

424 Microsoft, *Microsoft Corporation Annual Form 10-K* (2022), 3, accessed May 15, 2023, https://www.sec.gov/Archives/edgar/data/789019/000156459022026876/msft-10k_20220630.htm
425 Microsoft, *Microsoft Corporation Annual Form 10-K*, 8.
426 Microsoft, *Microsoft Corporation Annual Form 10-K*, 40.
427 Microsoft, *Microsoft Corporation Annual Form 10-K*, 56.
428 Microsoft, *Microsoft Corporation Annual Form 10-K*, 43.

Columbus, Ford, and Gates: No Business to Industrial Business to Post-Industrial Business

Comparing the form of entrepreneurship of Columbus, Ford, and Gates provides some final important insights. Notably, each shows entrepreneurship's essential nature did not change as the transition through the eras progressed. At the core of each entrepreneur's actions was a vision to accomplish something not done before, a role regardless of when or where entrepreneurs lived. That all three became astoundingly wealthy also underscores that entrepreneurial returns are also independent of the time they are earned.

Compared with Columbus, however, Ford and Gates show entrepreneurship's evolution. Unlike Columbus, who used hard power to acquire assets through force and plunder, Ford and Gates relied on entrepreneurship not plundering in nature, but commensurate with the eras where productive exchanges between buyers and sellers—on the supply side as workers and on the demand side as customers—became the norm.

This kinder, gentler entrepreneurship, expected in times that were kinder and gentler than the Pre-Industrial Era, was possible only because productive capacity improved and scalable business became possible. Ford perfected the scaling of goods production, and Gates perfected the scaling of knowledge and information captured in computer code.

A case can also be made that Gates's entrepreneurship was even kinder and gentler than Ford's. In Ford's world, the original financiers and Ford enjoyed the entrepreneurial returns from Ford Motor Company's successes, while most workers earned living wages on the assembly line, which, though far better than subsistence farming, still had drawbacks. Humans performing as biological machines meant assembly line work was physically exacting, mentally boring, and challenging to sustain. Workers on the shop floor also labored for decades to amass savings to retire at around 65 years of age.

In Gates's world, though work hours were longer than the typical five-day, eight-hour-a-day workweek in the Industrial Era, they were not as physical, were more mentally stimulating, and took advantage of our most valuable asset—the human brain. Workers at Microsoft not only had the opportunity to earn significantly more than those in the Industrial Era; many amassed the wealth to retire early. Compared with Ford's industrial organization, Microsoft's post-industrial organization was kinder, gentler, and considerably richer!

That workers were more empowered, received greater respect, and earned more at Microsoft was because what they did was central to Microsoft's success. Wealth did not come from economic capital converting raw materials into physical goods along assembly lines, where manually dexterous humans did mostly routine, supportive assembly work. Instead, wealth emerged from careful instructions developed by workers at the core of Microsoft's value-adding processes. Workers as members of the creative core became the primary sources of value.

Two additional differences between Gates's experience compared with Ford's and Columbus's relate to the difficulties raising the initial capital to fund each venture and the time it took to generate the wealth eventually accumulated. Both Columbus and Ford took years to raise the finance needed to fund their ventures, and in the case of Ford, 27 years passed before his first notable product reached the market. Because of its complexity, Ford took decades to perfect his first vehicle, which involved considerable trial and error and production of working prototypes.

Gates encountered far fewer constraints. He did not face years of negotiation to fund Microsoft's startup, and neither did he wait long for his wealth to accumulate. At the age of 31, he was the youngest self-made billionaire in American history, and at 38 (in 1994, 19 years after starting Microsoft), he became the world's wealthiest man, a position held for 13 years. Why Gates did not face the stresses of Columbus and Ford at their ventures start, and why his wealth accumulated so quickly and was so substantial, reveal important differences between industrial and post-industrial business.

Gates and Allen sought no external capital to found Microsoft in 1975, and though some external financing was received before the company's IPO—Technology Venture Investors, a Silicon Valley venture capital firm advising Microsoft when it went public, acquired 6.2 percent of Microsoft from Gates and Allen in 1981[429]—this financing was sought more to build credibility among institutional investors than to raise funds,[430] just as going public was more to provide liquidity for Microsoft stock than to raise capital. Microsoft's business, unlike Ford's, was not capital intensive. It was labor and ideas intensive.

There was no need to finance a sprawling Rouge plant; offices with desks in cubicles where *super smart Einsteins* wrote computer code were needed. What made it even easier was Microsoft learned early on how to price and sell code, meaning that the funds generated internally from sales easily financed growth. Finally, Microsoft's origin as a self-funded startup produced a frugality that persisted for decades. Expenses were kept as low as was possible, and cash was carefully preserved for rainy days that were always expected soon.

That Gates's wealth accumulated so quickly derives from the fact that intangible ideas captured in computer code are imminently scalable. To increase output at Ford Motor Company once full capacity was reached required new investment, done mostly on a lumpy, stepwise basis. Capital-intensive businesses inevitably face scale constraints. In contrast, *burning* MS-DOS onto computer hard drives or selling Microsoft Word or Excel on floppy disks or streaming software over the internet requires little capital once the code is written. Few, if any, scale constraints are encountered.

In addition, once development costs are covered, the low marginal cost of producing additional software copies means profits grow very quickly with sales. In managerial accounting terms, with most produc-

---

429 Lowe, *Bill Gates Speaks*, 39–40.

430 John Callahan and Steven Muegge, "Venture Capital's Role in Innovation: Issues, Research and Stakeholders Interests," in *The International Handbook on Innovation*, ed. Larisa V. Shavinina (New York: Elsevier, 2003), 643.

tion costs fixed and the variable cost per unit of new product low, cash flow once fixed costs are covered is considerable. Add products that become standards used on most computers, and the result is a highly profitable and hard-to-dislodge market incumbent.

Gates and Microsoft also created products that immediately benefited businesses and individuals around the world.

> And while it wasn't his primary intent, Bill Gates himself was far from the main beneficiary of his industrial endeavor. By creating a de facto standard in computer operating systems, he unlocked widespread cross-compatibility of applications and files, which boosted global workforce productivity throughout the 1980s and 1990s to historically astronomic levels. The same work output that had previously required a bank of financial analysts poring over hand calculations or a pool of typists hammering away at carbon-copied memos could be accomplished by a single office worker in a fraction of the time, and then disseminated instantly to a worldwide audience using a compatible DOS or Windows-based PC.[431]

An alternative explanation of this success relates to the concept of *network effects*, which holds that the value of any good or service depends on the number of people using it. Ultimately, a large proportion of Microsoft's value derived from the fact that the vast majority of computers use the same software, meaning that, regardless of where you are or what you are working on, you will be able to access your data on almost any computer.

This was the model that produced the world's wealthiest person in less than two decades and made many thousands around him millionaires and some billionaires. The human intensity and imminently scalable nature of Microsoft's business are why Gates's wealth accumulation was quicker than Ford's and also explain why so many employed by Microsoft accumulated wealth working there. These and the assessments

---

431 Andrew Greta, "The Persecuted Titan," 134.

noted previously permit the contrasting of industrial with post-industrial organizations. Table 12 provides such a comparison.

Table 12: Industrial versus Post-Industrial Organizations

Industrial	Post-Industrial
Dependent on physical capital; asset and labor intensive	Dependent on intellectual capital and ideas; mostly labor intensive
Based on physical/tangible products	Based on intangible, high-value-added services/solutions
Employs mostly in the factory	Employs on the campus, at home, or anywhere
Hard to scale	Easy to scale
Balance sheet orientation	Income statement orientation
Low net income per person	High net income per person
Low market value per person (MVP)	High market value per person (MVP)
Slow wealth creation dispersed to outside suppliers of financial capital; few inside shareholders	Fast wealth creation, also dispersible to inside suppliers of knowledge; many inside shareholders

Table 12 indicates industrial organizations are typically physical capital dependent, are asset and labor intensive, and produce physical/tangible products. They employ many workers, mostly in factories, and face scale constraints. In addition, managers operating these businesses have more of a balance sheet orientation, meaning measures such as return on capital employed (ROCE) or return on assets or investment (ROA or ROI) measure them, and their core task is to make the considerable assets they control *sweat* (i.e., generate as much return as possible). Further, if net income (profits after tax) is divided by number of employees, the ratio tends to be low, as does the ratio of market capitalization (stock price multiplied by the number of shares in issue) divided by the number of employees to produce the market value per person (MVP). Finally, compared with post-industrial counterparts, industrial organizations display slower wealth creation dispersed mostly to founders and outside suppliers of financial capital; fewer inside shareholders are enriched.

Post-industrial organizations, in contrast, are human and intellectual capital intensive and employ smarter people producing intangible, higher-value-added services and solutions that are far easier to scale. Employees can work in an office or virtually, and those operating these businesses have more of an income statement than balance sheet orientation. Because the physical assets they manage are limited, measures such as ROCE, ROI, and ROA are less important; sales minus costs (i.e., an income statement orientation, reflected by measures such as net income on sales) is more important. Finally, because of their intellectual capital dependency, net income per person and MVP are higher, and a faster wealth creation more dispersed to inside suppliers of knowledge is observed. More inside shareholders are present in the post-industrial organization.

Table 13 presents data reflecting the differences noted in Table 12. Data on six post-industrial organizations—Apple, Microsoft, Google (Alphabet), Cisco, Nike, and Amazon—is compared with data on three industrial organizations—Caterpillar, Ford, and General Motors. The year of establishment, employee number, market capitalization (Market Cap), MVP, net income/sales (Net Inc/Sales), and net income/employee (Net Inc/Emp) are provided, with MVP ranked from lowest to highest. This MVP, as of May 16, 2023, is only a single point in time estimate and fluctuates as share prices change. The data clearly shows how MVP differs among industrial versus post-industrial companies.

Table 13 underscores the differences highlighted in Table 12. Post-industrial MVPs (excluding Amazon's) range from US$2.31 million to US$16.46 million per person, while industrial MVPs range from Ford's US$263,006 to Caterpillar's US$978,918. Caterpillar's high MVP compared with Ford or GM may to some degree be attributed to the move the company has made from provider of physical machines to the seller of complex, network-based solutions such as those seen in its joint venture with Trimble.

Table 13: Comparative Industrial versus Post-Industrial Organization Data

	Year Founded	Employee Number	Market Cap (US$)	MVP (US$)	Net Inc/ Sales (%)	Net Inc/ Emp (US$)
Ford	1903	173,000	45.5 bn	263,006	–1.25	–11,451
GM	1908	167,000	44.04 bn	263,713	6.34	59,485
Amazon	1994	1,541,000	1.18 tn	765,737	–0.53	–1,766
Caterpillar	1925	109,100	106.8 bn	978,918	11.28	61,457
Cisco	1984	83,300	192.2 bn	2.31 m	22.90	141,801
Nike	1968	77,239	178.9 bn	2.32 m	12.94	78,277
Google	1998	190,234	1.5 tn	7.89 m	21.20	315,254
Microsoft	1975	221,000	2.3 tn	10.41 m	36.69	329,131
Apple	1976	164,000	2.7 tn	16.46 m	25.31	608,555

Data from fiscal year 2022 annual reports or annual SEC 10-Ks. Market capitalizations are from May 16, 2023, reported by Google Finance. This value changes when stock prices change.
In the table, *m* indicates *millions*, *bn* indicates *billions*, and *tn* indicates *trillions*.

In addition, net income on sales for Apple, Microsoft, Google, Cisco, and Nike ranges from 12.94 to 36.69 percent, while Caterpillar, Ford, and General Motors vary from –1.25 to 11.28 percent. Net income per employee for post-industrial organizations ranges from US$78,277 to US$608,555, while the three industrial numbers vary from US$11,451 to US$61,457, respectively. The value of employees, measured either by net income or MVP, is far higher in post-industrial than in industrial organizations.

While the generalizations in Table 12 account for differences between the two categories of organizations, they do not always hold. With a market capitalization of US$1.18 trillion and a relatively low MVP (below Caterpillar's US$978,918 at US$765,737), Amazon also operates with negative net income to sales and net income to employee ratios.

This anomaly is caused both by industry effects and by Amazon decisions. An early entrant into e-commerce as a books-only retailer, Amazon's biggest source of revenues remains retail, with its 2022 annual shareholder letter boasting that "Amazon sells nearly every physical and digital retail item you can imagine, with a vibrant third-party seller ecosystem that accounts for 60% of our unit sales, and reaches customers in virtually every country around the world."[432]

But being a retailer competing with online and traditional retailers means margins are tight to the extent that for FY 2022, Amazon retailing posted an operating loss of US$10.59 billion on revenues of US$433.89 billion (–2.44 percent). AWS, accounting for US$80 billion of Amazon's US$513.9 billion revenues (16 percent), reported an operating profit of US$22.8 billion, with its 28.5 percent margin similar to other Table 13 post-industrial firms.[433]

Moreover, as America's second largest private-sector employer, Amazon's 1,541,000 employees are close in number to the largest US private-sector employer, Walmart, with 2,100,000 associates who each generated net income of US$5,561 (lower than all but Ford and Amazon) and who showed an MVP of US$175,652 on May 16, 2023, lower than all MVPs in Table 13.[434] Because it does not have an AWS equivalent, Walmart must generate profits in its retail and online businesses to stay afloat. Its Net Income to Sales in FY 2022 was 1.85 percent, confirming again the thin retail margins.

The work done by most Walmart in-store employees (stocking shelves and working at fulfillment centers, greeting and checking out customers, etc.) is of a lower value and, in most instances, manual in nature. Those responsible for the design, maintenance, and improvement of likely the world's most efficient traditional retail logistics supply chain—the IT-based core of Walmart's business—are likely to earn remuneration closer to those at Microsoft or Cisco.

A similar dichotomy is seen at Amazon. Those responsible for the company's extremely efficient, technology-based e-commerce retail platform or for operating AWS, "the world's most comprehensive and

---

432 Amazon, *Amazon Annual Form 10-K* (2022), accessed May 17, 2023, https://s2.q4cdn.com/299287126/files/doc_financials/2023/ar/Amazon-2022-Annual-Report.pdf.
433 Amazon, *Amazon Annual Form 10-K* (2022).
434 Walmart, *Annual Form 10K, 2022* for the fiscal year ending January 31, 2023, accessed May 17, 2023, https://s201.q4cdn.com/262069030/files/doc_financials/2023/ar/Walmart-10K-Reports-Optimized.pdf.

broadly adopted cloud, offering over 200 fully featured services from data centers globally,"[435] are post-industrial workers that create considerable value. Those in the over 1,300 Amazon fulfillment centers ensuring the right product is in the right box and reaches the right customer create far less value and are less generously rewarded. Amazon fulfillment centers employ between 1,000 to 1,500 full-time associates,[436] meaning the company has far more employees in these lower-value-added jobs, again similar to Walmart.

That Nike has relatively low net income to sales and net income per employee is also because Nike is in the low-margin shoe and apparel businesses, but regardless, its US$2.32 million MVP confirms its status as a post-industrial enterprise. With shoe and apparel production outsourced to low-cost manufacturers from inception, Nike's core business revolves around product design and development and marketing and brand management, all high-value, post-industrial, knowledge-based competences.

Lastly, while revealing differences between industrial and post-industrial organization, the comparisons in Table 12 and the data in Table 13 are, strictly speaking, misdirected. Comparing Ford Motor Company with Cisco, Apple, or Microsoft, or Caterpillar with Nike, is not comparing apples to apples. Better is comparing organizations to competitors; for example, how does Ford Motor Company's MVP or net income per person compare with Toyota's or Tesla's?

Also insightful is observing what has happened over time. For example, at Microsoft, has the MVP increased, remained stable, or decreased over time? At Caterpillar, how are MVP and net income per person trending over time? Hopefully both have increased steadily, indicating Caterpillar and its workers are becoming more post-industrial in makeup and contribution. This should be a goal of all organizations,

---

435 Amazon, "Cloud Computing with AWS," accessed May 18, 2023, https://aws.amazon.com/what-is-aws/.
436 Amazon, "Our Facilities," accessed May 19, 2023, https://www.aboutamazon.com/workplace/facilities.

industrial or post-industrial: continually upgrading the capabilities and performance of those working for them. By so doing they will drive employees to lift their value added and become post-industrial too. We now turn to the last topic covered in this chapter—the political economy of the Post-Industrial Era.

Post-Industrial Era Political Economy: Divergence and Convergence with the Possible Triumph of Democracy

Chapter 3 notes that the political economy suitable to an era involves the regime type and economic policy that manages the complexities arising as the often-competing forces of stability, growth, and development are dealt with and balanced. Post-industrial nations also face and balance these forces: too little growth may eventually hinder development and impact stability, while too generous development following pandering political choices and insufficient growth may similarly affect stability. How such situations are present in and might impact the United States and other Leaders over the coming decades is mentioned briefly later and considered more comprehensively in Chapter 5.

With around half of humanity still living in pre-industrial rural or urban subsistence and awaiting input-led growth to industrialize, the smaller percentage in or at the cusp of post-industrial production must strive to maintain innovation-led growth. Based on material in this chapter, competitive post-industrial nations will boast well-educated workers and focused producers, supported by partners and suppliers who provide supply chain elements they do better. Competition ensures work remains high quality and low cost, and at the top of any competitiveness wish list are excellent education and IT infrastructures and efficient producers focused on their areas of proven competitive advantage.

Economically literate nation-state leaders aware of where countries fit in the global productive order will also lead the most competitive nations and will know that social costs should be continually compared with competitors. Higher subsidies for uncompetitive workers in time renders nations uncompetitive if competitor costs are lower. Higher healthcare costs may impair similarly. More about these is said in Chapter 5 when America's global competitiveness is considered.

Fukuyama's *End of History* thesis, proposed after communism's collapse, was among the first to suggest twenty-first-century political economy would converge around a single model. Trumpeting Western liberal democracy as the one best form of government—and qualifying that the reason why is because it protects universal rights to freedom and exists only with the consent of the governed—Fukuyama insisted deregulated, free-market capitalism would be the liberal economic order accompanying the democracy he expected to dominate.[437]

This forecast was more robust at the twentieth century's end when America was at the height of its global power. Its economic collapse in 2007 and the economic and political adjustments that have since followed—prominent among these being America's drift toward isolation and authoritarianism under Trump and the appearance of a China-led alliance in 2023 that includes Russia, Brazil, India, South Africa, and others—pauses Western liberal democracy's inevitable advance and superiority. Chapter 5 also considers how these developments may impact global stability and commerce over the twenty-first century.

Other challenges Western democracies face over coming decades could undermine democracy's preeminence even further. Regardless of industrialization level, nations must not live beyond their means. This occurs when public spending exceeds taxes to produce enduring fiscal deficits, when imports exceed exports such that endemic current account deficits follow, or when borrowing to sustain consumption leaves debt challenging to repay.

Facing an aging population, persistent trade and fiscal deficits, and a ballooning national debt, America is out of balance. To rebalance, reductions in publicly funded benefits and entitlements, tax increases, or

---

437 Francis Fukuyama, "The End of History? As Our Mad Century Closes, We Find the Universal State," *Washington Post*, July 30, 1989, C1. Fukuyama's views were more comprehensively presented in Francis Fukuyama, *The End of History and the Last Man*, (New York: Free Press, 1992).

both, are required. The twentieth-century record shows modern distributive democracy is good at handing out benefits, but whether it is able to impose discipline and economic pain is still to be tested. Inability to impose these may place Western democracy in further jeopardy. Chapter 5 focuses on how the US imbalances appeared, what it will take to redress them, and what is required of political leaders to ensure that the rebalancing takes place.

Those awaiting fulfillment of Fukuyama's *End of History* convergence must also accept multiple forms of democracy and capitalism exist. Chapter 3 notes that European and US social welfare expenditures are higher than in Asia, where provision for the aged is more a familial than a state responsibility. Only public education in Asian democracies matches Western expenditures.

This and other data show at least three forms of democracy exist: Scandinavian welfare social democracy (e.g., Denmark and Sweden); continental European/East Asian corporatist social insurance/familial democracy (e.g., Germany and Japan); and Anglo-Saxon lower taxes/limited welfare/free-market democracy (e.g., Britain and the United States).[438] Given these, a theory centered around capitalism's varieties in practice questions if "increasing international economic integration will force the institutions and regulatory regimes of diverse nations into convergence on a common model."[439]

The *Varieties of Capitalism* thesis holds different forms of capitalism arise from the advantages national institutions offer and explains through five domains (industrial relations, vocational training/education, corporate governance, interfirm relations, and coordination vis-à-vis employees) the practices organizations follow to resolve common coordination problems in the varying forms.

---

438 Gøsta Esping-Andersen, *Social Foundations of Post-industrial Economies* (Oxford: Oxford University Press, 1999), 170.
439 Peter A. Hall and David Soskice, eds., *Varieties of Capitalism: The Institutional Foundations of Comparative Advantage* (New York: Oxford University Press, 2001), vi.

Three distinctive forms of capitalism have resulted, two of them being the extremes between which most countries reside: liberal market economies (LMEs), comprising the United States, Britain, Canada, Australia, New Zealand, and Ireland, and coordinated market economies (CMEs), comprising Germany, Japan, Switzerland, Netherlands, Belgium, Sweden, Norway, Denmark, Finland, and Austria. A third form between LMEs and CMEs, Mediterranean economies (MEs), comprising France, Italy, Spain, Portugal, Greece, and Turkey, possess relatively large agrarian sectors and extensive state interference involving nonmarket coordination in corporate finance (closer to CMEs), coupled with more liberal labor relations (closer to LMEs). Comparing LMEs with CMEs, GDP growth rates, GDP per capita, and unemployment from 1961 to 1998 were the same.[440] LMEs and CMEs both report satisfactory long-run economic performance while supporting characteristics unique to each.

Important differences between the two extreme forms are also noted: CME work hours are shorter and income distribution is more equal, LME worker involvement in paid work is higher and income distribution is more unequal, and LMEs produce more radical innovation, while CMEs deliver more incremental innovation.[441] LME organizations are less encumbered or assisted by regulation and focus more on open markets and prices to order operations, while CME organizations rely more on non-market-based mechanisms and less on open markets to foster theirs. In the terms previously encountered in these pages, LMEs rely more on markets and CMEs more on plans. MEs, in the middle, rely on both markets and plans.

That all 22 nations in the *Varieties of Capitalism* analysis are democratic means democracy's dominance over other regime types is where post-industrial political economy convergence may occur, but a single economic policy or form of capitalism is soundly rejected by the data. As nations possess different resources and capabilities and as their producers occupy different market niches, multiple forms of capitalism

440 Hall and Soskice, *Varieties of Capitalism*, 20–21.
441 Hall and Soskice, *Varieties of Capitalism*, 41.

and economic policy will likely continue to coexist alongside democracy in post-industrial political economies.

Important for business leaders and business professionals is an ability to operate within the rules and regulations of each form. For example, in European settings, labor is closer to a fixed cost, while in America, it is more a variable cost, hired and fired at will. Conducting Anglo-Saxon-type labor cost cutting in Europe with stronger unions and more protected workers is inadvisable. Similarly, hoping to hire American CEOs at European remuneration levels is as misdirected. America's more market-based, unequal shareholder capitalism differs from Europe's more equitable stakeholder capitalism, and CEO pay differs markedly too. In post-industrial political economy, both convergence and divergence will be present; one model will not fit all.

One weakness in the *Varieties of Capitalism* analysis is that only political economy choices of industrialized nations are depicted. As nations commence industrialization and as Chapter 3 explains, those directed by economically literate authoritarian developmentalists or democracy light regimes in nations operating typically from competitive weakness means more interventionist, state-led, CME/ME-type orientations are better. LME choices under modern distributive democracy at such times is inadvisable.

Finally, though every authoritarian developmentalist state industrializing over the twentieth century became democratic, China may not. As long as the Chinese Communist Party delivers rising living standards, it may remain in power. In addition, the Economist Intelligence Unit's 2022 Democracy Index named only 24 of 167 countries as full democracies: 48 were denoted flawed democracies (the United States among these), 36 were called hybrid regimes, and 59 were listed as authoritarian.[442] Many authoritarian regimes hold power, and one or a few may industrialize without becoming democracies. But not one has done so yet, and time will tell if Fukuyama's democratic convergence explains all

442 Economist Intelligence Unit, "Democracy Index 2022," accessed May 22, 2023, https://www.eiu.com/n/campaigns/democracy-index-2022/

nations. Absent Chapter 5's cataclysmic global meltdown scenario, it will certainly explain most.

Conclusion and Synthesis

The Post-Industrial Era started around 1950 when computers appeared and then changed the characteristics of the goods, services, and solutions on offer, how they are produced, and even the nature of organization and human work itself. To illustrate an era still developing before our eyes, five vignettes present lessons from the front lines of post-industrial business and show how industries change as production is automated and user-led communications online expand. What Cisco pioneered in the early 2000s is now used in orders placed online every day, where digital tents mediate and control transactions as they move from placement to completion. Further, to protect competitive positions, Leaders are moving to offer complex services and solutions so that physical products are bought because of technology-enabled solutions offered around them.

Rather than complementing them as was the case in the Industrial Era, machines are replacing humans, who are left to do work machines cannot do. Under such conditions people are now doing three types of work: post-industrial creative work, post-industrial transformative work, and post-industrial manual work.

Post-industrial creative work is typically done in organizational creative cores, and all should aspire to become members of these high-value teams. Three routes to membership exist: through an understanding of the industry or business domain involved (the industry/business route), through possessing expertise about the scientific or technical aspects of an innovation (the scientific/technical route), or through creating new industries from scratch (the visionary route).

Post-industrial creative work goes to the heart of competitive strategy by developing new goods, services, or solutions that customers demand and competitors struggle to imitate, while post-industrial transformative work focuses on improving existing operational efficiency. Moreover, high-performing firms rely on different processes to control tightly coupled business operations versus more loosely coupled and iterative strategy formation.

Post-industrial transformative work focuses on improving conditions in the known world but still requires innovation. Because they possess leading-edge knowledge of a functional domain, business-oriented post-industrial transformative workers may find new ways to market goods or better ways to manage supply chains, and this work also helps vertically integrated industrial organizations transition to the network-based organizations now characterizing post-industrial commerce. Transformative scientific/technical workers may find better ways to use technology in existing products.

Unlike vertically integrated industrial organization that is controlled by human-mediated hierarchies, and because of business process automation and the ease with which activities are now coordinated across internet-based networks, post-industrial organization is better described as a collective of focused, specialized partners responsible for specific niches. Moreover, with the internetworking of business operations, organizational scope narrows as outsourcing increases, hierarchy diminishes, head count and operational costs drop, and operational efficiency improves.

Post-industrial organizations are also typically less capital intensive than industrial organizations, and asset-based measures like ROCE, ROI, and ROA are less important in their management. Net income and MVP, also higher in post-industrial than in industrial organizations, are more important. In addition, faster wealth creation is seen in post-industrial firms, with more inside shareholders present too. Not just supporting acts to machines, software engineers and coders became Microsoft's source of value and made Bill Gates the world's richest man at the age of 38. Heralding the arrival of post-industrial entrepreneurial capitalism, thousands at Microsoft also became independently wealthy, often in less than a decade.

Both convergence and divergence at the political economy level will likely occur as the Post-Industrial Era continues. The dominance of one economic model is unlikely. At least three forms of capitalism have been identified, with LMEs and CMEs being the extremes between which most reside. More importantly, while each form has unique characteristics, both report satisfactory long-run economic performance. As nations possess different resources and capabilities and their producers occupy different market niches, these multiple forms of capitalism and economic policy will likely continue to coexist. Key for those working across borders is an ability to operate within the rules and regulations that each form of capitalism mandates.

As other nations join the post-industrial world, democracy's dominance over other regime types may be where convergence occurs. All industrialized nations today are democracies, and no autocracy is yet fully industrialized. Time will tell if China or other autocracies will industrialize and remain nondemocratic. Should this occur, regime type convergence will not occur either.

We turn now to the challenges of sustaining the human struggle for productivity over the foreseeable future. Current global diversity, imbalances nations now or sometime in the future may face, and our urgent need for clean energy provide the context within which three scenarios for the century ahead are presented. Then, insights and actions readers should draw and take from the information in these pages concludes this book.

Chapter 5

SUSTAINING THE HUMAN STRUGGLE FOR PRODUCTIVITY

Global Diversity, Remedying Imbalances, Our Search for Clean Energy, and Scenarios for the Twenty-First Century

The first paragraph of this book asks readers to grade mankind's economic progress over the past 7,000 years, and the description of the human struggle for productivity that follows permits our advance to be summarized as follows: millennia of stumbling around as hunter-gatherers or subsistence farmers, capped by 225 years of astonishing progress and abundance. Over the last two centuries—and as the model perfected by First Movers collectively denoted as the European Exception was improved upon by nations best labeled Fast Followers—the economic world expanded into the three categories framing this book: Leaders, Followers, and Failures.

The distance between Leaders at the leading edge of productivity and Failures at the lowest level of human output is now wider than ever. While some are creating the smart products, services, and solutions to accompany life in our automated, networked, technology-intensive post-industrial world, others still face the scarcity that has plagued man for all his time on Earth. The inequality and diversity characterizing our economic world now must be understood to fully appreciate the complexity of the ongoing struggle.

In addition, after 150 years of industrialization and 75 years of post-industrial progress, the human struggle for productivity faces short-term impediments beyond the transition from Failure to Follower to Leader. Some Leaders are exhibiting behaviors more typical of Failures or struggling Followers and need to regain balance. Western democracies—including the United States and Asia's most advanced democracy, Japan—face rebalancing.

But accounting for the present inequality and facilitating entry of those excluded while rebalancing those already industrialized are not the only challenges faced. Industrialization has relied on fossil fuels, and climate scientists conclude this is a major contributor to the increase in CO^2 in the Earth's atmosphere. Anthropogenic global warming/climate change is the third impediment facing the ongoing human struggle for productivity, and absent notable technological leaps, this longer-term problem will take generations to resolve.

This chapter is divided into four sections. First, the economic diversity encountered around the world is summarized. Then, data on the United States embodies the imbalances resulting from recent choices made by Leaders that characterize a now upside-down world. Appreciating how these imbalances arose and what is required to rectify them is especially pertinent to these societies. Third, the challenges of global warming/climate change are noted. Nothing is more important to sustaining the human struggle for productivity than our search for cleaner energy. Finally, after considering the diversity and imbalances that characterize the status quo, and once the challenges revealed by our warming planet are understood, three scenarios describing the paths the human struggle for productivity might follow over the twenty-first century are presented. The book concludes by equipping readers to take actions in their spheres of influence to ensure the best scenario eventuates for us all.

Early Twenty-First-Century Global Diversity: Not as Flat a World as Some Think

Table 14 reports International Monetary Fund (IMF) GDP and GDP per capita for seven regional groups and eight countries. China, the United States, and India on a GDP PPP basis account for 41.78 percent of global output, ranking first, second, and third in GDP size by this measure, respectively. Nominal GDP places America first and China second, with India behind Japan and Germany in fifth.[443] Germany and Japan are included as they are the biggest economies in the European Union and developed Asia, respectively, and data on Brazil, Russia, and South Africa complete the BRICS. To underscore how unequally production is distributed, the table also lists population size by region and country.

Indicative of the gap between richest and poorest on a PPP basis, the IMF reports #1 Ireland's US$145,196 GDP per capita is 281 times that of #196 South Sudan's US$516.[444] While Irishmen live on almost US$400 a day, the world's poorest in South Sudan subsist on less than US$1.50 a day. Table 14's US$80,035 GDP per capita of 335 million Americans and US$56,929 of 446 million European Union citizens compared with the US$23,382 of 1.411 billion Chinese and the US$9,073 of 1.429 billion Indians highlights the diversity even further.

443 Nominal GDP measures GDP at market exchange rates and better reflects international financial flows and internationally traded goods and services, but as exchange rates vary, it is more volatile than PPP measures. PPP compares the cost of a standard basket of goods in each country in local currency against those in US$ and uses this ratio for the exchange rate used. The same hamburger selling for €4 in Berlin and US$4 in New York would imply a PPP exchange rate of €1 for US$1; German nominal GDP and PPP GDP would be the same in US$. Developing economy PPP GDPs are typically higher than nominal GDPs in US$ because their costs of living are lower than in the United States. This explains why Indian or Chinese PPP GDPs increase in US$ compared with their nominal US$ GDP measures.

444 The International Monetary Fund, "World Economic Outlook," April 2023, accessed May 28, 2023, https://www.imf.org/external/datamapper/datasets/WEO.

Table 14: 2023 GDP, GDP per Capita, Population, and Gini Indices

Region/Analytical Group	GDP PPP (%)	GDP Nominal US$tn*** (%)	GDP/ Capita US$ PPP	Pop. (m)	Gini **** (Rank)
North America (3) *	18.63	30.728 (29.1)	63,789	509	-
Central and South America (18)**	5.31	4.532 (4.3)	17,378	489	-
European Union (27)	14.56	17.819 (16.9)	56,929	446	-
Africa (54)	5.10	2.995 (2.8)	6,363	1,398	-
Emerging & Developing Asia (30)	33.58	27.148 (25.7)	15,572	3,757	-
G7 Advanced Economies (7)	29.89	45.915 (43.5)	67,166	776	-
Emerging/Developing Economies (155)	58.89	45.100 (42.7)	15,183	6,746	-
World	100	105.569	na	7,836	-
Country					
China	18.92	19.374	23,382	1,411	38.2 (69)
United States	15.39	26.855	80,035	335	41.5 (46)
India	7.47	3.737	9,073	1,429	35.7 (91)
Japan	3.70	4.410	51,809	125	32.9 (126)
Germany	3.18	4.309	66,132	84	31.7 (137)
Russian Federation	2.86	2.063	34,837	143	36.0 (88)
Brazil	2.30	2.081	18,686	204	48.9 (15)
South Africa	0.57	0.399	16,091	62	63.0 (1)

Unless otherwise indicated, data is from the IMF's *World Economic Outlook* (April 2023), accessed May 28, 2023 https://www.imf.org/external/datamapper/datasets/WEO. Population data, which are continually changing, are 2023 IMF estimates for the regions and countries concerned.
*Numbers in parentheses are the number of countries in each region/analytical category. For country data in each category, see reference, accessed May 28, 2023, https://www.imf.org/external/datamapper/region.htm and https://www.imf.org/en/Publications/WEO/weo-database/2023/April/select-aggr-data. Countries are excluded if not IMF members and not monitored by the IMF, or if their databases are not fully developed, or if the IMF does not receive data from them.
**GDP estimates for Central and South America averages those in each region. Brazil's dominance means weighted averages would yield higher estimates.
***Data in parentheses in each region's nominal GDP as a percentage of World nominal GDP.
****"Gini Index coefficient—distribution of family income," *The World Factbook*, accessed February 28, 2023, https://www.cia.gov/the-world-factbook/field/gini-index-coefficient-distribution-of-family-income/country-comparison. According to this data, South Africa is the world's most unequal society with a Gini of 63, though two islands have lower Gini's according to CIA (Faroe Islands and Jersey); Slovakia is the lowest country at #176 with a Gini of 23.2.

Most concerning in Table 14 is Africa's average US$6,363 GDP per capita, about one-third of Central and South America and Developing Asia. Average Africans survive on less than US$20 a day. Finally, 6.746 billion of the world's 7.36 billion people have on average US$15,183 in annual purchasing power but command only 58.89 percent of world

GDP on a PPP basis. The nominal GDP gap is even wider: the 6.746 billion people in the emerging/developing world command only 42.7 percent of nominal global GDP. Nominal measures indicate the advanced G7 economies produce more than 155 developing economies do.

Income disparities within nations are also often substantial and must be accounted for. Table 14 reports the Gini coefficients of the eight countries and shows the more unequal income distributions often seen in developing countries. South Africa (#1 of 178 countries) and Brazil (#15) display high Gini coefficients compared with the more equal European nations. Notably, behind South Africa, 8 of the 10 most unequal nations are African.[445] Small groups of elites control most of the income and wealth in developing countries, meaning the material quality of life for the majority in these societies is even lower than average GDPs reflect.

A rank of #46 with a 41.5 Gini confirms (as already noted) that inequality is part of the American story too. European nations (e.g., Germany 31.7, #137) and Japan (32.9, #126) are far more equal. Even fellow Anglo-Saxon economy Britain is #99 at 35.1, while neighbor Canada is #121 at 33.3, close to the Europeans. Southern neighbor Mexico, like other developing nations, is #25 at 45.4.

Table 14's diversity indicates that the world is not as flat as some think. This notion of a flat world was popularized by *New York Times* columnist Thomas L. Friedman after he observed how developments in India and China were threatening American commerce and employment. Friedman noted:

> The flattening forces are empowering more and more individuals today to reach farther, faster, deeper, and cheaper than ever before, and that is equalizing power—and equalizing opportunity, by giving so many more people the tools and ability to connect, compete, and collaborate. In my view, this flattening of the playing field is the most important thing happening in the world today.[446]

---

445 *The World Factbook*, "Gini Index Coefficient—Distribution of Family Income."
446 Thomas L. Friedman, *The World Is Flat: A Brief History of the Twenty-First Century* (New York: Farrar, Straus and Giroux, 2005), x.

Friedman is reflecting on how emerging Followers were affecting Leaders and writes mostly from a Leader's perspective. From this viewpoint, concluding that the "flattening of the playing field is the most important thing happening in the world today" is understandable. Contending the world is flat is not. In addition, whether the world will indeed be flat by the end of the twenty-first century is also debatable. Only one of the three scenarios concluding this chapter, balanced global growth, predicts a flat world by 2125. Unbalanced global growth and global meltdown will not result in the flat world that Friedman may be worrying about.

Twenty-First-Century Global Diversity: BOP to MOP to TOP, or Competing in Low-End, Good-Enough, and Premium Markets

That income levels still vary widely both within and between nations means consumption patterns differ within and between them too. Low-income consumers often lack the means to afford the basic needs of food, shelter, and clothing. In contrast, developing economy elites and the middle and upper classes of developed societies have the purchasing power to afford the amenities of comfortable post-industrial lifestyles. These include spacious, well-built houses; abundant food to eat at home or in restaurants; fashionable clothes to wear; safe, reliable cars to drive; the most recent "cool" consumer electronic devices to remain connected; education when and where required; and healthcare when and where needed.

The diversity in incomes gave rise to Prahalad and Hart categorizing worldwide income across three levels: Bottom of the Pyramid (BOP), Middle of the Pyramid (MOP), and Top of the Pyramid (TOP).[447] In the early 2000s, 4 billion humans were thought to populate the BOP, all living off less than US$1,500 annually, while 1.5 to 1.75 billion people were placed in the MOP, earning between US$1,500 and US$20,000 per annum. Only 75 to 100 million were allocated to the TOP, earning more

447 C. K. Prahalad and Stuart L. Hart, "The Fortune at the Bottom of the Pyramid," *Strategy + Business*, January 10, 2002, 2–4.

than US$20,000 annually. Accepting 4 billion, 1.75 billion, and 100 million as estimates of population dispersion at the twentieth century's end, 2 percent would be in the TOP, 30 percent in the MOP, and 68 percent in the BOP.

Chapter 1 reveals that around half the world's population is yet to start the struggle for productivity, so placing just under 70 percent of the world's population in the BOP a generation ago is unsurprising. Updating Prahalad and Hart's estimates means around 50 percent now survive in pre-industrial rural and urban subsistence at the BOP, around 40 percent live in industrial conditions in the MOP, and 10 percent enjoy TOP post-industrial levels of consumption.

Prahalad and Hart also divided the MOP 1.75 billion into two tiers—the relatively poor in developed nations and the rising middle classes in developing countries—and argued the rising middle classes in developing countries were primary targets for Leader MNCs emerging market strategies. They also stressed fortunes awaited those selling to BOP consumers. Though living rurally or in urban slums, owning few if any assets, with little or no formal education, and being harder to reach using conventional distribution, credit, and communications methods, these poorest of the poor allegedly represented a large, untapped market MNCs had ignored, hence their phrase: "The fortune at the Bottom of the Pyramid."

Prahalad and Hart's 2002 article prompted substantial literature on how to serve BOP consumers,[448] though there were dissenters. One labeled Prahalad and Hart's BOP thesis "logically flawed and inconsistent with the evidence" and asserted misfortune, not fortune, awaited

448 See for example: C. K. Prahalad, *The Fortune at the Bottom of the Pyramid: Eradicating Poverty through Profits* (Upper Saddle River, NJ: Wharton School Publishing, 2004); Stuart L. Hart, *Capitalism at the Crossroads: The Unlimited Business Opportunities in Solving the World's Most Difficult Problems* (Upper Saddle River, NJ: Prentice Hall, 2005); Ted London and Stuart L. Hart, *Next Generation Business Strategies for the Base of the Pyramid: New Approaches for Building Mutual Value* (Upper Saddle River, NJ: FT Press, 2010); and Eric Kacou, *Entrepreneurial Solutions for Prosperity in BoP Markets: Strategies for Business and Economic Transformation* (Upper Saddle River, NJ: Wharton School Publishing, 2011).

MNCs at the BOP.[449] The dissenter also noted small- to medium-sized local companies, not Leader MNCs, were best suited to exploiting these BOP opportunities.

Figure 15 contains the familiar curve showing the Pre-Industrial, Industrial, and Post-Industrial Eras in Figures 1 and 3 with the BOP, MOP, and TOP included as well as markets depicted in low-end, good-enough, and premium segments.[450] These three segments are similar to dividing purchasing power into BOP, MOP, and TOP and also list the products that the income levels permit. Low-end products are of low quality and meet basic needs of consumers with low incomes; good-enough products are of good quality for value-seeking consumers with midlevel incomes; and premium products are high-end products purchased by discerning customers with considerable purchasing power.

In Figure 15, the BOP/low-end segment is placed in early industrialization as the process starts, and the MOP/good-enough segment develops and matures as industrialization is accomplished. Finally, the highest level of consumption is attained by those at the TOP/premium segment, placed in the Post-Industrial Era. In the early twenty-first century, TOP/premium consumers are post-industrial consumers in the developed world and developing-nation upper classes who enjoy industrialization's early gains. Those living in urban and rural subsistence with purchasing power demand low-end products, while lower and middle classes of industrializing societies consume mostly good-enough products.

---

449 Aneel Karnani, "The Mirage of Marketing to the Bottom of the Pyramid: How the Private Sector Can Help Alleviate Poverty," *California Management Review* 49, no. 4 (August 2007): 91.
450 Orit Gadiesh, Philip Leung, and Till Vestring, "The Battle for China's Good-Enough Market," *Harvard Business Review*, September 2007, 81–9.

Figure 15: The Human Struggle for Productivity: From BOP to MOP to TOP

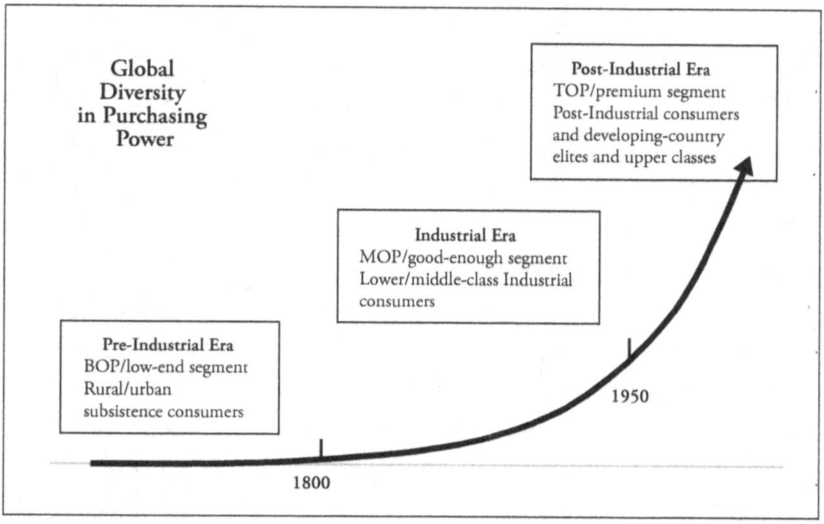

Global Diversity in Purchasing Power

Post-Industrial Era
TOP/premium segment
Post-Industrial consumers and developing-country elites and upper classes

Industrial Era
MOP/good-enough segment
Lower/middle-class Industrial consumers

Pre-Industrial Era
BOP/low-end segment
Rural/urban subsistence consumers

1950

1800

Applying low-end, good-enough, and premium segments to the Chinese consumer market in the 2000s revealed local Chinese enterprise was more suited to exploit the two lower segments, while Leader MNC brands served premium markets.[451] Neither China's poor nor its rising middle class were Leader MNC target markets. The Chinese elite at the TOP with purchasing power to enjoy the premium products Leader MNCs offered were.

SABMiller, the world's second-largest beer brewer at the time, encountered these tiers entering China in the late 1990s.[452] Supporting the idea that MNCs did not compete in low-end/BOP or good-enough/MOP markets, the premium segment, which accounted for 5 percent of beer volume in China, was dominated by Leader MNCs. Upscale urban

451 Gadiesh, Leung, and Vestring, "The Battle for China."
452 Information on SABMiller's entry into China is from Donna Everatt and Niraj Dewar, *South African Breweries International: Devising a China Market Strategy*, Ivey Case 9B00A024 (London, ON: Ivey Publishing, Richard Ivey School of Business, The University of Western Ontario, 2000).

consumers quaffed global brands of their choice, though only paying an average 64 US cents per 640-mL bottle.[453]

The good-enough and low-end segments, which accounted for 55 and 40 percent of beer volume, respectively, sold for an average of RMB2.50 (30 US cents) and RMB1.50 (18 US cents) per 640-mL bottle. Low-end and good-enough Chinese beer consumers paid far less than American consumers at the time. Local producers also served the good-enough and low-end segments, and with prices among the lowest in the world, they found making money difficult too.

The Chinese TV market of the mid-2000s was similar. Leading vendors in the premium segment—which like the beer premium market only constituted a small segment, at 13 percent of the overall Chinese TV market—included Panasonic, Philips, and Sony, all offering state-of-the art, feature-rich LCD and plasma screen TVs at premium prices.[454]

Local producers such as Hisense, Skyworth, and TCL in the good-enough niches and Konka in the low-end niches dominated the lower segments, selling LCD, plasma, and large cathode ray tube screens with limited features to good-enough consumers and cathode ray tube screens with basic, standard features and low-cost components to low-end consumers.[455] Good-enough TV prices undercut foreign brands; low-end TVs were priced even lower.

The Tata Nano is an example of a good-enough Indian automobile. Developed by Tata Motors using local "frugal engineering," the Nano was launched in 2009, and by 2012 the base BS III at a list price of Rs.141,898 (US$2,798) and the upscale metallic LX BS IV for Rs.200,360 (US$3,950) were offered.[456] A term coined by Renault CEO

---

453. . . The Chinese renminbi (RMB)/US$ exchange rate in 2000 was around RMB8.27 to US$1.

454 Gadiesh, Leung, and Vestring, "The Battle for China," 83.

455 Gadiesh, Leung, and Vestring, "The Battle for China," 83.

456 Tata Motors, "Price List," April 3, 2012, but no longer accessible. http://tatanano.inservices.tatamotors.com/tatamotors/price_list.php. Rupees were converted to US$ at the prevailing rate on April 3, 2012, (US$1/Rs50.6400).

Carlos Ghosn in 2006 to describe how Indian engineers developed the Nano, "frugal engineering" was defined as:

> . . . an overarching philosophy that enables a true "clean sheet" approach to product development. . . . It recognizes that merely removing features from existing products to sell them cheaper in emerging markets is a losing game. That's because emerging-market customers have unique needs that usually aren't addressed by mature-market products, and because the cost base of developed world products, even when stripped down, remains too high to allow competitive prices and reasonable profits in the developing world.[457]

Seating four and intended as a family vehicle for urban Indians in crowded cities, providing an alternative to motorbikes, the Nano boasted a 623-cc two-cylinder gas engine offering 67 mpg, had a manual transmission, could reach a top speed of 65 mph (but took more than 35 seconds to get there—three times longer than the average family sedan), and lacked modern safety features such as airbags. Underscoring Nano's good-enough status, the four-door Nissan Versa 1.6 S at US$11,750 was the cheapest American automobile at the time, offered with air conditioning and CD stereo. Three Nanos could be purchased for the price of one Versa.[458]

Placing consumers in the BOP, MOP, and TOP while dividing markets into low-end, good-enough, and premium segments, combined with data from the Chinese beer or TV market or the Indian automobile market, captures the diversity as struggles for productivity begin and proceed to higher levels of productivity. A similar transition from low-end to good-enough to premium markets occurred in America.

---

457 Vikas Sehgal, Kevin Dehoff, and Ganesh Panneer, "The Importance of Frugal Engineering," *Strategy + Business*, May 25, 2001, 1.

458 After a decade of production, the Tata Nano was judged no longer good enough for urban Indian consumers. Made from 2008 to 2018, the Nano was discontinued in 2019, though Tata Motors expects to offer a low-priced Nano EV in 2023 or 2024; see "Tata Nano Ends 2019 with Zero Production," *Economic Times*, last updated January 7, 2020, accessed May 30, 2023, https://economictimes.indiatimes.com//industry/auto/auto-news/tata-nano-ends-2019-with-zero-production/articleshow/73131247.cms.

Though beginning to industrialize in the nineteenth century, only after the economically devasting 1930s and World War II did middle-class Americans join the MOP across suburban America by consuming what now would be denoted good-enough products.

When moving to the suburbs in the 1950s in search of the American dream, middle-class houses were between 1,200 to 1,500 square feet in size, with one and a half bathrooms shared by a family of four. The two or three bedrooms in the single-story ranch house were small, and the kitchen and dining room were insufficiently comfortable to accommodate a small TV watched by all at night. The TV was in the formal living room of the five-room dwelling.

Being closer to 1950s America than to middle-class Americans now, middle-class Chinese or Indian consumers today purchase good-enough products. This means that the average middle-class consumer in the United States differs on a purchasing power basis from the average middle-class consumer in each country too. With global diversity more completely described, how Leading MNCs might compete globally can now be considered, starting in premium and followed by good-enough and low-end markets.

Premium-Market MNCs: World-Class Products and Supply Chains with Global, Regional, National, and Local Operations

Leaders Apple and Nike, among the best-performing MNCs over the past 25 years, remained in premium markets and did not offer low-end or good-enough products to developing-world consumers. Nike shoes and apparel and Apple iPads, iPhones, and Macs are sought by TOP consumers worldwide. Both have significantly outperformed the S&P 500 and the Nasdaq index and serve premium markets with world-class products that rich consumers value and competitors struggle to match.

Moreover, as competitiveness means relying on the best from everywhere, few premium-market products originate from single organizations in single geographies. Consistent with the dispersed, interconnected networks that characterize post-industrial commerce, design may occur in America, manufacturing may take place in China, software may originate from India, and global logistics may be coordinated from Hong Kong.

To determine the optimal Leader MNC organizational structure, the activities required to produce products must be specified and the best location for each activity found. Four locations capture this activity-based structuring: global, regional, national, and local. Global activities are done in one or few locations. Regional activities are performed at locations best for a region. National activities are common to a country and done in the best location in that country, while local activities are executed locally to fit unique local conditions.

Table 15 reports Nike activities (in italics) and where they are performed geographically. At Nike, product creation and development and manufacturing are global; European, Middle East, and Africa (EMEA) logistics are regional; environmental health and safety is national; and in-store retail sales may be local to permit in-store purchasing or adjustment for local conditions.

That Nike product creation and development and manufacturing are global means they are located in specific locations that excel at that activity. Nike describes product creation and development as follows:

> The first spark of a product idea sets the NIKE, Inc. Product team into motion. The team of developers, testers, engineers, designers and managers obsess over Nike's iconic silhouettes and create groundbreaking new styles. They collaborate, ideate and refine products' construction, fit and materials. They maintain a keen understanding of consumer and market trends. They skillfully operate at the intersection of buyer needs, technical feasibility and business objectives.[459]

459 "Become a Part of the NIKE, Inc. Team," accessed May 30, 2023, https://jobs.nike.com/job/00634579. The job link is removed once the job is filled.

Table 15: Categorization of Nike Activities: Global, Regional, National, and Local

Nike Activity (shown *in italics*) and Location	
Global	*Product Creation and Development*: Done in Beaverton, Oregon *Manufacturing*: Factories in China, Vietnam, Indonesia, and other locations globally
Regional	*EMEA Logistics:* Nike European Logistics Campus, Laakdal, Belgium, supplying Nike sports clothing, shoes, and accessories to over 50 countries in the region*
National	*Environmental Health and Safety Specialist—Korea:* Nike Facilities, Seoul, South Korea, requires knowledge of occupational health and safety regulations and relevant environmental regulations in Korea and demonstrated experience managing relationships and issues with local regulatory authorities**
Local	*Offline Retail Sales:* In the United States, done in Nike stores, Foot Locker, and DICK'S Sporting Goods, among others***

* Flanders Investment and Trade, "How Nike Made Flanders Its Logistics Gateway to Europe," November 27, 2020, accessed May 30, 2023, https://invest.flandersinvestmentandtrade.com/en/news/how-nike-made-flanders-its-logistics-gateway-europe. EMEA stands for Europe, the Middle East, and Africa.
** "Search Jobs," Nike, accessed May 30, 2023, https://jobs.nike.com/job/32091. The specific job link is removed once the job is filled.
*** Nike US-owned stores operate under formats including Nike Factory and Nike Clearance stores, https://www.nike.com/retail, accessed May 30, 2023; Foot Locker has stores in over 25 countries, including the United States, https://stores.footlocker.com/, accessed May 30, 2023; and DICK'S Sporting Goods has over 800 stores, https://www.dickssportinggoods.com/s/stores, accessed May 30, 2023.

Most product creation and development jobs are at Nike's world HQ and are held by Nike employees. These workers join teams that are part of Nike's creative core and do the post-industrial creative work that keeps Nike ahead of competitors. On May 30, 2023, three jobs in this activity were advertised, all based in Beaverton, Oregon.

Manufacturing's global categorization also provides clues into the company's business model. Nike started as an American distributor of running shoes made in Japan; from its founding its business model excluded manufacturing. This activity was outsourced to offshore manufacturers, first in Japan and then moving to South Korea and Taiwan. In the early 1980s, Nike entered into supply contracts with Chinese state-owned factories.[460] As of May 31, 2022, Nike sourced footwear from 120 contract finished goods footwear factories in 11 countries, with 94 percent made in Vietnam, Indonesia, and China; 279 contract finished goods apparel factories located in 33 countries made Nike apparel.[461]

Had Nike located its manufacturing operations in the United States, its running shoes would have cost more, consumers would have purchased fewer, and shareholders would have enjoyed poorer returns. More importantly, Nike may have been driven out of the market by lower-cost suppliers sourcing from other countries. But its focus on product design and development and brand management—two intangible, hard-to-copy, high-value activities—permitted Nike to build its core competence and global competitive advantage while partnering with external suppliers focused on theirs. This explains Nike's high market value per person of US$2.32 million (page 310), equivalent to Cisco's, who like Nike outsourced manufacturing from its founding. Nike's MVP was also far higher than Amazon's US$765,737, and almost ten times General Motors's or Ford's.

Nike built a business perfectly positioned and structured for post-industrial commerce. Labor-intensive manufacturing was outsourced to the cheapest hands globally while employees focused on product development and maintaining and extending the value of the Nike brand. Decades ahead of its time, Nike focused its human capital on high-value, knowledge-intensive, creative activities. The company was post-industrial before the phrase was even coined.

That Nike logistics in EMEA function out of Laakdal, Belgium, indicates a regional activity. More than likely the location was chosen because of its geographic centrality and because connections to the Middle East and Africa were easy from there. To qualify as regional, an

---

460 James E. Austin and Francis Aguilar, *NIKE in China*, Harvard Business School Case 9-386-065 (Boston: Harvard Business School Publishing, September 1985, revised October 1988), 2.
461 Nike, Inc., *Nike Annual Form 10-K* (May 31, 2022), accessed May 30, 2023, https://d18rn0p25nwr6d.cloudfront.net/CIK-0000320187/de1a2596-13c0-452e-9122-fee481da40ad.pdf.

activity should be common to a region and extend beyond the boundaries of a single nation.

Environmental health and safety are denoted national as this activity complies with local regulations and practices, which differ across nations. Finally, store retail activities in the United States are designated local as these occur where the rubber hits the road, executed by associates familiar with local language, consumers, cultural practices, and demand conditions. The ways in which local weather, sports icons and teams, and leisure preferences impact demand is part of the knowledge required in the execution of Nike retail activities. Further, for doing business across the United States, some retail activities may be national, some regional, and some local—Nike online sales are not local. Classifying retail as local does not account for the retail function's diversity. Correct activity classification requires paying attention to the details of each.

All MNCs serving consumers globally face the questions Nike did as it built one of the most successful post-industrial enterprises in business history. Primary among these is what product to offer (premium, good enough, low end); how, where, and by whom will these products be produced, delivered, and serviced; and which activities will the enterprise focus on and which will be outsourced?

In addition, the global organizations relied upon to serve customers should be controlled by digital networks like those seen at Cisco, and forming these structures requires analysis to determine the activities that make up the extended supply chain and where each activity falls along the global, regional, national, or local spectrum, concluding with whether it should be outsourced or done internally. Leading MNCs serving premium markets require this activity-based structuring to stay in business and thrive. Leaders operating advanced networked enterprises means Followers must connect to these digital networks, and underscores that Followers must possess the post-industrial infrastructure to participate in global commerce.

Determining whether an activity is global, regional, national, or local and whether it should be done within or outside a firm's boundary is not only important for organizations. Individuals must also ask if their jobs are global, regional, national, or local. As a global activity has the potential to be scaled everywhere, the value added—and remuneration—is higher than those scaled regionally, just as local roles are typically of a lower value than roles serving a national customer base. Readers aspiring to lead in global, competitive post-industrial organizations should focus on mastering global activities.

Lastly, also key to note is that activity location is not static. At Nike, manufacturing jobs were routinely relocated to where cheaper labor was available. Just as Nike does for shoe production, individuals must watch job trends to maintain their competitiveness. To stay ahead in an increasingly competitive post-industrial world, Americans must not only do what machines cannot do; what Indians, Chinese, or others across the world cannot do is also where they should focus. As they have done since the mid-twentieth century, others across the world will continue to seek high-paying Americans jobs, doing them for less than Americans ask. If high salaries are the goal, Americans should focus on global activities others cannot do.

MNCs Competing in Low-End or Good-Enough Markets: Avoiding Square Pegs in Round Holes

Whether Leader MNCs are able to compete in low-end and good-enough markets is controversial. Some allege fortunes await in these markets; others conclude local firms possess advantages difficult to dislodge. Clear is that Leader MNCs are not naturally equipped for these markets and that to compete requires at the very least alteration of practices followed in premium markets. For them, competing in the lower segments means avoiding being square pegs in round holes.

Though praised for competing in premium markets, being a square peg in a round hole did occur to Nike. It offered a "World Shoe" to low-income Chinese consumers for US$10–15 a pair in the late 1990s, but the venture failed, and Nike exited the market in 2002. Many reasons explained this failure, including Chinese suppliers selling identical products in Beijing and Shanghai,[462] Nike not adapting margins to suit the low-margin business typical of these markets, and executives being uncomfortable with a low-priced product that conflicted with Nike's brand.[463] Using Nike's legacy suppliers, business model, and famed swoosh was also incorrect, and the World Shoe ended up a square peg in a round hole. Even with the right product, a different brand that offered lower returns was needed.

SABMiller's entry into China's low-end and good-enough beer markets in the 1990s shows an MNC effectively competing in these segments. Being from South Africa and having operated breweries in sub-Saharan Africa and Eastern Europe, more than anything, might explain the success. While Nike legacies placed it at a disadvantage, SABMiller's decades-long developing economy experience prepared it for China.

The company entered via a joint venture with a local partner well versed in the market—appropriate, as beer relies on local taste and distribution. Armed with the ability to operate breweries anywhere at world-class levels while knowing how to partner with insiders in developing markets meant SABMiller was a round peg in a round hole, well prepared for China's low-end and good-enough beer markets. It had capabilities the local partner needed, and the local partner had some that SABMiller relied on.

Conditions beyond its Chinese operations, however, eventually hampered SABMiller in China. Anheuser-Busch InBev's acquisition of London-listed SABMiller in 2016 forced SABMiller—then the world's second-largest brewer—to sell its 49 percent stake in China Resources

---

462 Stuart L. Hart and Sanjay Sharma, "Engaging Fringe Stakeholders for Competitive Imagination," *The Academy of Management Executive* 18, no. 1 (February 2004): 14.
463 Adam Morgan, *The Pirate Inside: Building a Challenger Brand Culture Within Yourself and Your Organization* (West Sussex, England: John Wiley & Sons, 2004).

Snow Breweries, and the company received far below analysts' expectations for its holding in the brewer of the world's top-selling beer. Further, the 22-year-old joint venture produced "voluminous vats but punier profits,"[464] consistent with conditions in hypercompetitive low-end and good-enough markets. General Electric also followed a strategy closer to SABMiller and engaged scientists and engineers in India and China to develop good-enough products later modified and distributed globally.[465] Here, as GE's internal "frugal engineering" developed the innovation, the company was not threatened by a launch at home.

Leader MNCs, as they enter developing-country markets, can remain in premium markets as Apple and Nike did and bet they can extend their hold as consumers move to the MOP and TOP in these nations. Or like SABMiller or GE, they can enter a lower market segment and hope to build market share and trade up as local conditions evolve. Moreover, for developed country MNCs and as was seen with Nike's World Shoe, legacies often get in the way. Products that meet the needs of low-end or good-enough consumers require production at a cost meeting the limited purchasing power of the consumers and marketing and distribution to reach the consumers where they live. Such design, production, and marketing methods do not easily match the costs and capabilities of Leading MNCs.

But staying out of low-end and good-enough markets leaves the arena open for good-enough and low-end producers to build share domestically and later move up the value chain as purchasing power increases, eventually competing with MNCs in premium markets internationally. US tractor manufacturers may face this scenario at the hands of Mahindra & Mahindra. Based on sales of tractors manufactured by Mahindra in India and China, by 2005 Mahindra had claimed 6 percent

464 James Fontanella-Khan and Patti Waldmeir, "China Brewer Sale Clears Path to AB InBev's £71 Billion SABMiller Deal," CNBC, March 2, 2016, accessed May 31, 2023, https://www.cnbc.com/2016/03/02/china-brewer-sale-clears-path-to-ab-inbevs-71-billion-sabmiller-deal.html.

465 Jeffrey R. Immelt, Vijay Govindarajan, and Chris Trimble, "How GE is Disrupting Itself," *Harvard Business Review*, October 2009, 56–65.

of the under-70-hp tractor market in the United States.[466] Mahindra used its Indian and Chinese good-enough market experience to enter the American market; it sells more units by volume than any other tractor manufacturer worldwide and now has five US-based assembly plants. This outcome may form part of the unbalanced global growth scenario considered later in this chapter and underscores the first major imbalance that may eventually characterize twenty-first-century global commerce, this being that while Followers progress, Leaders stumble.

The competition between local incumbents and MNCs in China's good-enough markets is testimony to the battle between internal and external competitors in the world's biggest developing market and underscores that Mahindra & Mahindra is not the only aspiring global competitor Leading European and American MNCs may face from the developing world. For Leader MNCs, competing in China or India is beyond making fortunes serving the poorest at the BOP. Defending premium-market positions while attacking incumbents dominating good-enough markets is the more immediate challenge.

MNCs entering the low-end or good-enough markets in countries like India and China while possibly gaining access to growth in these contexts still face risks. They may fail because they offer the wrong product, use the wrong business model, or have too high return expectations. Or they may enter and gain traction but find the victory pyrrhic: economic returns may be low or the country concerned does not negotiate the transition from Failure to Follower to Leader smoothly, and instead of getting more productive and richer, average consumers only get older. This outcome is also part of the unbalanced global growth scenario considered later, under the second major imbalance that may characterize events until 2125: while Leaders rebalance and retain economic footing, Followers stumble.

Armed with an understanding of global diversity and what it will take to remain competitive in the emerging twenty-first-century post-in-

466 Tarun Khanna, "China + India: The Power of Two," in *Harvard Business Review on Thriving in Emerging Markets* (Boston: Harvard Business School Publishing, 2011), 113–4.

dustrial global economy, we turn to human-induced imbalances that may threaten progress. These include imbalances resulting from the largest market failure in history—this being our use of fossil fuels as industrialization's primary energy source—and imbalances that have resulted from some Leaders living beyond their means. We turn first to global warming/climate change and how it threatens our collective progress. The threat is better framed as an energy rather than a climate crisis. New forms of clean energy (e.g., wind, solar, hydrogen, and hydroelectric) are needed to power the world we all live in. The energy status quo must change for all, and quickly!

Global Warming/Climate Change: A Massive Disruptor to Mitigate at All Costs

Industrialization has had an unintended, unwelcome effect: atmospheric carbon dioxide (CO^2), a greenhouse gas that traps heat and causes planetary warming, has increased 150 percent from 1750 to 2023,[467] mostly from our past century's burning of fossil fuels (oil, coal, and natural gas). If CO^2 continues growing atmospherically at current rates, global average temperatures will increase by over 2° above pre-industrial levels by 2100, with calamitous effects on all inhabitants of our world.

Though a 2022 study found increases could be contained to 2° if nations acted as they had promised, even with this goal met, conditions will still be challenging.[468] This two-degree-warmer world represents what scientists characterize as a profoundly disrupted climate with fiercer storms, higher seas, animal and plant extinctions, disappearing coral, melting ice, and people dying from heat, smog, and infectious diseases.

The Intergovernmental Panel on Climate Change (IPCC), established in 1988 to assess the science relating to climate change, provides

467 "Global Climate Change Vital Signs," NASA's Jet Propulsion Laboratory Earth Science Communications Team, California Institute of Technology, updated May 25, 2023, accessed June 4, 2023, https://climate.nasa.gov/vital-signs/carbon-dioxide/.

468 Seth Borenstein, "Study Finds Nations Can Keep Global Warming to 2 Degrees If Pledges Are Met," PBS Newshour, April 13, 2022, accessed June 12, 2023, https://www.pbs.org/newshour/world/study-finds-nations-can-keep-global-warming-to-2-degrees-if-pledges-are-met

periodic assessments of global warming/climate change's scientific basis and advises on its risks and impact. Representing 195 nations and mobilizing the world's leading climate scientists, the IPCC noted the following in its 2023 Sixth Assessment Report:

> Widespread and rapid changes in the atmosphere, ocean, cryosphere and biosphere have occurred. Human-caused climate change is already affecting many weather and climate extremes in every region across the globe. This has led to widespread adverse impacts and related losses and damages to nature and people (high confidence). Vulnerable communities who have historically contributed the least to current climate change are disproportionately affected (high confidence).[469]

Markets fail when a product's full price is not covered by those consuming it, and negative externalities are incurred when products place costs on third parties unrelated to their production or consumption. On this basis, global warming/climate change is the most widespread market failure ever and is imposing externalities on poor developing countries for industrialization enjoyed by developed countries over the past two centuries.

But externalities are not only being levied on the most vulnerable and least responsible for them. Mitigating the effects of rising sea levels and dealing with the destructive effects of extreme weather events are externalities our fossil fuel use is imposing on people everywhere. The children and grandchildren of the industrialized world will face these over the rest of this century, the magnitude depending on how quickly clean energy emerges and carbon neutrality is reached.

The key questions are how quickly will we act as scientists advise, and as a result, how much of our reaction will be mitigation versus adaptation? Timely action means more mitigation will occur. Tardiness means more adaptation than mitigation, and given how slowly mitigation is

---

469 Hoesung Lee et al., "Summary for Policymakers," A.2 in *Climate Change 2023: Synthesis Report*, Intergovernmental Panel on Climate Change, Geneva, Switzerland, accessed June 6, 2023, https://www.ipcc.ch/report/ar6/syr/downloads/report/IPCC_AR6_SYR_SPM.pdf.

occurring, significant adaptation costs are already being encountered around the world. Moreover, as global warming/climate change affects all across our planet, a global solution is also needed. If the industrialized world moves to clean energy, but the developing world does not, the problem will persist, and with national self-interest always stronger than global interests, achieving cooperation on this scale is difficult.

Also frustrating the emergence of a global solution was a delayed and poor response from the world's most influential nation and then biggest polluter. Though apparent by the mid-1990s that fossil fuel use was an existential threat requiring urgent action, US-based global warming/climate change deniers held any serious response at bay. Exceptional America to learn from or follow does not apply here.

By 2023, China emitted the most CO^2; America was second, ahead of the European Union and other developed countries, which collectively emitted a little more CO^2 than America. Where the European Union differs is it accorded global warming/climate change the prominence it deserved decades ago and has taken far more steps to find solutions. Hopefully, with extreme weather events on the rise and with temperatures across the country now consistently at new record levels, Americans are finally recognizing global warming/climate change is indeed human induced and requires urgent action from all to resolve.

The intent here is neither to explain the science behind global warming/climate change nor cover the mitigation or adaptation needed. Climate scientists and other experts must provide these. Required here is to place on record the situation's urgency and to leave readers with no doubt about its seriousness. In a review of the economics of climate change commissioned by the UK government in 2006, Nicholas Stern, former chief economist of the World Bank, underscored the need for immediate action to avoid the threat from becoming irreversible. Stern noted:

> The investment that takes place in the next 10 to 20 years will have a profound effect on the climate in the second half of this century and in the next. Our actions now and over the coming decades could

> create risks of major disruption to economic and social activity, on a scale similar to those associated with the great wars and the economic depression of the first half of the 20th century. And it will be difficult or impossible to reverse these changes.[470]

With Stern stressing the urgency, American tardiness in the first two decades of the twenty-first century is especially egregious, and it is difficult to estimate where the world might be now had Americans taken the threat as seriously as others did in 2000.

Opportunity abounds, however, as global warming/climate change is mitigated. Estimating that an annual investment of 1 percent of global GDP would mitigate the crisis, Stern continued:

> Action on climate change will also create significant business opportunities, as new markets are created in low-carbon energy technologies and other low-carbon goods and services. These markets could grow to be worth hundreds of billions of dollars each year, and employment in these sectors will expand accordingly.
>
> The world does not need to choose between averting climate change and promoting growth and development. Changes in energy technologies and in the structure of economies have created opportunities to decouple growth from greenhouse gas emissions. Indeed, ignoring climate change will eventually damage economic growth. Tackling climate change is the pro-growth strategy for the longer term, and it can be done in a way that does not cap the aspirations for growth of rich or poor countries.[471]

Confirming the investment needs are higher in lower-income countries that face greater exposure to climate risk (often exceeding 5 percent of GDP), in 2022 the World Bank noted that developing economies annually investing 1.4 percent of their GDPs would cut emissions by 70

---

470 Nicholas Stern, "The Price of Change," in *IAEA Bulletin* 48, no. 2 (March 2007): vi, accessed June 12, 2023, https://www.iaea.org/publications/magazines/bulletin/48-2.
471 Stern, "The Price of Change," viii.

percent by 2050.[472] Accordingly, while all countries must change their behaviors, developed countries, which bear the major responsibility for the crisis, not only must decarbonize their economies but also should assist developing countries as they move to counter the threat.

Given these opportunities, the biggest price America may pay for its climate intransigence is others will lead the way into the clean economy. Then, instead of exporting technology it might have developed, the country will have to import clean technology, deepening its already high dependence on external production.

With progress currently less than is needed, in the short to medium term the status quo will likely worsen as adaption more than mitigation dominates, leaving the least able and most exposed to global warming/climate change's punishing effects. One of the three scenarios presented later in this chapter, global meltdown, presumes the global warming/climate change battle is lost and leaves our children and grandchildren in an apocalyptic world most imagined would only occur in the movies.

We turn now to the second human imbalance that might derail progress over coming decades, this being that while Followers catch up, Leaders fall behind. A United States living beyond its means typifies the challenge here.

Leaders in Retreat: Democracy and Hospital Passes in an Upside-Down World

Nations, like individuals, must live within their means, and imbalances in America since 1981 reveal a nation living beyond its means both publicly and privately. These imbalances went largely unnoticed until 2007, when credit irresponsibly advanced over a housing bubble forced the federal government to take unprecedented steps to prevent the American and global financial systems from failing. The US government spent

472 World Bank, "Countries Could Cut Emissions by 70% by 2050 and Boost Resilience with Annual Investments of 1.4% of GDP," press release no. 2023/028/CCG, November 3, 2022, accessed June 12, 2023, https://www.worldbank.org/en/news/press-release/2022/11/03/countries-could-cut-emissions-by-70-by-2050-and-boost-resilience-with-annual-investments-of-1-4-of-gdp

over US$3.7 trillion in financial bailouts and bond-buying operations, and all steps taken by federal authorities to deal with the crisis exceeded US$14 trillion.[473]

The assistance given by the American government meant public imbalance measured by federal debt reached levels unseen in peacetime. Even more indicative of America living beyond its means long before this time, the federal government had spent more than it raised in most years since 1981, when federal debt as a percentage of US GDP started rising. Before this, there had been a 34-year decline from its 106 percent high in 1946 to a 30.60 percent low in mid-1981.[474] Federal debt as a percentage of US GDP increased in every administration after Carter except for Clinton's second term, and as Figure 18 shows, most significantly after 2008 under Obama, Trump, and Biden. Both Republicans and Democrats are responsible for the fiscal misbehavior.

Figure 16 reports US data on home prices, building costs, interest rates, and population from 1890 until 2014, and this data, viewed with Figure 17's mortgage equity and private consumption data, shows how American private sector imbalances arose from the mid-1990s through the mid-2000s.[475] As Figure 16 shows, after dropping in the first half of the twentieth century and remaining flat over the second half, American home prices suddenly almost doubled in less than a decade, and then quickly declined back to 114 by 2012, with 100 being the index level for house prices in 1891.

473 Claus Vogt and Roland Leuschel, *The Global Debt Trap: How to Escape the Danger and Build a Fortune* (Hoboken, NJ: John Wiley & Sons, 2011), 2.

474 Federal Reserve Economic Data, "Federal Debt: Total Public Debt as Percent of Gross Domestic Product (GFDEGDQ188S)," US Office of Management and Budget and Federal Reserve Bank of St. Louis, accessed June 20, 2023, https://fred.stlouisfed.org/series/GFDEGDQ188S.

475 Figure 16 is from an Excel spreadsheet in Robert J. Shiller, *Irrational Exuberance*, 2nd ed. (Princeton, NJ: Princeton University Press, 2005), accessed June 15, 2023, http://www.irrationalexuberance.com/index.htm.

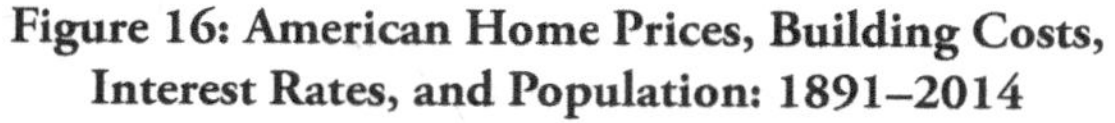

Figure 16: American Home Prices, Building Costs, Interest Rates, and Population: 1891–2014

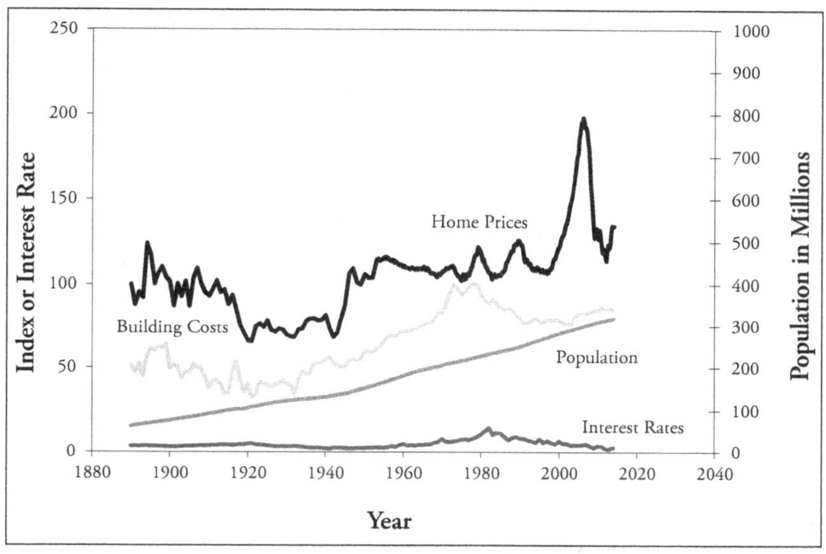

Figure 17 depicts mortgage equity withdrawals (MEWs) and private consumption as a percentage of US GDP from 1953 to 2007 and shows how the housing bubble enabled Americans to live beyond their means. The left-hand scale and lighter line depict MEWs, and the right-hand scale and darker line is private consumption. Compelling is how consumption remained constant at 64 percent or less of GDP for the 40 years from 1953 to 1993 and then from the mid-1990s rose to over 70 percent by 2001, a rapid increase in a very short time. The close correlation between consumption and MEWs shows how the housing bubble supported an increase in private consumption over the first five years of the twenty-first century. Moreover, a return to pre-1993 levels has not transpired.

Figure 17: Private Consumption Spending and Mortgage Equity Withdrawals as US GDP Percentages: 1953–2007[476]

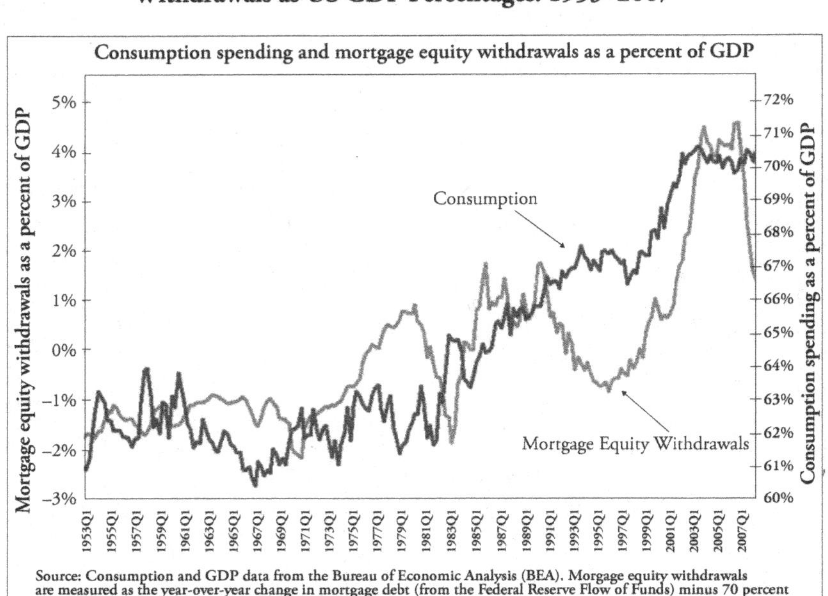

Source: Consumption and GDP data from the Bureau of Economic Analysis (BEA). Morgage equity withdrawals are measured as the year-over-year change in mortgage debt (from the Federal Reserve Flow of Funds) minus 70 percent of residential investment spending (from the BEA).

Unlike the 1990's dot-com investment bubble that caused some economic expansion, a consumption binge with no associated productivity gains followed only five years later. Americans simply borrowed their prosperity. When the bubble burst and home prices plummeted, so did the ability to repay debt, leading to widespread default. To prevent financial collapse, the federal government had to intervene, with this intervention keeping demand stable as overindebted Americans regained financial footing. As consumption from private borrowing fell, consumption sustained by federal borrowing filled the gap. Americans continued borrowing their prosperity, funded instead by public borrowing.

And hopes that the housing bubble would remain the high-water mark of federal intervention were dashed only a few years later. The 2020 COVID-19 pandemic caused an economic crisis of even greater magni-

476 Josh Bivens, "As Consumption Goes, So Goes the American Economy," Economic Policy Institute, March 19, 2008, accessed June 15, 2023, https://www.epi.org/publication/webfeatures_snapshots_20080319/.

tude than the housing bubble, and to sustain an economy literally shut down overnight, intervention was again needed.

This second major intervention in less than a decade lifted federal debt as a percentage of US GDP to levels far beyond the previous 1946 postwar record. Figure 18 reports federal total debt as a percentage of US GDP from 1966 to 2023.

Figure 18: Federal Total Debt (% of US GDP): 1966–2023[477]

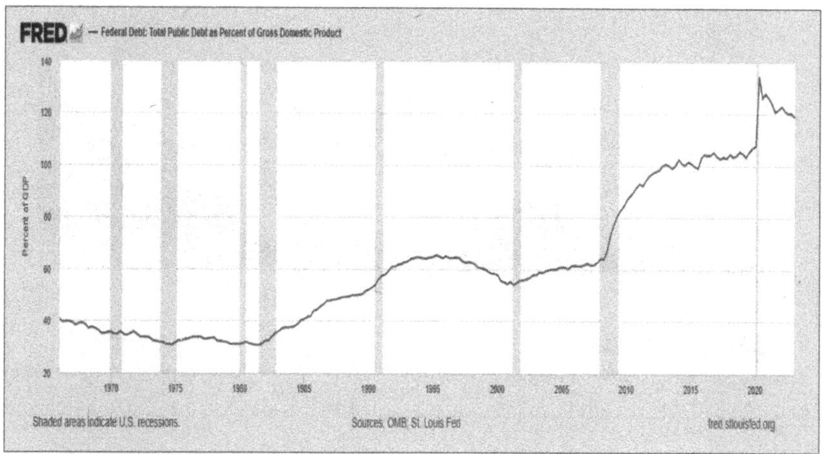

The impact of the 2008 and 2020 interventions on federal debt are easy to see. After hovering around 60 percent of US GDP from the early 1990s until 2008, 100 percent was reached in Q4 2012, and a record 133 percent was recorded in Q2 2020. By Q4 2022, federal total debt had declined to 119 percent of US GDP, still far above the previous record in 1946 of 106 percent.[478]

A graphic from the US Government Accountability Office (GAO)'s sixth annual report on US fiscal health,[479] Figure 19 reports federal public

477 "Federal Debt: Total Public Debt as Percent of Gross Domestic Product." This data differs slightly from similar data provided in Table 16, given it is from a different agency (Federal Reserve Bank of St. Louis vs. the IMF) and likely reports a different date.

478 "Federal Debt: Total Public Debt as Percent of Gross Domestic Product."

479 US Government Accountability Office, "The Nation's Fiscal Health: Federal Action Critical to Pivot toward Fiscal Sustainability," Annual Report to Congress, May 2022, accessed June 20, 2023, https://www.gao.gov/assets/gao-22-105376.pdf,

debt held from 1900 to 2022 and projects this debt will increase alarmingly over the coming decades without revenue and spending changes. In Figure 19, the increases in federal debt from the housing bubble and COVID-19 crisis are easily seen and mimic those in Figure 18.

Figure 19: GAO US Public Debt Projection (% GDP): 2022–2050

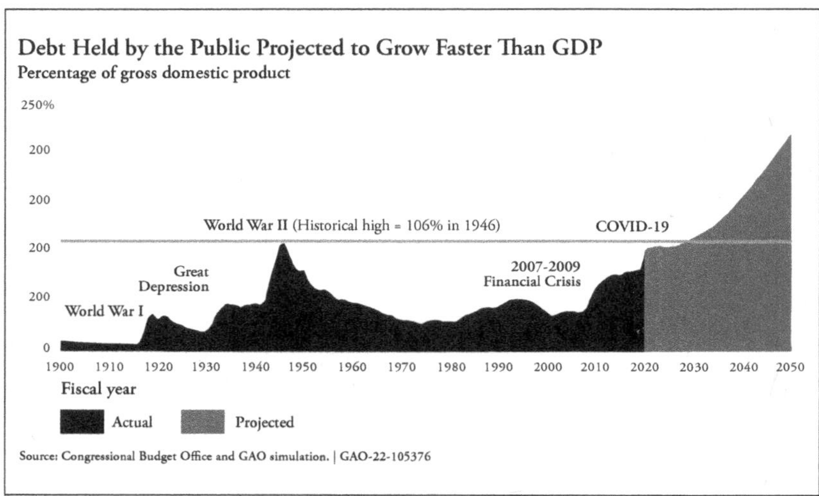

But unlike Figure 18's total federal debt, government debt held by other federal entities is excluded in Figure 19. Social Security, civilian retirement, military retirement, and Medicare trust funds, among others, have for decades invested surplus receipts in federal securities, meaning some US federal debt is intergovernmental (the government effectively owes itself). On June 1, 2023, of the US$31.5 trillion federal total debt (in Figure 18), US$24.7 trillion (78 percent) was held by the public[480]

480 This debt is "all federal debt held by individuals, corporations, state or local governments, Federal Reserve Banks, foreign governments, and other entities outside the United States Government less Federal Financing Bank securities"; see "U.S. Treasury Monthly Statement of the Public Debt (MSPD)," US Department of the Treasury and the Bureau of the Fiscal Service, June 2023, accessed June 18, 2023, https://fiscaldata.treasury.gov/datasets/monthly-statement-public-debt/summary-of-treasury-securities-outstanding.

and US$6.8 trillion (22 percent) by government entities.[481] This explains why Figure 19's federal debt is less than 100 percent of GDP while Figure 18's is just under 120 percent. Figure 19 debt excludes the sum the US federal government owes itself.

Without revenue and/or spending policy changes, the GAO forecasts interest will grow to 14 percent of federal spending by 2035 and 27 percent by 2050, up from 8 percent in 2019. Facing a significant increase in debt carrying costs, total federal spending is expected to reach 34 percent of GDP by 2035 and 46 percent by 2050, which further underscores the unsustainability of current policy. In 2019 it was 21 percent. The federal government mediating almost half of American economic expenditure is unwelcome under any circumstances. Adding intergovernmental debt to the GAO numbers will make a bad forecast even worse.

Regrettably, America is not alone among industrialized nations with excessive government debt. Table 16 shows government public debt, government revenues, government primary balances, and interest paid on public debt as percentages of GDP for 24 nations in two groups: the 20 most indebted and 4 less indebted. Government revenues as a GDP percentage are also reported, as are primary balances, which show the difference between government revenues and expenditures excluding interest costs. The IMF considers the primary balance the best measure of government fiscal policy decisions. Interest payments combine with primary balances in the last column to show overall budget surpluses/deficits.

A generation ago, developing countries dominated the most indebted list. In 1990, of the top 20 most indebted countries, only 4 were developed: Israel at #4 (at 138 percent), Belgium #5 (130 percent), Italy #15 (95 percent), and Ireland #16 (93 percent). In 2023, Japan at #1, Greece

481 This debt is "Government Account Series securities held by Government trust funds, revolving funds, and special funds; and Federal Financing Bank securities. A small amount of marketable securities are held by government accounts"; see "U.S. Treasury Monthly Statement of the Public Debt."

at #3, Italy at #5, the United States at #9, and 6 other developed countries (in bold) in the top 20 reflects our now upside-down economic world.

Developed countries are now 50 percent of the top 20 most indebted nations. Unlike in the twentieth century when developing countries were the main cause of financial instability, the baton may soon pass to developed nations. Rather than being examples to follow, some Leaders may in time find themselves in need of financial assistance.

Table 16 shows how high government indebtedness has become; all top 20 hold debt above 100 percent of GDP, far higher than the 64 percent average of the 149 countries ranked. The top four exceed 150 percent. America's 2022 4 percent budget deficit shows how far government expenditures exceeded taxes with interest included. In 2021, its primary balance was –7.96 percent of GDP, and in 2020, –11.90 percent, with its budget deficit about 3 percent higher. Figure 20 shows government revenues as a percentage of GDP for nine nations, providing one explanation for industrialized nation debt increases.

Table 16: Government Debt, Revenues, Primary Balance, Interest (% GDP): 2022

Top 20 Indebted Countries	Gross Public Debt* (% GDP)	Gross Public Debt Ranking	Govt. Revenues (% GDP)**	Govt. Primary Balance (% GDP)***	Govt. Interest (% GDP)#	Govt. Budget Surplus/ Deficit (–) (% GDP)
Japan	261	1	37	–5	1	–6
Sudan	186	2	15	–2	0	–2
Greece	178	3	50	0	2	–2
Venezuela	158	4	6	–6	0	–6
Italy	144	5	49	–4	4	–8
Cabo Verde	127	6	22	–2	2	–4
Bhutan	125	7	27	–6	1	–7
Barbados	123	8	30	3	5	–8
US	121	9	33	–1	3	–4
Suriname	120	10	28	1	4	–5
Bahrain	118	11	23	–2	4	–6
Sri Lanka	116	12	8	–4	6	–10
Maldives	115	13	30	–8	4	–12
Portugal	114	14	44	2	2	–4
France	112	15	54	–3	2	–5
Spain	112	16	42	–2	2	–4
Canada	107	17	41	2	3	–5
Belgium	105	18	50	–2	2	–4
UK	101	19	39	–2	4	–6
Rep. of Congo	100	20	32	12	3	–15

Select Less Indebted Countries	Gross Public Debt* (% GDP)	Gross Public Debt Ranking	Govt. Revenues (% GDP)**	Govt. Primary Balance (% GDP)***	Govt. Interest (% GDP)#	Govt. Budget Surplus/ Deficit (–) (% GDP)
China	77	41	26	–7	1	–8
Germany	67	58	47	–2	1	–3
South Korea	48	98	27	–1	1	–2
Norway	37	119	64	26	0	10
Sample Average	64	-	**29**	**–1**	**2**	-

All data from Public Finances in Modern History Database, International Monetary Fund, 2022, accessed December 20, 2023. The IMF notes the following regarding the database: "The Public Finances in Modern History Database documents two-hundred years of the history of budget deficits and government debts. The current version covers 151 countries over the period 1800–2022, subject to data availability," https://www.imf.org/external/datamapper/datasets/FPP. Table data is rounded to the nearest whole number.
* *IMF, "Gross Public Debt, Percent of GDP,"* https://www.imf.org/external/datamapper/d@FPP/USA/FRA/JPN/GBR/SWE/ESP/ITA/ZAF/IND?.
** *IMF, "Government Revenues, Percent of GDP,"* https://www.imf.org/external/datamapper/rev@FPP/USA/FRA/JPN/GBR/SWE/ESP/ITA/ZAF/IND?.
*** *IMF, "Government Primary Balance, Percent of GDP,"* https://www.imf.org/external/datamapper/pb@FPP/USA/FRA/JPN/GBR/SWE/ESP/ITA/ZAF/IND?. *The IMF defines the primary balance as* "the difference between a government's revenues and its non-interest expenditures."
# IMF, *"Interest Paid on Public Debt, Percent of GDP,"* https://www.imf.org/external/datamapper/ie@FPP/USA/FRA/JPN/GBR/SWE/ESP/ITA/ZAF/IND?.

Figure 20 reflects the European Exception's twentieth-century triumph and tribulation. After World War II, higher government economic involvement across western Europe delivered more stable and equitable societies over the second half of the twentieth century but at a cost not fully borne by those benefiting. Government debt has, to some extent, funded the increase, meaning the next generation will likely pay for these benefits.

Figure 20 also offers insight into why America is in such jeopardy for its fiscal choices. As a leading LME (page 316) with low government revenues as a percentage of GDP, it has less capacity to deal with crises. With aggressive intervention since 2008, the country's high federal debt is to be expected.

Figure 20: Select Government Revenues: 1950–2021 (% GDP)[482]

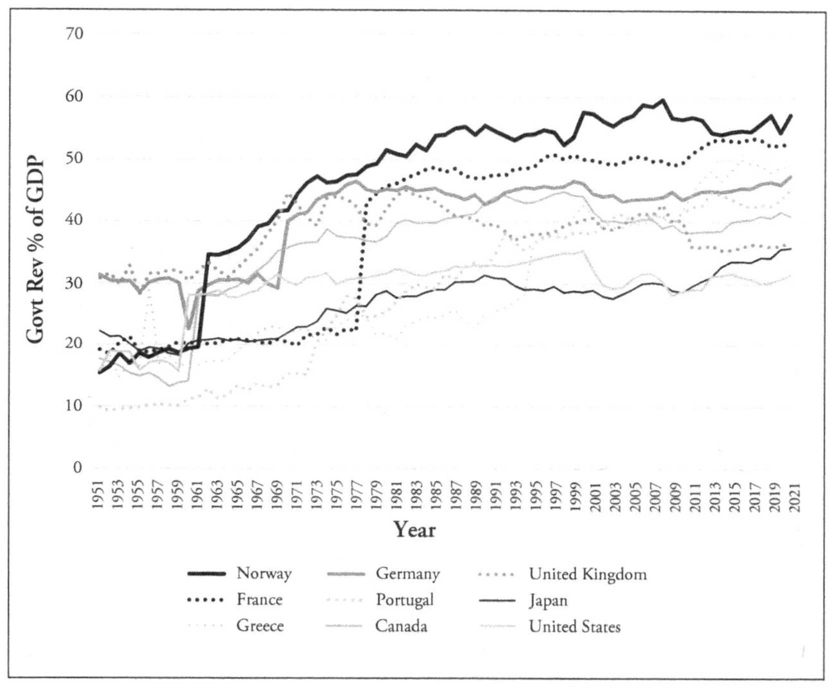

Figure 20 also validates the LME versus CME distinction that separates the European economies from Canada, the United States, and the United Kingdom. All European economies, from Portugal's 45.32 percent to Norway's 57.30 percent, show higher government engagement in economic activity than do the United States (at 31.46 percent), the United Kingdom (at 36.89 percent), or Canada (who falls midway at 40.96 percent). Japan, with government revenues at 35.86 percent of GDP (below the United Kingdom), is not as engaged as other CMEs are. Its fiscal expenditures, like America's, have outrun its fiscal appropriations.

Figure 21 shows four nations' primary balances from 1950 to 2021 as a percentage of GDP, two fiscally responsible (Norway and Germany, in black and gray thick lines) and two irresponsible (the United States

482 IMF, *"Government Revenues, Percent of GDP."*

and Japan, in black and gray thin lines). The dotted linear trend lines show each country's average slope over the 71 years.

Figure 21: Select Government Primary Balances: 1950–2021 (% GDP)[483]

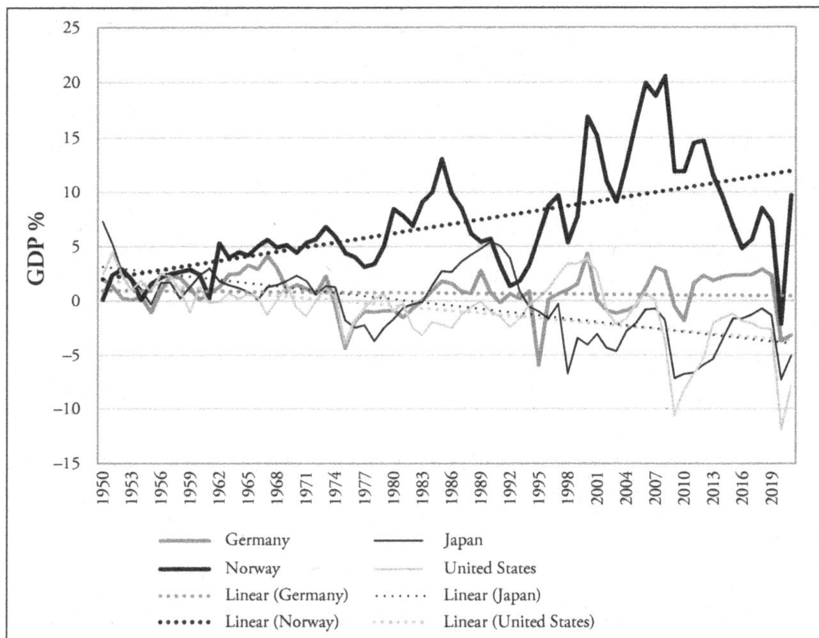

Norway, with a population of 5.6 million, has the highest government economic engagement of the four, but with the world's largest sovereign wealth fund from state-owned petroleum sales,[484] the country has the means to run budget surpluses while offering generous public services. Being industrialized before its oil reserves were fully exploited, Norway avoided the resource curse and is likely the world's most financially secure nation. A 2021 over 9 percent budget surplus while most if not all others were running deficits to deal with the pandemic underscores its remarkable endowment.

483 IMF, "*Government Primary Balance, Percent of GDP.*"

484 "Top 100 Largest Sovereign Wealth Fund Rankings by Total Assets," The Sovereign Wealth Fund Institute, accessed December 4, 2023, https://www.swfinstitute.org/fund-rankings/sovereign-wealth-fund.

Its strength is so profound that Norway went into primary balance deficit only once over the 71-year period: in 2020, when running a 2.14 percent deficit following the COVID-19 shutdown. For the remaining 70 years, its primary balance averaged an impressive 6.97 percent of GDP. Its upward-sloping trend line shows that not only have Norwegian primary balances remained positive, but they have increased over time too. Norway both lives within its means and saves for tomorrow. Its fiscal management deserves an unreserved A+.

Germany, while not endowed with Norwegian natural resources, has been responsibly managed and in Figure 21 shows a negative primary balance for 20 of the 71 years, with a positive average primary balance of 0.72 percent of GDP. Its linear trend line is flat and above 0, a good pattern to see. This data, together with Germany's 2022 gross public debt at 67 percent of GDP, shows a nation living within its means and a government intervening responsibly when needed. Germany earns an A for fiscal management.

Japan and the United States show fiscal management generously denoted as irresponsible. Of most concern in Figure 21 is that both show not cyclical but permanent primary deficits. As their downward-sloping trend lines indicate, Japan's primary balance went negative in the 1970s and has remained there ever since, excluding between the mid-1980s to the mid-1990s, when it was positive. America's primary balance went negative in the early 1980s, and except for the windfall from the dot-com boom from the mid-1990s until the early 2000s, it remained negative too.[485] Both earn a D or D– for fiscal management.

The conditions under which America, Japan, or any other industrialized nation might succumb to their fiscal impropriety is considered later in this chapter. Needing emphasis here is how major industrialized democracies are looking more like struggling developing countries than members of a modern elite enjoying the fruits of their labor. In the unbalanced global growth scenario, the challenge is framed as balancing

485 Pages 367–369 and footnote 495 provide more details on the economics of the dot-com boom and why America deserves a D for fiscal management.

promises with discipline when fiscal reality means promises cannot be met. Some may face intergenerational conflict as promises and fiscal reality collide in the tragedy of societal *hospital passes*.

Hospital pass is a sporting metaphor. In rugby, only those holding the ball may be tackled, and seeing a big forward looming, at the very last moment a player passes the ball to a teammate who is then tackled and ends up in the hospital. Key is passing players knowingly place compatriots in danger; they receive the debt ball and face the risk of default and fiscal hospitalization. Borrowing sets up the conditions for societal hospital passes when the following generations are called to service and repay the debt. Politicians taking the more politically expedient route to fund benefits through borrowing and not taxes are more guilty than those enjoying the benefits they did not pay for. But culpability notwithstanding, if a debt crisis results, innocent bystanders land in the hospital long after those causing the damage are gone and forgotten.

As noted in the unbalanced global growth scenario, being poor at imposing pain means democracies may adjust too little too late, and an external force (e.g., the IMF or a similar agency) may have to intervene. Hopefully, voters and responsible leaders will prevent the United States or Japan—or others—from facing such a crisis. We now turn to the economic scenarios that may transpire over the next 100 years. As is explained, how Leaders, Followers, and Failures act individually and collectively will influence which prevails.

Twenty-First-Century Economic Scenarios: Peace with Scarcity Vanquished (BGG), Imbalance with Instability Enduring (UGG), or an Inhospitable, Apocalyptic World (GM)

The first economic scenario, balanced global growth (BGG), presumes Leaders maintain innovation-led growth, while input-led growth continues among Followers as Failures too become Followers and catch up. This best-case scenario predicts that by the end of the century or soon thereafter, most if not all nations are fully engaged in the human struggle for productivity, and that with scarcity mostly vanquished, abundance reigns and the Leader/Follower distinction is of little use as Failures disappear and economic competitive advantage determines the relative economic position of prosperous nations not that far apart in wealth.

The second scenario, unbalanced global growth (UGG), contains two sources that may cause imbalance: either Leaders fail to sustain their innovation-led growth and decline as Followers and Failures ascend; or as Leaders sustain innovation-led growth, Followers fail to catch up, and Failures remain. A combination of these imbalances is also possible. If Leaders are the source of imbalance, their prosperity will decline as Follower and Failure prosperity increases, and if Leaders maintain growth while the rest struggle, Followers and Failures will be the primary source of instability instead. Either way, economic growth will be lower than in BGG, and the world will be more unstable and less prosperous. Rich and poor will still be far apart.

The third scenario, global meltdown (GM), predicts neither Leaders nor Followers maintain growth as expected, and that once the full cost of global warming/climate change is incurred, global output and living standards peak and then decline in our hot and inhospitable world. In this dystopian world the twentieth-century conditions will seem a wistful, unattainable dream. Global output will be lower and more volatile than in BGG or UGG, and while Leaders and Followers will experience diminished economic choices, Failures will pay the biggest cost. These three scenarios are now more fully considered.

Balanced Global Growth: Emergence of a Stable, Prosperous World

As First Movers into the Industrial and Post-Industrial Eras, it was inevitable that the European Exception would set the pace from 1800 until the end of the twentieth century. But a twenty-first-century BGG world will depend less on America and Europe and more on developing nations like China, India, Brazil, Mexico, Indonesia, and Nigeria. As Africa is expected to account for about 25 percent of global population by 2050,[486] progress in China and India followed by changes across Africa will drive events should BGG unfold.

Because of economic progress, scale, and differences between youth and maturity, irreversible change will occur as BGG proceeds. China will be the first to dominate, but as other Followers rise while Leaders continue growing, China's influence will dilute. Then, as scarcity's scourge is finally eliminated and a prosperous multipolar world emerges, no region or nation will dominate. Under BGG, the twenty-first century will be described as the global century, underscoring that the triumph was not due to any single nation or region but to widespread global progress.

The differences between input-led and innovation-led growth and that the industrialized have higher living standards and more mature economies are the primary socioeconomic causes of the change under BGG. Aging populations, saturated markets, and lower economic growth means Leaders will inevitably be outpaced as their percentage of the world population declines. With relatively young populations and material needs unmet, Followers under BGG will drive most of the economic growth over the coming century.

Industrialized markets will still grow at around replacement rates or at the rate innovative new products persuade well-served consumers to try something new, and once all nations are fully industrialized, global growth will slow to the natural innovation-led growth rate. Though what this rate will be exactly is unknown, it will not be the 5 to 10 percent annual GDP growth Fast Followers enjoyed in their input-led growth. Between 1 to 3 percent is more likely.

BGG assumes that by the twenty-first century's end or soon thereafter, economic capability is widely spread such that most, if not all, nations will have negotiated their input-led growth and caught up. With physical infrastructures and housing established, and with key services

---

486 Declan Walsh, "The World is Becoming More African," *New York Times*, October 28, 2023, accessed November 12, 2023, https://www.nytimes.com/interactive/2023/10/28/world/africa/africa-youth-population.html.

such as education and healthcare widely accessible, all will reside in stable, prosperous societies. And as productivity's spread leads to production at similar levels worldwide, high average GDPs per capita will mean a global middle class with smaller differences between rich and poor.

With differences both within and between nations less significant, a nation's percentage of global output will be determined by population size and not by per capita GDP. India and China will be the biggest economies, and if America is 5 percent of the global population, it will command around 5 percent of global output. Should BGG transpire, no country will again have the power and influence America had over the twentieth century. China, because of its recent economic growth, has already joined America as a contending great power, and it is likely that cooperation and competition will characterize the relationship between these two nations over the coming decades. But as others catch up, the influence of single nations will decline, and once parity is reached in our multipolar world and previously powerful nations revert to becoming first among equals, coalitions like that governing the European Union will likely be how global political power, where needed, is exercised. And as all are prosperous, peace and stability will reign. Figure 22 shows global output should BGG prevail.

Figure 22 is similar to the S Curve in Figure 7. Indicative of the billions joining the struggle for productivity over the next 75 to 100 years, and shown in the line's steep ascent, is that growth is high until around 2100. By 2125, growth slows to the natural innovation-led growth rate, and as this is expected to be around 2 percent, the line continues sloping gently upward after 2125.

Figure 22: The Human Struggle for Productivity: Balanced Global Growth

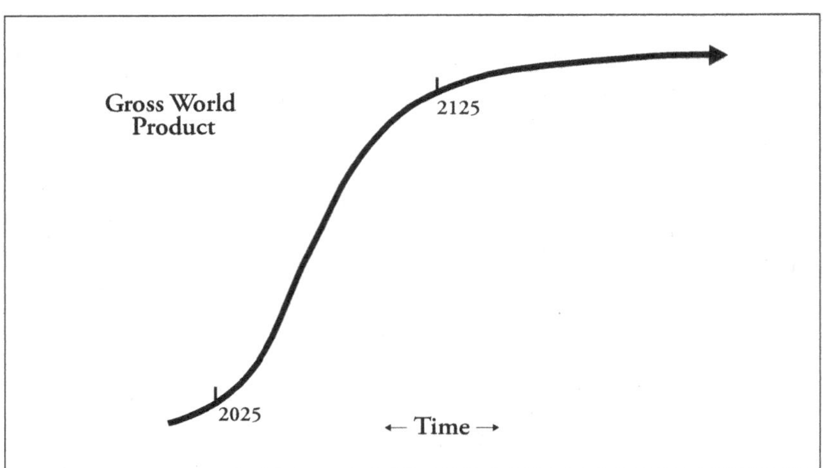

This future may seem threatening to developed country residents, but no economic law holds Leaders will cease to prosper as others catch up. If your neighbors get rich, you will too, provided you have something to sell to them. After World War II, the United States produced almost half the world's output, and as American living standards improved over the next two generations, Fast Followers industrialized by relying on growing American purchasing power. Made in Japan but consumed in America was followed by made in Hong Kong, Singapore, Taiwan, and South Korea until made in China and consumed in America became the status quo at the twentieth century's end. And as Europe and Japan recovered after World War II and Fast Follower productive capacity emerged, Americans still grew richer.

Postwar American wealth increased as the country continued to offer high-value products others wanted. Mainframe and personal computers, MS-DOS, Microsoft Word and Excel, the internet, and Google, among other innovations, emerged from the country in the twentieth century's last decades. More recently, the move to the cloud, AI, and other advances continue to propel the country forward while American purchasing power still permits others to diversify through export-led growth to American consumers.

Applying to individuals, companies, and nations alike, the lesson is clear: whether Leader, Follower, or Failure, to engage in economic exchange, what you produce must be purchased by others, and if salable items are not produced, your living standards will drop unless you have savings—a store of past productivity—to rely on. Without these, largesse from others is needed to survive.

Even in a balanced, multipolar BGG world, however, some nations will be wealthier because their competitive advantage will permit them to produce higher-value products (in today's world: aircraft from Boeing/Airbus, luxury cars from BMW/Mercedes-Benz, advanced semiconductor chips from TSMC, appliances from Samsung or LG, electric vehicles and other green products from China), but competitive advantage should always be considered temporary, lest better products appear.

In competitive global markets, the temporary monopoly positions producers hold erode as others copy or find ways around the advantage; staying ahead is only possible through unrelenting innovation and continuous improvement. Innovating faster than others replicate is the mantra to thrive by in a world of innovation-led growth. Those wishing to maintain production of high-value goods and services in the multipolar BGG world must follow this principle. What advantages nations and their citizens will possess in a century's time is unknown; all that can be said is global competition will force a focus on what each does best.

In 2022, exports of goods and services accounted for 30 percent of national GDP, meaning that 70 percent of output remained domestic.[487] Coverage of global, regional, national, and local activities in Chapter 4 notes that the more focus is on global and regional than national or local activities, the richer producers will be. Notably, high-income countries export 33.7 percent of their GDPs; middle-income, 25.9 percent; and

487 World Bank, "Exports of Goods and Services (% of GDP)," World Bank national accounts data and OECD National Accounts data files, 2023, accessed July 11, 2023, https://data.worldbank.org/indicator/NE.EXP.GNFS.ZS.

low-income, 20.8 percent.[488] Those wishing to be among the wealthiest must focus on global competitiveness and offer products purchased around the world. Products, services, and solutions that stay at the efficient frontier of global commerce must be offered by them. Those at this level will enjoy a living standard among the highest in our balanced prosperous world.

BGG is the best-case scenario for the human struggle for productivity, and skeptics may argue that to assume all nations will transit to industrialized states over the next 100 years is optimistic. But 2125 is only one point in time; 2150 could be when BGG is reached. Key over the next 50 years or so is to place us squarely on this preferable path. The second and third scenarios identify inhibitions that may prevent BGG from prevailing, and the best response to skeptics who worry BGG is infeasible is to encourage them to work to ensure that the other two scenarios do not dominate. Recording the impediments that may allow UGG or GM to do so provides important information to ensure BGG is eventually the road taken by us all.

We turn now to the second scenario, UGG, with inhibitors that may lead to the scenario prevailing divided into two: UGG problems of wealth that stall Leaders, and UGG problems of poverty that slow Followers and derail Failures. These two problem sets are considered consecutively.

Unbalanced Global Growth and Leader Problems of Wealth: Inequity amid Wealth and Excess without Discipline

As Chapter 4 indicates under "Leaders in Retreat," problems of wealth among industrialized nations may arise from many sources, including aging societies not saving enough to cover retirement/healthcare costs; a failure to provide the education workers require to remain competitive, causing economic growth that is insufficient to sustain that society; and societies that because of cornucopia lose their productive edge and cannot compete with those getting up earlier and working harder. Soci-

488 "Exports of Goods and Services," World Bank Group.

etal hospital passes that restrict economic growth may also result from nations living beyond their means.

In the United States, Social Security and Medicare/Medicaid will likely be the crucibles for hospital passes, and should these occur, discretionary income will be restricted as those lacking means are supported. Of most concern is that taxes paid into Social Security have not, as is the case in Norway, been invested in a sovereign wealth fund to cover future obligations. Social Security and Medicare trust funds have already been lent back to the US federal government and spent to meet current obligations. Being underfunded, Social Security may become means tested, meaning wealthier American contributions will essentially become a tax rather than an investment. Declining Medicare trust funds may also mean wealthier Americans will be required to pay more for government-mediated health insurance.

Compared with other developed countries, American taxes are low. OECD 2020 data comparing 39 countries shows US taxes were seventh lowest at 25.54 percent of GDP; 5 of the 6 countries below the United States were developing countries.[489] The sample average was 33.5 percent, and the European Union average was even higher. The US 25.54 percent of GDP does not align with a great power that accounts for almost 40 percent of global military expenditure and that since 1980 has run fiscal deficits.

Though what occurs when nations default is understood, less clear is how much government debt is too high. Financial markets have remained stable with Japan's debt over 260 percent of GDP and Italy's at 150 percent, and the United States has borrowed easily with debt at 120 percent of GDP. These countries are listed because their default would impact global financial markets seriously. As oilman J. Paul Getty noted: "If you owe the bank $100 that's your problem. If you owe the bank $100 million, that's the bank's problem." Should Japan, America, Italy, or a similar sized country default, both the country and the world have a

489 OECD, "Tax-to-GDP ratios, 6/12/2021," accessed July 23, 2023, https://www.oecd.org/coronavirus/en/data-insights/tax-to-gdp-ratios.

problem. When the bank is owed US$24 trillion—the 2023 US federal public debt—all will feel the impact.

In May 2023, Americans held their breath as Republicans and Democrats negotiated an increase in the US federal borrowing limit, leading to speculation about what would happen under limited default:

> The repercussions of a first-ever default on the federal debt would quickly reverberate around the world. Orders for Chinese factories that sell electronics to the United States could dry up. Swiss investors who own U.S. Treasurys would suffer losses. Sri Lankan companies could no longer deploy dollars as an alternative to their own dodgy currency.
>
> Zandi and two colleagues at Moody's have concluded that even if the debt limit were breached for no more than [a] week, the U.S. economy would weaken so much, so fast, as to wipe out roughly 1.5 million jobs.
>
> And if a government default were to last much longer—well into the summer—the consequences would be far more dire. . . . U.S. economic growth would sink, 7.8 million American jobs would vanish, borrowing rates would jump, the unemployment rate would soar from the current 3.4 percent to 8 percent and a stock-market plunge would erase $10 trillion in household wealth.[490]

Financial markets are built on trust and confidence, and should these be lost in an American default, the impact would be immediate, catastrophic, and hard to overestimate. Banking systems worldwide would collapse as credit markets freeze and interest rates spike; a significant US dollar depreciation would make US imports more expensive as American living standards plummet, and global economic growth would grind to a halt and likely contract. Repercussions greater than the Great Depression are possible.

The American government will also be unable to rescue the global financial system as it did in 2007 and 2008. Fires cannot be extinguished by the material causing them, and stopping the panic ball rolling after an

490 Paul Wiseman, "Here's What Would Happen to the Global Economy If the U.S. Defaults on its Debt," PBS Newshour, May 22, 2023, accessed July 13, 2023, https://www.pbs.org/newshour/world/heres-what-would-happen-to-the-global-economy-if-the-u-s-defaults-on-its-debt.

American default is almost impossible as events cascade upon themselves. When markets turn and bolt, reversing sentiment is difficult. America acting responsibly so market confidence loss is not flirted with—and to avoid even slightly opening the door to default—is eminently preferable.

Financial markets do, however, indicate displeasure in other ways before default occurs. Fearing its creditworthiness is in jeopardy, rating agencies may downgrade America's credit rating and increase the country's borrowing costs; in the extreme, investors may decline to invest at all. Foreign investors dumping their investments would cause the US dollar to weaken and the wealth of those holding US Treasurys to decline. Severe damage to the global banking system might also result.

Since World War II, America has been considered the most stable and lowest-risk national economy, with federal interest rates being the lowest-risk rate against which all others are set. As a result, the US dollar is recognized as a reliable store of value and an international means of exchange. In addition, as international investors sought the safe haven of US Treasurys in times of crises, foreign ownership of US federal public debt grew from US$14 billion (5 percent of total public debt) in 1970 to US$7.3 trillion (30 percent of total public debt) by 2022.[491] In December 2022, Japanese investors held US$1,76.3 billion of federal debt (14.71 percent of foreign holdings) while Chinese investors held the second-highest amount at US$867.1 billion (11.85 percent of foreign holdings).[492] Should American fiscal laxity cause foreign investors to seek other safe havens, the domestic capital market is unlikely to be deep enough to replace this group quickly.

How long the US dollar will remain in its position of global primacy is hard to determine. As happened to the British pound sterling as the British Empire dissolved, the status of the currency will likely decline as

---

491 Peter G. Peterson Foundation, "The Federal Government Has Borrowed Trillions, but Who Owns All That Debt?," *Fiscal Blog*, May 11, 2023, https://www.pgpf.org/blog/2023/05/the-federal-government-has-borrowed-trillions-but-who-owns-all-that-debt.

492 Marc Labonte and Ben Leubsdorf, *Foreign Holdings of Federal Debt*, Congressional Research Service report, updated June 9, 2023, accessed November 3, 2023, https://sgp.fas.org/crs/misc/RS22331.pdf.

others grow. As this book goes to press, the BRICS and others are moving to de-dollarize, hoping to remove the use of US dollar for the purchase of critical commodities like oil. Regardless of this effort, responsible fiscal and economic management is even more fundamental as American influence wanes. Rather than being buoyed by demand for US Treasurys, as it is the *cleanest dirty shirt*, economic fundamentals will more and more determine America's economic standing in the world. And the best defenses are a government living within its means and a strong economy.

To balance US federal books, likely both an increase in taxes and a decrease in expenditures will be needed, medicine that is hard to deliver in a democracy. Because of the pain they cause, mandates to increase taxes and cut expenditures are rare, and to occur voluntarily, America's two political parties will likely need a maturity absent at this time. They will have to jointly canvass on a platform that revenue increases and expenditure cuts are imperative so that voters have no choice. Sadly, coalition politics at this level is unthinkable with the American electorate and political parties so divided.

Adding insult to injury, out-of-power politicians often argue that containing debt is imperative, but once back in power, they cut taxes and continue spending recklessly, forgetting their earlier protestations. Other economic slights of hand to offer pain-free solutions are also used; for example, promising higher economic growth will permit rebalancing without any increases or cuts. This promise is even more egregious when to attain the growth, tax cuts are said to be essential.

Called "voodoo economics" by George H. W. Bush when contesting the Republican primary in 1979, this mantra became the supply-side economics Ronald Reagan relied upon after his election in 1980. But economic gains over the Reagan years were not from any supply-side magic. They were from classic countercyclical Keynesian economics: cut taxes to put money in private hands and increase government spending (supported by public borrowing) to stimulate economic growth.

That above-average growth assists rebalancing was, however, shown over the dot-com boom, as US GDP growth from 1996 to 2000 of 3.8 percent, 4.4 percent, 4.5 percent, 4.8 percent, and 4.1 percent flooded state and federal coffers.[493] But estimates of the gains proved to be "irrationally exuberant," and the boom became an investment bubble. As GDP growth slumped to 1 and 1.7 percent in 2001 and 2002, respectively, the collapse impacted investors and the nascent businesses they supported.[494] Tax revenues from stock option grants and capital gains disappeared with the stock market's collapse, significantly impacting fiscal balances of the federal government and many states.[495]

The fiscal surpluses that had led to 1999 forecasts that federal debt would be mostly repaid by 2006 vanished quicker than they appeared.[496] Also important to note is that the higher growth, though to some extent illusory, was when tax rates were far higher than they are in 2023, refuting charges that American tax rates are too high and restrict investment. This was not the case in the second half of the 1990s, when, with US tax rates far higher than today, innovation was readily funded. High taxes were not the problem; the quality of the innovation was.

Over most of American history, federal debt increased to pay for war or to counter economic crises and then decreased once hostilities ended or the crisis was mitigated. This pattern has not been followed from 1980 on. Over the 20 years from 1980 to 2000, a time of peace and prosperity that included the Cold War's end, federal debt increased. Then in the

---

493 World Bank, "GDP Growth (Annual %)—United States," 2023, accessed July 18, 2023, https://data.worldbank.org/indicator/NY.GDP.MKTP.KD.ZG?locations=US.

494 World Bank, "GDP Growth (Annual %)—United States."

495 California was at the center of the 1990s boom/bust cycle, and its personal income tax revenues increased from US$28 billion in 1997–98 to nearly US$45 billion in 2001–01, before plummeting to below US$34 billion in 2001–02. See Legislative Analyst's Office, "California's Economy and Budget in Perspective," December 2002, accessed July 18, 2023, http://www.lao.ca.gov/2002/cal_facts/budget.html.

496 In 1999 the Congressional Budget Office estimated the US federal government would pay off its "reducible debt" by 2006. This was a high point of the irrational exuberance of the era. See Alan Greenspan, *The Age of Turbulence: Adventures in a New World* (New York: Penguin Press, 2007), 217.

early 2000s, America went to war and faced a financial crisis second only to the Great Depression, but taxes were cut as debt increased.

This summary of American fiscal behavior provides the underlying reasons for the D or D– grade awarded for American fiscal management in these pages, and odds are high that this fiscal impropriety will continue such that an F is soon warranted. From today's vantage point, it seems only financial market refusal to continue funding will impose the discipline needed, at considerable cost to America and the world.

Indicative of another problem of wealth that may mean UGG is the path followed over the coming decades as Leaders struggle with problems of wealth is that the United Kingdom's aging population and austerity following its European Union exit has placed its much-heralded National Health Service in danger of collapse:

> As it turns 75 this month, the N.H.S., a proud symbol of Britain's welfare state, is in the deepest crisis of its history: flooded by aging, enfeebled patients; starved of investment in equipment and facilities; and understaffed by doctors and nurses, many of whom are so burned out that they are either joining strikes or leaving for jobs abroad.
>
> The fate of the N.H.S. matters beyond Britain. Rising health care costs are bleeding public finances in almost every country, regardless of their political systems.[497]

No country faces more draining healthcare costs than the United States, with 18 percent of 2021 GDP devoted to healthcare compared with 1960's 5 percent.[498] In 2022, the United States spent US$12,555 per capita compared with an average US$6,414 by 12 other wealthy OECD countries.[499] US healthcare outcomes are also below average in

---

497 Mark Landler, "A National Treasure, Tarnished: Can Britain Fix Its Health Service?," *New York Times*, July 16, 2023, accessed July 17, 2023, https://www.nytimes.com/2023/07/16/world/europe/uk-nhs-crisis.html.

498 Peter G. Peterson Foundation, "Why Are Americans Paying More for Healthcare?," *Fiscal Blog*, July 14, 2023, https://www.pgpf.org/blog/2023/07/why-are-americans-paying-more-for-healthcare.

499 Peter G. Peterson Foundation, "How Does the U.S. Healthcare System Compare to Other Countries?," *Fiscal Blog*, July 12, 2023, https://www.pgpf.org/blog/2023/07/how-does-the-us-healthcare-system-compare-to-other-countries.

all OECD measures. A threat to national economic security, unabated healthcare costs have the potential to financially ruin America. And with healthcare costs so high, America will likely be unable to treat its way out of its current crisis.

Absent technological advance that automates healthcare and reduces costs significantly, the best way forward is for Americans to eat less and exercise more. Healthy living will mean healthcare costs drop on their own. If another generation ages as unhealthily as baby boomers have, bankruptcy by healthcare is almost guaranteed. While drugs and other procedures may help those already addicted to carbohydrates and struggling with obesity, ensuring young Americans eat the right quantity and quality of food and exercise to remain healthy is an infinitely better way forward. A national initiative on healthy living, equivalent to the war on drugs or the struggle against tobacco, is urgent. Viewing 1960s and 1970s American movies shows overweight America was not the case then; returning to this state is essential.

That healthcare costs might financially ruin Leaders is compounded when population decline accompanies aging populations. Here, not only will higher healthcare costs have to be met; fewer workers to generate the wealth to meet the costs will be available. Encouraging immigration and ensuring these immigrants are able to sustain higher-than-average economic growth is one way to escape this quandary. Relying on technology and automation to serve aging seniors is another.

Another potential cause of imbalance as UGG problems of wealth are considered is how failure to educate impacts growth and competitiveness. In Chapter 3, the role education played to develop industrial workers is emphasized, and it is revealed there that poor education was failing Americans at the end of the twentieth century. However, claims about poor education must be viewed with care.

Analysis of the 2009 PISA scores (the Program for International Student Assessment administered by the OECD, which compares reading, science, and math scores of 500,000 fifteen-year-olds in 65 countries), shows that after controlling for poverty, American reading score rose remarkably. American students in public high schools with less than 10 percent of students on free and reduced lunch scored 551, higher than any OECD country; schools with between 10 to 25 percent of students qualifying for free and reduced lunch ranked only behind South Korea and Finland.[500]

If after controlling for poverty American math and science proficiency improves as much as reading proficiency did, the data shows the need to attend to poverty more than to education per se. Importantly, this association is confirmed elsewhere. Analysis of 2012 and 2018 PISA scores show a strong negative correlation between PISA math scores and poverty across an international sample.[501]

As was the case in American reading proficiency scores, average math scores strongly depended on the share of low-performing students, which depended on the degree of relative poverty. The solution to poor education may be wider than improving only what happens in schools. Poor education and its effects appear similar to the lack of broadband adoption due to demographic factors highlighted earlier. Dealing with poverty is a bigger problem than addressing education only.

Moreover, an inability of American workers to compete has led to forecasts that a "structural budget deficit of more than 3% of GDP every year over the foreseeable future"[502] is likely, needed for unemployed workers unable to survive in a world where their skills no longer match the jobs available. Wealthy countries must either invest in education to retrain uncompetitive workers so they return to the workforce, or support over the remainder of their natural lives from public funds may

---

500 Howard L. Fleischman et al., *Highlights from PISA 2009: Performance of U.S. 15-Year-Old Students in Reading, Mathematics, and Science Literacy in an International Context* (NCES 2011-004), National Center for Education Statistics, US Department of Education (Washington, DC: US Government Printing Office, 2010): 15, table 6, accessed July 18, 2023, http://nces.ed.gov/pubs2011/2011004.pdf.

501 Vittorio Daniele, "Socioeconomic Inequality and Regional Disparities in Educational Achievement: The Role of Relative Poverty," *Intelligence* 84, (January–February 2021): 101515, accessed July 18, 2023, https://doi.org/10.1016/j.intell.2020.101515.

502 Jim Manzi, "Keeping America's Edge," *National Affairs*, Winter 2010, 17.

be required. Though education costs, a lack of education unquestionably costs more.

The last concern that may cause Leaders to stumble such that UGG prevails is both cultural and economic and pertains to what happens when cornucopia lulls societies into false senses of economic security and dulls their productive edge such that they are unable to compete. This relates especially to competing with Followers who are hungrier, get up earlier, work harder, and leave Leaders unable to produce high-value products and services others demand.

This concern may relate more to southern European nations than it does to the United States or other industrialized Asian nations, but it may also eventually apply to nations such as France, with its 35-hour workweek and average worker desires to retire between 58 to 62 years of age. Wealthier nations and their workers must be aware of competitor costs and ensure they remain competitive with competitor work ethic, cost, and capabilities.

Finally, all nations balance social needs for equity with economic needs for efficiency, similar to the balancing of growth and development as explained in Chapter 3 when the economic nation-building triangle was presented. Even built nations must balance growth and development to ensure stability is maintained, and it could be argued America places too much weight on economic efficiency (growth) and too little on social equity (development), while Europe's concern for social equity (development) is outpacing its economic efficiency (growth).

America's Anglo-Saxon capitalism that favors markets over plans and shareholders over other stakeholders may lead to inequality that produces political instability and eventually causes the nation to stumble. Less focus on growth and more on development will likely be needed to restore stability. Under these conditions, America's economic growth will suffer.

In contrast, some more generous welfare states in Europe's CMEs may face social welfare costs that are too expensive, causing them to reel under the weight. With Asian and other economies operating with less generous welfare and less costly workers, uncompetitive European producers may be priced out of international markets and left to produce only local or national lower-value-added goods and services. With too little growth and too much development, some in Europe are in danger of becoming museum and tourist destinations wealthy outsiders enjoy while instability grows as populations demand public services that their economies cannot afford to deliver.

We now turn to UGG and problems of poverty, which are divisible into two categories: Followers failing to fully industrialize and Failures remaining unable to embark upon a path to industrialization. Followers not achieving full industrialization may be caused by internal factors inhibiting their growth or by factors beyond their control that make it difficult to continue their progress. Failure inability to begin the march toward industrialization is typically caused by more basic considerations, mostly failures of leadership as civil war or other conflict drags them down. Follower problems of poverty are first considered, followed by Failure problems of poverty that may leave them as enduring Failures.

Unbalanced Global Growth and Follower/Failure Problems of Poverty: Economic Takeoff Stalled or Growth Never Started

Many factors may cause Followers to stumble. First, a phenomenon known as the middle-income trap has already been identified as a potential impairment of economic development. This trap occurs when labor costs rise too high to permit a country to continue exporting low-cost manufactures, but it still cannot compete in the higher-value industries others dominate in. Incomes do not progress to higher levels and growth stalls.

The World Bank classifies countries as middle income with gross national incomes between US$1,005 and US$12,275, and in 2013 it noted that of 101 middle-income countries in 1960, only 13 had reached high incomes by 2008.[503] The other 88 remained trapped in middle incomes, confirming that reaching high-income status is by no means guaranteed. Making matters even worse, developing economy workers early in industrialization typically add little value, meaning unlike Ford's five-dollar day workers, they cannot afford the products they are making.

Other inhibitors may be more specific to countries themselves. China, though remarkably successful over the past 50 years, is not yet out of the woods. Information suppressed by Chinese internet censors suggests nearly 1 billion Chinese live on less than US$300 per month.[504] If even remotely close to the truth—often absent in authoritarian societies—this shows a worrying inequality in Chinese income distribution and that the average worker is still unproductive.

Adding to this concern, with an aging and soon-to-decline population following implementation of the One Child Policy, China may get old before it gets rich. To keep populations constant, 2.1 births per woman is required, and according to its 2020 census, China's rate was 1.3, below Japan at 1.4.[505] With a population expected to drop precipitously, One Child couples may face the daunting task of supporting four aging parents and themselves while raising what is likely to remain only one child, compounding the population decline further.

> A key problem will be the rising number of retired people for each person in work, the old age dependency ratio. As this rises, there are fewer workers able to pay taxes to support the health needs and pensions of the elderly. And by 2050 China's old age dependency

---

503 World Bank and Development Research Center of the State Council, P. R. China, *China 2030: Building a Modern, Harmonious, and Creative Society* (Washington, DC: World Bank, 2013): 12, accessed August 2, 2023. https://doi.org/10.1596/978-0-8213-9545-5.

504 Aadil Brar, "China Tries to Censor Data about Nearly 1 Billion People in Poverty," Newsweek, December 28, 2023, https://www.newsweek.com/china-article-censorship-1-billion-people-monthly-income-2000-yuan-poverty-1856031.

505 Peter Hartcher, "China Could Be the First Country to Get Old Before It Gets Rich and the Implications Are Profound," *Sydney Morning Herald,* May 18, 2021, https://www.smh.com.au/world/asia/china-could-be-the-first-country-to-get-old-before-it-gets-rich-and-the-implications-are-profound-20210517-p57sj6.html.

ratio is expected to be higher than Australia's, America's, Britain's or Germany's.[506]

Estimates place China's population at 800 million by 2100, while India's is expected to peak at 1.7 billion in the 2060s and fall back to 1.5 billion by the century's end.[507] Resources will likely be needed to provide for China's fast-aging and declining population, impairing economic growth as senior needs crowd out others. A low per capita income for the majority of Chinese coupled with a declining population does not auger well for the country's future.

Misallocation of capital is another challenge China may face. For example, the overbuilding of apartments, probably driven by bureaucrats seeking to promote employment, has led to estimates that vacant homes sufficient for three billion people are available in the country, with many purchased in the 2016 property upturn still vacant seven years later.[508] Further, in 2023, Chinese automobile producers had the capacity to produce 40 million units while annual domestic demand was about 15 million units less.[509] This overcapacity is bigger than annual vehicle sales in the American automobile market.

Economic growth will suffer as the country absorbs the cost of its misallocated capital, and the Chinese regime's reputation as an efficient economic manager will suffer too. China's path may even follow that of the Soviet Union, which showed that authoritarian growth and plans were superior in the early stage of industrialization, but as an economy grows in complexity and diversity, central planning is harder and harder

---

506 Hartcher, "China Could Be the First Country."

507 Michael E. O'Hanlon, "China's Shrinking Population and Constraints on Its Future Power," Brookings Institution, April 24, 2023, accessed August 2, 2023, https://www.brookings.edu/articles/chinas-shrinking-population-and-constraints-on-its-future-power/.

508 Reuters, "Even China's 1.4 Billion Population Can't Fill All Its Vacant Homes, Former Official Says," September 24, 2023, accessed October 4, 2023, https://www.reuters.com/world/china/even-chinas-14-bln-population-cant-fill-all-its-vacant-homes-former-official-2023-09-23/.

509 Christiaan Hetzner, "Europe's Biggest Car Show Was Long the Stomping Ground of German Brands—But It's Now 'Become the China Show,'" *Fortune*, September 5, 2023, accessed September 7, 2023, https://fortune.com/2023/09/05/iaa-munich-car-show-china-byd-nio-tesla-xpeng-germany/.

to do. Moreover, and as is pointed out in Chapter 3, in early industrialization, state assistance is necessary. But as nations and their businesses stand up, governments should stand down and leave producers to rely on their own resources to compete. Time will tell if the Chinese authorities negotiate this transition successfully.

With its population expected to increase until midcentury, India by contrast may lack the investable surplus to grow as fast as its increasing population needs, meaning it continues underperforming and fails to fully industrialize. Chapter 3 underscores India's need for democracy light, primarily so that surplus is invested to provide the foundation for the higher growth its growing population needs. Like China not escaping the middle-income trap as it suffers from low productivity and capital misallocation (and eventually falters from a rapidly aging and declining population), India may fail to achieve economic escape velocity because of the weight of its growing population. Both may remain stalled in middle-income traps: too few people in China, too many in India, and both also suffering from doses of economic mismanagement. BGG will not be realized for as long as either falter.

Another factor impairing Followers is if post-industrial technology automates human work to the point that those hoping to rely on labor-intensive manufactures to enter the global economy find this route closed. With robots replacing hands and software automating services, new ways to enter the global economy will be needed. And facing education gaps too big to equip workers with skills to produce exportable goods or services, later Followers may fall behind those reaching economic takeoff before low-value added, export-led growth ceased as a starting point.

A further inhibitor, even if the export-led manufacturing door remains open, is at the other end of the value chain. America's dominance after World War II permitted it to open its domestic market so that Fast Followers could rely on American purchasing power to kick-start their industrializations. To keep its workers employed, China, which will not account for around half of global output as America did after World War II, may instead move toward self-reliance over the coming decades.

China will not be, as America was, the global consumer of last resort providing purchasing power for others to rely on should it move toward in China, by China, for China. Aspirant Followers will be left without a munificent market of the sort Fast Followers—China included—had access to in their early dashes for growth. UGG may result as Followers fail to reach the scale needed to fully industrialize.

Inhibitions that might cause Followers to stumble over the remainder of the twenty-first century such that UGG endures have now been identified, and we now turn to the problems of poverty that Failures may face. These are mostly from leaders not understanding the economic nation-building task itself, and instead of using power to eliminate scarcity's scourge, they use it to enrich only themselves or cronies; or, relying on mankind's basest instincts, they use it to protect their tribe or sacrosanct beliefs.

Why civilizations, nations, and societies fail is extensively written about, and there is no need to repeat this literature here.[510] An appraisal of Failures across the world reveals nations punished by the absence of that scarcest of goods: competent leadership. For as long as authoritarian plunderers, extractive elites, corruption, and crony capitalism persist, Failures or struggling Followers will remain. Terrorist groups, drug cartels, organized crime, and gang violence also disrupt stability such that economic nation-building and growth remain in the wings. The Taliban of Afghanistan, basing their leadership on the imposition of fundamentalist notions that disempower women and brutally enforce social rules, will not move Afghans from Failures to Followers. A civil war such as the one now seen in Syria robs Syrians of stability, an essential element required before any consideration of growth or development is feasible.

510 Readers interested in this literature should start with Jared Diamond, *Guns, Germs, and Steel*; David S. Landes, *The Wealth and Poverty of Nations*; and Daron Acemoglu and James A. Robinson, *Why Nations Fail: The Origins of Power, Prosperity, and Poverty.*

Finally, to join the human struggle for productivity, economic literacy regarding how Fast Followers industrialized is imperative for most African, Latin, and South American nations closer to Failure than to Follower (whether autocracies or democracies or somewhere in between). By laying out the transition from pre- to post-industrial production and by describing the routes First Movers and Fast Followers chose to industrialize, this book captures choices Failures face as they contemplate what is required of them to join the struggle for productivity. Not following this advice will mean enduring Failure.

Figure 23 details how UGG output will proceed over the coming century. Figure 22's BGG is compared with the dashed line, which shows UGG GWP where Followers advance while Leaders stumble, and with the dotted line, where Leaders sustain but Followers struggle. Both the quantum of GWP and the rate of economic growth (shown by each line's slope) will be higher should Followers stay on track while Leaders do not. The major difference between the dashed and dotted lines is the slope. One trends slightly upward and the other slightly downward.

Figure 23: The Human Struggle for Productivity: Unbalanced Global Growth

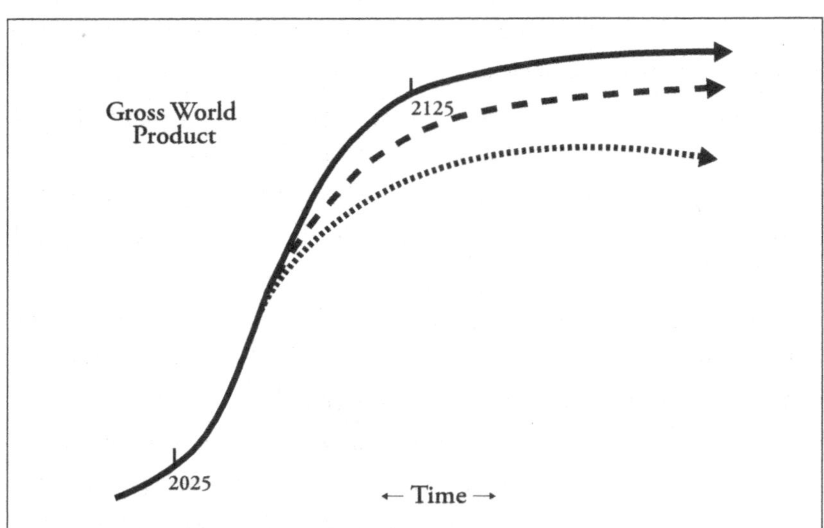

Though UGG GWP is not as abundant as it would be under BGG, progress will still be made in a world that remains poorer and more unequal and unstable, and whether BGG or GM is eventually reached depends on the choices made as history unfolds. If the advice in this book is heeded, the better future will eventually be reached. If not, a worse future may be in the cards. We turn now to the third scenario, global meltdown. As BGG describes the best case for the human struggle for productivity, GM captures the worst that may transpire over the twenty-first century and beyond. After describing GM's characteristics, the scenario that will likely prevail concludes the scenario coverage.

Global Meltdown: Everything Everywhere All at Once, a World to Avoid at All Costs

Global meltdown is the worst future mankind may face. This scenario predicts that both UGG problems of wealth and poverty persist such that Leaders and Followers continue struggling and that our failure to mitigate makes global warming/climate change the final straw that causes economic meltdown and collective failure. Relying on the title of a film that won seven 2023 Oscar awards, *Everything Everywhere All at Once* leads to global catastrophe.

Record heat, out-of-control wildfires, worsening hurricanes/tornadoes, warming oceans and changing currents, punishing droughts and floods, deforestation, disappearing ice packs and glaciers, and rising sea levels are already being experienced. GM predicts these will worsen, and when combined with struggling nations and low economic growth, living standards peak midcentury and then decline inexorably. Uninhabitable geographies and increasing food and water insecurity lead to additional climate refugees in the apocalyptic world emerging.

With the worst of UGG eventuating, Leaders struggle to rebalance as their debt-driven economic growth becomes more and more unsustainable and declines even further as financial default occurs. Followers stumble as too little growth and too much development limits their prosperity also. Declining Leader wealth means Follower markets for export-led growth diminish, and as aspirant Followers find it more difficult to establish economic footholds, poverty increases among them too. In the face of Leader/Follower decline, Failure conditions continue worsening.

Mass migration will continue. North Africans will seek to escape to Europe, South and Central Americans will consider America their haven of choice, and developing Asians will move anywhere close by that might offer upliftment unavailable at home. Sub-Saharan Africans will lack an easily accessible location to migrate to and may pay the highest price for the unfolding tragedy. Should GM prevail, rising inequality both within and between nations will occur, as will increases in conflict, displaced persons, and mass refugees.

Five mass extinctions are noted in the Earth's geological record, and a sixth, the Holocene extinction, now underway, is a direct result of human action over the past two to three centuries:[511]

---

511 The Holocene epoch is the past 12,000 years from the last ice age, and the Holocene extinction is the flora and fauna extinction caused by human activity.

> The current extinction event also differs in that it is driven by the concurrence of phenomena unique to human actions including changes in land and sea use; direct exploitation of animals and plants; climate change; pollution; and invasive alien species.[512]

With climate scientists now searching for tipping points that may cause the Atlantic Meridional Overturning Circulation to collapse and foster a new European ice age,[513] there is no shortage of doomsday predictions regarding global warming/climate change. What is certain is that anthropogenic extinction has already decreased global biological diversity, and hundreds of millions of human lives are at risk as the crisis deepens. Also certain is that quality of life will continue to be impaired, and at worst societal collapse is possible. In the extreme, human lives may revert back to as Hobbes had described in the mid-seventeenth century: "solitary, poor, nasty, brutish, and short," but good government will be unable to reverse the damage should our mitigation prove to be too little, too late. Man will be left atop a diminished and spluttering food chain, master of an inhospitable domain he alone created.

Figure 24 shows GWP should GM prevail (dashed line) compared with Figure 22's BGG output. Global output growth peaks lower than either UGG or BGG and then declines. Where the new—and possibly sustainable—low is encountered, and how fast and to where output recovers, is hard to determine. This will depend upon how inhospitable our hot planet is, how ingenious human adaptation is, and how many humans are left when the dust settles. The smaller human population is, the lower global output is likely to be.

---

512 Nick King and Aled Jones, "An Analysis of the Potential for the Formation of 'Nodes of Persisting Complexity,'" *Sustainability* 13, no. 15 (July 2021): 8161, accessed August 13, 2023, https://doi.org/10.3390/su13158161.

513 Damian Carrington, "Gulf Stream Could Collapse as Early as 2025, Study Suggests," *Guardian*, July 25, 2023, accessed August 13, 2023, https://www.theguardian.com/environment/2023/jul/25/gulf-stream-could-collapse-as-early-as-2025-study-suggests. The 2004 science fiction disaster film *The Day After Tomorrow* depicts such a catastrophe and is based on the 1999 book *The Coming Global Superstorm* by Art Bell and Whitley Strieber.

Figure 24: The Human Struggle for Productivity: Global Meltdown

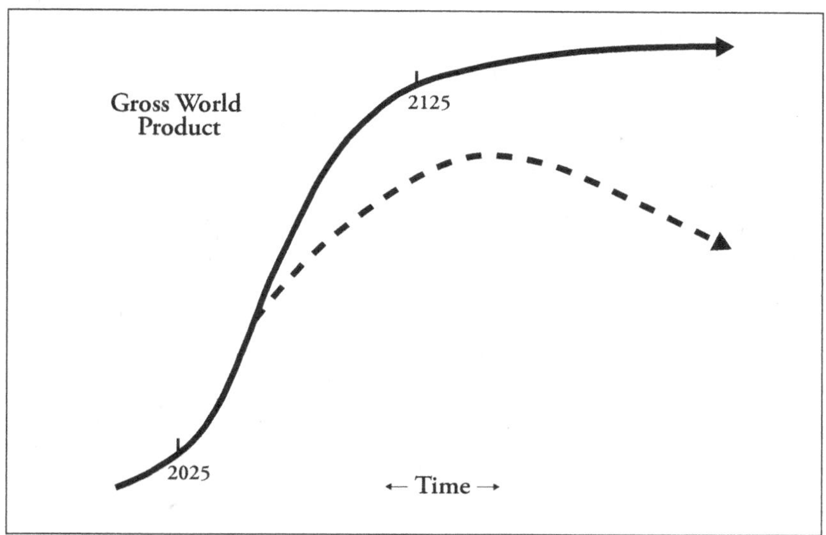

We now turn to considering which scenario is most likely to prevail. But readers are warned, as many from Yogi Berra to allegedly Mark Twain cautioned: forecasting is difficult, especially about the future. As you will see, UGG is considered most likely to prevail, but again counsel is warranted: BGG or GM might still prevail; all the next section does is speculate about which is most probable. And if, as is suggested, UGG does prevail, whether the UGG glass is half-full or half-empty becomes an important consideration. This book ends by suggesting how all who read it should act or react to ensure a more optimistic, glass-half-full UGG transpires so that BGG eventually comes to pass. Good news is always the best way to frame a message, and this is why it concludes this book.

Most Likely Scenario: Unbalanced Global Growth in a World Muddling Through

For BGG to transpire by 2125, every nation must make the right choices to maximize its economic conditions over the next 50 to 75 years and by 2125 be industrialized or close to this state. The likelihood of this occurring is low. Some nations may follow the correct path, but others will likely not, leaving BGG less likely and UGG as better describing the world in place at this time. This does not, as was highlighted when BGG was initially outlined, mean BGG never transpires. BGG may arrive later, say by 2150 or 2175, giving life to a glass-half-full interpretation of UGG. Nations may continue to struggle but learn from their mistakes and others' successes, meaning all do reach the BGG promised land, only slower than forecasted here.

Similarly, for GM to prevail, Leaders, Followers, and Failures all make the wrong choices such that the worst possible economic conditions result. Similarly, steps taken to mitigate global warming/climate change all turn out to be too little, too late, and as a result, the most punishing effects of our warming planet are imposed. Just as a prediction that all the right choices are made so that BGG prevails is unlikely, so is the prediction that all the wrong choices are made to ensure GM prevails.

But caution is again warranted: if our mitigation is so ineffective that widespread punishing results appear sooner and more intensely than expected, GM may still prevail because the global warming/climate change effects are so profound that our struggle for productivity is seriously impaired, notwithstanding any positive steps Leaders, Followers, or Failures take in the interim. GM, though less likely than UGG, may be more likely than BGG.

It is difficult, if not impossible, to provide estimates of how likely each scenario is, but logic dictates UGG is most likely. If GM is second most likely, mitigating global warming/climate change quickly is imperative. But absent a global warming/climate change knockout punch that forces us into GM, it is likely that as UGG unfolds over the coming century, nations will continue muddling through as Leaders and Followers face problems of wealth and poverty and as Failures struggle to raise themselves to aspirant Followers and join the modern world as industrialized nations.

Most important when 2125 is reached is that the UGG that has transpired is a glass half-full, meaning mankind only faces a century or more of UGG that eventually leads to BGG being attained. Also critical to this outcome is that the worst effects of global warming/climate change are avoided. How our collective actions may ensure this outcome concludes this book.

Unbalanced to Balanced Global Growth: Global Insights and Our Need to Work Together

Climate change/global warming is a global problem that demands a global solution. Only Leaders reaching carbon neutrality while Followers continue fossil fuel use is insufficient. Some Followers may even argue those already industrialized did so without energy limits, and it is their turn. Such actions, however, will lead to the "tragedy of the commons," where rational decisions made by a few are irrational when the interests of all are taken into account.

Effective mitigation requires nations commit to the unnatural act of placing global interests above national interests, and national governance has shown an evolution from tribes to kingdoms/principalities to nation-states, the latter two often forged on the anvil of conflict. Representing more civilized governance, two international institutions emerged from the twentieth-century world wars: the League of Nations, superseded by the UN.

Then, the 1948 General Agreement on Tariffs and Trade eventually led to formation of the World Trade Organization (WTO), an intergovernmental organization mandated to establish, revise, and enforce rules governing international trade. WTO rules are laid out in agreements, and members are guaranteed their exports will be treated fairly and consistently by other members and promise to treat imports similarly in their home markets. Finally, and indicative of regional as opposed to national governance, the European Union was forged after World War II, initially to promote economic integration. By 2023, it included 27 nations that had agreed to the largest peacetime transfer of national sovereignty ever to build regional political governance at a depth unmatched previously.

These global institutions collectively point to the governance needed to mitigate global warming/climate change. Moreover, the move toward more supranational governance means diplomacy will rest less on the shoulders of strong individual nations and more on alliances and coalitions.

Further, those dismissing institutions such as the UN or IPCC (pages 341–342) should think carefully about their sentiments. Only all nations working alongside institutions such as the IPCC will ensure that the world's best climate scientists, and not politicians or biased vested interests, develop the required solutions. So that the worst effects of climate change/global warming are mitigated and our best future is ensured, global governance backed by all nations is essential. Unless detractors have credible alternatives to quickly replace these international institutions, they must support them and work from within to ensure the mitigation agreed to is appropriate and implemented. An isolationist or climate-denier America that spurns global governance is especially unfortunate at this time, and not only will its rational voice be missed, the country will also lag in the technology needed to scale clean energy and will again have to import what it does not do at home.

But well-directed global governance, though necessary, is insufficient. Tangible resources that help poorer nations deal with the immediate effects of a crisis not of their making are also called for. This is not only the right action to take. It will equip Failures and Followers to support the mitigation asked and be especially beneficial if aiding in their industrialization too. Taxpayers worldwide must recognize that public funds allocated to climate change/global warming mitigation and adaptation both within and beyond their borders are essential. To safeguard the future for their children and grandchildren, Americans must appreciate that both national and international investment of their tax dollars is necessary.

To ensure BGG comes to pass after a time of UGG, economic nation-building as depicted in these pages and the lessons Fast Followers offer must be learned from to ensure economic nation-building investments are made for the right reasons and in the right manner. A more regional approach might be advisable, with the United States facilitating the modernization of Central and South America and Europeans focusing on Eastern Europe and northern Africa while industrialized Asia helps less developed Asian nations. Assistance for sub-Saharan Africa might best be facilitated from Johannesburg. Ensuring all nations move from Failure to Follower and join the cadre of industrialized nations is the best way to stop unwanted refugees flooding neighbors, and locating advisors close to the sources of such immigration might better align incentives and capabilities.

Hoping to build a so-called Global South counterweight to Western dominance of the past two centuries, in January 2024 the BRICS added Argentina, Egypt, Ethiopia, Iran, Saudi Arabia, and the United Arab Emirates to their five-nation alliance. In addition, established in 2015 with a Shanghai HQ and enabling Followers to assist Followers, the BRICS New Development Bank (NDB) may be an additional vehicle through which responsible economic nation-building occurs. Previously established development agencies such as the World Bank and IMF might be more effective if working alongside the NDB; such cooperation may be foundational to the *pax mundi*, or world peace, that BGG hopefully leads to.

With Brazil, Russia, India, China, and South Africa still engaged in economic nation-building to industrialize, an NDB/IMF/World Bank consortium focusing on economic nation-building across the developing world will not only increase policy quality. Representing nations more like them than industrialized nations are, Failures and Followers will likely be more receptive to advice from such a collective institution than from the IMF or the World Bank alone.

Any alliance that narrows the gap between the Global North and South or between our world's rich and poor—and encourages a more multipolar rather than bipolar world—is better than alliances that do not. As this book is completed, fears of a new global conflict between America/Western powers and an emerging Russian/Chinese/BRICS alliance are growing. Any steps to encourage BRICS/global engagement through peaceful means must be encouraged. Readers at this time may find these ideas about global engagement and governance incredulous. Our history of conflict and how our basest instincts often dominate and prevent cooperation with others unlike us supports this disbelief. Regardless, we must find ways to engage our better selves globally to solve the urgent crisis our warming planet presents, and if our steps add ways to help Failures become Followers, so much the better.

How the global balance of power is maintained over the coming century is an important final question to conclude these global insights. The first half of the twentieth century saw the world's great powers engaging in two global conflicts, followed by a cold war between the United States and Russia from 1947 until the Soviet Union's dissolution in 1991. But the last half of the century also saw rapprochement between former enemies and a peaceful European integration that offers lessons to all. In addition, America as policeman of last resort ensured Allied victory in World War II and stopped communism's drive for dominance through a conflict that thankfully remained *cold*. This maintenance of peace, though imperfect, accompanied progress unmatched in human history.

Russia's role in Germany's defeat meant playing a more significant role in world affairs than it would have had World War II not happened. Though its state-led autarkic economic model failed in four decades, Russia still has much military power, enduring from its former great power status. Regretfully, in the twenty-first century this hard power has been deployed to disrupt and destabilize failed states from Afghanistan to Syria and has reached from the Central African Republic to Burkina Faso. Its most recent use of hard power, Russia's failure to defeat Ukraine after its February 2022 invasion has led to a conflict more intractable than Russia expected. Important for the global balance of power is that China has become a partner as Russia struggles militarily against Ukraine, who has exhibited unexpected bravery, fortitude, and resilience while relying on Western weaponry and aid to resist the Russian aggression.

China's support of Russia is understandable given Russia's ability to provide oil and other raw materials while it imports Chinese manufactures in exchange and given they are both led by authoritarian regimes. But rivalry that leads to conflict between China and its acolytes and America and the West means regression back to where the world was in the last century. Resources, rather than being deployed for the more pressing needs of mitigating global warming/climate change or assisting Failures to become Followers, will be squandered for security and/or war.

The hope is that China remains true to its history in that it has never invaded another nation, and that as it continues to grow in power, its nationalism and ethnocentricity become muted so that more soft than hard power is used to expand its influence. As is noted on pages 59–60, this was the model China employed when the dominant great power of the early fifteenth century. Maintaining such a record will mean China will be far more responsible than great powers before it, surpassing the British, Americans, Germans, Japanese, and Russians as the Eurocentric world emerged and blossomed and as global conflict played out over the twentieth century.

How China is exercising its growing global power is seen in its Belt and Road Initiative, started in 2013 to enhance transport, communication, and political links with over 150 countries. China by mid-2023 had provided close to US$1 trillion to mostly developing countries to build power plants, roads, airports, telecommunications networks, and other infrastructure.[514] Time will tell whether this engagement better fosters local economic development than Western assistance did so before. Page 177 underscores that no nation has ever been built by foreigners and lays out conditions that must be in place before international assistance more helps than hinders. At the least, aspirant Followers' local workers must be enabled to produce.

In Chinese offshore investment to date, debt-funded projects are typically completed by Chinese companies, meaning little capability transfer occurs. As their international hosts borrow to fund projects, recycled renminbi pays Chinese companies and labor. Left with debt to pay for infrastructure built by foreign interests, decades will pass before export proceeds are freely available for local use. Early infrastructure projects in Africa used the same model, where the major (if not only) beneficiary was China itself. And to obtain this influence, China is now the developing world's largest lender. Part of its US$1 trillion developing-nation investment might also form part of the capital misallocation it faces over the coming years.

If internal economic or other pressures build in China, one way to divert national attention is war. Moreover, as China (because of its One Child Policy) has a surplus of male over female, utilizing this surplus energy on the battlefield may be even more attractive. In 2022 China had 2,000,000 active military personnel, the world's largest; India was second at 1,450,000, the United States third at 1,390,000, followed by North Korea at 1,200,000, and Russia fifth at 830,000.[515] Regretfully, and as has been seen many times over history, unbridled nationalism usually ends poorly for most involved.

---

514 Keith Bradsher, "China's $1 Trillion to Gain Global Influence. Can That Go On?," *New York Times*, October 17, 2023, accessed November 10, 2023, https://www.nytimes.com/2023/10/16/business/chinas-belt-and-road-initiative-bri.html.

515 Statista Research, "Largest Armies in the World Ranked by Active Military Personnel in 2022," August 29, 2023, accessed September 3, 2023, https://www.statista.com/statistics/264443/the-worlds-largest-armies-based-on-active-force-level/.

An equal sadness from this reasoning is that American military readiness will have to be maintained, with its 2022 US$867 billion[516] investment being nearly 40 percent of global military expenditure.[517] In a more peaceful world, these funds may be invested elsewhere. If American military expenditures—currently about 3.5 percent of US GDP—are lowered, sizeable US federal debt reduction may result. Regardless, America as policeman of last resort for the democratized, industrialized world may again be called upon if Chinese or other aggression threatens world peace.

America will likely remain first among equals over the coming decades but will not again have the unilateral power it had over the twentieth century. *Pax Sinae* (or the Peace of China) may take the stage briefly, but it will not be as enduring or strong as American influence was. This possibility is considered in the next section. Nonetheless, the hope is *pax mundi* eventually reigns in our multipolar BGG world. We turn now to insights these pages offer nations as they move from Failure or Follower and join the fully industrialized world.

Unbalanced to Balanced Global Growth: Followers and Failures Led by Those Understanding the Long Road Ahead

This book explains the political economy of industrialization and the economic nation-building task more completely than ever done so before. For Followers, how regime type helps or hinders industrialization is clarified, and the economic policies deployed by those already industrialized are compared. The comparison shows that the paths taken by industrialization's First Movers, though impressive, should not be followed. Instead, and to ensure Failures become aspirant Followers and Followers become Leaders so that UGG becomes BGG, twentieth-century Fast Follower industrializations should be studied and learned from.

516 Footnote 28 reports 2022 US military expenditures.

517 Peter G. Peterson Foundation, "The United States Spends More on Defense Than the Next 10 Countries Combined," *Fiscal Blog*, April 24, 2023, accessed September 3, 2023, https://www.pgpf.org/blog/2023/04/the-united-states-spends-more-on-defense-than-the-next-10-countries-combined.

For China, the message is both congratulatory and cautionary. The world's second most populous nation and biggest economy on a PPP basis accomplished the fastest industrialization and most significant reduction in poverty ever, and while doing so it became the factory of the world, with prowess now at Leader levels in industries from electric vehicles to solar energy. But its industrialization has led to overcapacity and capital misallocation, and China as surplus supplier to the world may hinder more than help others' efforts. Opposite to the role America played over the past 50 years as consumer of last resort to the global economy, aspirant Followers may be unable to industrialize as their ability to attain the scale needed from export-led growth is stymied.

China may even prevent Leaders from competing by exporting subsidized surplus goods at below cost. In a political economy where creating jobs leads to political advance and may have contributed to capital misallocation, state-owned enterprises remaining in operation rather than facing the pain of restructuring may confound the country for years. Moreover, and as already noted, China also faces possible income inequality challenges and a declining and aging population, and with too little wealth being generated, the country may, like others before it, be caught in a middle-income trap. Some have concluded that China's economy may show a pattern similar to the one seen in Japan beginning in the second half of the twentieth century: an impressive advance followed by unexpected stagnation ever since, never overtaking the American economy.[518] Under such circumstances, UGG will persist. For China's economic advance to continue, increasing worker productivity so that wealth is more widely created and income more widely distributed, at a minimum, is imperative.

Caution is also warranted for India, which, as Chapter 3 points out, requires a more growth-oriented democracy so that capital and labor

---

518 Jasmine Ng, "China Slowdown Means It May Never Overtake US Economy, Forecast Shows," Bloomberg, September 4, 2023, updated September 5, 2023, accessed September 9, 2023, https://www.bloomberg.com/news/articles/2023-09-05/china-slowdown-means-it-may-never-overtake-us-economy-be-says.

are mobilized to produce the enduring input-led growth needed to foster faster economic growth. Like China, population levels may again prove significant, except too many people may be the drag preventing India from catching up. Too many people may present similar drags to sub-Saharan nations, meaning many across the subcontinent will remain trapped in overcrowded urban enclaves, unable to flee their post-industrial urban subsistence. Some may escape to South Africa, the only more developed country accessible to them, adding to that country's already overwhelming domestic challenges.

Moreover, South Africa may find stability and growth hard to maintain unless its extractive elite is brought to heel and more attention is paid to the excluded in the country. More economically literate leadership that better appreciates how to meet basic development needs while maintaining stability and fostering stronger growth is required for the country's fragile democracy to consolidate into a stable, more equal society.

Similar prescriptions pertain to Failures under the harsh boot of authoritarian plunderers. For as long as leaders are more concerned about self-enrichment or maintaining control through hard power and corruption, industrialization will be hindered. To move from Failure to Follower, leaders who understand the stability/growth/development nexus, what it takes to mobilize capital and labor so that industrialization gets underway, and what economic policies are best to foster early economic growth, are essential.

Further, if authoritarianism is the regime type utilized, these leaders should also know how plunderers differ from developmentalists and be cognizant of the economic paths twentieth-century Fast Follower authoritarian developmentalists followed in their dashes for growth. Lee Kuan Yew's clean government in Singapore, the mistakes made by South Korea under President Park as the chaebol were built and then restructured in the face of the opening of the South Korean economy, and the discipline and hard work of the Chinese people as their economy was built almost from scratch after 500 years of isolation, all can be learned from.

Failures and aspirant Followers intent on catching up must also identify what their initial economic engagement with the outside world will be. Will it be based on high-quality, low-cost manual labor in products for export-led growth as was the case for Fast Followers? Will it be primary product exports, or will it be through tertiary services such as tourism, to name three choices?

If based on raw material exports, to avoid the resource curse, export receipts must be invested to diversify the economy. These, falling into the hands of a corrupt, extractive elite or deployed to lift living standards without productivity alongside, may mean the resource curse eventually hampers growth. Should oil demand decline, oil exporters with an economy built and maintained by foreign inputs may not be able to sustain the living standards nature's bounty alone affords. Income from investments outside of oil may replace lost wealth, provided the sums invested are sufficient. Well-invested trust funds assist at any level, from trust fund babies to trust fund nations.

Failures and Followers also should recognize they will need industrial leaders and industrial workers to build the businesses that become their industrialization's cornerstones, and given this, building the education infrastructure that provides the human capital to provide this workforce is also essential. Relying on education from others ahead of them, especially for tertiary education, is feasible too. South Korea's brightest were doing graduate work in engineering and other disciplines and attending custom business executive education courses at leading American universities in the 1980s and beyond. Similarly, over the past 20 years, millions of Chinese and Indians have attended universities in the United States, Europe, and Australia. In 2021–22, over 290,000 Chinese and 199,000 Indian university students studied in America.[519]

That all Failures become aspirant Followers and all Followers become Leaders in markets they can defend is the hope of this book. Moreover,

---

519 Statista Research, "Number of International Students in the U.S. 2021/22, by Country of Origin," June 2, 2023, accessed September 12, 2023, https://www.statista.com/statistics/233880/international-students-in-the-us-by-country-of-origin/.

advice and help from those in industrialized societies is useful as aspirant Failures step up to the arduous task of nation-building, but for nations to move forward in the manner prescribed in these pages, the initiative must come from within. South Korea was built by South Koreans, and the Chinese and Indians are now building their nations just as the Americans and Japanese did before them. And during this process, leaders must step up to move their countries forward as their people defer gratification and do the work to remove the scourge of scarcity from their midst. An understanding of the long road to industrialization and how government, organizations, and individuals contribute along the way is essential and will greatly increase the likelihood of success.

Unbalanced to Balanced Global Growth: Leaders in Balance Showing the Way to a Cleaner World

Four key ideas are presented in this book for industrialized nations. First, those with structural and/or ever-increasing government debt must regain fiscal balance and not promise more than they can afford. Expenditure cuts or tax increases—or both—are the only way to accomplish this. Second, many must maintain balance as their populations age and decline. Third, for those with businesses with Leadership positions, help to sustain competitiveness may at times be needed. This assistance may include targeted public investment in basic research that the market will not do. In addition, part of innovative competitiveness at the nation-state level is ensuring education at the efficient frontier of industry positions is accessible and part relates to ensuring other costs do not outpace those of competitors. If covered by public funds, these include healthcare costs.

Finally, nations should understand and acknowledge the risk all face from global warming/climate change and make carbon neutrality an objective governments, businesses, and citizens alike strive for. Leaders must recognize the role all play in the mitigation of and adaptation to the crisis and allocate resources to poorer nations to assist their adaption and mitigation too.

For the United States, the implications are clear: with taxes below the world average, an increase of between 3 to 5 percent of GDP in federal taxes and a decrease in federal expenditure of around the same amount would likely protect future generations from fiscal hospital passes and the calamity of financial default. Voters should only elect leaders who acknowledge the extent of the fiscal imbalance and consequences if left unattended, and these leaders should build a coalition to codify the changes needed.

To avoid political pandering or interparty outbidding to retain or regain power, Republicans and Democrats must jointly stand behind the solution. As noted on page 368, only such a coalition will likely deliver the discipline required. Finally, the percentages described here are only informed guesses; a panel of impartial experts working with the Congressional Budget Office must be formed to produce estimates of the tax increases and expenditure cuts needed. This panel's mandate could include first seeking to balance the country's books through tax increases alone. Expenditure cuts should be added only if unavoidable.

Its ability to attract, absorb, and equip immigrants provides America an inestimable advantage. Immigrants bring energy and skills that have sustained the country from its beginning. Initially from the United Kingdom, Germany, Ireland, and other European countries, they first came to escape oppression or grinding poverty to farm the rich soil of the New World. Later they flooded factories of the Northeast and Midwest as industrialization gathered steam. Most recently, armed with skills placing them among the best and brightest, they came to study at the country's world-renowned universities and remained to do work that few Americans could do.

Observing that Chinese and Indian engineers ran nearly 30 percent of Silicon Valley high-tech companies in the 1990s, one commentator noted: "Over time, terrorism is less a threat to the US than the possibility that creative and talented people will stop wanting to live within its borders."[520] Moreover, Central and South American immigrants harvest the bounty of American farms and build homes across the nation. By the early twenty-first century, immigrants were core to American post-industrial competitiveness while also providing manual labor in places Americans chose not to work.

Immigration can also ensure America's population does not decline as it is in Germany, Japan, and Italy, among others. The US Census Bureau, in its middle-immigration scenario, estimates the country's population will reach 370 million by 2080 before dropping to 366 million by 2100.[521] Its high-immigration scenario places the 2100 number at 435 million, while its low-immigration scenario peak is 346 million in 2043, with a decline to 319 million by 2100. Using middle-series estimates, the non-Hispanic White population will be 44.9 percent of the total population in 2060, with Hispanics at 29.6 percent and Black Americans at 13 percent. Non-Hispanic White was the most prevalent group in 2022 at 58.9 percent, followed by Hispanic at 19.1 percent and non-Hispanic Black at 12.6 percent. There will be more non-White than White Americans by midcentury.

But with some wanting to build walls to keep immigrants out, illegal immigration has been an enduring political flashpoint and a second issue needing bipartisan congressional attention. Comprehensive immigration reform to provide sufficient visas for skilled and less-skilled immigrants is essential, as is securing the borders to stop illegal entrants from entering the country en masse.

Regardless of this challenge and the politics of the day, important to recognize is that America's ability to attract and absorb immigrants so they become productive, engaged Americans is a vital economic, social,

---

520 Florida, "America's Looming Creativity Crisis," 8.

521 United States Census Bureau, "U.S. Population Projected to Begin Declining in Second Half of Century," Press Release CB23-189, November 9, 2023, accessed February 25, 2024, https://www.census.gov/newsroom/press-releases/2023/population-projections.html.

cultural, and political advantage that must endure.[522] Should it do so, by 2100 America will have a larger and hopefully stable population, more diverse and economically sustainable than it otherwise would have been. Closer to global demographics than it is now, the country will still be exceptional when compared with others.

Conditions are more challenging with aging and declining populations. Slower economic growth and rising healthcare costs accompany this demography, and depending on how wealthy the aging population is, tax increases to cover retiree subsistence and healthcare costs may be levied on slower-growing and even contracting economies. With a shortage of human caregivers, technology and automation may meet some senior needs and address the human shortage a declining population presents. Either way, many nations will have to balance slowing growth and increasing development costs while still ensuring future generations produce the wealth their aging societies need.

Americans should also only elect leaders who accept the science behind global warming/climate change and who recognize that the crisis is of our making and ours to fix. Climate change naysayers or deniers have no place anywhere; their dangerous, ill-informed, often vested-interest rantings will likely lead to a climate-based tragedy of the commons and possibly to a worldwide hospital pass that plagues mankind for generations, if not indefinitely.

Federal assistance where and when needed to aid American business competitiveness is suggested only because China provides considerable assistance to its producers, and to level the playing field, intervention may still be required. If Chinese surplus is offered at prices lower than local manufacturers can match because of government subsidy, it is only a matter of time before trade or other barriers to protect threatened local industries arise. Should China move toward a more market-oriented

522 Recent research confirms that upward mobility has continued in the United States for immigrants from countries such as Mexico or Guatemala and that recent immigrants have moved up the economic ladder at the same pace as European immigrants did before them (Ran Abramitzky and Leah Boustan, *Streets of Gold: America's Untold Story of Immigrant Success* [New York: Hachette Book Group, 2022]).

economy and withdraw state assistance, the corresponding need for American federal intervention will decrease too. We turn now to insights individual readers might draw from this book.

Unbalanced to Balanced Global Growth: Individual Insights as We All Build a Better World

Summarizing the individual insights offered in these pages fittingly concludes this book. Rather than discussing how nations and their leaders and organizations should act to ensure UGG evolves to BGG, this final section focuses on what individuals might do, think, and expect while envisaging their futures in our changing world. As is true for nations and their leadership, individual insights differ depending on location and level of economic development, though many apply regardless of where readers live or work.

For readers in industrialized nations, remaining ahead of Follower competition is paramount. Americans, for example, must be able to do work Indians and Chinese cannot do. With remote work even more possible after the COVID-19 pandemic, Follower-based workers are hungrier, get up earlier, work harder, and are significantly cheaper than those in richer nations. All at universities in the industrialized world should graduate with skills those studying at universities in the industrializing world do not have.

Moreover, for more specific guidance on jobs for Americans over the foreseeable future, the US Bureau of Labor Statistics *Occupational Outlook Handbook* projects the 20 occupations with the highest expected numeric growth over the coming decade. Over 2022 to 2032, and indicative that both high- and lower-value jobs will be in demand, home health and personal care aides with a 2022 median pay of US$30,180 per year are projected to have the highest increase at 804,600 jobs over the decade. Software developers at a median pay of US$127,260 are second at 410,400, and restaurant cooks with a median pay of US$34,110 are third at 277,600.[523]

Many of the top 20 high-growth occupations are high paying and include registered nurses, general and operations managers, medical and health services managers, financial managers, nurse practitioners, computer and information systems managers, accountants and auditors, and lawyers. Given the country's unhealthy and aging population, that 7 of the top 20 (35 percent) are in healthcare is unsurprising. In addition, many of these top 20 jobs are not easily outsourced. Americans should consult this type of data as they consider employment choices and their futures.

Technological advance is the second factor all should be conscious of when considering skill development and employment over the foreseeable future. As widely noted earlier, technology has been automating human work and replacing humans since the mid-twentieth century. This trend continues with AI, the technology du jour causing most consternation as this book is completed.

McKinsey & Company allege activities accounting for up to 30 percent of hours currently worked in America could be automated by 2030, though AI is expected to more enhance how STEM, creative, business, and legal professionals work than eliminate employment in these job categories.[524] Lower-value work in office support, customer service, and food service is more likely to decline, though as noted previously, the US Bureau of Labor Statistics projects restaurant cooks will not be among the jobs automated.

Though likely to be significant, how extensive AI's impact will be is indeterminable at time of writing. The best premise to keep in mind is that as soon as an activity is reduced to a series of *if this . . . then that* statements, it is only a matter of time before that activity is automated. For

---

523 US Bureau of Labor Statistics, "Most New Jobs," *Occupational Outlook Handbook*, modified September 6, 2023, accessed September 18, 2023, https://www.bls.gov/ooh/most-new-jobs.htm.
524 Kweilin Ellingrud et al., *Generative AI and the Future of Work in America*, McKinsey Global Institute, July 26, 2023, accessed September 18, 2023, https://www.mckinsey.com/mgi/our-research/generative-ai-and-the-future-of-work-in-america.

example, most medical diagnoses and treatments may eventually be automated, meaning even medical doctors face risks. Doctors already perform *if this . . . then that* analysis evaluating symptoms, and machines confirm their initial diagnoses through tissue analysis or diagnostic tools such as X-ray, ultrasound, MRI, and PET scans, among others. In time, software will likely be better than human minds for this work. Disease etiology and treatment may eventually be reduced to computer code based on AI and machine learning, an AI subset that uses algorithms and data to build models to explain interactions among variables. Such automation also may help America evade bankruptcy through healthcare.

An additional possibility is that machines eventually take over most productive work so that human contribution significantly reduces. No law says humans will always work 40 hours a week; should automation reduce human input work hours will also decline. This would aid aging societies facing population decline, and with more free time, quality of life might improve as automated production makes scarcity of less concern than it is now.

Should automation pervasively accompany production, purchasing power may eventually depend less on what individuals alone produce. Today, purchasing power is mostly determined by the value of what humans produce and the wages they earn. Should humans be arbitraged out of production, what is left to determine is how individual purchasing power is calculated. At the extreme, if machines produce everything and scarcity is eliminated, production may become free. All humans will need to do is place orders and await delivery from the machines. Under such conditions, individual purchasing power becomes moot.

Regardless of this possible longer-term development, technological advance until now has created more than destroyed jobs, with these new jobs always requiring higher skills than those replaced. Readers everywhere must recognize that the human contribution to productive work must continually be improved and enhanced. As noted on page 235, data is the post-industrial oil, and the ability to manipulate and work with large datasets using advanced analytics are capabilities all humans should seek to acquire, regardless of where they live or work. Massive amounts of data are now being generated in almost every domain, from the hard and social sciences to business, medicine, public health, public policy, and law, among others. Being able to analyze and use this data to improve operational efficiency and decision-making or offer new products or services is invaluable.

Over my nine-year tenure as dean of the University of South Carolina's Darla Moore School of Business, acquiring advanced business analytics proficiency was made central to the work of the over 5,300 undergraduates at the school. By 2022, all were leaving data proficient, analytically capable, and functionally based, armed with work ethics and business analytics skills that singled them out against business undergraduate students across the United States. A functional base was insisted upon, as finance analytics differs from marketing analytics or operations and supply chain analytics or analytics in human resources management.

Salary and placement data show the effect of these advanced analytical skills. For the Class of 2015, soon after I became dean, undergraduate placement 90 days after graduation was a paltry 62 percent at an average reported salary of US$47,290. The Class of 2022 reported a record 96 percent placement at a record salary of US$66,163, and the Class of 2023 recorded a 90 percent placement at a record salary of US$70,268. Able to tell stories through data and relying on analytics skills central to many aspects of high-value post-industrial work, these graduates were ready to do post-industrial transformative work on day one of their first jobs.

For Followers catching up, the concern must also be that smart machines are fast replacing humans in manual work and the routine elements of service work, and that the route to the middle class is no longer accessible through manual assembly line work or routine office work. Better-educated workers working alongside smart machines is where higher-value manual and clerical work is going. Education systems worldwide must adjust to this reality as they mobilize human capital for industrialization's input-led growth.

Global warming/climate change also presents unique challenges for all to be conscious of at home. My advice is to not buy near water, whether river, dam, or ocean. Be especially aware of floodplains and low-lying land close to coasts. But many own properties acquired before the effects of global warming/climate change became apparent and cannot easily relocate. These legacy investments may mean costs owners never expected to face, and not much can be done to avoid them apart from insurance—if available—and having savings for damage they hope to never face.

Home insurance prices will also go up with the increasing flood, fire, and storm damage, and funds to repair damaged and destroyed infrastructure will also be increasingly required. Extensive damage may mean investment almost akin to the initial investment to build the infrastructure is needed. In addition, given the wind effects of stronger storms, burying rather than leaving utility cables above ground may also be worthwhile. Finally, demand for construction services to repair damaged homes, factories, offices, and infrastructure will increase as the effects of global warming/climate change worsen. As a result, less will be available for other uses.

A word about American consumption is also warranted. As a First Mover into the Industrial Era and beneficiary of the high-quality, low-priced goods emerging in the second half of the twentieth century, America's past 40 years will likely be written about in history books as the golden age of conspicuous consumption in the country. But as is noted in these pages, some of this consumption was supported by a borrowed prosperity sustained by debt. Making matters even worse, the market failure arising from ignoring the full cost of carbon over the past two centuries means goods were underpriced too. IMF analysis reveals fossil fuel subsidies surged to US$7 trillion in 2022 and that consumers did not pay for over US$5 trillion of environmental damage in 2022 alone.[525]

Many economists support a carbon tax to remedy the market failure that cheap fossil fuels have caused, with these proceeds used to mitigate global warming/climate change or invested to develop clean energy alternatives. Equally, a carbon tax may also increase oil prices when producers cut them to prevent cleaner alternatives from coming to market. One way to ensure alternatives don't reach the market is to keep fossil fuels cheap, and oil producers have for decades manipulated prices to achieve this end. These behaviors not only protect market positions; they also increase the likelihood that GM is the scenario we all eventually face.

Cheap energy also kept transport costs low, and these permitted production's globalization so that goods made in China could be transported to the United States at an affordable price. Should energy prices rise, global supply chains will become less attractive as producers relocate to areas geographically closer to their markets. Regional as opposed to global production, a trend already underway following supply chain disruptions in the pandemic, is likely. Instability in China, or increasing political tension between China and the West, is likely to add to the impetus for more regional production.

Prices increasing and borrowed purchasing power decreasing will signal the end of the American golden age of consumption, and the next generation of Americans will likely have lower material living standards than their parents did. This change will not occur immediately but will unfold over time. Yet, when compared with the living standards of other industrialized nations, cutting American living standards even by 20 percent will still mean Americans are materially better off than most in the world.

Average American home size before the 1960s was 1,500 square feet and by 2022 had reached 2,566; homes 20 percent smaller at 2,000

---

525 Simon Black, Ian Parry, and Nate Vernon, "Fossil Fuel Subsidies Surged to Record $7 Trillion," *IMF Blog*, IMF, August 24, 2023, accessed September 26, 2023, https://www.imf.org/en/Blogs/Articles/2023/08/24/fossil-fuel-subsidies-surged-to-record-7-trillion.

square feet—the year 2000 median—will not end life as it is known.[526] Americans driving 20 percent smaller cars, eating 20 percent less food, and having 20 percent less clothing will not either. In fact, 20 percent less food will mean healthier Americans.

Cutting consumption to ensure Americans live within their means and increasing taxes while cutting expenditures to ensure the federal government lives within its means will result in a more balanced and stronger America. Once basic needs are met and all have food, clothing, shelter, education, and healthcare, the meaning of life is not determined only by the additional possessions accumulated.

Given the challenges of climate change/global warming and the need to wean off all from fossil fuels, American consumers must expect to pay more for energy and be required to use energy more carefully while also becoming more conscious of recycling and material usage in general. As the excluded billions join the human struggle for productivity, demand for raw materials will grow significantly, and new models of consumption must accompany this increased demand. Routinely sending old consumed goods to landfills will become harder and harder to justify. Recycling and reuse will instead become the order of the day.

Another way to ensure American purchasing power stays strong is to address the country's increasing wage inequality. The CEO-to-worker compensation ratio for the 350 largest public firms in the United States in 2021 was 389, meaning that chief executive annual compensation was almost 400 times more than the average salary of production and nonsupervisory workers, up from 20.4 times in 1965.[527] In 1990 the ratio was 77.30 and by 2000 had climbed to 371.7, reaching this at the height of the dot-com boom. By 2010 the ratio had dropped back to

---

526 Michael Kolomatsky, "Houses Are Still Big. Prices Are Much Bigger," *New York Times*, August, 17, 2023, accessed September 25, 2023, https://www.nytimes.com/2023/08/17/realestate/housing-prices.html.

527 Statista Research, "Aggregated CEO-to-Worker Compensation Ratio for the 350 Largest Publicly Owned Companies in the United States from 1965 to 2022," January 30, 2023, accessed September 26, 2023, https://www.statista.com/statistics/261463/ceo-to-worker-compensation-ratio-of-top-firms-in-the-us/.

178.3, indicating that much CEO pay depends on stock price performance and is variable. But regardless of its contingent nature, top executive compensation close to 400 times that of the average worker is hard to support.

Underscoring how much more American CEOs are paid than CEOs in other countries, in FY 2019, data from 429 large companies in Japan, France, Germany, the United Kingdom, and the United States revealed American CEOs annually earned 1,041 million JPY, while United Kingdom CEOs earned 285 million JPY, German CEOs 273 million JPY, French CEOs 174 million JPY, and Japanese CEOs 55 million JPY (the lowest).[528] Japanese CEOs earned 5 percent of their counterparts in America, while United Kingdom CEOs received only 27 percent, this percentage also being above German and French CEO pay packets.[529] Faced with this data, almost 9 in 10 Americans agree that the growing gap between CEO and worker pay is problematic; 73 percent think most CEOs of America's largest companies are paid too much.[530]

CEOs and market-oriented persons in the United States often state the market sets the price and that the remuneration is correct, primarily because the market says it so. But just because a market sets a price does not make the price right or moral. Markets are forums where buyers and sellers meet to transact, and asking if they are moral and know right from wrong is the wrong question. The correct question is are people moral or immoral as they transact in markets? Given people may be moral or

---

528 Using the Japanese yen/US$ exchange rate of 148.90 JPY for US$1 (as of September 26, 2023) means American CEOs in 2019 would have earned US$6,991,269, while Japanese CEOs took home US$369,375. German CEOs would have banked US$1,833,445. American CEO remuneration is not only high compared with the average worker; it is also high compared with CEO remuneration elsewhere.

529 Sumio Morita et al., "CEO Pay Landscape in Japan, the U.S. and Europe—2020 Analysis," Willis Towers Watson, December 9, 2020, accessed September 26, 2023, https://www.wtwco.com/en-us/insights/2020/12/ceo-pay-landscape-in-japan-the-us-and-europe-2020-analysis.

530 Jennifer Tonti, *Companies Should Reduce Income Inequality by Raising Minimum Wage to Living Wage and Capping CEO Compensation*, JUST Capital, April 2022, accessed September 26, 2023, https://justcapital.com/wp-content/uploads/2022/05/JUST-Capital_Worker-CEO-Pay-Survey-Analysis_May-2022-min.pdf.

immoral, markets do transact immorally—for example, drug trafficking. In that case, regulation addresses a behavior all consider wrong.

No moral equivalency exists between drug cartels and American CEO remuneration. Drug trafficking shows markets permit wrong behaviors and that market fundamentalists who claim the market is always right do not understand how markets work. Indicative of market misbehavior, CEO remuneration in large public companies in the United States have reached levels that need attention. And again, referring to my time as dean—or CEO—of the Darla Moore School of Business, upon taking the appointment in January 2014, the first item I verified was that my remuneration was not more than 30 times greater than the lowest-paid full-time worker at the school. If it was, I would have dropped my pay accordingly.

Nothing stops American CEOs from adopting this position at a ratio they deem correct. They could allocate the remuneration they would have received to workers, making raises not inflationary. Further, paying lowest on the pay scale more will immediately affect consumption, given employees at lower pay scales spend more of extra income than they save. CEO remuneration is far more likely to be saved and invested than consumed. Paying the bottom 10 percent more may increase consumption so much that the stock prices of companies supplying the goods and services rise, and with their substantial holdings of company stock, CEO wealth will also increase.

The solutions needed to remedy American CEO pay abuse is beyond this book's scope. America's rising inequality since the 1970s is highlighted on pages 264–265, and CEO remuneration is part of the bigger story of rising inequality in the country. The jeopardy societies face when inequality gets too wide is clarified on page 179, and all Americans should be conscious of this as they consider the state of their country. Time will tell if Trump's MAGA movement endures as a result of rage made more stringent by rural Americans being left behind economically, as has been claimed.[531]

531 Tom Schaller and Paul Waldman, *White Rural Rage: The Threat to American Democracy*, (New York: Random House, 2024).

In addition to its rising inequality, America's overall social contract, like its fiscal health, also needs recalibration. The rich will not be irreparably damaged if their taxes are increased, and CEOs will not suffer unbearable loss if their pay is cut to 250 rather than 400 times average worker pay. But increasing only the taxes of the rich will likely be insufficient to remedy America's fiscal imbalance. In 2022 about 40 percent of American households paid no federal tax. One issue the panel of experts formed to set the tax increases and expenditure cuts needed to remedy the imbalances must consider is how many households are permitted to pay no federal taxes. It may be better if more American households pay some taxes. Most should have some skin in the game.

Neither will Americans suffer unbearable harm if their consumption is moderated to take into account the market failure that 200 years of fossil fuel use have caused and if their federal government shows the discipline to live within its means. Higher energy prices will mean American consumers, like their European counterparts, act more judiciously when heating or cooling houses and driving motor vehicles. Free or cheap goods are typically overconsumed. As seen in the decade after the 1973 OPEC oil shock, when vehicles shrunk and miles per gallon improved to account for the more expensive gas, Americans adjust and consume more carefully when prices rise.

These changes should be considered investments in the stability and sustainability of the world's most admired nation and will place the country back on a path for its exceptionalism to continue. With an economy still the envy of the world focused on becoming carbon neutral and powered by clean energy, and with a workforce ready to continue its innovation-led growth and produce the goods, services, and solutions that others marvel and demand, America will continue to be an example for others to follow over the twenty-first century.

But only with their country's political economy back in balance and with its social contract better calibrated can Americans confidently work alongside others to ensure GM is avoided, UGG becomes BGG, and scarcity is eliminated from our world. And this will not be *great power America* keeping Pax Americana in place but America as first among equals working alongside others as previously indelible problems of Failures are resolved and Followers prevail over the challenges they face so that *pax mundi* becomes the high state humanity reaches and enjoys.

I arrived in America in 1989 to restart my professional life and, like most immigrants, am deeply thankful for the opportunities I have enjoyed since then. The United States, though imperfect and a work in progress, was then, as it is now, the most successful country in history and is in no need of being made great again. For at least the past century it has been so. Its biggest enemy now is not the Chinese or those crossing its borders illegally in search of better lives. Instead, it is found in those wishing to isolate the country from a changing world as their insecurities and fears are pandered to.

Only leaders acknowledging the challenges facing the country and who offer bipartisan solutions to conquer them will mobilize Americans to save the country from itself. Americans do not back down from challenges demanding sacrifice, and given the right information, they are more than able to meet in the middle to work together so that the coming century is even better than their country's storied past. And not only Americans will benefit. The world will regain an advocate ready and able to work alongside others for the common good. One objective of this book is to make this outcome more likely.

Footnote 1 highlights humans emerged out of Africa somewhere around 200,000 years ago, and that in this sense, we are all Africans. Superficial differences in skin color and other external physical characteristics evolved as humans moved away from the equator and represent a miniscule part of our genetic makeup. Absent these superficial differences, we are all the same and seek comparable outcomes for our families and communities.

Our overwhelming similarities hopefully mean that over the remainder of the twenty-first century, cooperation more than competition characterizes human engagement. As this book emphasizes, this, too, is needed to ensure our better selves work together so that the best future prevails for us all.

Author's Biography

DR. PETER J. BREWS

Peter J. Brews stepped down as dean of the Darla Moore School of Business (DMSB) in December 2022 after nine years in office and left academic life as dean emeritus in December 2023.

His professional career started in investment banking and moved into higher education, where while earning graduate degrees in law and business and two PhDs, he taught business law, economics, finance, corporate strategy, and international business and conducted research at three leading universities: the University of the Witwatersrand, Johannesburg; Duke University; and UNC-Chapel Hill.

His accomplishments include being a world-class researcher/teacher and individual contributor (he holds multiple awards for both); being an academic entrepreneur in the proposal and leadership of innovative, high-value academic programs; and being a transformative leader of DMSB, the premier, 6,400-student-strong academic brand of the University of South Carolina.

His early research investigated corporate growth through M&As and how environmental volatility moderated strategic planning and performance. He then pioneered research into internet generation companies and was first in the world to show how internet enabling affected firm strategy, structure, scope, and performance. He has also written or supervised 23 cases on strategy formation, corporate finance, and most recently on international and post-industrial business, each case capturing leading-edge business practices for others to adopt.

Companies invite Brews to address topics such as the evolution of the global economy and our struggle for productivity (focusing on how nations, firms, and people maintain competitiveness in the fast-changing global economy), on how the internet/IT and networking of business operations are altering business, and on strategy formation and capacity building in an innovation-led world.

He has also taught widely and consulted internationally in these fields. Firms he has worked with include Barclays, Boeing, Caterpillar, Eastman Chemical, Ford Motor Company, General Motors, Grant Thornton, Lucent Technologies Asia/Pacific (H. K.) Ltd., Merrill Lynch, Progress Energy, Siemens AG, Mandarin Oriental Hotel Group of Hong Kong, LG of South Korea, and Standard Bank and Telkom in South Africa.

Index

A

AccuGrade, 230, 231, 270
Africa, v, 7, 11, 12, 20, 23–25, 51, 54, 58–60, 63, 64, 70–73, 76, 105–107, 183, 185–191, 204, 209, 248, 251, 265, 314, 323–325, 333–335, 338, 359, 360, 387, 390, 393, 409, 412
airports, 82, 89, 172, 201, 202, 254, 389
Amazon, v, 5, 221, 223, 224, 252, 253, 309–312, 335
Amazon Web Services (AWS), v, 252, 253, 311
America, 2, 5, 7, 11, 12, 16, 19, 23, 25, 26, 38, 50, 51, 53, 54, 59, 60, 63, 71, 72, 75, 76, 82, 84, 86–89, 92, 93, 99–101, 103, 107, 111, 125, 134–136, 139, 140, 142–145, 168, 169, 172, 173, 192, 202, 209, 221, 222, 236, 254, 256, 257, 259–261, 264, 269, 311, 314, 317, 323, 324, 331–333, 343, 345, 346, 351, 352, 354, 355, 357, 359, 361, 362, 365, 367, 368, 370, 371, 373, 376–378, 381, 386–389, 391, 392, 394, 396–398, 400, 401, 403, 405–409
American exceptionalism, 2
Apple, 235, 272, 289, 294, 295, 309, 310, 312, 332, 339
artificial intelligence (AI), v, 235, 400, 401
Asia Pacific, 23
Atlantic Meridional Overturning Circulation, 382
AT&T, 89, 235
authoritarian developmentalist, 6, 130, 131, 165, 180, 183, 185, 190, 191, 205, 317
authoritarian plunderers, 6, 131, 378, 393
Avions Marcel Dassault, 240

B

Ball, Lucille, 95
Bank of Japan, 150
Barbados, 353
Beijing, 73, 202, 338
Belgium, 258, 316, 334, 335, 351, 353
Bell, Daniel, 212
Bell Laboratories, 235
Benz, Karl, 90
Berlin, 73, 323
Bernanke, Ben, 15
Best Buy, 224
Bhutan, 353
Biden, Joseph, 37, 261, 346
BMW, 229, 363
Boeing, 5, 89, 218, 219, 224, 240, 241, 363, 412
Boeing GoldCare, 5, 218–220
Bosack, Leonard, 244
Brazil, 58, 59, 63, 73, 127, 183, 185–187, 189–191, 209, 314, 323–325, 359, 387

BRICS, 323, 368, 387, 388
broadband, i, 255–263, 372
Built Robotics, 232, 233
Bush, George H.W., 368

C

Cabo Verde, 353
Cambridge University, 50
Canada, 11, 100, 155, 223, 224, 258, 260, 316, 325, 353, 355
Carter, Jimmy, 346
Caterpillar, 5, 157, 230–233, 270, 272, 309, 310, 312, 412
Catholic Church, Spain, 68
CEO (Chief Executive Officer) pay, 317, 406, 407
Champy, James, 6, 277
Chandler, Alfred, 6, 86, 87, 134–136, 138
Chaplin, Charlie, 95
Charles VIII, 68
Chicago, IL, US, 73
China, i, iii, 11–13, 20, 23, 31, 32, 35, 36, 47, 48, 51–53, 55, 59–61, 73, 82, 83, 87, 88, 103, 107, 125, 126, 148, 158, 161, 167, 173–176, 183, 184, 191, 194, 197, 199–206, 208, 209, 254, 314, 317, 320, 323–325, 329, 333–335, 338–340, 343, 353, 359–363, 375–378, 387, 389–393, 398, 404
Christian Church, 49
Cisco, 235, 244–248, 250, 251, 276, 309–312, 318, 335, 336
Clayton Act, 88, 98
clean energy, 2, 38, 320, 321, 341–343, 386, 404, 408
Clinton, Bill, 346
Club of Rome, 36, 37
coal, 86, 102, 103, 106, 107, 113, 119, 187, 207, 341
Columbus, Christopher, 60, 61, 66–71, 75, 76, 110, 123, 124, 286, 304, 305
competitive advantage, iii, 22, 161–165, 191, 279, 313, 335, 359, 363
computer numerical control (CNC), v, 236–240
computer-aided design (CAD), v, 217, 236–241
computer-aided manufacturing (CAM), v, 237–241
computer-integrated manufacturing (CIM), v, 237–239, 241, 242
copper, 106, 107, 254
corruption, 53, 191, 193, 199, 378, 393
Council for International Economic Cooperation and Development, 151
COVID-19, 16, 26, 33, 204, 222, 348, 350, 357, 399
creative core, 6, 211, 269–274, 285, 298, 300, 305, 318, 334
Cuba, 69

D

Daimler, Gottlieb, 90
Darla Moore School of Business, v, 402, 407, 411
de la Cerda, Don Luis, 68
Dell, 279
democracy light, 6, 142, 144, 146, 167, 198, 209, 317, 377
Dhaka, Bangladesh, 73
DHL, 222
Diamond, Jared, 378
Digital Research, 291
DiLorenzo, Thomas, 88
Dimension Data, South Africa, 248, 251
Drucker, Peter, 6, 213, 267
Dutch Golden Age, 59

Dwight D. Eisenhower System of Interstate and Defense Highways, 89

E

early industrialization political economy, 6, 43, 55, 126, 128, 144, 190, 198, 391
East India Company, 59
Eastern Europe, 11, 12, 25, 338, 387
Economic Development Board, Singapore, 152, 157
Economic Planning Agency, Japan, 150
Economic Planning and Development Council, Taiwan, 151
Economic Planning Board, South Korea, 150
Economic Planning Council, Taiwan, 151
Edison, Thomas, 89, 111
energy consumption, 102, 103, 106, 201
Engelberger, Joseph F., 215
England, 48, 49, 51, 57, 63, 68, 98, 133, 145
entrepreneurship, 45, 46, 66, 67, 70, 71, 75, 79, 109, 110, 123, 212, 285, 291, 304
European exceptionalism, 51, 60
European Union, 14, 31, 197, 259, 323, 324, 343, 361, 365, 370, 385

F

Fair Labor Standards Act, 98
Fanuc, 236, 244
FedEx, 222, 243, 248, 253
fertility rates of women, 35, 56
feudalism, 47–49, 51, 55, 57, 75
fiscal management, 357, 368, 370
Ford, Henry, 58, 71, 89, 110, 111, 113, 114, 270
Ford Motor Company, 58, 89, 109, 110, 113–115, 118–121, 123, 124, 136, 138, 207, 226, 243, 285, 306, 312, 412
fossil fuels, 102–105, 207, 322, 341, 404, 405
France, 48, 57, 68, 73, 102, 103, 142, 145, 146, 155, 173, 258, 316, 353, 355, 373, 406
Friedman, Thomas L., 325, 326

G

Gates, Bill, 71, 272, 285, 287–289, 293, 294, 297, 301–303, 305–307, 319
General Agreement on Tariffs and Trade, 385
General Electric, 89, 245, 287, 339
General Motors, 89, 100, 109, 120–123, 136, 157, 207, 215, 227, 243, 244, 309, 310, 335, 412
Germany, iii, 22, 73, 90, 136, 137, 142, 146, 147, 155, 173, 223, 258, 284, 315, 316, 323–325, 353, 355–357, 376, 388, 396, 397, 406
Gini coefficients, 265, 325
global activities, 333, 337
Global Positioning System (GPS), v, 220, 227, 228, 230, 232–235, 270
global warming/climate change, 3, 4, 29, 37, 38, 43, 81, 322, 341–345, 359, 380, 382, 384–386, 389, 395, 398, 403–405
good-enough markets, 18, 326, 328, 329, 331, 332, 337–340
Google, 235, 252, 253, 309, 310, 362
Great Britain, 8, 23, 59, 100, 125, 132–134, 139, 141, 142, 173, 198, 208, 370

Great Depression, 8, 16, 142, 143, 350, 366, 370
Great Moderation, 14–16
Greece, 63, 258, 316, 351, 353, 355
gross world product (GWP), v, 10, 11, 21, 39, 154, 362, 379, 380, 382, 383
guilds, 62, 64–66

H

Hammer, Michael, 6, 276, 277
Hart, Stuart, 326, 327
Henry VII, 68
Hobbes, Thomas, 6, 8, 62, 382
Honda, 155, 227
Honeywell, 279
Hong Kong, iii, 5, 125, 147, 148, 152, 154, 158, 160–164, 166–168, 170, 171, 173–175, 194, 196, 208, 333, 362, 412
hospital pass, 6, 345, 358, 365, 396, 398
human population, 3, 29, 33, 35, 38, 43, 382
hunter-gathering, 3, 17
Hyundai, 22, 156, 268

I

immigrants, 82, 115, 161, 371, 396–398, 409
India, i, iii, 11, 12, 19, 35, 59, 73, 104, 107, 183, 197–206, 209, 254, 314, 323–325, 333, 339, 340, 359–361, 376, 377, 387, 390, 392, 393
Indian Ocean, 70
Industrial Revolution, 8–10, 12, 13, 17, 23, 39, 60, 66, 74, 133–135, 139
informal sector, 21, 74, 194
infrastructure as a service (IaaS), v, 252, 302
innovation-led growth, 2, 6, 21, 22, 41, 173, 175, 176, 313, 358–361, 363, 408
input-led growth, 6, 21, 22, 41, 166, 172, 173, 175, 176, 178, 198, 208, 313, 358, 360, 393, 403
Intel, 235, 289, 291
intergovernmental debt, 350, 351
Intergovernmental Panel on Climate Control (IPCC), v, 341, 342, 386
International Business Machines (IBM), 235, 239, 244, 279, 286, 290–295, 297, 301
International Monetary Fund (IMF), 201, 323, 324, 349, 351, 354, 358, 387, 388, 403
Internet for All initiative, 261
Internet of Things (IoT), v, 5, 6, 220, 229
Iran, 387
Ireland, 258, 259, 269, 316, 323, 351, 396
Isabella I, Queen of Spain, 68, 69
Istanbul, Turkey, 72, 73
Italy, 65, 155, 258, 316, 351–353, 365, 397

J

Japan, iii, v, 5, 23, 24, 26, 31, 36, 48, 51, 55, 73, 96, 100, 103, 104, 107, 125, 126, 136, 137, 147–150, 153–156, 159, 160, 163–167, 173–175, 196, 208, 236, 258, 268, 315, 316, 322–325, 334, 351, 353, 355–358, 362, 365, 375, 392, 397, 408
Japan Export-Import Bank, 150
JCPenney, 223
Jefferson, Thomas, 92
John II, King of Portugal, 68

K

Karachi, Pakistan, 73

Keynes, John Maynard, 6, 13, 40, 143
Koninklijke Philips Electronics, 90
Krugman, Paul, 171, 172
Kuznets, Simon, 6, 77, 78, 80, 108, 109

L

Latin America, 11, 12, 23, 72, 171, 194
League of Nations, 385
Lerner, Sandra, 244
Lexus, 228, 229
Life Cycle Model, i, 3, 28, 29, 38–40, 43, 44
life expectancy, 49, 57, 91, 130, 201, 203
literacy, 49, 91, 130, 201, 203, 379
local activities, 333, 363
London, 51, 73, 84, 97, 166, 338
low-end markets, 326, 329, 332, 337, 339, 340

M

machine learning (ML), 235, 401
Maddison, Angus, 6, 13, 55, 60, 77
MAGA (Make America Great Again) movement, 407
Maldives, 353
Malthus, Thomas, 6, 34
Manchester, United Kingdom, 73
Manila, Philippines, 73
market capitalization, 300, 308–310
market failure, 195, 341, 342, 403, 404, 408
market value per person (MVP), 308–312, 319, 335
Marx, Karl, 6, 57, 58, 65, 84–86
McDonnell Douglas, 89
median age, 201, 203
mercantile capitalism, 47, 51, 53, 75
Mercedes Benz, 90, 227, 229, 363
Mexico, 50, 172, 173, 176, 258, 260, 289, 325, 359, 398
Michigan, United States, 96, 111, 113, 117, 119
Microsoft, 5, 235, 245, 252, 253, 272, 285, 286, 288–303, 305–307, 309–312, 319, 362
Middle East, v, 11, 12, 23, 33, 107, 333–335
middle-income trap, 374, 377, 392
Ministry of Agriculture and Forestry, Japan, 150
modern distributive democracy, 6, 144, 197, 207, 208, 317
Moscow, Russia, 73
Mumbai, India, 73

N

national activities, 333, 363
National Aeronautics and Space Administration (NASA), 30, 31
National Highway Traffic Safety Administration (NHTSA), 229
National Labor Relations Act, 98
National Wages Council, 152
nation-building, i, 176–180, 183, 189, 190, 208, 209, 373, 378, 387, 391, 395
natural gas, 102, 106, 207, 212, 341
net income per employee, 309, 310, 312
net income to sales, 309–312
Netflix, 252, 253
Nevins, Allan, 88
New York, 73, 84, 134, 159, 225, 323, 325
Nike, iii, 5, 87, 222, 309, 310, 312, 332–339
non-Asian G5, iii, 173–175
Norway, 258, 260, 316, 353, 355–357, 365
numerical control (NC), v, 236–239

O
Obama, Barack, 37, 346
Old Navy, 223
One Child Policy, 35, 203, 375, 390
Organization for Economic Co-Operation and Development (OECD), i, 155, 156, 171, 222, 255, 256, 258–260, 365, 370–372
organizational creative cores, 6, 270, 272, 273, 318
organized labor, 97, 98, 100

P
Pacific Ocean, 70
Pakistan, 35, 73
Paris, 50, 73
Pax Americana, 409
pax mundi, 387, 391, 409
Pax Sinae, 391
Philadelphia, 73, 98
Philips, Anton, 90
Philips, Gerard, 90
Philips Electronics, 90, 159
PISA (Program for International Student Assessment), 371, 372
plague, 8, 33, 49, 57, 189, 398
platform as a service (PaaS), 252, 302
political economy, 4, 6, 43, 47, 48, 53, 55, 125, 126, 138, 147, 165, 202, 212, 285, 313, 314, 316, 317, 320, 391, 392, 408
population decline, and its effects, 36, 360, 371, 375, 401
Porsche, Ferdinand, 90
Portugal, 59, 68, 258, 316, 353, 355
post-industrial creative work, 6, 263, 269, 270, 274–276, 298, 318, 334
post-industrial manual work, 263, 283, 284, 318
post-industrial robotics, 4, 215
post-industrial transformative work, 5, 6, 242, 269, 271, 274–276, 282, 283, 298, 318, 319, 402
Prahalad, C.K., 326, 327
premium markets, 326, 329, 331, 332, 336, 337, 339
President's Information Technology Advisory Committee (PITAC), 260
primary balances, i, 351, 355–357
printing press, 49

R
railways, 142, 161, 201, 202
Reagan, Ronald, 368
refugees, 381, 387
regional activities, 333, 335, 363
renewable energy, 82, 102
Republic of Congo, 353
resource curse, 108, 109, 356, 394
RFID, 221
roadways, 201, 202, 220
Rockefeller, John, 88
Roebuck, Alvah, 89
Roman Empire, 12
Russia, 23, 24, 31, 32, 73, 107, 314, 323, 387–390
Russia/USSR, 23, 24, 27

S
S Curve Model, i, 3, 28, 39, 43, 44
SABMiller, 329, 338, 339
Salesforce, 252
Samsung, 22, 156, 268, 363
Say, Jean Baptiste, 6, 110, 117, 141
Sears, Richard Warren, 89
Sears Roebuck, 89
Seattle Computer, 286, 292
Shanghai, China, 73, 167, 338, 387
Sherman Antitrust Act, 88
slavery, 62–64, 66, 75, 82, 84, 97
Sloan Jr., Alfred P., 89, 120

Smith, Adam, 6, 41, 52, 54, 56, 65, 87, 94, 95, 98, 134, 139, 141, 145, 277
software as a service (SaaS), 252, 302
Solow, Robert, 6, 169, 170, 173
South Africa, 20, 24, 59, 73, 106, 183, 185–191, 209, 248, 251, 265, 314, 323–325, 338, 387, 393, 412
South Korea, iii, v, 5, 22, 55, 87, 125, 131, 147, 148, 150, 156, 157, 159–164, 166, 170, 171, 173, 174, 183, 190, 192–194, 196, 208, 209, 257–259, 262, 263, 268, 334, 353, 362, 372, 393–395, 412
Spain, 59, 68–70, 231, 258, 316, 353
Sri Lanka, 353
St. Petersburg, Russia, 73
Standard Oil Trust, 88
Stanford University, 244
Stern, Nicolas, 343, 344
sub-Saharan Africa, 11, 12, 23–25, 204, 338, 381, 387, 393
Sudan, 323, 353
Suriname, 353
Sweden, 258, 315, 316
Syria, 378, 389

T

Taiwan, iii, v, vi, 5, 22, 32, 125, 147, 148, 150, 151, 156, 158–164, 166, 170, 171, 173, 174, 196, 208, 334, 362
Taiwan Semiconductor Manufacturing Company, 22, 159
Taliban, 127, 181, 378
Tata Motors, 330, 331
Tata Nano, 330, 331
Taylor, Frederick Winslow, 6, 94, 95
Tianjin, China, 73
Toffler, Alvin, 17
Tokyo, Japan, 72, 73
Totaltech, 224. *See also* Best Buy
Toyota, 96, 155, 227, 312
trade union, iii, 97–100
tragedy of the commons, 385, 398
transaction cost economics (TCE), vi, 118
Treaty of Tordesillas, 59
Trimble Navigation, 5, 230, 243, 270, 272, 309
Trump, Donald, 37, 314, 346, 407

U

Ukraine, 389
United Nations, vi, 35
United Parcel Service (UPS), 222, 243, 248
United States, iii, 8, 13, 14, 16, 23, 24, 27, 32, 36, 37, 63, 72, 85, 88, 89, 93, 97–100, 103, 107, 125, 126, 132–135, 137–139, 141, 142, 146, 153, 155, 160, 168, 170, 171, 173, 177, 201–203, 208, 221, 223–225, 236, 258, 260, 262–266, 301, 303, 313, 315–317, 322–324, 332, 334–336, 340, 345, 350, 352, 355–358, 362, 365, 366, 370, 373, 387, 388, 390, 394, 396, 398, 402, 404–407, 409
United States Code, 88
urban subsistence, 18, 21, 47, 72–74, 76, 97, 313, 327, 329, 393
urbanization, 72, 74, 90, 201–203
US Census Bureau high-immigration, middle-immigration, and low-immigration scenarios, 397
US federal debt, 346, 349–351, 354, 366, 367, 369, 391
US Treasurys, 366–368

V
Varieties of Capitalism, 315–317
Venezuela, 70, 353
Volkswagen, 90

W
Walmart, 222, 311, 312
Wayfair, 223, 225
West Africa, 63
West Indies, 63, 70
Western Europe, 11–14, 48, 50, 51, 55, 72, 89, 100, 125, 354
Williamson, Oliver, 6, 120, 121
wood, fuel source, 106, 107, 187
world population, i, 20, 21, 33–37, 154, 156, 327, 360
World Trade Organization (WTO), vi, 385
World War I, 31, 118, 144, 145
World War II, 16, 25, 27, 31, 90, 120, 121, 125, 142, 147, 156, 168, 173, 176, 199, 332, 350, 354, 362, 367, 377, 378, 385, 388

X
Xerox PARC, 235

Y
Yucatan Peninsula, 30